C0-AMY-953

JEREMIAH SULLIVAN BLACK

A Da Capo Press Reprint Series

THE AMERICAN SCENE
Comments and Commentators

GENERAL EDITOR: WALLACE D. FARNHAM
University of Illinois

JEREMIAH SULLIVAN BLACK

A DEFENDER OF THE CONSTITUTION AND THE TEN COMMANDMENTS

by

William N. Brigance

DA CAPO PRESS · NEW YORK · 1971

A Da Capo Press Reprint Edition

This Da Capo Press edition of
Jeremiah Sullivan Black
is an unabridged republication of the
first edition published in Philadelphia
in 1934.

Library of Congress Catalog Card Number 72-139196

SBN 306-70078-6

Published by Da Capo Press
A Division of Plenum Publishing Corporation
227 West 17th Street, New York, N.Y. 10011

Manufactured in the United States of America

JEREMIAH SULLIVAN BLACK

JEREMIAH SULLIVAN BLACK
At About Fifty-five Years

JEREMIAH SULLIVAN BLACK

A DEFENDER OF THE CONSTITUTION AND THE TEN COMMANDMENTS

by

William Norwood Brigance
Wabash College

UNIVERSITY OF PENNSYLVANIA PRESS
Philadelphia
1934

LONDON: HUMPHREY MILFORD: OXFORD UNIVERSITY PRESS

Manufactured in the United States of America

To

R. J. B. and J. M. B.

Haply, for I am black . . . *I am abused . . .*

Yet

I have done the state some service, and they know't.

OTHELLO

PREFACE

HERE is a story, previously unwritten, of a dynamic and colorful public character who wrought more influence on American history than many Presidents.

As a young man he held high office—District Judge and Chief Justice of Pennsylvania, Attorney-General and Secretary of State of the United States. His influence was commensurate with such offices.

As an old man he held no office. But as a private citizen his influence exceeded that which he wielded as an office holder.

He drafted Congressional messages for two Presidents of the United States.

Under his startling eloquence the Supreme Court overthrew trial by military commissions in the North at the close of the Civil War; drew the teeth from an Enforcement Act of the Thirteenth Amendment; and sawed off literally and bodily the ominous provisions of the first section of the Fourteenth Amendment, allowing us today to live under the boon of that amputation. "It is useless to deny it," said a Judge of that Court, "Judge Black is the most magnificent orator at the American bar."

He forced the Radical Congress of 1868 to repeal one of the Enforcement Acts of Reconstruction, "by trick, imposition and breach of courtesy," in order to save its Reconstruction policy from destruction.

Famed as an eccentric character, he reveled in his independence and his curiously egocentric life.

Besieged by clients, who showered him with huge fees, he scarcely stooped to gather in the golden shower.

Anathematizing the opinions of his political enemies—yet he held them fast as personal friends.

Once denouncing certain of the judges of the Supreme Court for having "made a covenant with death" and for being "with hell . . . at agreement," yet he continued to win decisions from that court.

At sixty, with his right arm crushed and rendered forever useless, he learned at once to shave and to write a beautiful script with his left (see p. 232).

Born with a natural taste for disputation, and gifted with the most terrible invective since Junius, he reveled in magazine and newspaper controversies. Public men from Stephen A. Douglas to Robert G. Ingersoll were his victims, yet the wounds inflicted were clean and cauterized, healing without fester.

Colorful, eloquent, eccentric—for a quarter century in the most tragic era of American history he remained upon the public stage, an independent gladiator, hand on sword, ready on the instant to champion minority causes and to lead forlorn hopes.

In writing this biography, I am indebted to the following persons for aid given in locating historical material and for verifying certain facts regarding the life of Jeremiah S. Black: Judge Francis J. Kooser of Somerset, Pennsylvania; Mrs. J. V. L. Finley, Mrs. William Stair, Mr. Carey E. Etnier, and Judge W. F. Bay Stewart, of York, Pennsylvania; Mr. John G. Ogle and Dr. Roy F. Nichols of Philadelphia.

To Dr. Mary Clayton Hurlbut of Lockport, New York, I am especially indebted for the loan of the invaluable collection of newspaper clippings and pamphlets treating of Black's life, which was made by Dr. Hurlbut's mother, Mary Black Clayton.

To Judge Henry C. Niles of York, Pennsylvania, I also am especially indebted both for his wide knowledge upon the subject of this book and for granting freely of his time in verifying many of the details.

To Dr. A. C. Baird, Dr. H. J. Thornton, and Dr. W. T. Root, of the University of Iowa, I am indebted for careful readings and frank criticisms of the manuscript.

W. N. B.

Crawfordsville, Indiana
June 15, 1934

CONTENTS

ILLUSTRATIONS

ABBREVIATIONS OF WORKS MOST FREQUENTLY CITED IN THIS VOLUME

C. F. Black—Chauncey F. Black, *Essays and Speeches of Jeremiah S. Black*; D. Appleton, New York, 1885.

Black Papers—Papers of Jeremiah S. Black, 1813-1904; 73 Vols., Manuscript Division, Library of Congress, Washington, D. C.

Clayton—Mary Black Clayton (daughter of Jeremiah S. Black), *Reminiscences of Jeremiah Sullivan Black*; Christian, St. Louis, 1887.

Clayton MSS.—A collection of newspaper articles and pamphlets relating to the life of Jeremiah S. Black, made by Mary Black Clayton; IV Volumes; now in possession of Mrs. Clayton's daughter, Dr. Mary Clayton Hurlbut, Lockport, New York.

Hensel—W. U. Hensel, "Jeremiah Sullivan Black"; *The Green Bag*, II, May 1890, pp. 189-197. Hensel was a personal acquaintance of Black.

Niles—Henry C. Niles, "Jeremiah Sullivan Black and His Influence on the Laws of Pennsylvania," *9th Annual Report of the Pennsylvania Bar Association,* 1903, pp. 400-471. Niles also was a personal acquaintance of Black.

1

SCHOOL AND FARMING

IN THE year 1810 fell the twenty-first birthday of the American national government. Although James Madison, "Father of the Constitution," sat at the helm, nevertheless this twenty-first year marked the passing of control in Congress from the Revolutionary fathers into the more aggressive hands of a younger generation—the "war hawks," typified by Henry Clay and John C. Calhoun, by William Crawford and Felix Grundy, who, two years later, were to force the issue with Great Britain and thereafter were to dominate the arena of politics until the eve of the Civil War.

Legal principles incident to this new form of government were yet but faintly crystallized. Of the political issues that were to shake the foundations, only the faint rumblings occasioned by the Virginia and Kentucky resolutions had yet been heard. The more ominous eruptions —Hartford Convention, Nullification of South Carolina, Slavery Compromises of 1820 and 1850, Dred Scott, Secession, Civil War, and Reconstruction—were yet in the future. Only to astute minds were warning signals visible.

Jeremiah Sullivan Black was born in this momentous twenty-first year of American national life. We shall follow his life, as he grew and developed with these legal and political issues in which he was to play a part, as he wrought an influence upon them, and was in turn influenced by them.

The date of his birth was January 10. The place was "Pleasant Glades," a farm in Stony Township, Somerset County, in western Pennsylvania.[1]

This unique section of Pennsylvania is not quite a valley, nor yet a basin, but is a high level tableland cupped between the crests of the Allegheny Mountains and Laurel Ridge, 2,000 feet above the sea. It abounds in glades—wet level lands about the headwaters of streams —and is characterized by short seasons, early snows, delightfully cool summers, and wild beautiful scenery. Braddock's historic road passes

[1] C. F. Black, p. 7; Clayton, p. 12.

At the end of this volume will be found a bibliography which lists the complete publication details of all general works, public documents, and magazine articles cited herein; the essential information concerning the manuscripts cited is also listed. For the additional convenience of the reader a short list of abbreviations of works most frequently cited is placed opposite the first page of the text.

through the county. Its people at this time were chiefly of German descent; indeed of its numerous churches, nearly two-thirds were Lutheran or German Reformed. Villages were fairly numerous, but small. Its county seat and largest center, Somerset, numbered less than 500 persons. Its people were distinctly rural, separated from communities toward the seaboard by the barrier of the Alleghenies.[2]

In Jeremiah Black were mingled the strains of the two nationalities who were prominent in colonizing western Pennsylvania, German and Scotch-Irish. His paternal great-grandfather, John Black, had landed at Philadelphia, from North Ireland, about 1730, and had at once pushed westward. One of the sons of John Black was James. All that we know of James can be stated in a few words: He married a Jane McDonough in 1770; he moved still farther west than his father had lived, and settled in Somerset county; he became unusually prosperous and owned several farms; to him and his wife was born a son, Henry Black, on February 25, 1783. This Henry Black was the father of Jeremiah Sullivan Black. We shall return to him later.[3]

Upon the maternal side, Jeremiah Sullivan Black's grandfather was Patrick Sullivan, who was born in Ireland on St. Patrick's day, 1754. He came to America at the age of fifteen. Later he served as a captain in the Pennsylvania line during the American Revolution and, coming to York upon some military duty, he there met and married Barbara Bouser, a German girl who had but recently landed in America. For a while they lived in York. There a daughter, Mary Sullivan, was born to them. Later, however, they removed to Somerset County and settled upon a farm in the neighborhood of the Black family. Sullivan was a stern Federalist and prominent in local politics. For some years he was a representative in the State Legislature from Somerset County. He seems to have been the type of man who brooked no opposition from friend, foe, or menial; who used to "knock down arguments upon all occasions."[4]

Henry Black, meanwhile, had met and married Mary Sullivan. Together they had taken up their abode on the Black homestead in Somerset County. Jeremiah Sullivan Black was their eldest child. He was named for his mother's brother, a flourishing tobacco merchant of Baltimore.[5] Two other children also were born to them—another son, James, and a daughter, Mary Anne. James was drowned in the Allegheny River at Pittsburgh when a youth of nineteen. Of him it is impossible to learn much. Even his older brother, Jeremiah, never wrote or uttered his name in any reminiscence of boyhood. This aversion

[2] *Hazard's Register*, 1830-1836, lists Somerset almost annually as having the earliest snow in the state.

[3] Clayton, pp. 9-10.

[4] C. F. Black, p. 2; Clayton, pp. 11-12.

[5] Clayton, p. 12.

was typical of Jeremiah. "His nature could never voice any deep grief," said his daughter.[6]

The sister, Mary Anne, married a Somerset merchant and spent her entire life in this community.[7] Occasionally she flits across the historian's eye through letters, still preserved, to her brother.

The father, Henry Black, was a man of considerable prominence. He served from 1815 to 1818 in the State Legislature; from 1820 to 1840 he was a lay judge of Somerset County.[8] He ended his career by a term in Congress, being elected to that office in 1841.[9]

This prominence did not afford his son, however, educational facilities beyond the meager ones of this western community; nor, may we add, did it lift the mortgage from the family homestead. Both of these details were to be left to the resourcefulness of young Jere himself.[10]

Jere's schooling began at the age of five, when he was sent to school in the neighboring village of Stoystown. Two or three months later, however, the school system of Stoystown collapsed in midyear.[11] The schoolmaster had run away. Young Black was then taken to a second neighboring village of Berlin, some fifteen miles from Stoystown. "I learned nothing, or next to nothing, at either place," said Black, "except an intense dislike of confinement in doors. It sticks to me yet."[12] And he adds that, after several years of attending school in Berlin, he joined hands with other boys in seeking relief by searching for nails and pieces of iron among the ashes of a barn that had been struck by lightning and burnt down. Firm in the belief that these were objects of proven and tested power in drawing the lightning, they deposited them with great care under the schoolhouse and withdrew in serene confidence that the building would be demolished and their troubles ended for some time at least.[13]

There seems to have been more than mere horseplay in the prank. It was the day of "lickin' and larnin'," of gerund grinding and word wrestling, when subjects often were deliberately made a grind and human interests in the subject-matter were as often systematically stifled. "I loved books," said Black in speaking of this period of his life; and in the same breath he exclaimed, "I hated school."[14]

[6] *Ibid.*, p. 16.

[7] New York *Tribune*, August 20, 1883. The information for this article was furnished by Black's son Chauncey.

[8] *Ibid.*

[9] *Conspectus of National Cyclopedia of American Biography*, p. 39.

[10] Hensel, p. 189.

[11] Black's Autobiography; Clayton, p. 13. Black's daughter, Mary B. Clayton, states that Black began an autobiography in 1876 but never finished it. This autobiography is no longer extant, but large portions of it, all treating of his youth, are quoted by Clayton. Subsequent citations to it will refer both to it and to the pages in Clayton in which it appears.

[12] Autobiography, Clayton, p. 13.

[13] *Ibid.*, p. 13.

[14] *Ibid.*, p. 14.

Yet he attended school withal. From Berlin he later removed to Somerset, boarded with a friend of the family and attended the village school. Here he was offered the highest level of instruction in the county, and, upon finishing, he was looked upon by his former classmates of Berlin as having attained the pinnacle of educational standing.[15]

Still the youth was dissatisfied. Out of school, he had read much, in fact had exhausted the substantial libraries of his father and grandfather. Perhaps in Somerset he had met with one of those rare teachers, some unknown Mark Hopkins, who had discarded the traditional methods of the day and revealed to him the distant heights of learning. We do not know. But we do know that he felt that even the county's best at Somerset was not enough.[16] His eyes turned eastward. In Brownsville lived an uncle, David Black. In Brownsville also was a classical academy. So to Brownsville he went and attended the academy.[17] When he graduated here at the age of sixteen or seventeen he had completed all of the education he ever received at the hands of regular masters.

This education was the common, traditional one for that day. Chiefly it had included the Latin classics, mathematics, philosophy, and the natural sciences. Of Latin he was especially fond, and at fifteen or thereabouts had become a skilled Horatian. He committed Horace verbatim; translated it into English prose, and then turned his English prose into English verse of his own. Throughout his life, he remembered all three—Latin, English prose, and English verse—though neither of the English versions had ever been put into writing.[18] One of his amusements in leisure moments was to compare his youthful version with the numerous published translations.

In literature he had made the acquaintance in school with Dryden, Pope, and some of the minor poets. Outside of school, he says, "I had learned the whole Bible, and thought myself versed in its historical parts very well. I was not wholly ignorant of law. I had come across the Trial of the Judges . . . and read with intensest interest all the speeches and all the journal proceedings as well as the evidence."[19] This familiarity with the phraseology and content of the Bible was to

[15] F. A. Burr, Philadelphia *Press*, August 20, 1883. Burr was a well-known journalist who in 1881 published Black's Memoirs in the Philadelphia *Press*. His material was largely taken first hand from letters, documents, and verbal testimony of Black and other men with whom Black was associated. Burr also published supplementary articles in the *Press* on these interviews during 1882 and 1883.

[16] *Ibid.*

[17] C. F. Black, p. 2.

[18] *Ibid.*, p. 3.

[19] Clayton, p. 22.

prove, by all odds, the most potent in future use of any subject he had yet covered. It, with Shakespeare, was to form the backbone of a vivid and remarkably forceful style. But Shakespeare was yet undiscovered by him. Like the Bible, it was to be discovered outside of the classroom.

At that time in general appearance, he was pale and spare and freckled. His mother often said of him, "Jere looks as if the wind would blow him away." Commenting in later life upon his appearance as a young man, Black remarks, "I must have been very ungainly. My associates did not venture any remarks to me on such a subject, but later in life many of them said, that while I was a student I seemed to them most awkward and unpromising. When a half grown boy I boarded at Captain Webster's whose wife watched me with much interest. One evening she sat knitting at the fire place while I was opposite her, absorbed in the study of my lessons. After giving me a long look she said with a sigh, "Well, Jere, you may be a very good man some day; I hope you will; but, bless my soul, you will never be handsome!"[20]

He never felt the desire to learn the ordinary amusements of youth, never learned to swim, shoot, skate, or to play cards.[21] His only recreations seemed to be reading and conversation. The latter he developed to a high art, not only as a mode of expressing his own views but also as a source of acquiring knowledge, until a friend later wrote of him, "He plunders everybody he meets of all they know, and then it is his forever. . . . He talks all the time, but he wouldn't bore you if you made the trip with him from here to Pittsburgh by canal boat."[22]

Yet upon completing his academic studies, this youth—who had no interest in outdoor life or pursuits, who had an intense interest in books and thoughts, and already a faint intimation of his unusual power of intellect—turned his footsteps back to the Somerset farm and took his place behind the plow. But turning of the earth could never attract him. It served him only as an accompaniment to the recitations of some verse, of Dryden or Poe, Horace or Virgil. He continued his education, as Burns made his songs, "behind the plow and to the music of the crumbling soil." His body was maturing into the strength of manhood; the spare, lean frame was filling into the proportions of an unusually large man, tall, straight, supple, with the strength of a giant. His mind was a pace ahead of his body.

"Mental inactivity is to me a great pain," he said many years later. "Work for the mind is as essential to my health as food for the body. Conversation will suffice for a time. Even light reading will satisfy

[20] Autobiography, Clayton, p. 24.

[21] Clayton, p. 18.

[22] Undated letter, William Elder to Colonel Wolff, Black Papers, Vol. I.

me for a time. But I must have law or metaphysics for substantial food."[23]

Neither of these substantials was to be found behind the plow, and his father's attitude toward his attendance upon that implement may be suggested in the story which made its rounds, that when starting for Harrisburg on horseback to attend the state legislature, Henry Black asked each of the family what he should bring them. To Jere he said, "And what do you want, my son?" Jere promptly and earnestly replied, "Shakespeare's Plays, father." Whereupon the father retorted, "Oh, no, Jere, I had better bring *you* somebody's *Works*."[24] Young Jere always denied with some heat the insinuation thereby conveyed that he was guilty of physical idleness. "I learned to work on the farm as creditably as any boy of my age . . . I think I disappointed nobody by lack of physical exertion."[25] Still, all in all, he freely admitted that he "did not promise well as a field hand." Every hour of leisure was occupied in reading or reflection.

[23] F. A. Burr, Philadelphia *Press* August 20, 1883.
[24] David Paul Brown, *The Forum,* II, p. 104.
[25] Clayton, p. 17.

2

THE YOUNG LAWYER

YOUNG Jere had turned his thoughts toward a career in medicine. His father's thoughts ran to law. The two were agreed upon one point—that he showed poor promise as a farmer. The law won, partially because his father's mind was fixed, but more perhaps because at Somerset there was an excellent opening for a student of the law in the office of Chauncey Forward.[1]

Chauncey Forward was one of the most genuinely brilliant lawyers in western Pennsylvania, with a wide practice and a wider acquaintance. He was a Democratic leader of his district and at this time, 1827, also a member of Congress, serving in that body from 1825 to 1831.[2] He was a brother of Walter Forward of Pittsburgh who served as Secretary of State in Tyler's administration, and of Judge Oliver Forward, an early and prominent citizen of Buffalo. Some impartial observers regarded him as the most able of this distinguished trio.[3]

This contact of young Black with Chauncey Forward was fraught with tremendous consequences. Not only did it lead to an exceptionally severe and thorough training in the law, but it started him out as a young attorney with the prestige of Forward's name. Later it influenced his choice of a wife and set the trend of his religious thinking. Taken altogether, it was one of the most significant episodes of his life that he was, at the age of seventeen, brought under the tutelage of so able and prominent a master.

But the young student of law was not at first encouraged by these possibilities. His shoulders were weighted down with the seemingly hopeless task of mastering the principles and practice of his new profession. For one whose exceptional mentality was already apparent, he possessed a surprising lack of confidence in his own powers. Through most of his life, as we shall see, this lack of self-confidence followed him into every new vicissitude, and it was not until he was beyond middle age that he came to a conscious realization of his true powers. As a youth, this lack of confidence was disturbing to his peace of mind. "My heart sank within me," he wrote, "when I looked at the catalogue of books and saw how many branches of abstruse learning

[1] Clayton, p. 21.

[2] *Conspectus of National Cyclopedia of American Biography*, pp. 40-41.

[3] Clayton, p. 45.

were required to make up a lawyer . . . Mr. Forward knew that I needed encouragement, and he intended to give it, but his earliest lectures and conversations depressed me still more by the vastness of the knowledge which he himself possessed. He seemed to be talking to me from a height, so great and inaccessible that I could never reach it."[4]

He did, however, after much struggling, make what he termed "slow progress." Chauncey Forward, as we shall observe, entertained a much more favorable opinion of this rate of progress than the subject himself.

Black's habit of devouring every book of any description that came to hand continued with unabated vigor, and the library of Chauncey Forward offered him a greater opportunity in this direction than he had heretofore enjoyed. It was not, however, until the second year of his study of the law that he made the discovery which was to cast so significant a shadow upon his style of writing and speaking. I refer to his discovery of Shakespeare. When once he had tasted of the savor of this literature, however, he devoured it to the last line. Not content with merely a single reading of these plays he reread them again and again until he was so thoroughly familiar with the major characters that, throughout life, he could quote accurately at will even from obscure passages. This discovery, he says, "was to me almost a new world."[5] To him it gave lessons both in expression and in philosophy that influenced, not only his literary style, but even his view of human concerns.

His memory was so exact that he was never known to have misquoted a passage. It annoyed him to hear others do so. When he was a member of the Constitutional Convention of Pennsylvania in 1873, each time some member quoted incorrectly he would stalk down the aisle, twirling his famous tobacco box, and say to the reporter: "My son, the gentleman from so-and-so has just made a citation from the great dramatist from Avon. It was not quite correct. It should have been thus. See that you get it correctly in the record." Apparently there must have been too many such offenders for his comfort, for one day he addressed his friend George M. Dallas to this effect: "Dallas, I expect to be away for a week. I desire your assurance that in my absence you will be present at each session of the Convention and for me and in my place, protect and defend the memory and reputation of my friend, William Shakespeare."[6]

Shortly after Black first began his reading of Shakespeare, he turned also to Milton. "Milton disappointed me at first," he said, "but Para-

[4] Autobiography, Clayton, p. 23.
[5] Clayton, p. 23.
[6] Niles, pp. 464-65.

dise Lost took me like Niagara. It gradually filled me with a sense of its awful grandeur."[7]

His zest for these new discoveries in literature, however, did not cause him to abandon his earlier favorites, Horace and the Bible. His admiration for the latter, at this time, sprang less from his regard for it as a chart of faith than from his interest in the turns of thought and the terseness of expression to be found in the King James version. Above all things, the coining of phrases, the stamping of thought into unmistakable patterns, attracted him. Cameos of expression irresistibly fascinated him. So drawn was he to this pursuit that it left him with some distaste for Coke and Blackstone and rendered his progress in law slower than it might otherwise have been.

Yet it cannot be said that the time devoted to literature was unprofitable. Nor was it unwisely balanced with his immediate purpose of studying law. He was setting the foundation upon which he was to build a style remarkable for its vigor and clarity of statement, and singular for its Anglo-Saxon purity. This style, in turn, became one of the direct sources of his power, not only as a controversial writer, but also as a lawyer and jurist. In his maturity, it was a continuous source of comment and surprise to those who were acquainted with the paucity of his early schooling. David Paul Brown, an author and lawyer who often appeared as counsel before the Supreme Court of Pennsylvania during the time that Black sat as Chief Justice of that body, was continuously impressed with his facility and vigor of expression. "The style of Judge Black's composition is unlike any other with which we are acquainted," he writes. "If we were asked to say in what the chief merit . . . depends, we should answer, in the perfect clearness in which he exhibits his thoughts—whether right or wrong, no man can misunderstand him." "It is to our mind, a beautiful style, and the wonder is, where he should have formed it. There certainly could have been no temptations within the ordinary jurisdiction of a county court to lead to so much perfection in composition; nor could his opportunities while at the bar account for his literary excellence. . . . He had not had the advantages Franklin, and many others, enjoyed in a printing office which, in itself, with a bright pupil, is the best of schools. Where, then, did he obtain it?"[8]

Allowing always for the influence upon style of the vigor and lucidity of thought itself, the answer to Brown's query is to be found in Black's early and intensive contact with unexcelled masters of English and Latin prose and poetry. Horace and Milton, Shakespeare and the Bible—these four—were the exemplars which served as models for his style. So intensely did he study them, that they forever served him as reservoirs from which he could draw, at random and at will,

[7] Clayton, p. 23.

[8] David Paul Brown, *The Forum*, II, p. 106.

to "startle or thrill with a variety of apt quotation." It is not without significance that he was thoroughly at home with all of these sources before the age of twenty.

His first prominent appearance as a speaker was upon July 4th, 1830. The Mountain Cavalry of Somerset had planned a celebration for the occasion and were looking for a speaker who could give phrase to their inarticulate thought and sentiments of the day. Who could serve them better than this twenty-year-old grandson of a Revolutionary captain? So to him they turned, drafting him as chief speaker of the day. How much labor of the lamp went into this effort, we do not know. Likewise the curtains are drawn over whatever measure of success the occasion may have brought him. But at least the crowd gathered, he spoke, and a copy of the carefully prepared address was preserved for us through its publication in the next issue of the Somerset *Whig*.

It is a speech typical of what might be expected of any precocious twenty-year-old youth. It is marked at times with a buoyant exaggeration—a quality, it should be noted, which is not always confined on such occasions to youth. The topic of this day, he tells us, can never be hackneyed or exhausted, "as long as the bosom of an American contains one pulse that beats with public spirit, or one chord that vibrates with patriotism." The day itself is still the most important on the calendar. "Every philanthropist hails it with joy; every advocate of the rights of his race, points to it as an example; and every lover of freedom from Zembia to Cape Horn, glows with delight at a retrospective glance to the Fourth of July Seventy-six."

The impelling necessity of speaking in concrete language at all costs and all times, has not yet impressed him. He pays gilded and glowing tribute to Washington, Franklin, Jefferson, and Henry without stooping to mention any one of these characters by name. In Washington, for example, "We see the glory of the ever-admired commander-in-chief of the army in its fullest splendor. We admire the hero, who, elevated above all his compeers, bared his head to the storm, and 'in naked majesty defied the shock.'"

The figurative language is rough-cut, though none of it is grossly mixed or wholly incongruous. Taken as a whole it serves its purpose well. Like every youth, he draws lessons from Rome—yet only three times and each but briefly, which is a low record for speakers of his age.

With all of its immaturity, this speech bears the unmistakable stamp of Black's personality and is marked with certain characteristics which are later developed and refined by him into trademarks of style. Outstanding among these, is the ability—already here marked—to sprinkle his language with apt and startling quotations that are woven into the woof of his own language and text. With sudden effect, he here dramatized the words of Patrick Henry: "I am not worth buying, but such as I am, the King of England is too poor to do it." That monarch, continued Black, "learned 'what constitutes a state;' that it is not—

> High raised battlement, strong tower, or
> moated gate;

No, not even their floating bulwarks of British oak—but men,

> High minded men, who know their rights,
> And, knowing, dare maintain."

All in all, it is doubtful if his moderately educated audience could fully follow all of his abstruse allusions or grasp all of his abstract phrasing of ideas. Yet this ideal is seldom realized in speeches of such occasions, not even by the much-touted Bunker Hill orations of Webster himself. If the effort on the whole was sophomoric it must be said in extenuation that his was exactly the age of a sophomore. The wonder was not that the effort was sophomoric, but that it was made at all.[9]

If his law studies suffered from his preference for literature, the neglect did not fatally impair progress. Before he had reached his twentieth birthday, Forward felt that the tutor's task was done and urged Black to take examinations for the bar. The young man was reluctant. His confidence in himself was in no whit improved, but under Forward's insistence he yielded and passed his bar examinations.[10] No sooner were the examinations finished than Forward did a most remarkable thing. He advertised his own large practice into the hands of young Attorney Black. This was his answer to that young man's fears of his own ability. Having done this, Forward betook himself to Congress and left Black to work out his own salvation under the load of an assured practice.[11] "My anxiety and trouble under this load of responsibility," said Black, "were greater than I can express. I would have thrown it off and gone at anything that promised half the pay; but I had no such chance, and so I kept on in the law for the mere lucre of it, until I began to love it for its own sake."[12]

But it would seem that Forward's practice was not the only source of business. Henry Black, his father, was a man of wide political and personal influence. Many of his friends brought their business to his son's office. And as if these sources of practice were not enough to keep a young attorney busy, the offices of both deputy sheriff and prosecuting attorney were thrust upon him. There was scarcely a case

[9] A full copy of this speech is found in Clayton, pp. 30-44.
[10] Clayton, pp. 20-21.
[11] C. F. Black, p. 4.
[12] Clayton, p. 25.

that came before the local court in which he was not, in some capacity, forced to serve. "And I would rather have mauled nails," he said.[13]

Under ordinary circumstances an able young attorney in a small village might expect to find his way easier at the start through the lack of opposition from other able lawyers. But Somerset in that day was a notable exception. Among the attorneys at this bar was a group of men of unusual ability and wide experience. If Chauncey Forward was perhaps the ablest, he was not the only one. Left behind to confront and confound young Attorney Black was Charles Ogle, who later attained a national reputation before the bar and who, in Congress, was a central figure in assaulting Van Buren's administration and driving it from power. Ogle had few equals in his day in the use of invective—a weapon unduly powerful in frontier communities. Also there was Joseph Williams, already established in law practice, who was later to become a federal judge in Kansas and chief justice of the Supreme Court of Iowa. Following him were nearly half a dozen others who rose later to state prominence in law and politics.

"How, under the circumstances, I kept along with a full practice and a fair success is a little mysterious," said Black.[14] But in truth, it gives us the key to his early success. Cases were thrust upon him. He was forced into the court room, forced day after day into mental combat with men older in experience and recognized in attainments. Shrinking from the dread of these contests, yet he was driven perforce to carry on, until finally he mastered his fear, and grew in power and in skill. His weaknesses of argument were exposed by skillful opponents until he learned to leave few flanks exposed. He was driven to use his tongue in quick and ready repartee, and he discovered in that member a stinging weapon of attack. Completely he justified the confidence placed in him by Forward. By the time he was twenty-six years of age, most of his seniors at the bar had disappeared from the stage and had left him with a still larger practice and a reputation that was extending to other parts of the state.

In beginning the study of the law, "I did not know the value of general principles, or how legal problems could be solved by the application of fundamental maxims," said Black. But already he was seeing that law, in all its myriad of minute details, could not be mastered by one man; or even if it could be so mastered, courts and juries could never be led to disentangle themselves from its intricacies. Already he was reducing the law to a few fundamental principles—clear in general outline to both lay and legal mind—and was drawing upon his growing power of language to apply those maxims to questions of law in strikingly vivid and convincing phrases. Thus were

[13] F. A. Burr, Philadelphia *Press*, August 20, 1883.

[14] Clayton, p. 29.

the hours spent with Horace, Milton, Shakespeare, and the Bible henceforth related with his advancement in law.

In the formative years from twenty to twenty-five, the tenor of his life had been set. Intensely had the law possessed him. To the end of his life he remained a lawyer and a lawyer only. Business held no moment of inducement. Mere money-getting offered little allurement. Politics attracted him strongly, but always and only in its relation to law. He seldom viewed a political question apart from its legal aspect. With all of his attachment to politics, he cared less than common for political office. The law had fired in him a burning zeal which consumed all lesser desires. Under its banner there was, there could be, no philosophic calm; none of the cool and leisured dignity of the scholar. It was rather the bugler's note, the trumpet call, the "clang of steel on shield." The law for him was the militant patriarch of justice. It spoke with the voice of the prophets.

3

MARRIAGE

THE eldest of Chauncey Forward's eight children was Mary. When Black came to study law under her father, Mary was eight years of age; the young law student was seventeen and a half. This disparity of age put them at once upon familiar terms. The tall youth brought her presents, petted her, and treated her as a very nice and very young child. He was a frequent visitor at the Forward home, where he borrowed books, paced the floor in conversation "wearing out carpets," and talking with his mentor upon "every subject between heaven and earth," while young Mary sat and listened and admired both of them.

In 1831, Forward returned from Congress to resume his practice of law. Black continued his struggles as a young attorney, and resumed his visits to the Forward home. Shortly thereafter Mary left home to attend a boarding school at Cumberland, Maryland. When she returned, she had grown from childhood to young womanhood. Black ceased petting her, but his visits continued unabated; he conversed with her father as often and as vigorously as ever, and wore out carpets by his pacing with accustomed zeal. Books and conversation apparently were still the prime motives for his visits.

Yet there were perceptible differences. Soon he took to visiting the Forward home on Sunday mornings when, as he well knew, Mr. and Mrs. Forward were attending church, and Mary, as the dutiful eldest child, was at home in charge of the seven younger Forwards. The books, of course, were still in the library and he would take one from the shelves, reading it and discussing it with her. But books were not uppermost in the minds of either of them.

Mary was only sixteen when they were formally engaged to be married.

This event was hastened by tragic circumstances. Mary's mother, in the winter of 1835-36, had caught a "fever" from a son who had been in Washington, and after a devastating and lingering illness, died. Her father's practice took him away from Somerset for such frequent and extended periods, that he feared to leave his home in the unaided hands of a youthful daughter. He therefore urged an immediate marriage of the engaged couple, suggesting that they make their home with him so as to care for the family during his absences.

The young couple needed little urging, so fifteen days after her mother's death, Mary Forward was united with Jere Black in marriage. There had been no time for the usual preparation of wedding things. There was no merry-making, no wedding feast.[1]

The date of the marriage was March 23, 1836. It was the day preceding Mary's seventeenth birthday.[2]

For more than a year the young couple lived in the Forward home. Domestic relations appear to have been wholly harmonious, but other circumstances eventually led to a separation of the two families. The Blacks longed for a home of their own. Their eldest child, Rebecca, had arrived on March 7, 1837. The young mother, not yet eighteen, no doubt felt that it would be easier to care for her child out of sound and reach of her seven younger brothers and sisters. Finally, Chauncey Forward brought a second wife to his home, relieving the Blacks of their duty toward the Forward family.

At the same time another circumstance also hastened their decision. Forward had moved from the home in which Mary Black had been born, but she had long wanted to live there again. The house itself had burned, probably in the great Somerset fire of 1833 which destroyed nearly a quarter of the town.[3] But a new house had been built upon the old grounds. The tall poplars were still there, the hedges, the old garden. It still wore the air of home. "The place was just on the edge of town, the house was set back from the road among fine old trees, in an inclosure of several acres—an ideal home for a romantic couple with rural tastes."[4]

Meanwhile Mr. Hamden, a lawyer who now lived there, decided to leave for Pittsburgh. Eagerly the Blacks bought the place, moved in, and began homemaking. New walks were laid out; new trees and hedges, arbors and vines, soon improved the beauty of the old familiar grounds. For a time, even literature and law were neglected for fruits and vegetables. The couple acquired some local reputation for the excellence of their strawberries, raspberries, grapes, and plums. They kept horses, cows, chickens, pigs. "One night Mr. Black got home from a distant court too late to see how his garden grew," his daughter tells us. "He asked his wife if some plum trees which he had planted before he left had grown in his absence. She said, she thought not much. The next morning he said, 'Mary, those plum trees have grown several inches.' 'How do you know?' she asked. 'Why, I went out last night after you were asleep and *felt* them.' "[5]

In this home they lived for twenty years—until Black went to Washington in 1857 as Attorney-General in Buchanan's Cabinet. Here all of their children, save Rebecca their eldest, were born—Chauncey

[1] Clayton, pp. 45-52.
[2] Forward-Black Family Bible.
[3] *Hazard's Register,* XII, p. 280.
[4] Clayton, p. 54.
[5] Clayton, p. 55.

Forward Black, in 1839; Henry, in 1842; Mary, in 1845; and Anna (always known as Nannie), in 1852.[6] It is to Mary Black, later Mrs. Clayton, that we are indebted for so many of the details of her father's early life.

Here we might pause for a glance at the personal features and characteristics of the man. Hensel tells us that he was six feet tall and "straight as an arrow."[7] David Paul Brown, however, places his height at "about five feet, ten inches."[8] Both men knew him well, both on the whole are accurate writers. Black's daughter supports Hensel's judgment; "he was six feet high."[9] Still, his exceptionally erect carrriage may have given the illusion of greater height than he actually possessed, although it is almost certain that Brown underestimates his height. "Just under six feet," seems to be the more general estimate.

Brown speaks of his "strong, compact, and active frame, apparently capable of enduring great physical toil." Undoubtedly he was a man of uncommon physical strength. Hensel adds that he had a "ruddy complexion," and "shaggy eyebrows." The latter feature is markedly emphasized by his photographs. To call them "shaggy," gives only a hint of their true characteristics. They were bushy, immense, overhanging. Beneath them glittered a pair of grey eyes that drew attempted descriptions in every portrait ever written of him. They were luminous, volatile, quizzical. His friends speak of them as sparkling with geniality, and expressive of his finest shades of feeling. Court-room reporters mark the withering effect of their glittering wrath upon witnesses, opposing counsels, and even the court itself at times.

Already the eccentricities for which he was later famous were being manifested. "He wore out a good many carpets," his daughter tells us, for when "he thought deeply or became interested in conversation, he rose to his feet and paced up and down the floor . . . generally keeping on exactly the same path, and soon leaving a bare place at both ends where he turned about."

Yet all of his pacing was not done indoors, for down "in the lowest part of his garden, he allowed the hedges to grow very thick and high, making a sort of barricade for one long, quiet, shaded walk. Here he paced and pondered by the hour, wearing with his feet a white track in the gravel. When his wife wanted him to come to dinner or some other sublunary purpose, she sent one of the children to put a small soft hand in his and lead him to the house."[10]

These eccentricities soon gave rise to newspaper legends, until it

[6] Forward-Black Family Bible.
[7] Hensel, p. 196.
[8] D. P. Brown, *The Forum,* II, p. 108.
[9] Clayton, p. 46.
[10] Clayton, pp. 47, 56.

is now impossible to separate the true from the false. Black's daughter, Judge Henry C. Niles, and Mrs. J. V. L. Findley do, however, agree in their testimony from personal recollection that the "shirt story" was true. Mrs. Black, it seems, could never convince her husband of the importance of frequent changes of linen while attending court. So accustomed was he at home of having her exchange fresh shirts for soiled ones, that he never observed the changes. Away from home, he continued to wear the same linen, regardless of time or condition. Finally she packed him four shirts as he was leaving on a four-day trip to court. "Now Jere," she admonished, "you simply must wear these shirts. Do you hear me?" "Yes, Mary," he replied. "And do you promise?" she persisted. "Yes, Mary," he promised.

He left home, attended court and returned. His wife unpacked his traveling bag. Not a shirt was to be found. "Jere, where are those shirts?" she demanded. "You said for me to wear them," he grumbled. "Yes, but what did you do with them after you wore them?" she demanded. "Nothing," he replied with a twinkle in his eyes. He had spoken the literal truth. All four shirts were upon his back, the clean ones over the soiled ones. He had kept his promise and had appeared each day at court with a fresh shirt.[11] Mary Black never fully trusted her husband again in such matters. Many years later, when he was attending court in Washington, she sent the following significant telegram:

Sent clothes today. I will come Saturday if you don't come home. Answer.[12]

In truth, Black was indifferent to any external force, sound, or thought when he was engrossed in court work or any work. "He seemed oblivious to all else in the world," writes his brother-in-law, Judge Francis J. Kooser. "Mealtime and bedtime differed in nowise from any other hours of the day or night. Force or particularly urgent language alone could get him from his task, and yet I heard him say once he believed he was the best loafer in the land. This was based on the fact that on his farm, in good weather, he would tramp about, refusing to attend to any business. Sometimes, for weeks, he would not open or read a letter or a telegram, one or another of his family doing this service, and nagging him into directing what replies, if any, should be made."[13]

[11] Clayton, (p. 56), places the date of this episode as sometime during Black's early married life. Judge H. C. Niles and Mrs. J. V. L. Findley (to the writer, January 11, 1930) each recall the incident. They were residents of York, Pa., and well acquainted with the Black family. Since Black did not move to York until 1861, the incident must have occurred after this date.

[12] Black Papers, April 16, 1874.

[13] Francis J. Kooser to the writer, January 23, 1930.

4

POLITICS AND RELIGION

BLACK'S interest in politics began at an early age. At sixteen he read Randolph's collection of Jefferson's letters and already was a trenchant Jeffersonian Democrat.[1] At eighteen he marched in the ranks of Jackson followers during the campaign of '28, and forever remained his ardent and militant defender. Before he was twenty-one, when the Anti-Mason issue arose, he leaped to the defense of Jacksonian Democracy with a series of articles in the local Somerset papers.[2] Through the vicissitudes of party triumphs and disasters, of Secession and Civil War, he never wavered from his first political faith. "He believed in the principles of Democracy as he did in a demonstration of Euclid," wrote James G. Blaine of him in later years. "All that might be said on the other side was necessarily absurd."[3] A more precise statement might be that he believed that the Bill of Rights was the most sacred portion of the Constitution, and that the rights of man should be set above the rights of money. He could see but one party which championed this principle.

His adherence to the Democratic Party, and especially his militant championship of Jackson, is all the more remarkable in the light of his father's views. That gentleman once had been a Democrat himself, but gradually he had been estranged from the party. The election of Jackson, which elated the son, was to the father the last straw. He went over to the Whigs. The effect of his views upon his son, if any, served only to strengthen the latter's loyalty to Jackson and Democracy. He plunged at once into political strife—corresponding, organizing, campaigning with the utter abandon which he gave, when aroused, to any enterprise.

Significant results sprang from these early political activities. At some period in the Thirties it led to a meeting between Black and James Buchanan. Black was twenty years the younger, but the two men struck a warm and lasting friendship. Black's first admiration for Buchanan was from the latter's skill as a lawyer. He felt that Buchanan was one of the greatest lawyers of his day. His argument in the impeachment case of Judge Peck before the United States Supreme Court, Black

[1] New York *Tribune*, August 20, 1883. Material for this article was furnished by Black's son, Chauncey.

[2] C. F. Black, p. 4.

[3] J. G. Blaine, *Twenty Years*, I, p. 230.

claimed, was the greatest legal argument ever made upon the power of a court to punish for contempt. In truth, he admired Buchanan more as a lawyer than he ever admired him as a statesman and executive. In later years he said, "he ought to have been Chief Justice of the United States. He would have made the greatest jurist that ever graced the bench."[4]

On his side, Buchanan was attracted to Black. Through the many earlier disappointing years of aspiring to the Presidency, he confided his hopes and ambitions to Black to an extent accorded to few other men. After 1836 the two men were in continuous correspondence. On March 22 of that year Black, in writing to Buchanan for a copy of the latter's reply to Webster, undertook to offer this bit of pungent advice regarding the latter's political course: "Cox's friends would consider it an honor to him to be kicked by you. I don't think either he or they ought to be gratified in that way any further."[5]

From under the hard-cider and log-cabin Whig landslide in 1840, he again wrote Buchanan: "We are near about as badly beaten as our enemy ever wished us to be." "When the anti-popular party in a republican government 'stoop to conquer,' God knows they stoop low enough for any purpose."[6]

As early as 1841, he was writing to Buchanan in this vein: "Your friends in the western part of this state are making a strong and I think well concerted movement in your favor for the Presidency."[7]

Meanwhile other political movements were afoot which had more immediate results. In 1841 the Democrats of western Pennsylvania decided to nominate Black for the vacancy in Congress caused by the death of Charles Ogle. But the Whigs again "stooped to conquer" by hastening to forestall the nomination through putting up Black's father, Henry Black, for that office. The maneuver had the desired result. The son refused to run against the father and the latter was triumphantly elected to Congress.[8]

Political recognition was not long denied the son, however. The following year, 1842, saw a vacancy in the office of President Judge of the 16th Judicial District of Pennsylvania. This district was composed of Franklin, Bedford, and Somerset Counties (to which Blair and Fulton counties were later added when these counties became organized). Because of his active political services, Black felt that he had some claim in disposing of this vacancy and wrote Governor Porter urging the appointment of James X. McClanahan, a Chambersburg attorney.[9] At the moment, however, there was a tangle in Pennsylvania

[4] New York *Tribune*, August 20, 1883.

[5] Black File, Buchanan Papers, March 22, 1838.

[6] Black File, Buchanan Papers, November 28, 1840.

[7] *Ibid.*

[8] F. A. Burr, Philadelphia *Press*, August 20, 1883.

[9] Niles, p. 401.

politics which prevented the Governor from appointing any of the candidates urged for the office. He therefore cut the knot by appointing the man who had never sought office in his own behalf.

So Black, at the age of thirty-two, became President Judge of that same 16th Judicial District in which his father formerly had served for twenty years as a lay judge.[10]

He was the youngest judge in the State. Many older men had coveted the honor. Many gray-haired lawyers felt it a little lowering to their dignity to address such a youth as "Your Honor." Extreme courtesy and tact were needed to prevent giving offense. Courtesy Black ever had, but not always tact. His tongue was quick; already he had acquired an audacity and quaintness of wit; his sarcasm could be as sharp and deadly as a rapier. Inevitably, at first, he gave offense to a few who appeared before his court. Yet the tongue that gave unwitting offense could also adroitly make amends. In a neighboring county was a leader of the bar whose name was Chambers, "gray in the law, and jealous of his professional dignity." In the very first case tried, the young judge and the old lawyer came to a sharp difference on a question of practice. Black's ready tongue gave offense to the venerable Chambers. But when other lawyers explained to the young judge how deep a wound had been given, he put aside his judicial dignity and offered an open apology in his court, closing with the irresistibly apt words of Othello: "Haply, for I am *black*, and have not those soft parts of conversation that *chamberers* have."[11]

Such amend won the heart of the older man. It gained a recognition for the young judge. Perhaps it also taught him the virtues of tact. At any rate, we hear of little thereafter but high respect and admiration for his qualities as a judge.

There were no railroads in his district. Black enjoyed riding and was fond of a spirited horse. So off from his wife and family he went horseback, traveling among the hills and valleys from court to court. Save for Shakespeare and the Prophets, he was much alone . . . meditating . . . growing . . .

His decisions acquired a note for "terseness and purity of style" and for their correct interpretations of law. Few went to higher courts, and few of these were reversed. He rose to a state-wide legal prominence.[12]

Turning aside from this thread of political events, we may now observe the influence of another force in Black's life. During the autumn of 1839 an epidemic of mountain fever had swept the vicinity of Somerset. Mary Black fell dangerously ill of the disease. Her father, Chauncey Forward, was stricken before she recovered. Black was in

[10] Black Papers, March 30, 1842.
[11] Clayton, p. 83.
[12] F. A. Burr, Philadelphia *Press*, August 20, 1883.

court at Ebensburgh when the news reached him that Forward was dying. Through daylight and darkness he spurred his horse, but when at last he reached his father-in-law's side, at three o'clock in the morning of October 9th, the end was at hand. Forward "made one agonizing, unsuccessful effort to speak his wishes to the man on whom he relied to carry them out, and died."[13]

As Forward's life, his legal learning, and his political views had deeply influenced the career of the younger man, so now his death in the prime of life, at forty-three, left a lasting impression. Black began to ponder upon the religious views of his counselor. His mind was still wrapped in these views when, seven weeks later, a son was born. The son, as a matter of course, was given the name of Chauncey Forward Black.[14]

Forward had been a devout and faithful member of that sect founded by Thomas and Alexander Campbell, and known officially as Disciples of Christ. Indeed, Thomas Campbell himself, upon one of his tours, had ridden into Somerset and before leaving had baptized Mr. and Mrs. Charles Ogle and Mr. and Mrs. Chauncey Forward. To the day of his death, Forward remained an eloquent and constant worker in the cause.[15] Black often had heard Alexander Campbell, the famous son of Thomas Campbell, preach in Somerset, and he had enjoyed his companionship not only in Forward's home but also in his own home. Toward this sect his mind was now turning in grave reflection.[16]

A second incident spurred his decision. Toward his father, Black felt a warm parental love and admiration. He had refused, it will be remembered, to accept the Democratic nomination for Congress in 1841 after his father had been placed on the Whig ticket. He had been overjoyed at his father's election. But shortly after that event—indeed upon November 28 of that year—his father was found dead in his bed at the Stony Creek farm. This shock, coming so directly upon the death of Forward, affected him uncommonly. He became possessed with the idea that he too had not long to live. He read much on religion. Once he said to his family: "I want you to be able to say when I am gone what Samuel said when he left the judgeship: 'Whose ox have I taken? or whose ass have I taken? or whom have I defrauded? whom have I oppressed? of whose hand have I received any bribe to blind mine eyes therewith? and I will restore it unto you. And they said, Thou hast not defrauded nor oppressed us; neither hast thou taken aught of any man's hand.' "[17]

He was now thinking of Christianity, not abstractly, but as a per-

[13] Clayton, p. 58.
[14] Forward-Black Family Bible.
[15] Clayton, p. 59.
[16] Clayton, p. 79.
[17] Clayton, p. 81.

sonal force in his life. It was characteristic of his dynamic nature to do nothing by halves. So he decided to visit Alexander Campbell at Bethany, Virginia, and to talk with him in person upon this subject now oppressing him. In May 1843 he set forth, taking his wife, his seven-months-old son Henry, a nurse, and Mrs. Charles Ogle, now a widow. Over the mountains to Pittsburgh they drove, thence down the valley to Bethany. Black was always a reckless driver, his daughter tells us, and upon more than one occasion upset his wife and family. But they reached Bethany with no bones broken.

For some days he and Campbell wrestled over the great problem. At the end, he was led out into the little stream and baptized by Campbell himself.

Ever afterward, when asked to what church he belonged he replied, "To the sect first called Christians at Antioch."[18]

To the end of his life, he remained a staunch adherent to this faith. Niles, who knew Black well in his later life, tells us that he "was a Christian, unostentatious and sincere. . . . But not of the churchman sort. His knee was too sturdy and his head too high to bend at any ritual or bow at cleric's nod. Lords spiritual had no more authority over his independent soul than princes temporal. . . . To him there was no distinction between things religious and secular. . . . Theology was no more sacred to him than law."[19]

[18] Clayton, pp. 84-85.
[19] Niles, p. 427.

5

BOOMS

FOLLOWING the death of Andrew Jackson, Black was called upon to deliver a Jackson eulogy at an important Democratic commemoration at Bedford. The address was given on July 28, 1845. Fifteen years had passed since his first sophomoric effort at Somerset. He was now thirty-five. His style had not yet reached its height, either in power or polish. Yet it was impelling and direct. He spoke with a movement and precision of language that marked the influence of long and continued association with masters of English style.

The subject was one to Black's liking; perfectly fitted to his nature, for in dealing with his Jackson's "memory there is no middle way. He himself is not a halfway man." He thereupon set forth his view of the man and his public character. "Andrew Jackson is entitled to stand higher on the list of public benefactors than any other man of his time. . . . He was a soldier unrivalled . . . a patriot pure and faithful, and a statesman uniting the greatest and best qualities of a republican ruler."

From Jackson's birth, through his youth, his early political and military career, the speaker unfolded his character. He lifts us to an epic drama where Jackson alone, unaided, overawed a whole mutinous army and turned its swelling discontent into a tide of loyalty, winning with it the decisive battles of the Seminole War. He depicted the man at New Orleans, confronted by "the finest army that ever landed on American soil." "And that city was not a Gibraltar or a Quebec—it had no natural advantages of position—no military works —no wall—no

> . . . high-raised battlement
> Strong tower, or moated gate,

and followed him through to his thrilling triumph.

The Presidency was next discussed, where "nullification reared its head—the Union was to be severed, because one of the States was displeased with a law," and where it failed because this man "spoke not in the language of expostulation, advice, or entreaty, but in the decisive and unequivocal tone."

Of Jackson's character, "he had been called ambitious . . . This accusation of his enemies coincides exactly with the praises of his friends. He *was* ambitious. But his was the ambition of a noble nature

. . . and intense desire to leave behind him a name hallowed by its association with great and beneficent actions. . . . Let those who object to such ambition make their worst of it." Let them remember "that there never was a period, from Jackson's arrival at the age of twenty-one till the day of his death, when he might not have been in the public service if he had so chosen; yet he spent more than half his time in private retirement. . . . His countrymen pressed upon him eleven different offices, without any procurement of his. Some of them he accepted with reluctance, and *all of them he resigned* before the term expired, except one; that one he surrendered back to the people after having held it as long as Washington had held it before him. . . . But I have done. It was, perhaps, unnecessary to say so much."[1]

The address was received among the Pennsylvania Democracy with acclamation. Copies of it were widely circulated. It brought Black prominently before the eyes of the State. David Paul Brown, who never before had heard of him, first came into contact with his name through "one of the literati, who had a right to judge," informing him "that the best biography or memoir of General Jackson that was ever produced, was written by *one* Black, from the backwoods of Pennsylvania, whom he had never seen, but should always admire."[2]

Meanwhile, the friendship and correspondence between Black and Buchanan had continued. The latter was now a member of Polk's Cabinet, and sought to be influential in his counsels. There was a vacancy upon the Supreme Court bench and Buchanan was attempting to fill it with a suitable man from Pennsylvania. But there was a thorn in the side of Buchanan's political flesh in the person of Simon Cameron. That gentleman had defaulted from the ranks of the Pennsylvania regulars, seized the balance of power between the Whigs and Democrats in the Legislature, and sent himself to the United States Senate.[3] He was there a standing menace to the political aspirations of Buchanan, for he stood in a position to oppose Buchanan's distribution of patronage in Pennsylvania.

Polk, likewise, was not anxious to enhance Buchanan's prestige by delivering the Federal patronage of Pennsylvania into his hands.[4] Against Buchanan's wishes Polk sent the name of George W. Woodward to the Senate for appointment to the Supreme Court.[5] But Cameron opposed the confirmation and Buchanan lifted no finger to have it confirmed. Woodward's appointment was rejected.[6]

Anxiously Buchanan cast around for a man suitable both to Cam-

[1] C. F. Black, pp. 189-205.
[2] Brown, *The Forum*, II, p. 109.
[3] A. K. McClure, *History of Pennsylvania*, I, p. 99.
[4] *Diary of James K. Polk*, I, p. 137.
[5] *Ibid.*
[6] *Ibid.*, p. 194.

eron and Polk. His choice seems to have fallen upon Black. It may appear surprising that he should have entertained any notion of elevating a thirty-five-year-old country judge, wholly unknown outside of his own State and not even well known over all parts within it, to so high a station. Yet Joseph Story had been but thirty-two when he attained that level; Buchanan rested supreme faith in the abilities of this young judge "from the backwoods of Pennsylvania"; also, he badly needed an acceptable candidate. Black was known to be upon friendly terms with Cameron. Perhaps Polk might be persuaded. Black wrote to Buchanan upon the subject, in considerable agitation of mind, when the news reached him. Although he carefully refrained from touching upon his own ambitions, there was a suppressed, almost quivering intensity in the letter. One senses in it that, with every fiber of his being, he coveted the high honor thus dangled before his view. Yet the old doubts assailed him. Was his ability worthy of a seat—alongside of Taney, McLean, Wayne, and Catron—upon the highest judicial bench in the land? The sheer altitude left him dizzy, and he had a "solemn conviction that any man who sits on that bench ought to have far higher qualifications than I possess."[7] He believed Robert C. Grier to be the best qualified man for the place.

Polk evidently was of the same mind as Black. Grier was given the appointment. Black remained in the district court.

He continued, however, to be favored for many offices. From Washington, Senator Cameron wrote him in 1848 that, after interviewing persons all over the State, he found a sentiment "that your nomination by the convention is very probable."[8] This refers probably to the governorship, but whatever the position, it went to another man, and on October 23 Cameron again wrote to Black upon the subject, this time in disgust over the nomination of an inferior candidate.

Through 1850 Black was in steady correspondence with John W. Forney of Philadelphia, Democratic political leader of his district. It is not clear from Forney's correspondence whether he was promoting Black's candidacy for any office or feeling him out upon other candidates. It is certain, however, that Forney regarded him as a man to be reckoned with. William Hopkins, on October 23 of this year, wrote to Black complaining that there were too many Black booms—booms for Governor, for Senator, and for the Supreme Bench. They divided his following. Hopkins urged him to concentrate upon the governorship.[9]

[7] Black to Buchanan; Black File, Buchanan Papers, January 24, 1845. Evidently this letter was written in 1846 instead of 1845, since Polk was not President in January 1845. Also the Woodworth nomination was rejected in January 1846; see *Polk's Diary,* I, p. 194.

[8] Black Papers, August 10, 1848.

[9] Black Papers, October 23, 1850.

Black was not insensible to his opportunities. Yet he appears to have disliked maneuvering for a place. Whether this sprang from pride or from astute politics one cannot with certainty now say; but it seems to have been from pride. Sooner or later, some higher recognition he knew must be given him. It appears to have better suited his nature to wait until momentum was gathered without. He was not unmindful of this factor in Andrew Jackson's political life.

From a historical view, posterity is indebted to one of these booms for the most searching and analytical portrait of Black that exists at this stage of his life. A certain Colonel Wolff hungered to be a maker of governors. His search for a suitable subject led him across the trail of Black. Who this Colonel Wolff might have been, we cannot say with any certainty. Sufficient for our purposes is the fact that he wrote one Dr. William Elder for a frank and unvarnished opinion of his man. Elder, as it happened, had been born in Somerset and knew Black intimately. He had moved to Philadelphia to practise medicine. He likewise had gained wide prominence as an abolitionist orator and as a writer, both of editorials and books.[10]

Black, on the other hand, anathematized abolitionism and all of its allies. He was no friend to slavery. But in every fiber of his being he was a lawyer. He understood no liberty save "liberty *under* the law."

Bearing in mind, then, that Elder and Black were men of sharp political differences, let us come to the portrait of Black left us in Elder's hand:

Dear Sir:

You ask me, for information, what I know about Judge Black. I answer that I know as much of, in, and concerning him as I am capable of knowing an intimate friend. He was born within 7 miles of me; he went to school, studied law, and he has spent most of his life in my native place. I was, for several years of our earliest manhood in constant intercourse with him. I have seen him grow, heard him think, and felt him being, doing, and suffering through all of his moods and tenses. I have had all desirable opportunities for quarreling with him, and a thousand times tested his better qualities in cordial agreements . . .

He is, I think, about 37 years old, but . . . you may think of him as fifty. . . . When appointed to the bench, he was, perhaps, the youngest man that ever received such promotion in the Commonwealth. The friends of his competitors thought he was young enough to wait a year or two—they made no other objection—but the Governor thought otherwise and his judicial conduct has handsomely vindicated the propriety of his appointment, as you may well know.

I don't care whether you accept everything that I say about him or not. *I* know whereof I affirm, but you may, like a prudent man, as you are, make what abatements you must. . . .

[10] *Appleton's Cyclopedia of American Biography,* Vol. 2.

In certain respects he is a man of prodigious natural talents, and of most extraordinary attainments. For philological, statistical, historical knowledge, and for any department of the natural and exact sciences, Black has greater original abilities than any man I have known. . . . He has read as much of what we call literature as the first class of those who do nothing else. . . . His memory of words, facts, dates, events, things, excels anything on record. He plunders everybody he meets of all they know, and then it is his forever, and always at hand for use; in fact it is no exaggeration to say that he has all his mental forces under as good discipline and can array them as effectively as Napoleon ever did the "grande Armee.". . .

The only place where he breaks down is in his political principles. He is a desperate democrat, in *your* sense of the word. I know nothing else against him in either opinion or practice. I have labored with him for years in this matter, like a good man that has a soul to save, but I am further now from the hope of reclaiming him than when he was twenty-one. He is, I fear . . . past redemption.

As a companion he is capital. He talks all the time, but he wouldn't bore you if you made the trip with him from here to Pittsburgh by canal boat. He is absolutely free from egotism, and he has no pet subjects for conversational essays. He is, indeed, a comfortable fellow anywhere and comformable, but so prudent that the Supreme Bench in vacation couldn't get him drunk!

Nevertheless, alas—though I have read, . . . talked, eaten, drank (mountain spring water), slept . . . and wrangled with him, I never could get the political kinks out of him. In fifteen years, and more, we have never once voted for the same candidates and I have given him up to his fate.

I doubt much if you have another such piece of stuff to make a Governor of in Pennsylvania. I hope that you have not. One such man is enough to spare from the higher service. And as I have no hope of ever making any better use of him, I suppose you may as well make use of him now as after a while. If you don't secure him soon he will either be on the United States Bench, or in a foreign mission or somewhere else out of your reach.

Yours truly
William Elder.[11]

Meanwhile a sweeping change had been made in the judicial system of Pennsylvania. Prior to 1850, judges had been appointed by the Governor. But by a constitutional amendment of that year the elective judiciary was engrafted upon the Pennsylvania system.[12] This required the election in 1851 of a full bench of five judges for the State Supreme

[11] Black Papers. No date, but marked by the MSS. division as "183–?" This is an error since the letter refers to Black's appointment as Judge, which was not made until 1842. Since the writer refers to Black as "about 37 years old," the date must be about 1847. Other letters are found among the Black Papers from Elder to Black and this one is easily identified as in the hand of Elder himself.

[12] Hensel, p. 190.

Court. Black's delayed political recognition came at last. The Democrats cast about for five strong judicial candidates—and settled upon Black, Walter H. Lowrie, John B. Gibson, Ellis Lewis, and James Campbell. The election placed four of these candidates in office,—with Campbell, who gained the smallest number of Democratic votes, losing to the highest Whig candidate, Richard Coulter. Of the ten candidates, Black led the entire field.[13] He had 1,200 votes more than even the venerable John Bannister Gibson, Pennsylvania's Nestor of the Bench, who had been a member of the Supreme Court for thirty-five years and who, for twenty-four years, had served as its Chief Justice.

The term of office for justices was fifteen years, except that the five judges simultaneously elected in 1851 were to draw lots for terms to expire at successive three-year intervals. By law, the judge who drew the shortest term should serve as Chief Justice. Black's letter to his wife tells us the story of this drawing:

> We drew yesterday and the result is as follows: Black, 3 years; Lewis, 6 years; Gibson, 9 years; Lowrie, 12 years; Coulter, 15 years. So you see your husband is to be Chief Justice. I don't like it. This whole business has been like our old woman's soap. "Somehow I have no luck with it."[14]

Although Chief Justice in name and in fact, he refused in court to occupy the center seat of distinction accorded to his rank. In that seat, John Bannister Gibson had sat for twenty-four years, longer than any contemporary judge in America. Black had long revered him from afar; since Forward's death, Gibson had served him as model and ideal. He could not in comfort take the chair which Gibson so long had occupied while that man still sat upon the bench. At his insistence, the older man continued to occupy his accustomed seat during the year and four months of life that remained to him.

[13] *Tribune Almanac*, 1852, p. 40.
[14] Clayton, p. 90.

6

CHIEF JUSTICE

THE justices of the Supreme Court of Pennsylvania in 1851 led a strenuous life. The court sat for four terms each year, January, May, October, and December. It convened in four districts over the State—Harrisburg, Sunbury, Pittsburgh, and Philadelphia. Added to the legal burdens which this program entailed, its members also were in heavy demand as honored guests for social affairs. The fame of the young Chief Justice as a quaint character and a fascinating conversationalist had traveled abroad. He was unduly sought after. He enjoyed the social life and, doing nothing by halves, accepted all invitations, went everywhere. One day a friend took him to the Philadelphia markets. The next day the friend's butcher said, "Excuse me, sir; but was not that gentleman with you yesterday a butcher?" "No; he is Chief Justice of Pennsylvania," the friend replied. The butcher was disappointed, "I was sure he was a butcher. He knew so much about the business."[1]

Soon, however, the strain of social life proved too much. Even Black's vigorous health would not stand it, and for a time he was compelled to refuse all invitations.[2]

He still maintained his residence at Somerset, although he was now away from home more than ever. Two months after he came to office, his fifth and last child, Anna, was born. Already the older children were away at school, so circumstances were favorable for closing the Somerset house occasionally and taking his family with him on the circuit.

The reorganized Supreme Court began its life with the December term, 1851, at Philadelphia. Black delivered his first opinion of the court upon December 29, in the case of *McAllister* vs. *Samuel*.[3] This case involved the property rights of insolvent debtors. It had been hanging fire in the lower courts for thirteen years, but the young Chief Justice disposed of it in an opinion packed into twenty-three lines. Included in those twenty-three lines was also a notice to future counsels before the court that efforts to reopen settled practices of that court would be fruitless. "The same point upon precisely the same state of facts, arose in the case of Moncure vs. Hanson, decided April

[1] Clayton, pp. 19-20.
[2] Clayton, p. 92.
[3] Harris, p. 115.

last, and reported in 3 Harris, 385 . . . Where a question has been once deliberately settled after solemn argument, it ought not to be disturbed, unless it be so manifestly erroneous that it cannot be supported without doing violence to reason and justice." With this statement of position, he not only affirmed the judgment of the lower court in this particular case, but disposed of three other similar cases, by merely citing their names and tersely adding, "judgements in these cases are also affirmed."

The relations on the bench between Black and the venerable John Bannister Gibson were as pupil to master. Black respected the older man's overshadowing reputation, deferred to his great learning, and reverenced his character. When on May 3, 1853, Gibson died after serving upon the court for thirty-seven years, Black "sang for him a dirge," said Niles, "that has become a classic in legal literature."[4]

He spoke indeed in a different language than in his eulogy upon Jackson. Here he sounded no militant note, aligned no argument, arrayed no defense of the man. The subject of his eulogy was of a different type; the words of the eulogist were cast in a different mold. In the interim between the two occasions he had grown in *nuances* of language; here he paid a tribute simple and sincere, and voiced a lament that rises at times into poetry. In it one hears the overtones of David's lament over Jonathan: "I am distressed for thee my brother Jonathan: . . . Thy love to me was wonderful, passing the love of women."

Gibson's death at the age of seventy-six, began Black, was a blow not sudden but severe.[5]

We regarded him more as a father than a brother. None of us ever saw the Supreme Court before he was in it; and to some of us his character as a great judge was familiar even in childhood . . . He was a judge of the Common Pleas before the youngest of us was born and was a member of this Court long before the oldest was admitted to the bar. He sat here with twenty-six different associates, of whom eighteen preceded him to the grave. For nearly a quarter of a century he was Chief Justice, and when he was nominally superseded by another, as head of the court, his great learning, venerable character and overshadowing reputation, still made him the only Chief whom the hearts of the people would know.

From Gibson's career, the eulogist moved to those qualities of mind that lifted him above the commonplace—and anyone who knew the eulogist could have prophesied that high among these qualities he would rank the subtlety, originality, and power of language which the subject possessed. "His written language was a transcript of his mind. It gave the world the very form and pressure of his thoughts. It was

[4] Niles, p. 403.
[5] 7 Harris, pp. 10-14.

accurate because he knew the boundaries of the principles he discussed." His language was rich, but "he never sacrificed sense to sound, or preferred ornament to substance." "He had one faculty of a great poet; that of expressing a thought in language which could never afterwards be paraphrased. When a legal principle passed through his hands, he sent it forth clothed in a dress which fitted so exactly, that nobody ever presumed to give it any other form." "For this reason it is, that though he was the least voluminous writer of the Court, the citations from him at the bar are more numerous than from all the rest put together."

The peroration rises to an epic:

Doubtless the whole Commonwealth will mourn his death; we all have good reason to do so. The profession of law has lost the ablest of its teachers, this Court the brightest of its ornaments, and the people a steadfast defender of their rights. . . . For myself, I know no form of words to express my deep sense of the loss we have suffered. I can most truly say of him what was said long ago, concerning one of the few immortals who were yet greater than he: "I did love the man, and do honor his memory, on this side idolatry, as much as any."

Throughout this portrayal of Gibson, Black unconsciously was painting the picture of his own ideal of greatness. Because Gibson so completely fitted that picture, Black had long admired him. But at the point where Gibson did not fit that picture, he could not refrain from touching upon the shortcoming: "A little dash of bitterness in his nature would, perhaps, have given a more consistent tone to his character and a greater activity to his mind," he said. "He lacked the quality which Dr. Johnson admired. He was *not* a good hater." And whatever else might be said of Black by friend or enemy, it cannot be said that he suffered for want of this quality. If he had not yet acquired it, at least it soon was to be acquired in the turbulent years ahead when popular rights were menaced and open corruption sat in high places of government.

Black's term expired in 1854. In general the year was a disastrous one for the Democratic Party. The Know Nothings arose and swept the state. Governor Bigler, who had gone into office in 1850 upon a majority of 8,000, was now turned out of that office by a majority of 37,000. Black was the lone Democrat to survive the State ticket. Aided by a division between the Whigs and Know Nothings, he rode high above the shipwreck and was returned to office by an imposing lead of 47,000 over his nearest rival.[6]

His consistent policy of refusing to urge himself for office was now bearing fruit. "He is no mere politician," commented an editorial

[6] *Tribune Almanac*, 1855, p. 44.

writer, "no trader in party wares; no buyer and seller of votes by newspaper claptrap and speech-making humbug. He is one of the few statesmen of the present day who have kept their political garments free from the stains of the demagogue and the trimmer."[7]

His term was for fifteen years. According to law, that Supreme Court judge nearest the end of his term became Chief Justice. Beginning with the December term of court in 1854, Ellis Lewis therefore entered upon his term in that office and Black took his place among the associate justices.

[7] Clayton MSS. Unfortunately the source of this clipping is not given.

7

A JURIST OF THE COMMONWEALTH

AS A jurist of the Commonwealth of Pennsylvania, Black's services covered too short a period to approach such an influence as that of John Bannister Gibson. That he would have equalled this influence, however, had his career as a jurist covered so long a period, is hardly open to question. He possessed at least one attribute of highest judicial genius, namely, the ability to animate lifeless legal principles, to make vivid what formerly had been obscure. "His own vision of legal truth was clear," said Niles, "and he had the skill to state it and the reasons which made it necessary and unalterable, so convincingly as to compel submission of the mind, not to authority, but to overwhelming logic and self-evident right."[1]

His opinion of judicial pettifogging and hair-splitting would bear a pointed emphasis in our own day. In the case of *Bell* vs. *Ohio and Pennsylvania Railway*, he opposed the action of the majority of the court in refusing an injunction. Their reason for refusing the injunction, he said, "never entered the minds of either party or the counsel of either side or the judge of the District Court." It was too fine a point for any of them to see. "I think," he continued, "that the domain of the law is full enough of man-traps and spring-guns, without any assistance from me in setting them."[2]

A suit against a physician for malpractice in setting a leg was heard by the Supreme Court in 1853. The judge of the lower court had set himself up as an authority on medicine as well as law. Black handed down the decision reversing the lower court. "The judge fell into an error in stating the amount of skill required. We reverse it for that reason. . . . We are not authority on questions of surgery."[3]

So far as the permanent influence of his decisions upon the laws of Pennsylvania were concerned, none of Black's decisions were so important as those treating of the chartered rights of corporations. When he came to the Supreme Bench, corporations were in their infancy. Black foresaw their unexampled growth in the years to come, as he had read of their growth in the history of Europe. He feared that the power which they acquired would be used to the injury of the general public. His decisions endeavored to demarcate justly between

[1] Niles, p. 404.
[2] 1 Grant, p. 113.
[3] *McCandless* vs. *McWha*, 10 *Harris*, p. 274.

the chartered rights of growing corporations and the inherent rights of the people.

One of the earliest cases of this sort which came before the court was that of *Sharpless* vs. *Mayor of Philadelphia*, in 1853. It was a question of whether a city, as such, could issue city bonds for the purchase of stock in a railway company. In handing down the decision upon this famous case, Black recognized its far-reaching consequences in the following grave words: "This is, beyond all comparison, the most important case that has ever been in this Court since the formation of this government," he said.[4]

Carefully he stated the powers of the General Assembly. Then he stated the law, a specific Act authorizing the city of Philadelphia to purchase railway stock in these companies. "We are urged, however," he continued, ". . . to declare it unconstitutional if it be wrong or unjust. But we cannot do this. It would be assuming a right to change the constitution. . . . If we can add to the reserved rights of the people, we can take them away; if we can mend, we can mar; if we can remove the landmarks which we find established, we can obliterate them: if we can change the constitution in any particle, there is nothing but our own will to prevent us from demolishing it entirely."[5]

The city of Philadelphia, accordingly, was upheld in its right to purchase stock in a railway company.

Upon the other hand, no man ever could have been more unbending in his demand that corporations should keep within their charter limits. The case of the *Commonwealth* vs. *Erie & North East Railroad Company* makes clear his position upon the matter of charter rights. The original jurisdiction of the Supreme Court had been invoked to compel this railway company to remove its tracks laid in a location not authorized in the charter. Black delivered the opinion of the Court upon September 7, 1854, in an opinion that leaves nothing to be desired:

> An act of incorporation is . . . so simple that no man whether lawyer or layman, can misunderstand or misapply it. What a company is authorized to do by its act of incorporation, it may do; beyond that all its acts are illegal. . . . It is strange that the Attorney General, or anybody else, should complain against a company that keeps itself within bounds, which are always thus clearly marked, and equally strange that a company which has happened to transgress them should come before us with the faintest hope of being sustained. . . . A doubtful charter does not exist, because whatever is doubtful, is decisively certain against the corporation. . . . The doctrine is maintained by the Supreme Court of the United States and in many states . . . even in New England. . . . But we do not mean to discuss

[4] 9 Harris, p. 158.
[5] 9 Harris, p. 161.

the subject over again. The lawyer who is not already familiar with the numerous authorities upon it . . . will probably never become so; and the citizen who does not believe it to be a most salutary feature of our jurisprudence, would hardly be convinced though one rose from the dead.

The railroad company here had patently exceeded its charter. Therefore it was ordered to take up its tracks within four months![6]

Although this decision was attacked by outstate writers upon corporation law, it remained the law of Pennsylvania, and as late as 1889 the Supreme Court in the case of *Graff* vs. *Bird* still adhered to this view.[7]

The Erie Railway Company continued to haunt the sessions of the Supreme Court. At last its abuses became so flagrant that the General Assembly repealed its charter and appointed a receiver for its property. The company appealed to the Supreme Court to enjoin the receiver from taking over its property, claiming that such an act was confiscation. The Supreme Court refused to sustain the appeal and Black punctured their confiscation claim with these apt words:

When a corporation is dissolved by the repeal of its charter, the legislature may appoint . . . a person to take charge of its assets for the use of the creditors and stockholders; and this is not confiscation any more than it is confiscation to appoint an administrator to a dead man, or a committee to a lunatic.[8]

But the day of the railroad was to be a long one and Black was not to live to see the end of the struggle to determine whether the people or the railroads were to rule the Commonwealth.

On the bench or off, Black was a spirited controversialist, and one of the breeziest controversies of his entire life arose with his colleagues upon the bench. The case, officially, was known as that of *Hole* vs. *Rittenhouse.* Commonly it was called the Barney Hole case. Barney Hole was a squatter, ejected from land claimed by James Rittenhouse and John Thompson. They showed a title out of the Commonwealth since 1793. But Barney produced evidence that the State had given title to one John Graeff so early as 1785, though now none could say who this Graeff was or what became of his title. Rittenhouse retorted by showing proof of possession for twenty-one years, and secured a judgment in the lower court.

The verdict, however, was for too much and the judges of the Supreme Court unanimously agreed upon a reversal, but they disagreed upon the direction which the retrial should take. Black delivered the opinion, citing as his authority a case previously decided by Judge

[6] 3 Casey, pp. 351-2.
[7] Hensel, p. 192.
[8] 2 Harris, p. 307.

Gibson in 1847. Gibson was still alive at the time and, of course, agreed with Black's opinion. One other judge joined with these two, making a three to two decision in favor of Black's plan of retrial.[9]

The case again was tried in the lower court, wherein the judge of that court followed carefully the directions for the retrial. Again the verdict was against Barney Hole. But the unterrified squatter again took a writ of error to the Supreme Court.

Meanwhile Gibson had died and one of the judges had changed his mind. Black alone adhered to the former view of the Court, and after the second hearing, Ellis Lewis, the new Chief Justice, delivered the opinion. He not only attacked Gibson's original decision of 1847, but even satirized Black's first opinion in the Barney Hole case, which had been based upon Gibson's opinion, as the attempt to "impart immortality to error."

To have been himself the subject of attack would have been enough for Black, but to include his idolized Gibson was too much. Though he stood alone in the minority he still possessed a hand to write. And write he did, a dissenting opinion that was perhaps the most remarkable indictment ever made by one member of a court against his brethren. So stinging was his satire that it is claimed that other judges discussed the propriety of holding him for contempt of the very court of which he was a member.[10]

"The judgment now about to be given is one of 'Death's doings,'" said Black in this opinion. "No one can doubt that if Judge Gibson and Judge Coulter had lived, the plaintiff would not have been thus deprived of his property. . . . But they are dead; and the law which should have protected these sacred rights has died with them . . . 'New Lords, new laws' is the order of the day. Hereafter if any man be offered a title which the Supreme Court has decided to be good, let him not buy if the judges which made the decision are dead; if they are living, let him get an insurance on their lives; for ye know not what a day or an hour may bring forth."[11]

His vindication came after he had left the court. The Barney Hole case came up for the third time, and the plan of retrial laid down by Lewis was also reversed.[12]

Although this incident is characteristic of the gusto with which Black entered any controversy, yet it must not mislead one to suppose that he was often at odds with other members of the Court. This was the one eruption in the six years during which he sat with that body. After the incident had closed, he remained as firm and fast a friend of the opposing judges as ever. One of them, Judge George W.

[9] 7 Harris, p. 306.

[10] Niles, p. 430.

[11] 2 Philadelphia Reports, pp. 417-418.

[12] 1 Wright, p. 116.

Woodward, was perhaps the most intimate friend of his life and remained so to the end. Their letters during the next twenty years mark the warmth of this lasting friendship. Black was a good hater, but he was not a hater of men. He might hate the views of another, might even anathematize his views as the blasphemy of truth, but the man himself was borne no malice. We have seen this attested to by Dr. William Elder. We shall meet it often again. "You and I," he wrote a friend in 1858, "do not look at the thing in the same way or see it in the same light . . . I can only say, live on in your faith and I will die in mine."[13] The two remained friends, although they never saw politics eye to eye.

The decisions of greatest interest to us, greater even than those treating of corporation rights, are those relating to issues which later arose in another form during the turbulent years of Reconstruction. Again and again, in expounding the laws of the Commonwealth, we find Black handing down decisions that foreshadow the legal opinions he later expounded with such rare success before the Supreme Court of the United States. Indeed these years upon the Supreme Bench of the Commonwealth may be regarded as the formative years in this field of jurisprudence, and the Court upon which he sat as the proving ground wherein his opinions were stimulated by the argument of counsel and refined by reflection upon his own part.

When Seward turned loose that baneful phrase of "a higher law than the Constitution," to fester in the public mind, Black seized the occasion in his decision of *McDowell* vs. *Oyer* to brand that "higher law" as a bastard in jurisprudence.

> Law is a fixed and established *rule*, not depending in the slightest degree upon the caprice of those who happen to administer it. . . . It is this law we are bound to execute and not any "higher law" manufactured for each special occasion out of our private feelings and opinions. . . . Of course I am not saying that we must consecrate the mere blunders of those who went before us, and stumble every time we come to the place where they have stumbled. . . . We change with the change of time. . . . [But] to set up our mere notions above principles . . . settled and established is to make ourselves not the ministers and agents of the law, but the masters and tyrants of the people.[14]

Lawyers will recognize his view as an adherence to the principle of *stare decisis*—of standing by decided cases. The weight of this principle with him was heavy. It formed the basis for his quarrel with other members of the Court upon the Barney Hole case. In the case of the *Bank of Pennsylvania* vs. *Commonwealth* he called it the "sheet anchor of our jurisprudence."[15] He could conceive no other method

[13] Black Papers, Nov. 15, 1858.

[14] 9 Harris, p. 423.

[15] 7 Harris, p. 151.

of erecting a stable code of jurisprudence. To him it remained unaffected either by Sumter or Appomattox, so long as the Constitution itself was unchanged.

In the case of *Finley* vs. *Aiken*, he dissented from the opinion of the majority of the court because he felt that their decision extended chancery powers at the expense of the right of trial by jury. "The right of trial by jury needs no vindication," he stated. "It is necessary (if for nothing else) to check the tendency of the judicial mind to run into metaphysical refinements. . . . No mode of ascertaining truth can be infallible. But with the jury that scorns all subtle evasions of plain justice and a judge who frowns upon vulgar prejudices, we come as near the right as any system in the world."[16]

This dissenting opinion later became the law of Pennsylvania upon the point involved.[17] In defense of this view, Black delivered in 1866 the greatest forensic effort of his life, if not indeed the greatest ever delivered in the Supreme Court of the United States, causing that body not only to declare military commissions illegal in zones of peace, but to go even further and declare that no proclamation or law by President or Congress could ever render them legal. He made the right to a trial by jury the bulwark of liberty to the American people for all time.

The case most immediately famous, however, which arose during his whole judicial career was that of Passmore Williamson. Williamson was secretary of the Pennsylvania Abolition Society. On July 18, 1855, the United States minister to Nicaragua, John H. Wheeler, was on shipboard in the Philadelphia harbor, en route to his post of duty. With him on shipboard were three slaves. Williamson, with a band of ten to twenty negroes, descended upon him. Some of them seized Wheeler while others dragged the slaves, protesting, on to Pennsylvania soil and then declared them to be free. Wheeler applied to Judge Kane of the United States District Court for a writ of habeas corpus to require Williamson to produce these slaves. But Williamson evaded the writ by declaring that at no time whatever had the slaves been in his power. By this he meant that they had not been in his physical clutches, since he had been merely the commander of the buccaneering expedition, leaving the physical labor to his followers. But Judge Kane was unimpressed by such refined reasoning and committed Williamson to jail for contempt of court.[18]

The actual legality of the question was disregarded by the abolitionist press. The New York *Tribune*, on July 28, led off in a bitter attack upon Kane. Thereafter the story could be followed in the headlines of any eastern metropolitan newspaper.

[16] 1 Grant, p. 94

[17] Niles, p. 413.

[18] New York *Tribune*, July 28, 1855.

Williamson appealed to the State Supreme Court to release him from jail, through a writ of habeas corpus. That body, sitting in banc at Bedford, heard the case in August 1855. Black handed down the decision.

It was not a question of slavery. Slavery was in no way involved in the controversy. It was an issue pure and simple of whether the Federal court was supreme within its own sphere, or whether a State court had the right to trespass in the Federal domain and overrule decisions of a Federal court. In such a light only was it viewed by Black. "We have no more authority in law to come between the prisoner and the Court, to free him from a sentence like this, than we would have to countermand an order issued by the commander-in-chief of the United States Army," he said. "We have no authority, jurisdiction, or power to decide anything here except the simple fact that the District Court had power to punish for contempt a person who disobeys its process—that the petitioner is convicted of such contempt—and that the conviction is conclusive upon us." "We must maintain the rights of the state and its courts . . . but we will do nothing to impair the constitutional vigor of the general government which is the 'sheet anchor of our peace at home and our safety abroad.' "[19]

This decision, of course, was sound law. It expounded the doctrine of national supremacy within its constitutional sphere, a doctrine that was determined for once and all by the Civil War. But high passions make strange bedfellows; the abolitionists ranged themselves alongside the nullifiers of South Carolina in denouncing such a view of Federal supremacy.

The newspapers were waiting expectantly for the decision. On August 26, the Philadelphia *North American* printed a special supplement giving the briefs and arguments in full of the case presented before the Supreme Court. On September 10, both the *North American* and the New York *Tribune* carried Black's opinion in full upon the front news page.

"Worse than contemptible," raged the *Tribune*. Such a decision not only refused to "defend her imploring citizens against outrageous oppression and injuries," but even was "insulting them in their day of affliction."[20] Even in November, this paper was still fuming about this "notorious decision in favor of Judge Kane and his right to shut up men in jail without either law or right."[21]

Passmore Williamson, meanwhile, was meditating in solitude upon the laws of his country.

For six years Black sat upon the Supreme Bench of the Commonwealth. In those years that body heard and handed down decisions

[19] 2 Casey, p. 9

[20] New York *Tribune*, September 11, 1855.

[21] *Ibid.*, November 5, 1855.

upon more than 1200 cases. The opinions for more than 250 of these cases were written by Black.

In them one reads his dynamic personality. Whatever was lacking in defective early education was hidden by the strength and independence of his thought, by his habit of reducing the law to simple principles and of setting forth those principles, through decision after decision, in language so "distinct and distinctive" that layman and lawyer alike could grasp its import. The decisions mark him as a vigorous, intrepid, and unique judicial character. "His influence upon the law of Pennsylvania," said Niles, "was extensive and permanent."[22]

Meanwhile, in these years, he had learned and greatly grown. His ability to translate his thoughts into adventurous and ringing phrases had reached its climax. "The judicial literature of the English tongue may be sought in vain," said James G. Blaine, "for finer models than are found in the opinions of Judge Black when he sat . . . on the Supreme Bench of Pennsylvania."[23] Blaine, of course, could not speak from his own knowledge. He merely voiced the current opinion of his time.

Likewise had Black grown in his grasp of the higher ranges of jurisprudence. There were none of the greater issues upon which he had not heard able arguments, made an acquaintance with able authorities, and refined his own opinions. There were few of the smallest details of law that at least he had not met.

The last decision he ever delivered from any court was a most commonplace one, involving an amicable action of debt between the Commonwealth and the City of Philadelphia.[24] Even before this decision was rendered, he had been called into higher service.

But of this story, we shall treat in its proper setting.

[22] Niles, p. 469.
[23] J. G. Blaine, *Twenty Years*, II, p. 230.
[24] 3 Casey, p. 501.

8

WARRING POLITICAL FACTIONS

BEGINNING about 1855 there seems to have been a strong tide among the Pennsylvania Democracy to take Black from the Bench and send him somewhere else—to the Governor's chair or the Senate. His survival of the shipwreck of 1854 had marked him as an effective candidate for any high state office. His persistent policy of never wrangling for any office had put him in the good graces of the several bitter factions now fighting for state control of the party.

There were, of course, other seekers for these offices. Each faction sought to entrench itself in state control and to elect its own captains. Not until this hope was lost were they willing to accept any compromise candidate. Meanwhile, all factions sought to learn Black's plans with great circumspection. "What is your determination in regard to the U. S. Senator?" wrote one of these feelers, J. C. Van Dyke, in 1856. "Will you be a candidate if Forney is one. He is in my opinion actively in the field. If you and he are both candidates, you will place many mutual friends in tight places to choose between you."[1]

John W. Forney, mentioned in this letter, was the political leader of Philadelphia and head of one of the factions seeking state control. Black evidently did not relish Forney using another man as a cat's paw and told him so. "I am capricious in my temper and I wrote an answer [to Van Dyke] which I am glad I did not send."[2] To Van Dyke himself he wrote ironically:

> I seem to be wonderfully strong for everything—so strong that I suppose I have nothing to do but make my choice between Senator, Secretary of State, and other high employment. Private solicitations have [illegible word] upon me the former place and the newspapers (some of them at least) have set me up for the latter. That of course settles the question.[3]

The election of a United States Senator was to be made by the legislature in January 1857. On December fifth preceding, Black wrote to Forney:

> You have been considering me as a candidate for Senator. I need not tell you, for you know it well enough already, that I should regard that as a most desirable place. But I could not be elected without the

[1] J. C. Van Dyke to Black, Black Papers, Nov. 9, 1856.
[2] Black Papers, Dec. 8, 1856.
[3] Black Papers, Nov. 15, 1856.

aid of both you and Mr. Buchanan. You are both against me. Be it so. I think no less of either because you can't or won't.[4]

But Forney replied at once that Buchanan had told him that he preferred Black to anybody. In an undated letter, Black answered Forney to the effect that if this were so, then since he, Forney, was already out of the race, Forney's interest would seem to demand that either Black or Dawson should be elected. But there was no chance for Dawson. The implication was obvious. This is the only letter of known record where Black ever set himself forth as a candidate for an office.

Developments also were brewing in national politics. For fifteen years James Buchanan had been a prominent and logical contender for the Presidency. He was now sixty-five, and should the Democratic National Convention pass him over in 1856, his chance would be gone forever. Under the administration of Franklin Pierce, Buchanan had represented American interests at the Court of St. James with a pronounced skill and success. His absence from his own country had allowed him to escape the consuming heat of the Kansas-Nebraska affair. Black saw the strength of this position and in 1855 wrote to Buchanan at London. "I think your return home is looked for with some anxiety. If you expect to be a candidate again, you ought to be on the ground."[5]

The two men saw the situation with the same eye. Buchanan returned to America in April 1856; was nominated in the summer, and elected in the autumn. Their correspondence throughout this campaign showed that the two men had held long and frequent personal conferences over the issues and plans of the campaign. This intimacy led Black's political friends to urge him for a place in the Cabinet, but the files of the Buchanan papers do not show that Black himself ever mentioned his name or that of anyone else in connection with Cabinet appointments. To Van Dyke he wrote that "Mr. Buchanan has very little to do with a cabinet appointment and of course will not presume to have a mind of his own."[6]

Fratricidal strife, however, was raging within the Pennsylvania Democracy. J. Glancy Jones, leader of one faction, had exacted a promise from Buchanan that if a Cabinet appointment was made from Pennsylvania, it should be given to Jones. Eventually Buchanan saw that this would be tantamount to wrecking the State party and upon February 17, 1857, wrote to Jones as follows:

I have finally determined on all the members of the Cabinet except the Attorney-General; and it may be desirable under all the circumstances that I should appoint Judge Black to that place. Would you

[4] Black Papers, Dec. 5, 1856.
[5] Black File, Buckanan Papers, Feb. 17, 1855.
[6] Black Papers, November 15, 1856.

object to this appointment, should I deem it advisable? I should certainly appoint no other person than him from Pennsylvania.[7]

J. Glancy Jones evidently objected, for five days later Buchanan wrote that "your letter and the whole affair gives me very great pain."[8] But the Honorable J. Glancy Jones still demurred, hoping yet perhaps to gain a Cabinet post for himself, until Buchanan wrote him on February 28th that "It becomes my duty to ascertain whether you will release me from my promise not to appoint a Cabinet officer from Pennsylvania, if I should not deem it proper to appoint yourself."[9] Apparently the desired release was given. Meanwhile more rumors of this rift in Pennsylvania politics had reached the ears of the nation, for whom political writers were busy forecasting the make-up of the new Cabinet. The Washington *National Intelligencer* announced the Cabinet personnel on February 26, giving a place to J. Glancy Jones. But on March 2 the New York *Times* warned its readers that in spite of the "seeming confidence and authority" with which the new Cabinet had been announced, its members had not been definitely chosen, adding that "Mr. Buchanan . . . expressed the intention of choosing Mr. Jones, if he took anybody from that state, but the persistent and violent opposition . . . by the faction which Forney leads in Philadelphia has caused some hesitation." *Harper's Weekly* for March 7—after the inauguration—carried its forecast of the Cabinet and gave one place as still undecided between Jones and W. C. Alexander. But in all of the wild rumors, not one rumor pointed to Black as a Cabinet member. The first hint of any kind came on the sixth of March, when the New York *Tribune* carried the story that Lewis Cass, known to be the new Secretary of State, "was inquiring about the acceptability of Judge Black," Cass having been "commissioned by the President" to ascertain if Black would be acceptable to party leaders. Even the Philadelphia papers missed this story until the following day.

Black himself knew that he had early been considered as a member, but was of the opinion that he long since had been dropped from the list. On March 2 his name was before the Democratic State Convention at Harrisburg as a candidate for Governor and the balloting showed him only five votes behind the leader.[10] On the twenty-fifth ballot the final choice fell upon Packer.

The Senatorship and Governorship had gone into other hands. Buchanan already had been inaugurated and presumably the members who were to make up his Cabinet long since had been privately informed. Doubtless Black felt disappointed. Certainly he felt, as he

[7] *Buchanan's Works,* XI, p. 511.

[8] *Ibid.,* XI, p. 512.

[9] *Ibid.*

[10] New York *Tribune,* March 3, 1857.

said, "in need of a rest," and so determined to sail for Europe. Already he had engaged his passage when the following letter was delivered to him:

Washington 6th March 1857.

My dear Sir:

I have this moment signed your commission as Attorney General of the United States, and I have done this with great pleasure. I hope you may find it agreeable to yourself to accept this important office; and I entertain no doubt that we shall get on harmoniously and happily together.

There were certainly great difficulties in the way of your appointment, and Mr. J. Glancy Jones has behaved very well in contributing to the result. I may also add that Governor Bigler is quite satisfied with it, and I venture to express the hope that any past difficulties between you and himself may pass away and be forgotten.

We must be a unit here if possible. I hope you will come to Washington immediately, and in the meantime, believe me to be always,

Very respectfully your friend,

JAMES BUCHANAN

Hon: J. S. Black.[11]

Black was taken wholly by surprise. "Not the slightest intimation," he said, "was given me, directly or indirectly, until after I was nominated to the Senate, confirmed and commissioned. Then I received the President's letter, urging me to accept it. . . . Until I went to Washington and saw him myself, he continued to express great fears that I would not accept."[12]

To Buchanan he wrote that the appointment "has taken me very much by surprise and to say the truth it dislocates some plans that were dear to me. I shall be at Washington in the course of the next week. . . . The unity of your administration will never be broken by me. I have neither quarrel nor cause of quarrel with either of the gentlemen you name."[13]

Black therefore did not rest in Europe nor did he revel in the antiquities of the Old World. But this was the least of designs altered by the letter of March 6. It changed also his life's pattern—came as a cleavage, sharp and distinct, between two epochs in his life. He was now forty-seven years of age. Fifteen of those years had been spent in judicial robes and the future had seemed to offer him only a continuation in that role. But destiny—or chance—had juggled the dice and in a twinkling he put aside the robes forever. Behind him he had left a pattern upon the history of his own State, but with all of its distinctive character the State boundaries marked its limits. Hence-

[11] *Buchanan's Works*, X, p. 114.

[12] Clayton, p. 99.

[13] Black File, Buchanan Papers, Two letters of March 7, 1857.

forth, in public office or out, he walked as a national figure, marked at times by tragic lines and at times by lines heroic. Caught in the most tragic dénouement of our national history, suffering the common lot of inevitable misunderstanding and execration and deliberate misbranding laid upon all who had stood at the vortex—yet he arose in towering form to haunt the malefactors of Reconstruction, even as he had challenged destruction in the guise of Secession.

With his first steps toward Washington in March 1857, came a presage of the storm ahead. The same dispatches that carried the announcement of his appointment as Attorney-General, carried also the announcement of the Dred Scott decision.[14]

[14] Philadelphia *North American*, March 9, 1857.

9

ATTORNEY-GENERAL

THE Attorney-General was, as the *Tribune* said, "new to the nation."[1] But the newness quickly vanished. He was not at this time so eccentric as he later was to become, yet even now he soon became known as a character. His tall, erect figure and slouching, loose-jointed gait quickly became familiar to Washington. Reporters soon learned that the sternness of expression given by shaggy eyebrows to his features in repose, quickly melted away as his keen grey eyes lighted up in conversation or as he broke out in infectious laughter.[2] His total avoidance of public social functions and his remarkable capacity for hard labor became the topics of newspaper comment.

It would not be surprising if I had totally forgotten to mention a prominent member of the Cabinet who is never seen or heard of in the fashionable world (wrote the Washington correspondent of the New York *Tribune*). It would be something very novel, and probably very diverting to see the Attorney General in the middle of a ball room. It was my fortune to see him in a predicament quite as bad. It was on the first day he arrived in Washington to take his place in the Cabinet and he was dining with a party of friends at Willard's Hotel. Some considerate person had probably impressed upon him the necessity of getting himself up a little expensively on his advent in Washington, where he was to play a high official part; so the judge turned out in a splendid suit of black, a glossy silk hat, and, *mirabile dictu!* a pair of patent leather boots.

These last were evidently too much for him; for his ready racy conversation all evaporated, and he sat, not unlike Patience on a monument, but restless, disturbed, and uncomfortable, as though something heavy lay on his conscience or stomach. He begged permission at last to go to his room in the same hotel for a few minutes, and when he returned the change in his mien was magical. He let the secret out at once by admitting that he had been persuaded into a pair of patent leathers for the first time, and, he hoped, the last time in his life, and he felt pretty much as Hercules did in the shirt of Nessus. It was soon clear that Richard was himself again, and the company had as much reason to rejoice as the Judge himself that he had escaped from the "durance vile" of his patent leathers.

Though you never meet the Attorney General at a ball or a *soirée*, you can find him all day in the Supreme Court, and nearly all night

[1] New York *Tribune*, March 7, 1857.

[2] Washington *National Republican*, August 20, 1883.

at his office, which he rarely leaves till two o'clock A. M. "Do you call it fun, such work as that?" asked a friend of his the other day. "I admit," replied the Judge, "it is rather a grave kind of sport." Yet he is one of those men who revel in work, if it only be hard enough and dry enough.

The neglect of the learned Judge is forgiven by a gay world for the good reason that he is so charmingly represented there by his handsome and well-bred wife. Lucky for him that he has so eloquent a pleader before the social tribunal to extenuate her manifold acts of *lêse Majesté*. Mrs. Black has cards out for a ball on the 16th.[3]

Patent leathers were not the only troubles of the new Attorney-General. Upon him, as upon all officials at such a time, descended a flood of office seekers. How many came in person can never be known, but the mails alone in the first two months and a half brought more than 500 petitions and recommendations for public office. The next seven months added another 500, yet Black was but one member of the whole Cabinet.

Among this army of applicants was George Gibson, Jr., son of Chief Justice Gibson of Pennsylvania. He was at this time a military store keeper in New Mexico, which position he fitly described as "a sort of military nondescript but slightly removed from the rank and file," and with no opportunity of advancement.[4] He now wanted to be a paymaster in the army. His mother joined her plea to that of her son, begging an appointment for him.[5] Whether Black endeavored to secure an office for Gibson is not known. But the army records show that Gibson did not enter the rolls until 1861, after which he rose to the rank of colonel, and continued in service for the remainder of his life.

A few office seekers sought more objective ways of pressing obligations upon Black. The following letter from one W. B. Johnston of Philadelphia is a sample:

Many weeks since . . . I sent you thru the medium of one of the Express Companies a demijohn of monongahela whiskey and one of madeira wine, but having received no acknowledgment of either liquids, or of the note accompanying them, I am left to infer that all have been miscarried, as I am unable to conceive any other reason for your long silence. . . . I know I was somewhat troublesome and annoying to you in sending so many missives for the purpose of enlisting your influence in behalf of some of my friends, but I felt warranted in doing so as *I knew* my services to be *at your* disposal in whatever way you might choose to command them.[6]

[3] New York *Tribune*; quoted in *Harper's Weekly*, February 19, 1859, p. 119.

[4] Black Papers, April 26, 1857.

[5] Mrs. Sarah Gibson to Black. Black Papers, May 7, 1857.

[6] Black Papers, May 15, 1857.

This gentleman was not the only correspondent to suffer from neglect. Others with better reason, as his closest friends, were neglected almost altogether until some relief could be gained from the swarm of office claimants.

Meanwhile another duty claimed his attention. The Attorney-General stands at the titular head of the American bar. His client is the most important single client in the land—the Government of the United States. The minor cases of his client he might delegate to subordinates, but in cases of graver importance he must represent this client in person. The Supreme Court of the United States is the forum of his activity. Black never before had appeared before this high tribunal. Indeed he had not argued a case, or represented a client in any capacity, in fifteen years.

Now suddenly he must once more become the advocate. Would his tongue have lost its cunning? Could he thrust and parry with the old skill, or had fifteen years dulled the edge? Was he indeed equal in ability to those encounters of intellect to be incurred in this great theatre where only master minds are engaged?

His friends were not without anxiety, and the profession as a whole was curious. Only a few of them, perhaps, had read those lightning thrusts which were strewn through more than 250 decisions of the Pennsylvania Supreme Court, nor had they reckoned with the severe discipline in refinement and precision of language which the writing of those decisions had given.

His first appearance before the Supreme Court was in the case of *United States* vs. *Cambuston.*[7] It was one of the famous California land cases, involving a spurious and fabricated title to nearly a hundred square miles of land in the Sacramento valley which was claimed by Cambuston to be a valid Mexican title acquired by him before American occupation of that State. Cambuston had secured a confirmation of his title in the District Court of California and the government had carried an appeal to the Supreme Court.

It was an ideal case, calculated to display the highest legal qualities that Black possessed. He was an intense man. He hated fraud; he loved a fight. Here was work for such a character.

The hearing was set for January 7, 1858. To the Washington correspondent of the Philadelphia *North American*—a newspaper politically hostile to Black—we are indebted for an invaluable account of the scene. "Although no public notice had been given," he wrote, "the attendance at the Supreme Court this morning disclosed that an occasion of more than ordinary interest had excited and drawn together a large representation of men eminent in the legal profession and in the walks of public life. It had become known that Judge Black was to make his debut before this august

[7] 20 Howard, p. 59.

tribunal in his official capacity of Attorney General, and the curiosity of the profession, as well as the anxiety of personal and political friends was necessarily stirred to witness that first appearance."[8]

The court was opened, the case was called. Black made none of the personal references so common and so misplaced on first occasions. He made no allusion to the circumstances which had drawn the crowd together, no apology for any awkwardness that he might show, no appeal for any indulgence.

The case (continued the *North American* correspondent) was well calculated to call out what may not be inaptly called and will be quickly appreciated by those who know his forte, as the *surgical ability* of the Attorney General . . . He went at once directly to its legal examination, reviewing and analyzing the testimony with searching precision, exposing its weakness, tearing aside the flimsy covering of false pretence, and with scorching sarcasm cauterizing the wounds so mercilessly opened.

The legal propositions seemed uttered with an abrupt consciousness of assured authority, and the points were presented in forcible, jerking, and sinewy sentences, that almost startled from their freshness of style and absence of accustomed prosy formality. What appeared most to fix the attention of the court and audience, was the continuous and consistent logic, in which the argument was sustained in all its parts, holding the mind of both with eager and excited interest from the premises to the conclusion.

The ability and skill so exhibited in this opening case "relieved all anxiety" of his friends and "established his position where it may be contemplated with pride and satisfaction by the people of Pennsylvania . . . whatever may be their differences of politics . . ."[9]

A more positive verdict was rendered eighteen days later when the United States Supreme Court handed down its decision, reversing the decree of the District Court of California, declaring the Cambuston claim tainted with fraud, and restoring the vast tract of land to the public domain.[10]

[8] Philadelphia *North American*, Jan. 8, 1858.
[9] *Ibid.*
[10] 20 Howard, p. 59.

10

PROTECTING THE PUBLIC DOMAIN

WHEN the United States acquired the territory of California, it obligated itself to recognize as valid all land grants that had been made by the Mexican government to settlers in this territory.[1] To determine the validity of land grants claimed by the people of this territory, Congress in 1851 passed an act creating a Board of three land commissioners. To this Board all persons claiming land under Mexican or Spanish grants had to present their claims within two years, together with such documentary evidence and testimony of witnesses as they relied upon in support of their claims. The board was empowered to hear and decide upon all claims. From the decision of this board, appeals could be had to the District Court of California, and in turn to the Supreme Court of the United States.[2]

Under this law 813 claims were presented to the board of commissioners.[3] They totalled 19,148 square miles of land—over 12,000,000 acres. They included a very large proportion of the best mineral and agricultural regions in California, important ports, commercial points, sites for fortifications and lighthouses. Claim was laid to the land upon which were standing the cities of San Francisco, Sacramento, Marysville, Stockton, Petaluma, Berkeley, and Oakland. Titles suddenly made their appearance for Goat Island, Angel Island, Alcatraz, and even to Fort Point where the American government already had erected a $2,000,000 fortification. "In all the territory . . . there seemed to be not an island or a place for a fort, a custom house, hospital, or post office, but must be purchased on his own terms from some private claimant under a pretended title."[4]

Soon it was evident that some gigantic and organized fraud was abroad in the land.

One of the most imposing of these claimants was one J. Y. Limantour, an adventurous Frenchman, who filed eight claims covering 958 square miles of land—one claim being for 630 square miles. The board of commissioners rejected six of these claims, covering 924 square miles, but confirmed the other two. One of the claims thus

[1] *U. S. Treaties, 1776-1909,* I, p. 1111.

[2] *Statutes at Large,* IX, p. 631.

[3] O. Hoffman, *Reports of Land Cases Determined in the District Court.* I, 1862, Appendix.

[4] J. S. Black, *Land Claim Report to House of Representatives,* May 22, 1860. Exec. Doc. 84, 36 Cong. 1st Session, pp. 30-38.

confirmed was for eighteen square miles in the city and county of San Francisco; the other confirmed claim included Goat and Alcatraz Islands in San Francisco Bay, the Farallone Islands just outside the Golden Gate, and one square league just opposite Angel Island at Point Tiburon where the United States was erecting important fortifications and lighthouses. It is difficult even to estimate the value of the land thus claimed, but Black placed the value of the public property claimed at from ten to twelve millions of dollars and that of private property claimed at three times as much more.[5]

The United States had appealed the two grants thus allowed to Limantour, and the cases were pending in the District Court of California when Black assumed office. Almost immediately one Auguste Jouan began writing to the Attorney-General's office that he was in possession of important information bearing upon the Limantour claims. Jouan was a roaming character who recently had drifted from California to Cincinnati. Obviously he was an adventurer. He seemed unduly anxious to secure a free passage back to California, and no other motive could be discerned at first for his interest in the case. Black, therefore, did not turn a cordial ear to his offers, although Jouan pressed his case with great insistence, writing on one occasion three letters within two days setting forth his high qualifications as a witness.[6]

Finding that veiled allusions could make no headway, Jouan at last came to the open facts. On May 18 he wrote, "I am the person, at that time in the employ of Limantour, who altered the *date* of the Grant of the Island, Alcatraz, Yerba Buena and upon which, the Government fortifications are now being erected, and which grant was *confirmed* to said Limantour by the U. S. Land commissioners."[7]

This letter brought results. Three weeks later Auguste Jouan was steamer bound for San Francisco, in the company of a United States District Attorney.

Meanwhile Black sought for a man to send to California as special counsel for the government. To find such a man was not an easy task. He must possess an independence of initiative and action, for he would be 3,000 miles removed from any source of instructions; yet he must be one in whom implicit trust could be imposed not to abuse this lack of supervised authority. He must be indefatigable in energy. He must be a lawyer of the highest caliber; he would be expected to succeed where previous attorneys had failed. Black was not long in finding his man. He had heard this man appear in counsel before him at the Supreme Court of Pennsylvania; he respected his great ability and his unflagging energy; he had watched with confidence his recent

[5] *Ibid.*, p. 3.
[6] Black Papers, April 19 & 20, 1857.
[7] Black Papers, May 18, 1857.

appearances before the Supreme Court of the United States, had seen how quickly he had gained standing as a lawyer of national repute. To this man he now turned, offering him employment as special counsel of the government in resisting the fraudulent land claims in California.

The man was Edwin M. Stanton.

To the historian who must follow Stanton through his devious and often double course as Secretary of War under Lincoln and Johnson, it is a pleasure to write of him at this stage of his life. "I would be pleased to render, under your direction, any service in my power to the government," he wrote Black in October 1857, after receiving the offer.[8]

Although tied up with cases in the Supreme Court until January, Stanton proposed in this letter to plunge at once into the 1,000-page record of the Limantour case, its digested documents and testimony; to familiarize himself with all grants that had been made in California; and to formulate an organized system of action for a thorough clean-up of all fraudulent claims.

Stanton's last case was heard in the Supreme Court upon February 16, 1858.[9] Upon the following day he received his official instructions from Black, as follows:

> Mr. Stanton shall proceed without delay to the City of San Francisco and . . . shall investigate such suits against the United States now pending in the District Court of California under alleged Mexican grants, as may be directed by the Attorney General and especially the claims of Jose Y. Limantour, and shall take such measures as, in his opinion, justice may require for the defense for those suits and to resist the claims which are believed to be spurious and fraudulent against the United States . . .

For this arduous undertaking he was to receive $25,000 and full expenses.[10]

Four days later he sailed from New York upon the *Star of the West* —that same *Star of the West* of the ill-fated relief of Sumter three years later. On March 19 he arrived at San Francisco.[11]

Either Black or Stanton, or the two in conjunction, had conceived the plan of collecting all of the widely scattered archives of the Department of California under Mexican rule, and to ascertain from them what grants had been made. All other claims could then be resisted as spurious and fabricated. Such a work, it seems, had never been attempted. The Board of Land Commissioners had completely ignored the existence of archives. On April 16, less than a month after his ar-

[8] Black Papers, October 26, 1857.
[9] G. C. Gorham, *Edwin M. Stanton*, I, p. 50.
[10] Official Instructions and Appointment, Black Papers, Feb. 17, 1858.
[11] Gorham, *op. cit.*, p. 50.

rival, Stanton wrote to Black telling of his location of the archives covering the years 1838-44. Already he had found evidence of fraud, and of theft of portions of the archives. He asked for three translators to carry on his project.[12]

"From Sacramento to San Diego" Stanton collected his archives.[13] He found a portion of them in loose boxes in the office of the United States Surveyor-General at San Francisco. He located four boxes at Bernicio that proved fatal to Limantour's claim. He found that the Mexican land records not only had been admirably kept but even indexed; the famous "Jimeno Index" was first found—with leaves torn and separated—but with the complete record of land titles to 1844. Later a second index was discovered for grants between 1844 and 1846.[14]

For eighty-nine days Stanton examined these records with the aid of interpreters. He arranged them into 400 large volumes. The most important documents of these 400 volumes were accurately translated and printed. Photographic copies were made of official correspondence, official seals, and fraudulent grants, and these were bound for the use of courts and the Attorney-General's department. Likewise photographic copies of all cases appealed to the Supreme Court were taken, to be compared with these earlier copies. Not content with mere records, Stanton went further. He made a collection of the names of all "professional witnesses,"—those supposed to have hired out to do business of swearing false claims through the courts—and a record was made of their past dealings.[15]

"The archives thus collected," testified Black, "furnish irresistible proof that there had been an organized system of fabricating land titles carried on for a long time in California by Mexican officials."[16]

Hubert Howe Bancroft, the California historian, thought this statement of Black to be an "exaggerated allusion," and "extravagant self-praise."[17] Yet Bancroft's attitude seems to be one of resentment toward any officer who enforced what he felt to be a vicious land policy of forcing all claimants to prove their titles. Once the reader of Bancroft passes this resentful chapter, he finds page after page of unwitting praise for the vigorous action of Black and Stanton in protecting honest owners of land from the frauds of spurious titles. He exults over Black's defeat of Cambuston's claim (of which we have read in the preceding chapter). "This was the first of the spurious claims before the Supreme Court," he said.[18] Of the Fuentes claim

[12] Black Papers, April 16, 1858.
[13] J. S. Black, *Land Claim Reports*, p. 31.
[14] Gorham, *op. cit.*, pp. 52-54.
[15] J. S. Black, *Land Claim Report*, p. 31.
[16] *Ibid.*
[17] H. H. Bancroft, *History of California*, VI, p. 574.
[18] *Ibid.*, VI, p. 550.

for ninety-nine square miles of land in the Sacramento Valley, he feels that justice has been vindicated. "This was one of the most impudent claims that ever went beyond the district court."[19] Such statements infer the presence of other spurious and impudent claims, many of which are given by name and, upon examination, prove to be claims defeated through the efforts of Black or Stanton. Not the least of these were the claims of Limantour.[20]

The hearing upon the Limantour claims came up in the District Court of California in the summer of 1858. Limantour produced an air-tight official title to the claims. There was, and could be, no doubt that the signature of the Mexican official was genuine, that the title upon its face was perfect. Alcatraz, Goat Island, the Farallone Islands, Point Tiburon, and even the city of San Francisco seemed doomed!

But let us not forget the roaming adventurer, Auguste Jouan, whom Black had sent from Cincinnati to San Francisco to testify in this case. Jouan took the stand. He testified that four years after California had been ceded to America, he went in person with Limantour to Mexico City. There Limantour secured eighty *blank* petitions and titles, *signed by Micheltorena,* the former Mexican Governor of California. Jouan also told of certain recognizable erasures which he made upon one of these blank titles in filling out a spurious claim for Limantour. The title was produced in court and the alleged erasures were found to exist upon this particular title. Jouan went even further. *He produced in court one of these blank titles signed by Micheltorana!*

Jouan had done his work. Stanton now adduced letters from the archives to prove that at the time Limantour's claims were dated, 1843, there did not even exist the special stamped paper upon which these claims were written. Limantour was so overwhelmed that even his own lawyers deserted him. Not a word was uttered in reply.[21]

Limantour was indicted for perjury, gave bail of $35,000 for his appearance—but forfeited his recognizance and left it to be paid by his sureties.[22] Bancroft, in writing the chapter of this attempted fraud, forgot his pique at Black. "The exposure was so complete," he exulted, that Limantour was "lucky to escape from the country."[23]

Stanton returned to Washington in January 1859, having been gone nearly a year. Black, with good reason, felt that he had not been mistaken in picking the right man for the task. Their relation during this enterprise became extremely close. It led directly to Buchanan's appointment of Stanton, at Black's insistence, as Attorney-General during the closing days of his administration. It was a potent factor

[19] *Ibid.,* VI, p. 552.
[20] *Ibid.,* VI, p. 554.
[21] Gorham, *op. cit.,* pp. 57-65.
[22] J. S. Black, *Land Claim Report,* p. 33.
[23] Bancroft, *op. cit.,* VI, p. 554.

in bringing Stanton before the eyes of the nation and in making him available to Lincoln as Secretary of War.

Meanwhile the California land cases were to burden the docket of the Supreme Court for more than a decade. Under the Act of 1851, either the government or the claimant might appeal from a decision of the District Court to the Supreme Court. Exactly ninety-nine cases were so appealed.[24] More than a score of these already had been appealed when Black assumed the office of Attorney-General. Stanton's collection of the archives gave a new complexion to the whole problem, and Black attacked the situation with his customary vigor. He felt the need of a knowledge of Spanish. Even the most expert of translators might miss the special legal significance of many Spanish terms and phrases. He must compel these terms to speak their legal import correctly. He must know himself, of his own knowledge, what the Spanish documents contained. No translation, however expert, could satisfy him.

Therefore he turned to a study of the Spanish language. Armed with a grammar, dictionary, and law dictionary, he attacked the documents pertaining to cases before the court. Before long he had mastered a sufficient command of the language to enable him to understand and expound the Spanish and Mexican laws and legal documents relating to California land grants.[25] Although his command of the language never became a critical one it seems to have been quite sufficient to serve his purpose.

During his term as Attorney-General, seventeen grants confirmed by the District Court of California were proved to be fraudulent and were rejected by the Supreme Court. The lands thus restored to the public domain or the rightful owners by these seventeen decisions of the Supreme Court amounted approximately to 1,000 square miles, in addition to Angel Island in San Francisco Bay and the Santillan claim to a section of the city of San Francisco.[26]

[24] *Ibid.*, VI, p. 542.
[25] Francis J. Kooser to the Author, Jan. 23, 1930.
[26] J. S. Black, *Land Claim Report*, pp. 33-37.

11

RUMBLINGS OF DISRUPTION

IN MENTAL outlook Black was a lawyer and a lawyer only. Every question of life he saw from a legal view. Problems of statesmanship and politics were not excepted. In them he sought the legal issues, applied the legal remedy. To him there were few, if any, questions of polity. They were questions of jurisprudence. To miss this, the most dominant motivating drive of his life, is to miss nearly all that guided his conduct.

If this legal set of mind limited at times the breadth of his vision, it at least extended the length. He was a man of marked passions—passions that upon some questions distorted his uncommon ability in sound judgment. Yet upon some of the most turbulent questions of his generation—Secession and Reconstruction—the unmalleable legal cast of his mind enabled him to rise higher above the storms of passion that whirled around it than most statesmen of this period were capable of doing. To him slavery was not a question set apart to be decided by any higher law, lower law, mob law, or nullification acts—but like all other questions it was a matter of plain law. Reconstruction was not a mode of revenge to be conceived in minds twisted with hate. It must follow the channels of legal procedure. People's rights, as State's rights, could exist only under the law—not above it, below it, or outside of it.

We shall follow this legal stamp of Black's mind, from small actions to large, through his career as Attorney-General. One of his many duties in this office was to supply official opinions to other members of the Cabinet upon legal questions. Early in his career a delicate, though not highly important, question arose in the State department. A man accused as a deserter from a Spanish ship had been arrested on complaint of a Spanish consul in America, but released by a judge who ruled that his detention was illegal. Secretary of State Cass appealed to Black for an official opinion. Black replied by citing the Spanish treaty on this point, then showed how the Spanish consul had not brought his proof of desertion within any provision of this treaty.

The conclusion of this opinion is characteristic:

It might be convenient, in cases like this, to . . . let the rights of the person claimed as a deserter depend on the mere certification of a consul; but a written compact between two nations is not to be set aside for a shade or two of convenience, more or less. The law is so written, and that is sufficient answer to all that can be said against this proceeding.[1]

Likewise in an opinion called for by Jacob Thompson, Secretary of Interior, he laid down the same inflexible view. In this case Congress had passed an act to pay a federal officer for services rendered from January 1835 to June 1838. But some clerk had written *fifty*-eight in place of *thirty*-eight, and the law with this error so stood upon the official statutes. Could they pay the man anyhow, Thompson wanted to know, for the services rendered?

"If you erase one word and substitute another," replied Black, "what shall hinder you from altering every sentence it contains? If you can go behind the enrolled statute to find out a meaning which Congress did not express, how far may you go, and what is the rule? Congress must correct its own errors. It is neither safe nor legal for the executive to do it."[2]

Such was the view taken by Black upon all public questions.

There were, however, rumblings of national disruption arising from those who held a different view. Echoes of the Dred Scott decision were still reverberating through the land, and out of the northwest came new mutterings to reinforce the general drum fire. Sherman M. Booth, an abolitionist editor in Wisconsin, had been caught in a violation of the Fugitive Slave Law and taken into custody by the United States marshal. This had been some years earlier, in 1854. Scarcely, however, had Booth landed in jail before he was discharged upon a writ of habeas corpus issued by Judge A. D. Smith of the Supreme Court of Wisconsin, claiming that the Fugitive Slave Law was unconstitutional.[3]

Later Smith's action was sustained by the full bench of the Supreme Court of Wisconsin. The marshal, Ableman, then sued out a writ of error to the Supreme Court of the United States. Upon this writ, Booth was then indicted, tried, convicted, and sentenced in the United States District Court.[4] Again, however, he was released by a writ of habeas corpus issued by the Wisconsin Supreme Court, holding that the Federal Court was without jurisdiction as the Fugitive Slave Law was unconstitutional.[5]

It was the old issue of Nullification—early raised in our history by New England and later made famous by South Carolina. Always the weapon of a radical minority, it now was being evoked to serve the cause of abolition. It was being expounded with vigor, if not

[1] *Official Opinions of the Attorneys General*, IX, p. 97.
[2] *Ibid.*, IX, p. 50.
[3] 21 Howard, p. 508.
[4] 21 Howard, pp. 509-510.
[5] 3 Wisconsin, p. 158.

learning, by a court which would have resisted it to the death had its own interest lain on the other side. Likewise it was receiving sympathy and encouragement from high officials in Washington who, within the next few years, were to reverse themselves and evoke the god of battles to stamp it out of our national life. One of them, Charles Sumner, wrote to Byron Paine on August 5, 1854, regretting that it was Wisconsin instead of his own Massachusetts thus defying Federal supremacy.[6]

Again the United States Supreme Court issued a writ of error. It was filed on March 6, 1857,[7] the day Black was appointed Attorney-General. Likewise it was the same day on which the Dred Scott decision was made known to the public.

Under the title of *Ableman* vs. *Booth*, this case came up in the United States Supreme Court on January 19, 1859, and upon Black fell the duty of appearing for the government. He did so in a thorough and characteristic manner. His argument was of the type that might be expected of the man who had upheld Federal authority upon the identical issue in the Passmore Williamson case. His language was far more calm than might be expected from a man of his temperament upon such a question; it exhibited no hint of any personal feeling toward the judges of the Wisconsin court who had thrust a knife into what he held to be the vital organs of government. But against this court and the whole issue of nullification he rolled up a tide of legal evidence and swept their case loose from all legal moorings. Briefly summarized, his statement of the case was as follows:

1. In resisting the Federal laws, the very groundwork of the Constitution was violated.

> The Constitution declares that the Federal courts shall try all offenses against the laws of the United States; and Congress has given exclusive jurisdiction of Booth's offense to the District Court. No law, State or national, has authorized the Supreme Court of Wisconsin to intermeddle with the business in one way or another. Yet the latter court asserts its own jurisdiction and denies that of the Federal tribunal. . . . *One blast upon that ram's horn and the whole structure of judicial authority built by this Government comes tumbling about our ears like the walls of Jericho.*

2. Such a resistance to Federal laws likewise violated the great principle of *stare decisis*—or of legal precedence formulated under Federal laws.

> Here was a rule of constitutional interpretation, acted on by the Father of his Country, and by all his successors; approved by the sec-

[6] Charles Warren, *The Supreme Court in United States History*, II, p. 533.
[7] 21 Howard, p. 512.

ond Congress that assembled under the Constitution and by every succeeding Congress; affirmed directly or indirectly by every judge that ever sat on this bench, and by all the Federal judges of the country; approved, moreover, by every State court (except that of Wisconsin) in which it was ever questioned; and all the people have said "so be it." . . . There is no current of authority here, but a torrent, rolling forward impetuously as the waters of the Niagara River, and pressed from behind by all the waters of the lake. And here stand one or two men on the shore who try to roll it back by throwing their handful of sand in it. But the mighty torrent still thunders onward.

3. This attempt to overthrow Federal authority through a mere habeas corpus is more menacing than methods used in other such crises in the past. Wherever a Federal court may sit, it is struck dumb if the issue of constitutionality of any law is even touched upon, for in such a case

If there should happen to be, among the spectators in a corner of the courthouse, a probate judge of the county . . . he is the judge of last resort. . . . He will mount his habeas corpus and charge down upon you. . . . One word of his will paralyze your power. . . . Even if you convince him, perhaps you will not have done the tithe of work you have yet to do. There may be a score of other judges in the neighborhood having just as much power over your judgment as he has. . . .

In 1796 the excise duty on distilled spirits was believed in western Pennsylvania to be not only oppressive but unconstitutional. But the men of that day threw themselves back on the moral right of revolution, and opposed the obnoxious law with arms in their hands. They never dreamed of carrying on the "Whiskey War" by firing off writs of habeas corpus at the Federal authorities. . . .

We all remember the great debate in the Senate on this subject. Mr. Webster won his victory, so far as it was a triumph of logic and of law, by pressing this very point upon his adversary. "How," he said, "will you release yourselves from the grasp of the Federal judiciary?" But the victory would have been on the other side, if General Hayne could have answered that State judges had a right to take every case into their own keeping by means of the habeas corpus. He could not say so; he was too wise a man to believe it. . . . President Jackson, in his proclamation, used the same unanswerable argument. . . . It saved the country from dismemberment then. . . . When it ceases to be maintained, the Union of the States will become a rope of sand.[8]

After reading this speech, Black's old friend George W. Woodward wrote him from the Supreme Bench of Pennsylvania:

Many thanks to you, my old friend, for your excellent argument in the Wisconsin case. I like it. . . . A more atrocious case than that Wisconsin proceeding is not on record. I am glad you chastized it and very glad that it fell into *your* hands for chastisement. But I fancy

[8] C. F. Black, pp. 417-30.

that their Honors of the old fogy Court never had their ears tickled before with such singing periods.[9]

On March 9 following, the Supreme Court handed down its decision upholding Federal rights against the Wisconsin assault. The opinion was written by Chief Justice Roger B. Taney. "It was," said Warren, the historian of the Supreme Court, "the most powerful of all his notable decisions."[10] The whole opinion can be summarized by two sentences from the pen of Taney.

So long . . . as this Constitution shall endure, this tribunal must exist with it, deciding in the peaceful forms of judicial proceeding the angry and irritating controversies between sovereignties, which in other countries have been determined by the arbitrament of force. . . . Neither writ of habeas corpus, nor other process issued under State authority, can pass over the line of division between the two sovereignties.[11]

The radical press assaulted the decision in bitter terms. The New York *Tribune* characteristically denounced it as "forming a part of the same system of usurpation," as the Dred Scott decision. The Wisconsin Legislature retorted by solemnly reënacting the Virginia and Kentucky Resolutions of 1798-1799 and the South Carolina Nullification Act of 1833. This Nullification Act of the Wisconsin Legislature declared the "assumption of jurisdiction by the Federal Judiciary" to be "without authority, void and of no force"; furthermore that the several States of the Union "being sovereign and independent have the unquestionable right to judge of its infraction; and that a positive defiance of those sovereignties, of all unauthorized acts . . . is the rightful remedy."[12]

But in the end, even the Supreme Court of Wisconsin yielded, and by its own decision admitted that a Federal law could not be attacked in a State court upon the ground that it was unconstitutional.[13]

Along with the Wisconsin flare-up came another from Kansas. Kansas was indeed the hornet's nest inherited by the Buchanan administration. It could neither be pacified nor let alone. Previous to Buchanan's election the preliminary steps had been taken for admitting Kansas to statehood. As customary, the territory was required to draw up a constitution and submit it for Federal approval. From Kansas now came the Lecompton Constitution. In a proslavery election, at which the antislavery faction refused to vote, it had been overwhelmingly approved. In an antislavery election, in which the proslavery faction refused to vote, it had been overwhelmingly defeated. Should the administration accept or reject it?

[9] Black Papers, February 18, 1859.
[10] C. Warren, *The Supreme Court,* III, p. 58.
[11] 21 Howard, pp. 521, 523.
[12] Warren, *op. cit.,* III, pp. 61, 63.
[13] 14 Wisconsin, p. 180.

Black urged its acceptance, for reasons quite legal and politic, but unacceptable to the abolitionists. The Federal government, contended Black, could never pacify the warring factions in Kansas. The politic thing, therefore, was to get out and turn the state over to the people living there. What kind of constitution it was mattered little. Whether it favored one faction or the other mattered little. Admit Kansas to statehood, then its people could take charge and the majority would be free to keep, amend, or abolish the constitution. In short, let the people rule.[14]

The Republicans bitterly opposed this. Naturally they would, argued Black. For four years they had made political capital out of Kansas. They had just lost heavily in the local elections of 1857 and were too young an organization to stand another such defeat. Should the Kansas issue be settled so simply by allowing its people to keep, change, or abolish the Lecompton Constitution, the Republican political thunder would be dissipated. The Democratic party would be the preserver of the union and be entrenched more firmly than before. Therefore the Republicans wanted the uproar over Kansas to continue. It was, said Black, a "knavish trick."[15]

Meanwhile out in Kansas opposition of a sinister nature was going on. Murders were almost daily affairs. The first five of John Brown's murders were done there.[16] His was the act of a mere fanatic, but there was now arising a new type of depredation which had a special significance. The most illuminating record of it is to be found in the report submitted to Black by Joseph Williams, a District Judge of Kansas, on December 24, 1857. Williams was formerly Chief Justice of the Supreme Court of Iowa. His story corroborates others. It is not contradicted by any known facts. It was attested and sworn to by the affidavit of four other citizens.[17] This attested document tells of abolitionist freebooters "who had gone along the Osage river, with Sharps rifles and revolvers, driving men, women and children from their homes; taking, appropriating their property to their own use and running them out of the Territory." A recent story had been blown about by abolition newspapers charging that certain cattle had been seized in a lawless manner by "three hundred Missourians." Williams, investigating the charge, had found that the cattle were the property of one "Mr. Curry" who had foully shot another man through the head, had been indicted for the crime and somehow had secured bail after putting up the cattle as a security. But before the trial, Curry fled the country and forfeited the bail. Another newspaper charge of persecution spread by abolitionists was also investigated and turned

[14] Letter of December 25, 1857, Clayton MSS.

[15] C. F. Black, p. 273.

[16] E. Thayer, *The Kansas Crusade*, p. 192.

[17] Black Papers, Dec. 24, 1857.

out to be a legal indictment of six men for a series of crimes. In one of these crimes they had driven a seventy-five-year-old minister from his home, "took and used his property, and by threats, compelled him to leave the Territory." This property soon became the rendezvous of two organized bands numbering 275 men who not only expelled the entire population in that area, but even intimidated the Federal troops. "These outlaws boldly informed the Marshal that there was no law in Kansas and that they were acting under orders from James H. Lane," who was the Republican leader of this part of Kansas. Lane's outlaws were being "kept, fed, and clothed by aid Societies which are busy in this business in the East."

"I have no affection in favor of Slavery, I assure you," concluded Williams, but "with all this, I must say that, since I have been here, no pro-slavery man has been guilty of violating the law, that I know of."

To Buchanan, three months later, Williams wrote that Lane's outlaws "are not citizens of the Territory with the exception of a very few," that they were "making requisitions for men and munitions of war," and averring that "The Missourians" are driving out free settlers "when I *know and aver* that there have not been any Missourians . . . since I have been here (June last)."[18]

To Black Williams had written that "the object of all this movement by Lane . . . is to get up an embryo civil war in Kansas to prevent Congress from accepting the Lecompton Constitution." To Buchanan he wrote: "If Kansas remains in the Territorial condition, and is not permitted under the constitution now before Congress, we may look for an end that will be traced in blood from this, the mere beginning."

During the summer of 1857, Black himself had visited Kansas to investigate the conditions.[19] What he reported to Buchanan as a result of his trip is not known, but he agreed with Judge Williams as to the cause of the civil war. To ex-Governor Porter of Pennsylvania he wrote that the abolitionists "have taken an appeal from the ballot box to the 'higher law' of brutality and violence."[20]

Buchanan agreed with Black and sent the Lecompton Constitution to Congress for approval.

But a new leader was arising within the Democratic ranks, and like George of England, he was determined to "be a king." He had driven the Kansas-Nebraska Bill through Congress in 1854 thereby reopening the whole Kansas issue. He had sought and failed to secure the nomination for the Presidency in 1856. He would not fail in 1860. Stephen A. Douglas planted himself upon his famous doctrine of

[18] Buchanan Papers, March 3, 1858.
[19] Black Papers, July 9, 1857.
[20] Black Papers, Feb. 9, 1858.

popular sovereignty, denying that any route to popular sovereignty lay through the Lecompton Constitution.

With ranks divided, the Democratic party wavered. Finally a bill was passed returning the Lecompton Constitution to the people of Kansas for a third vote. Should the people accept the constitution they were to have the usual land grant given by Congress to new states. An outcry arose that the land grant was a bribe to the people of Kansas to gain their vote in favor of the Lecompton Constitution. Perhaps the accusation served its purpose, but it persisted after its usefulness was over until an impartial historian, *from the State of Kansas itself*, exploded the charge by showing that the grant was similar in size to that given to Minnesota in the previous year, that it was identical to that given to Oregon in the year following, and likewise identical with the grant finally given Kansas three years later when it was admitted to statehood. So regular was the proceeding in offering Kansas this land grant that Senator Henry Wilson, who gave the charge its first impetus, was forced to rearrange the speech of a Congressman in order to manufacture evidence for his purpose.[21]

But the Douglas defection, the civil war, and intimidation in Kansas had done their work. The Lecompton Constitution on August 2, 1858, was defeated in Kansas by a vote of 11,812 to 1,926.[22]

The administration was now thrown on the defensive and Douglas, after his reëlection to the Senate over Lincoln in 1859, undertook to push his victory farther by an article in the September 1859 issue of *Harper's Magazine* upon "Popular Sovereignty in the Territories."[23]

Buchanan was forced to mend his political fences. He called upon Black for the task. Therefore in reply to Douglas's article Black set forth some "Observations on Senator Douglas's Views of Popular Sovereignty," which appeared in the Washington *Constitution* for September 10, 1859. "It is clear in its style, temperate in tone and exceedingly forceful and cogent in argument," commented the New York *Times*, adding that its positions "are stated with great clearness and leave no room for misunderstanding or controversy as to their meaning. Its ability and the cogency of some of its extracts from former speeches of Judge Douglas will probably constrain him to take notice of it."[24]

Douglas was indeed compelled to take notice of it, for Black had driven him into an unpleasant position. He first showed that Douglas had falsely stated the doctrine upheld by the Buchanan wing of the Democratic party. Where Douglas had asserted that the Buchanan faction held that "the Constitution establishes slavery in the Territories,"

[21] F. H. Hodder, *American Historical Association Reports*, 1906, I, pp. 201-210.

[22] T. C. Smith, *Parties and Slavery*, p. 226.

[23] XIX, pp. 519-31.

[24] New York *Times*, September 13, 1859.

Black replied that "The Constitution certainly does not establish slavery in the Territories, nor anywhere else." But that "it is an axiomatic principle of public law that a right of property, a private relation, condition, or status, lawfully existing in one State or country is not changed by the mere removal of the parties to another country, unless the law of that other country be in direct conflict with it. For instance: A marriage legally solemnized in France is binding in America; children born in Germany are legitimate here if they were legitimate there; and a merchant who buys goods in New York, according to the laws of that State, may carry them to Illinois and hold them there under his contract. It is precisely so with the status of a negro carried from one part of the United States to another." In support of this statement of law, he pointed out that statesmen of former times had held the same opinion, that such a view had been the basis for the passing of the Ordinance of 1787, and for the Missouri Compromise; that the Republicans admitted it so unanimously that "the ablest men among them are driven . . . to hunt for arguments in a code unrevealed, unwritten and undefined, which they put above the Constitution or the Bible, and call it 'higher law' "; that even the abolitionists held the same view, and because of this view of the Constitution they had disdained "to obey what they pronounce to be 'an agreement with death and a covenant with hell.' "

All of this might be embarrassing enough for Douglas, but Black did not stop here. He pressed his advantage to show that Douglas's own views, as set forth in this article were at war with themselves and with many axiomatic principles of constitutional law. Douglas had stated his own opinion of the constitutional law involved in a long, ambiguous statement which, summarized by quotations from it, is as follows: "The Constitution of the United States neither establishes nor prohibits slavery in the States or Territories," but it "leaves the people" free to "form and regulate" it, "subject only to the Constitution of the United States."

"This," said Black, "is sailing to Point No-point." "This carries us round a full circle, and drops us precisely at the place of beginning." In brief, it leaves us assured that "the Constitution leaves everybody subject to the Constitution," which "we have never heard . . . doubted, and expect we never will."

"The territorial government," continued Black, "is merely provisional and temporary. It is created by Congress for the necessary preservation of order and the purposes of police." Its power is wholly dependent on the grant of authority by Congress. But if Congress cannot legislate upon the subject of slavery in the territories, as Douglas claims it cannot do, *how can Congress grant such a power to a territorial government which is dependent on Congress for every iota of its authority?*

"Yet Mr. Douglas declares . . . that the *want* of power in Congress is the *very reason* why it can delegate it."

As a parting shot Black exposed the "wobbling pathway" that Douglas had followed during the past ten years. Eight months before he had accepted the Dred Scott decision in a speech at New Orleans, "admitted the right of a Southern man to go into any Federal Territory with his slave and hold him there *as other property is held.*" Yet in 1849, when the identical legal issue of congressional control of territories was before Congress, he had voted for the Walker Amendment to give the President "unlimited power, legislative, judicial and executive, over the internal affairs" of New Mexico and California. Still again, in 1857, when the issue arose once more, in the Territory of Utah, he had favored the "absolute and unconditional repeal of the organic law, blotting the Territorial government out of existence and putting the people under the sole and exclusive jurisdiction of the United States, like a fort, arsenal, dock-yard, or magazine." "He does not seem to have had the least idea," summarized Black in one devastating sweep, "that he was proposing to extinguish a sovereignty or to trample upon the sacred rights of an independent people." In the Senate, in 1856, Black continued, Douglas strenuously had insisted that "the sovereignty of a Territory remains in abeyance, suspended in . . . trust for the people until they shall be admitted into the Union as a state." He had repeated that view in Philadelphia in 1858; he had again repeated it a month later in the Senate. But his new stand on popular sovereignty denies all of this, confers complete sovereignty upon the people of the territory—with Douglas all the while insisting that he is standing where he always stood.

Such was the reply of Black to Douglas. The reaction over the country was instantaneous. The article was reprinted in whole or in part in substantially every important daily paper. Some newspapers which at first reprinted only extracts complied with the requests of their subscribers and later ran the full article. The edition of extra copies run off by the *Constitution* was soon exhausted and two more editions were put out in pamphlet form, one of them being for 11,000 copies.[25] The New York *Times* and the Washington *Republic*, both of which were opposition journals, admitted that it was the strongest document on the Territorial question that had yet been laid before the public.[26] James E. Harvey of the Philadelphia *North American*, another opposition paper, exulted that Douglas "is demolished in argument, statement, and style. . . . He is a doomed man at Charleston."[27] The Louisville *Courier* summarized the reaction of the administration press. This paper thought that Black had "added largely to

[25] Black Papers, October 17, 1859.
[26] Press Clippings, Clayton MSS.
[27] Black Papers, September 16, 1859.

his already high reputation as a close and massive reasoner and a profound statesman," and exulted that he had "achieved a most signal victory in his discussion with Judge Douglas."[28]

Robert Tyler, son of the ex-President, wrote that "your article in reply to Douglas . . . is as conclusive a paper as I have ever read," and begged for 500 copies for distribution.[29] The son of Alexander Hamilton wrote that, in his father's argument upon the United States Bank, Black would find a confirmation of his stand upon the constitutional law involved in the controversy.[30] Copies of the article appeared even in England, and a translation was made into the German language.[31]

Black had indeed delivered the final blow that spiked Douglas's guns at the approaching Democratic convention in Charleston—but there was no stemming the defection that now was scattering the Democratic ranks. In the elections of 1858 the dissevered Democrats had been sharply defeated and the tide against them rolled on into the State elections of 1859. Nowhere was the defection more serious than in Black's own state of Pennsylvania. John W. Forney had lost out in his fight to control the Democratic party of that State and thereupon had joined the ranks of the Republicans, established a newspaper, and dedicated himself to a crusade against the majority which had ousted him. Two letters to Black give us the key to the whole affair. One was from David Webster, a prominent attorney and politician of Philadelphia. "In the present situation of affairs," he wrote, "it needs but a spark to ignite a conflagration."[32] The other was from one Charles Heffley of the village of Berlin, Somerset County. He was ignorant of punctuation and utterly careless of spelling and capitals —but vigorous and picturesque in language and prophetic in his outlook.

Folks in our town are generally well But as regards Politicks everything appears to be going to the Devil. . . . Mitchell and those fellows at Somerset go in With those traitors Douglas & Forney . . . Sonners and those abbolitionists have got up a Big Club of Subscribers for Forneys paper as for my part I Was not Deceived in Forney for I Expected that he would try and Raise the Devil the first oppertunity that he would get Now Cant you Democrats at Washington get a head of those fellows and have those Kansas Matters Settled.[33]

[28] Press Clipping, Clayton MSS.

[29] Black Papers, September 13, 1859.

[30] Black Papers, October 6, 1859.

[31] See Black Papers, September 1859 to January 1860, for the exceptional reaction to this article. Other comments and requests for copies may be found as late as September 1863.

[32] Black Papers, December 30, 1857.

[33] Black Papers, December 18, 1857.

But the Kansas matters were not settled and the breach within the Democratic ranks was widened. Added to this came a period of unployment and tight money following the sharp financial panic of 1857. This was the last straw. Heffley's rustic prophecy was fulfilled. The Democrats of Pennsylvania were swept out of office in October 1859.

Buchanan in 1856 had expressed his fears that a crisis must come. "I had hoped for the nomination in 1844, again in 1848, and even in 1852, but now I would hesitate to take it," he had said. "Before many years the Abolitionists will bring war upon the land. It may come during the next Presidential term."[34]

The next Presidential term was his own. And clouds were darkening upon every horizon.

[34] F. A. Burr, Philadelphia *Press*, March 16, 1882.

12

BUCHANAN AND HIS CABINET

IT HAD been Buchanan's ambition to equip himself with a harmonious Cabinet. He had served in many public offices, had himself been in the Cabinet of President Polk. He knew the value of administrative harmony. In conferring the position of Attorney-General upon Black, he had written "we must be a unit here if possible,"[1] and so insistent was he upon securing men who would work in harmony that he left out of consideration all of the more radical leaders of the party and their immediate camp followers, including those of Douglas. In this one point, Buchanan succeeded. He did gather around him a group of men who worked willingly and harmoniously together —until the parting of ways in 1860.

Let us pause for a glance at these men. Besides, Black, as Attorney-General, Lewis Cass of Michigan was in the State Department; Howell Cobb of Georgia was Secretary of the Treasury; John B. Floyd of Virginia was Secretary of War; Isaac Toucey of Connecticut was Secretary of the Navy; Jacob Thompson of Mississippi was Secretary of the Interior; Aaron V. Brown of Tennessee, until his death in 1859, was Postmaster-General, and following his death he was succeeded by Joseph Holt of Kentucky.[2]

"This is not a strong cast," exclaimed Greeley,[3] and his Philadelphia coadjutor agreed.[4] What Greeley really meant was that there were no abolitionists in the group. He was quite right. But this group of men did bring into the Cabinet training and ability of a high order.

Lewis Cass was the oldest in years and experience. He had been a soldier in the War of 1812, rising to the rank of Major General of volunteers. For eighteen years he had served with distinction as Territorial Governor of Michigan and had come from that office into the Cabinet of Andrew Jackson as Secretary of War. Six years later Jackson had sent him to France as minister. In 1845 Michigan, now a State, had sent him to the Senate where he had urged the annexation of Texas, the occupation of all of the Oregon Territory, and had opposed the Wilmot Proviso. In 1848, he had been nominated for President by the Democrats, but was narrowly defeated by Zachary Taylor. Three years later, his State had returned him to the Senate. Even

[1] *Works of James Buchanan*, X, p. 114.
[2] *Ibid.*, XII, p. 93.
[3] New York *Tribune*, March 7, 1857.
[4] Philadelphia *North American*, March 9, 1857.

JAMES BUCHANAN AND HIS CABINET

Greeley grudgingly admitted him to be a man of ability.[5] Buchanan personally did not like Cass but felt that he was about as near to the Douglas wing of the party as he cared to go for a place in the official circle.[6] At the time of his appointment, however, Cass was seventy-five years of age and lacked much of his former vigor. Perhaps this inclined Buchanan to offer him the Secretaryship of State rather than some other post, since Buchanan, because of his long experience in foreign service, in reality served as his own Secretary of State.

Howell Cobb likewise brought to the Cabinet a long experience in political leadership. He had served ten years in Congress, two of them as its Speaker, and had been for one term Governor of his State of Georgia. He was a debater of skill, an aggressive leader, and a champion of slavery. "Howell Cobb of Georgia," said the New York *Tribune*, "is plainly to be the master spirit of the new Cabinet." He is "shrewd, strong, coarse, ambitious, intensely proslavery, but not a Disunionist"; he had "decided ability," and was a man of "strong sense, energy and indomitable will." This tribute comes in Greeley's acrimonious and uncharitable attack upon the Cabinet as a whole and may be taken as the worst opinion of Cobb's ability that Greeley honestly could bring himself to put into print.[7]

John B. Floyd, head of the War Department, brought to the Cabinet less political experience than any man of the original group, save perhaps Black himself. He had served three terms in the State Legislature and one term as Governor of Virginia. Of all the members of Buchanan's Cabinet, Floyd drew the most pitiless heat of irate Northern opinion. He was accused of being a Secessionist from the start, of selling arms to the Southern States, of misappropriating Indian money in the Department of Interior.[8] His actions, however, were investigated by a Congressional Committee "organized to convict," yet who were forced to dismiss the charges as founded in "rumor, speculation and misapprehension."[9]

He also has been acquitted before the bar of historical judgment.[10] In the actual administration of his own department, Floyd proved to be able and efficient. The army was kept in a good state, considering the funds allowed for its use. But he was not meticulous in financial management. When the army needed supplies in the "Utah War," he saw that supplies were delivered—even though he had to advance government money to agents in violation of departmental regulations.[11]

[5] New York *Tribune*, March 7, 1857.
[6] See *Buchanan's Works*, XI, p. 59.
[7] New York *Tribune*, March 7, 1857.
[8] Henry Wilson, *Atlantic Monthly*, February 1870, p. 234.
[9] C. F. Black, p. 266.
[10] See Rhodes, *op. cit.*, III, pp. 239, 240.
[11] P. J. Auchampaugh, *James Buchanan and His Cabinet*, pp. 92-3.

This led to a long series of litigations and to the final refusal by the Supreme Court to accept his action as legal.[12]

Isaac Toucey, Secretary of the Navy, had begun his national political career in the House of Representatives. He had arisen to be one of the ablest constitutional lawyers of his days and had served as Attorney-General under Polk. The common opinion was that Buchanan would ask him to take that post again.[13] This Buchanan would doubtless have done had it not been for the necessity of moving Toucey to some other post to make room for Black. Between the intervals in Polk's and Buchanan's Cabinets, Toucey had served in the United States Senate. He seemed to be a rather taciturn man, but his letters show him to be vigorous in statement.

Jacob Thompson, who held the post of Secretary of Interior, was a man of exceptional and remarkable personality. "Winning, able, persuasive in argument, affectionate, and warm hearted,"[14] one cannot, even in this day, read his interesting letters without feeling that here is a man of vigor and charm. For eighteen years he had served his State of Mississippi in Congress. Once he had refused to accept an appointment to the Senate, although later he willingly consented to become Governor of Mississippi. The contrast of these two actions is typical of the man, for he had a love for his State akin to that found in the intense patriotism of peoples of small nations like Switzerland and Belgium. "I went to Mississippi when a young man," he said, "and anything I am she made me." At the parting of ways in 1860, Thompson was torn between two loves. "If I remained with the Union I would be denounced as a traitor to my state. If I resigned when my state seceded I would be called a traitor to my country."[15] Like Lee of Virginia, he could not lift his hand against his State. He went with it; and tragedy was written upon his later life. He and Black had become close friends and, much as Black opposed his views of secession, the friendship remained. Their correspondence, although rudely severed by the Civil War, was again resumed after the bitter struggle was over. We shall meet him often again.

Aaron Brown, the Postmaster-General, does not stand out in the scenes of the Cabinet, since his death in 1859 removed him before the tragic crisis of the following year. He seems to have been a man of considerable ability, however. Once he had been a law partner of President Polk and in the law he had amassed considerable wealth. Then followed six years in Congress and one term as Governor of Tennessee. Joseph Holt, who succeeded Brown after the latter's death, had been a lawyer of some reputation, and had at different times re-

[12] 7 Wallace, p. 666.

[13] *National Intelligencer*, Feb. 26, 1857; *Harper's Weekly*, March 7, 1857.

[14] Auchampaugh, *op. cit.*, p. 115.

[15] Philadelphia *Press*, September 17, 1883.

sided both in Kentucky and Mississippi. In the latter state he had been a political opponent of the brilliant Sergeant S. Prentiss. He came to the Cabinet without political experience save in holding the office of commissioner of patents to which he had been appointed by Buchanan in 1857. He was an abrupt and somewhat vindictive man.[16] But no one questioned his ability, least of all anyone who followed him through the crisis of 1860, as did Black.

We come to Buchanan, the President himself. What sort of man was he? How able as a leader? Of all men in modern history, none is harder with whom to make acquaintance. Posterity has been given few portraits of him, save those colored in the hues of passion. Enemies of his own day set him down as a weak and doddering old man; his friends retorted that enemies had lied his life away. "Impartial" historians who opposed his school of thought have left us a picture taken only from the lips of his enemies.[17] Equally "impartial" historians who adhere to his school have repudiated such a picture as utterly misrepresentative.[17a] Let us add another attempt to the already numerous ones to see Buchanan, the man, who sat as President of the United States between the years 1857 and 1861.

A man's face at fifty is partly what his life has made it. We do not dare trust too far any judgment based upon physiognomy, of course, but the habits and experiences of half a century leave at least a few lines. And Buchanan was sixty-six when he assumed the Presidency. His hair was nearly white, but his face looked younger than his years. It was a face long and full, with an exceptionally high and bulging forehead, a heavy nose and a prominent chin. Its expression bespeaks vigor and determination—but not weakness.

His handwriting was fine and precise, suggesting a steel-cut engraving. At the beginning of his administration, although it had lost some of its former firmness, it was still legible and smooth. At the end, there was a nervousness in the stroke which told plainly of the strain that had been laid upon him.

It is not only interesting, but highly significant, to compare the portraits written of Buchanan before the crisis with those written later. The plainest, the most unvarnished, is given us by James K. Polk. In his diary, Polk wrote freely and frankly, apparently never dreaming that his thoughts thus put on record should ever be opened to the scrutiny of history. Of Buchanan he wrote as frankly as of most other men who crossed his path. Buchanan wanted to succeed Polk as President in 1848. So, Polk feared, did those altogether too suc-

[16] His bitter twenty-year quarrel with Jacob Thompson illustrates this trait. See Philadelphia *Press*, September 10, 1883.

[17] F. W. Chadwick, *Causes of the Civil War*, p. 164.

[17a] Auchampaugh, *op. cit.*, p. 2.

cessful Whig Generals, Taylor and Scott. But Polk had an opinion of his own upon this subject; he intended to succeed himself. Therefore he took care to remove the political patronage of Pennsylvania from the hand of Buchanan.[18] "He has been selfish," he wrote in that journal intended only for his own eye, "and all his acts and opinions seem to have been controlled with a view to his own advancement, so much that I have no confidence or reliance in any advice he may give upon public questions."[19] He refers to Buchanan's "weakness" in hungering for the Presidency, but that is the only weakness Polk found. Buchanan was altogether too stiff-necked for his liking.

Indeed this seems to be the universal opinion of him prior to December of 1860—that he was too rigid and set, too self-confident of himself. Especially does one find this view among those who knew him well. Ten days after he had assembled his Cabinet in 1857, the Washington correspondent of the New York *Herald* remarked "It is evident to the Cabinet that Mr. Buchanan intends to be the President in every sense of the word. He is self-determined, not consultive, with the Cabinet."[20] No man in public life was more noted for a stiff knee than Black. Neither public criticism nor fear of contempt of court could awe him. As we follow his relations with Buchanan during the crisis of Secession, we shall not want evidence of his willingness to cross swords with his chief when his grounded convictions were at stake. Yet Black's daughter Mary, who was fifteen at this time, was impressed by the respect that her father and others held toward Buchanan. "His Cabinet called him 'The Squire' behind his back and they stood in much the same awe of him as boys do of a schoolmaster," she wrote.[21] Black himself testified to the same fact. "No man ever filled the Presidential office who knew better than he how to enforce the respect due to his position and I know of no one more tenacious of his opinions when his judgment was fixed," he said.[22] Howell Cobb resented the unbending manner of his chief. "We were like a lot of school boys," he complained.[23] Finally we may take the testimony of Philip F. Thomas, who served for a short time in the Treasury Department after Cobb's resignation. Of all the men who have testified concerning these trying days, Thomas impresses one as perhaps the most undisturbed in his passions.

It is the usual thing to talk about Mr. Buchanan's weakness. When he made up his mind he was a very stubborn man. . . . He had a good opinion of his own ability and judgment and prided himself upon

[18] *Polk's Diary*, I, pp. 138, 144, 194, 201.
[19] *Ibid.*, III, p. 403.
[20] New York *Herald*, March 16, 1857.
[21] Clayton, p. 106.
[22] F. A. Burr, Philadelphia *Press*, September 10, 1883.
[23] F. A. Burr, Philadelphia *Weekly Press*, August 25, 1881.

his statescraft. Judge Black could come nearer to managing him than any man I know, but he could not always do it by any means.[24]

To one who follows Buchanan through his career, it must be evident that Thomas, more than any other critic, has given us the key to Buchanan's character. He was not a weak, vacillating, or doddering old man. His weakness lay in going to the other extreme. He was determined to run his whole administration, to be his whole Cabinet. He neglected to counsel with or to take the advice of his advisers as much as he might have done. He indeed prided himself upon his statecraft, felt himself more experienced than his constituted advisers, and therefore without need of their counsel. Before the secession of South Carolina one may probe in vain to find the charge of weakness. Rather was he charged with other and directly opposite faults; craftiness and stubborn tenacity of purpose. These were indeed his faults and they were his weaknesses in the crisis.[25]

Much of the legend upon Buchanan's weakness has come to us through the impetus of Stanton's duplicity. As the Southern members of the Cabinet withdrew during the process of Secession, new members were added from the North. One of these new members was Edwin M. Stanton, whom we have met before as the able and vigorous prosecutor of the California land frauds. Later he became Secretary of War under Lincoln, and his new admirers wove many a merry yarn about his domineering part in the Buchanan administration. We shall attend to the chief one of them in a moment. But let us first give our attention to Stanton himself.

Of his ability there can be no doubt or question. But his double role in history has been definitely and completely excavated. Black trusted him, even though his son-in-law, James F. Shunk, who had gone to California following Stanton's employment there, warned Black against him. "You may depend upon it that Stanton is *not a perfectly fair man. Don't start.* I have made up my mind upon that point not hastily or rashly but upon sufficient evidence. . . . He has not done the fair thing with you. He has suffered you to bear all the odium of any disagreeable things you may have done even at his suggestion . . ."[26] Buchanan personally distrusted him and objected to placing him in the Cabinet; he finally did so only because Stanton's knowledge of pending cases before the Supreme Court made it necessary to have him there.[27]

The moment Stanton entered Buchanan's official family circle, he voluntarily assumed the role of spy for the incoming administration, secretly reporting to Sumner's house at midnight and forwarding un-

[24] F. A. Burr, Philadelphia *Weekly Press*, August 18, 1881.

[25] See *Buchanan's Works*, XI, p. 63, for Black's letter to Buchanan's biographer, G. T. Curtis, upon this subject.

[26] Black Papers, end of 1860.

[27] *Buchanan's Works*, XI, p. 247.

signed letters by day.[28] His purpose seems to have been the bidding for a place in Lincoln's Cabinet, for when that Cabinet was chosen, with his name omitted from the list, he turned upon Lincoln with venom. To Buchanan, now retired, he poured a constant stream of letters giving him information that could have been gleaned only in high counsels, praising Buchanan's administration of the crisis, and attacking the new administration with satire. "So far . . . as your administration is concerned," he wrote to Buchanan, "its policy in reference to both Sumter and Pickens is fully vindicated by the course of the present administration for forty days after the inauguration of Lincoln."[29] Of the new administration he speaks cuttingly as "black Republicans," of "Cabinet intrigues and Republican interference," of the "neglect and insult" of able Democratic military leaders. "They all act as though they meant to be ready 'to cut and run' at a minute's notice," he sneered at the new Cabinet. And finally he disposed of them by commenting that "no one speaks of Lincoln or any member of his Cabinet with respect or regard."[30]

But the Stanton who ran with the hare could also hunt with the hounds. When Lincoln removed Cameron from the War Office and turned it over to Stanton the latter dropped Buchanan on the instant and began the vilification of his former political friends. His service in the War Office was of the highest order, although he did harass his chief by insubordination, and insult his generals in the field. Grant thought him a bully and said contemptuously of him, "He cared nothing for the feelings of others." "The enemy could not have been in danger if Mr. Stanton had been in the field."[31]

It is to this type of man that we owe much of the historical misinformation about Buchanan himself and about Buchanan's administration upon the eve of Secession. Thurlow Weed led off in making Stanton a double-barreled hero by publishing a story in the London *Observer* on February 9, 1862, which was later reprinted in the New York *Herald* and thereafter made the rounds in other American newspapers. The story was to the effect that on December 27, 1860, at the instant when Buchanan was weakly yielding to the demand of South Carolina in removing Anderson from Sumter, Stanton strode forward in a Cabinet meeting, cited two Cabinet members for financial dishonesty, and wound up by giving Buchanan the choice of standing firm or of accepting his resignation. His threat of resignation was seconded by Black, Holt, and Dix, which "opened the bleary eyes of the President" and forced him to stand firm.[32]

[28] H. Wilson, *Atlantic Monthly*, February 1870, p. 234.

[29] *Buchanan's Works*, XI, p. 211.

[30] *Ibid.*, XI, pp. 203, 213, 190. See also XI, pp. 166-213 for seventeen letters, Stanton to Buchanan, written within four months.

[31] *Grant's Memoirs*, II, p. 380.

[32] G. T. Curtis, *Life of James Buchanan*, II, pp. 518-9; *Buchanan's Works*, XI, p. 265.

The story created great excitement and Stanton was naturally appealed to for verification. To his friends, he admitted the veracity of the story, but when he was called upon to commit himself in print where the world could check his story, he wrote an account which was exceedingly, and apparently purposely, veiled and obscure. In this he modestly said that the account was "substantially correct."[33] But he refrained even from allowing this ambiguous statement to go in print over his own name. Black denounced the story as false. "Weed's letter is now *lying* before me," he wrote to Buchanan,[34] and when called upon for a public statement of the affair, he stamped it as "wholly fictitious."[35] General Dix, whose name was also mentioned as supporting Stanton, likewise denounced it, pointing out that he was not even a member of the Cabinet at that time.[36]

Lincoln brooked many an insult from Stanton, because Lincoln was a patient man and because he knew that Stanton was an able Secretary. But Stanton took liberties with Lincoln that he dared not take with Buchanan. "Stanton never but once ventured beyond the line of mere obsequiousness," said Black, "and then was driven back to his place cowering under the lash of the President's reprimand."[37] This statement is supported by the testimony of Secretary Thomas, who succeeded Cobb in the Treasury Department.

In spite of the lack of support to bolster the story, it was repeated in eulogies of Stanton after his death and was blown about by Senator Henry Wilson in two widely circulated magazine articles.[38] The latter offense was too much for Black. He addressed an open reply to Wilson, pointing out the lack of authority for the story. With a dash of satire he summarized the lone strand of circumstantial evidence upon which Wilson based his story:

> Failing wholly to get anything out of Mr. Holt, you naturally enough resorted to Mr. Dawes; and Mr. Dawes, willing, but unable to help you, called in the aid and comfort of his wife. "She," her husband says, "distinctly remembers hearing Stanton tell at our house the story of that terrible conflict in the Cabinet." That is the length and breadth of her testimony. She remembers that Mr. Stanton told the story, but not the story itself. It was about a terrible conflict; but we do not learn who were engaged in it, who fell, or who was victorious—how the fray began, or how it ended—only that it was terrible.[39]

[33] Gorham, *op. cit.*, pp. 151-158.
[34] *Buchanan's Works*, XI, p. 263.
[35] Black Papers, August 6, 1863.
[36] M. Dix, *Memoirs of John A. Dix*, I, p. 379.
[37] F. A. Burr, Philadelphia *Weekly Press*, August 25, 1881.
[38] *Atlantic Monthly*, February 1870, p. 234; and October 1870, p. 463.
[39] C. F. Black, p. 289.

13

THE SPIRIT OF SECESSION AND ABOLITION

IT IS difficult, if not impossible, for posterity to appreciate the forces which played upon the fears and passions of men in the turbulent period of Secession—for we view it complacently as a record of events, past and settled. But the future was not revealed to the anxious men who stood in those days at the helm. They saw only the beginning, but not the end.

The average person sees today a clear-cut moral issue—slavery against freedom, right against wrong. But the clear hues of our day have been produced only by the fading and whitewashing of other hues. We must, if we can, project ourselves into the living environment of that day, see the issues and sense the fears that moved the actors in this, the greatest tragedy of the American historical drama. Our task is not easy, for few of us have ever read the complete history of this period. The flush of victory and the bitterness of defeat have alike given us many eulogies and many partial histories, but few complete ones. Northern historians have told the story of Union victory. Southern bards have sung of the valor of the Lost Cause. But between the two there stood the little group of border-state men, or men with border-state ideas, whose valiant fight to stay the rushing torrent of disunion has been held in contempt by both sides, and who have been allowed to go down in history "unwept, unhonored, and unsung." Yet more clearly than partisans of either side, they saw the issues of both sides and the dangers of the triumph of either.

Let us then, if we can, understand the state of mind of these men on the crisis of 1860. Other issues stood before them which obscured and shrunk that of slavery. The greatest of these was the preservation of the Constitution, of its guarantees of liberty and property. Slavery was but the issue of the hour. The real menace was to the Constitution itself. Because of this fear, a new party arose in 1860 calling itself the "Constitutional Union" party, recognizing "no political principles other than *the Constitution of the country, the union of the states and the enforcement of the laws.*" It polled nearly 600,000 votes and testified to the concern of conservative men, North and South.[1]

Black was one of those who held a grave concern for the future of constitutional government. Secession, of course, meant open disruption, and that he would not admit could be constitutionally ac-

[1] *Tribune Almanac,* 1861, pp. 34, 64.

complished. But all of the danger was not upon the side of Secession. Far from it. He saw in abolitionism an equal, and more insidious menace. To him abolitionism was merely another of the many drainage tubes of festered fanaticism of Puritanism. And as he surveyed the history of that fanaticism in America, he exclaimed that "no such calamity has happened to the human race since the fall of Adam, as the landing of the Pilgrim fathers."[2] It cannot be said that he hated individual New Englanders, or descendants of Puritans. Among the warmest friends of his whole life were such New Englanders, or descendents of New Englanders, as Caleb Cushing, Isaac Toucey, James A. Garfield, and Matt H. Carpenter. He thought Webster had been "gifted with the most subtle and exquisitely organized intellect" of any man of his generation. He regarded Rufus Choate as one of the greatest lawyers in American history. He would not be consciously unfair to the virtues of the Puritans, and once when a bogus letter purporting to be from Cotton Mather was circulating, showing him to be engaged in kidnapping Quakers, Black was the first to discover and denounce its bogus character.[3] To Garfield he wrote many years later that "the vices and wickedness of the Plymouth colonists are not to be visited on the heads of their children, according to the flesh. Among them, in every part of the country, are great statesmen, brave soldiers . . ."[4] But this left him no less uneasy over the dangers of Puritan fanaticism. To him abolitionism was the mere nineteenth-century counterpart of that holy zeal which, two centuries before, had driven Roger Williams—the only exponent of religious freedom in America—into the wilderness, and had spent itself in witch burning, the hanging of Quakers, and the public stripping and whipping of inoffensive women.[5] Once it had established the cruelest slave code in America, branded Indians like cattle and sold them into slavery—even unto the wife and child of that famous Indian leader, King Philip—until these enemies were exterminated.[6] Later it had burned brightly in war against Masonry and had welcomed with zeal the attack upon the Catholic Church in the guise of Know Nothingism. Now slavery was its object—and already in the offing other fanatics were gathering to lead an attack against the Christian religion and still others against the convention of marriage. Fanaticism must have its firebrand of the hour.[7]

But the turn of circumstances had given to this particular outlet of slavery a grave political aspect. The old Whig party, never in touch

[2] Hensel, p. 196.
[3] *Ibid.*
[4] C. F. Black, p. 300.
[5] *Ibid.*, p. 293.
[6] *Ibid.*, pp. 295-297.
[7] Black to Woodward, Black Papers, November 24, 1860.

with the real issues in American political life, had finally died with scarcely a gasp. The great bulk of political leaders, now men without a party, had few private scruples about slavery. Their last President had been Zachary Taylor, who was himself a large slaveholder. But Harriet Beecher Stowe had written a book that advertised the slavery issue, and these ex-Whigs had seized the chance of opportunists to ride this new vote-getting issue. "It must be perfectly well known to you," Black wrote to his friend George W. Woodward, "that in 1856 there was a serious debate among them, (it was scarcely settled indeed at the time of the election) whether their rallying principle should be opposition to the Catholic religion or opposition to the slave-holders. It is as sure as death that in 1860 they would have gone to burning churches and convents, and smelling about female schools with just as much zest as they attack slavery in the southern states, if thereby they could have been equally certain of success."[8]

All of this was good politics—but the joining of ranks between abolitionists and Whig politicians produced a situation which, in the eyes of such a staunch and literal defender of the Constitution as Black, was fraught with danger. The political activities of the abolitionists had revealed them as respecters neither of law nor Constitution. Their leader had publicly burnt a copy of the Constitution in the streets of Boston, and this document, which Jefferson had once pointed to as our "sheet anchor of safety," he had denounced as a "covenant with death and an agreement with Hell." Following this, they had espoused the covenant of the "higher law," above and beyond the Constitution. A legal mind like Black's could not but shudder at what a higher law must mean to those who regarded real law as an agreement with hell. They had furnished John Brown with arms and money, full knowing that both were to be used in cold-blooded murder. When Brown was caught with blood upon his hands, tried, and executed for his crimes, the mass meetings, tolling of bells, and oaths of vengeance against the law which forbade murders in the name of abolitionism could not but disturb the mind of such a man, who had learned to look toward the Constitution for a guarantee of the rights of citizens.

If any final proof could have been needed to disturb such minds as Black's, the attack upon the Supreme Court supplied it. This is no place to review the Dred Scott controversy. But there were men of that day who solemnly held the Supreme Court to be the highest judicial tribunal of the land. In its full legal powers it had handed down a decision upon a question brought before it for review. Moderate men felt that such a decision did not reflect the personal views of the members of that court so much as it did their legal opinion of what was and was not law. But the abolitionists had arisen in wrath and announced their intention to smash the highest court in

[8] Black Papers, November 24, 1860.

the land. Finally there was the Wisconsin case of Ableman and Booth, where a state judicial body had planted itself coldly and deliberately upon the doctrine of Nullification and sought to overthrow the whole superstructure of Federal law.

Fanatics are always with us, and fanaticism of 1860 perhaps did not exceed that of any other day, but in the eyes of the moderates the danger lay in the fact that they had made a covenant with the old Whig party and had brought into their ranks many who rode the tide for political gain. How far would the politicians go with the abolitionists in their assault upon the Constitution? What chance had the Constitution to live if state courts should become entrenched in their contention to declare Federal laws unconstitutional and if the highest tribunal in jurisprudence could have its decisions overturned?

So there stood a body of moderate men in the center of the controversy—viewing upon one side the dangers of abolition, and viewing with equal alarm upon the other the patent and open assault of Secession. In neither direction could they see a rift in the clouds. "I see the beginning," said Black, "but not the end."[9]

Two weeks after the election of Lincoln, George W. Woodward, Black's old friend and former colleague of the Pennsylvania Supreme Court, sent him an outpouring of heart and mind.

> I have had no heart to write you or anybody else on politics since the election. But now as I have pen in hand let me say a few things I want to say to somebody and I don't care how faithfully you preserve what I write—nor when or how it may come up in judgment against me.
>
> Lincoln and Seward are right. The conflict *is* irrepressible.

After detailing the assaults upon the Constitution, the attack upon Southern rights, and the dangers in the future, Woodward closed,

> As a Northern man I cannot in justice condemn the South for withdrawing from the Union. I believe they have been loyal to the Union formed by the Constitution—secession is not disloyalty to that, for that no longer exists. The North has extinguished it.
>
> And if they do go out, don't let a blow be struck against them by the present administration. Dissuade them if you can, but if you can't let them go in peace. I wish Pennsylvania could go with them. They are our brethren. . . . They have been good and peaceable neighbors. . . . We have driven them off and if we raise an arm to strike, the "stones of Rome will move to mutiny." . . .
>
> But I stop. Why I have written you I scarcely know except that I wanted to pour out my heart into some ear and thought possibly I

[9] This summary of the state of mind is made partly from Black's decision in the Passmore Williamson case, his Ableman and Booth argument and his open letter to General Garfield (C. F. Black, p. 292), but mostly from the exchange of letters with his closest friend, G. W. Woodward (Black Papers, November 18 and 24, 1860).

might suggest something worthy of your consideration in this hour of peril.[10]

Black did not, and could not, agree with his friend upon the issue of Secession, but he sympathized with his view of the causes. Six days later he wrote to Woodward:

We are probably in the midst of a revolution, bloodless as yet. . . . This great country is to be dismembered. The Constitution that Washington gave his approbation to is to be broken up and destroyed. I see the beginning but not the end.

He agreed with Woodward as to the exceeding danger to the Constitution, should the abolitionists force the ex-Whig politicians to yield to their demands.

Mr. Buchanan, (he continued) has . . . the most delicate and difficult duty to perform that ever was assigned to a human being and when it shall be performed, no portion of this people will say, "God bless you." A few scattered and bold hearts here and there will dare to do him justice. But in the North, his life's life has already been lied away, and the South will adhere to him only so long as he expresses no opinion against the constitutional right of secession and no determination to abandon his sworn duty of seeing the laws faithfully executed.

As to Woodward's letter,

I took the liberty of reading it confidentially to several of my friends. Cobb said he would give a hundred dollars for a copy of it. Gen. Cass said that it made him feel gladder than ever for his vote in the Senate on your nomination. [To the United States Supreme Court. See supra, p. 24.] To these two I read it separately, and afterwards to the President and all the members of the Cabinet together. It excited universal admiration and approbation for its eloquence and truth . . . . They wanted to publish it very much . . .[11]

Meanwhile the North was divided in its opinion upon the coming crisis. Greeley was the most potent factor in the defeat of Seward's aspirations for the Presidency and in the choosing of Lincoln. His paper, the New York *Tribune*, was considered to be the most powerful organ of the Republican party. Three days after the election of Lincoln, the *Tribune* announced its policy toward Secession in unmistakable accents:

If the Cotton States shall become satisfied that they can do better out of the Union than in it, we insist on letting them go in peace. The right to secede may be a revolutionary one, but it exists nevertheless. . . . We shall resist all coercive measures.[12]

[10] Black Papers, November 18, 1860.
[11] Black Papers, November 24, 1860.
[12] New York *Tribune*, November 9, 1860.

Exactly one week later Greeley reiterated his stand: "If . . . the eight Cotton Sates . . . shall quietly, decisively say to the rest, 'We prefer to be henceforth separate from you,' we shall insist that they be permitted to go in peace."[13]

As yet not a State had seceded. But while the nation was holding its breath as before the storm, Greeley had hastened to put himself on record. On the morning that the South Carolina convention assembled to discuss Secession, he again iterated his position:

> If seven or eight contiguous States shall present themselves authentically at Washington saying "We hate the Federal Union; we have withdrawn from it; we give you the choice between acquiescing in our secession . . . and attempting to subdue us" . . . we could not stand up for coercion, for we do not believe it would be just.[14]

Finally, as late as February 23, 1861—after the formation of the Confederate Government at Montgomery—Greeley's powerful voice was still supporting the cause of Secession.

> We have repeatedly said . . . that if the Slave States, the Cotton States, or the Gulf States only, choose to form an independent nation, they have a clear moral right to do so. . . . We will do our best to forward their views.[15]

But Greeley's was not the only voice in the North lifted against the preservation of the Union. Lieutenant General Winfield S. Scott, in his famous "Views" of October 23, 1860, remarked that "To save time, the right of secession may be conceded." Henry Ward Beecher, in a famous speech at Boston on March 27, contended, "I hold it will be an advantage for the South to go off." Wendell Phillips' voice could not be expected to remain silent amid the tumult. We hear it in April 1861: "You cannot go through Massachusetts and recruit men to bombard Charleston or New Orleans."[16]

The sentiment at the north in November 1860 and for many months thereafter was not the sentiment found when the guns before Sumter opened the war. Before the Buchanan government lay the open menace of Secession. Behind it, lay the insidious danger of a divided people. Within the counsels of the loyal Cabinet members was the sickening feeling that if the conflict should be precipitated before the public opinion to sustain it was crystallized, the Union would be dissolved in a breath.

But we have run ahead of our story. Let us return to the narrative of events.

[13] *Ibid.*, November 16, 1860.
[14] *Ibid.*, December 17, 1860.
[15] *Ibid.*, February 23, 1861.
[16] *Buchanan's Works*, XII, pp. 273, 283; *Rhodes, op. cit.*, III, p. 141.

14

THE SECESSION OF SOUTH CAROLINA

LINCOLN was elected President on November 6, 1860. The Legislature of South Carolina, already assembled to await the outcome, at once authorized the election of delegates to a secessionist convention, and Buchanan drew the Cabinet around him in earnest consultation.

His harmonious official family had come at last to the parting of the ways. Cass, Toucey, Holt, and Black denied any constitutional right of Secession. Cobb and Thompson were out-and-out believers in the right. Floyd opposed it upon the grounds then existing, but believed in the constitutional right.[1]

Of Black's own particular view, the best summation of it is given us by W. H. Trescot, the Assistant Secretary of State, who had been Acting Secretary in that office during the absence of Cass from June until October 1860. He was intimate with the leaders of both sides of the struggle. Furthermore his narrative was written in February 1861, while the events were fresh in mind. "Judge Black," he tells us, "treated the question exclusively as one of the constitutional law. . . . What is the legal wrong involved in secession and what is the legal remedy? A question to be solved judicially, not politically."[2]

Buchanan assembled his Cabinet on November 9. Of this meeting Floyd wrote in his diary, "The President said the business of the meeting was the most important ever before the Cabinet since his induction into office. The question, he said, to be considered and discussed, was the course to pursue in relation to the threatening aspect of affairs in the South, and most particularly in South Carolina." Black, reported Floyd, "earnestly urged sending at once a strong force into the forts at Charleston Harbor, enough to deter if possible the people from any attempt at disunion."[3] Buchanan ordered Floyd to reinforce the forts, and this Floyd promised to do. But later Cass told Black that they had not been reinforced. Black thereupon went to Buchanan and begged him to draw up a peremptory order for reinforcements and let him take it to the War Department. But Buchanan, said Black, "was annoyed at what he called my interference in the

[1] Floyd's Diary, Nov. 10, cited from E. A. Pollard, *Lee and His Lieutenants*, p. 794; Black to Buckalew, Black Papers, Jan. 28, 1861.

[2] Trescot MSS.; quoted by S. W. Crawford, *The Genesis of the Civil War*, p. 24.

[3] Floyd's Diary; quoted in Pollard, *op. cit.*, p. 792.

business of another department." He was doubtful of the wisdom of reinforcements, but would not state his reasons.[4] Meanwhile General Scott had been called in upon the reinforcement issue. Unfortunately for the welfare of the nation, Scott was now seventy-four years old, and was prey to infirmities of age which left him incapacitated for active service. Added to this, he was at odds with Buchanan. The latter had been in Polk's Cabinet during the Mexican War and had sided with Taylor in the Scott-Taylor controversy. As if this were not enough, Buchanan had opposed Scott's presidential aspirations and also had criticized the action of Congress in making him a lieutenant general. So unreconciled was Scott to Buchanan that he kept his headquarters permanently in New York City instead of in Washington.[5] Throughout the genesis of Secession we shall find Scott and Buchanan at odds with each other, to the detriment of national welfare.

In his "Views" of October 29, 1860, Scott had recommended the reinforcing of the nine Southern forts, but had submitted no military plan for doing so. Being called upon for such a plan, he added a supplemental "view" the following day to the effect that there were "in all five companies only" which were available. Five companies would total some 400 men. This number, Buchanan felt, would, if scattered over six highly excited States, inflame them rather than intimidate.[6]

The whole army consisted of but 16,000 men, and of this force nearly all was scattered over the extended frontier for the protection of border settlements against marauding Indians.[7] Black, however, believed that Sumter should have been relieved under any circumstances, even if it had to be done with the five companies which Scott's report said were available. He also held that this report was incorrect as to the number immediately available, and furthermore insisted that the quiet along the frontier would allow troops to be drawn from that source.[8] As to the inaccuracy of Scott's report, Black was wholly correct—for the army reports of 1860 reveal that there were 1,048 men and officers in Northern posts. Added to this were 800 marines.[9] Scott's report shows the General-in-Chief of the army to be more ignorant of army affairs than any general ought to be and remain in office.

Meanwhile not a soldier was sent to the Southern forts. Black never became reconciled to the failure of prompt action. His opinion was best expressed in his letter to Charles R. Buckalew, a close personal friend then serving as American Minister to Ecuador:

[4] F. A. Burr, Philadelphia *Weekly Press*, August 11, 1881.
[5] Crawford, *op. cit.*, pp. 162-163.
[6] *Buchanan's Works*, XII, p. 88.
[7] *Ibid.*, XII, p. 89.
[8] Crawford, *op. cit.*, p. 168.
[9] Chadwick, *op. cit.*, p. 186.

If the skirts of the administration were altogether clear in this business, I should feel much more comfortable than I do. We might have throttled this revolution by taking the right steps to put it down where it first broke out at Charleston. The three forts there were manned by only seventy-one men in all, and the danger of their being taken was foreseen by the Cabinet three months before it was realized. Cass, Holt, and I urged the President continually and earnestly to reinforce them while Cobb and Thompson as violently opposed it on the absurd ground that it would be offensive to South Carolina and provoke a civil war. Toucey was non-committal. Floyd professed to be with us, but was taking the best possible care to see that our views were not carried out. . . . But nothing was done . . .[10]

Other questions of broader scope than the mere reinforcing of a single fort were before the administration. In November, Buchanan called upon Black for a legal opinion on the right of States under the Constitution and of the power of the executive to suppress rebellion. He called for the answer before it was ready and found that Black was drawing up a paper upon the general duty of a President, under the Constitution, who might be faced with a Secession crisis. This was more than Buchanan wanted, and he directed Black to confine himself solely to certain cold points of law.[11]

It seems that Black was unwilling to do this unless Buchanan would file with him official instructions which should limit him to such an answer. This Buchanan did, and in the Black File of Buchanan Papers in Philadelphia there is the original draft of the following letter from Buchanan to Black, written in *Black's hand*, with a notation upon the back in Buchanan's hand that it was "The form in which Judge Black desired I might propound the questions to him for his opinion." The letter requests answers upon the following legal points:

1. In case of a conflict between the authorities of any State and those of the United States, can there be any doubt that the laws of the Federal Government, if constitutionally passed, are supreme?
2. What is the extent of my official power to collect duties on imports at a port where the revenue laws are resisted by a force which drives the collector from the custom house?
3. What right have I to defend the public property (for instance, a fort, arsenal, and navy yard), in case it should be assaulted?
4. What are the legal means at my disposal for executing those laws of the United States which are usually administered through the courts and their officers?
5. Can a military force be used for any purpose whatever under the Acts of 1795 and 1807, within the limits of a State where there are no judges, marshal or other civil officers?[12]

[10] Black Papers, January 28, 1861.

[11] F. A. Burr, Philadelphia *Weekly Press*, August 11, 1881.

[12] Black File, Buchanan Papers, November 17, 1860; *Buchanan's Works*, XI, p. 20.

Three days later, upon November 20, 1860, Black delivered his reply. It was exactly one month before the secession of South Carolina. In reply to the first question he said:

The will of a State, whether expressed in its constitution or laws, cannot, while it remains in the confederacy, absolve her people from the duty of obeying the just and constitutional requirements of the Central Government.

Replying to the second question—that of collecting import duties—he said that

To the chief executive magistrate of the Union is confided the solemn duty of seeing the laws faithfully executed. . . . The law requires that all goods imported into the United States within certain collection districts, shall be received by the collector . . . If the custom house were burnt down, he might remove to another building; if he were driven from the shore, he might go aboard a vessel in the harbor.

On the third question—the defense of public property—he stated:

Your right to take such measures as may seem necessary for the protection of the public property is very clear. It results from the property rights of the Government as owner of the forts, arsenals, magazines, dock yards, navy yards, custom houses, public ships, and other property which the United States have bought, built, and paid for. . . . The right of defending the public property includes also the right of recapture after it has been unlawfully taken by another.

But these were mere preliminaries. The heart of the whole constitutional issue rested upon the answer to the fourth and fifth questions—the question of suppressing insurrection. "I come now to the point in your letter which probably is of the greatest practical importance," he said in taking up these questions.

By the Act of 1807, you may employ such parts of the land and naval forces as you may judge necessary, for the purpose of causing the laws to be fully executed, in all cases where it is lawful to use the militia for the same purposes. By the Act of 1795, the militia may be called forth "whenever the laws of the United States shall be opposed or the execution thereof obstructed by any State, by combinations too powerful to be suppressed by the ordinary course of judicial proceedings, or by the power vested in the marshals." This imposes upon the President the sole responsibility of deciding whether the exigency has arisen.

Yet Black held rigidly to the view that the *courts* were the ordinary means of enforcing law and that the "whole spirit of our system is opposed to the employment of any other except in cases of extreme necessity." If Federal officers in a State are reached by the influences against the Federal Government and resign, this will not allow any justification for sending in troops and making war upon the people of that State, for "You can use force only to repel an assault on the public property and aid the courts in the performance of their duty. If the means given you to collect the revenue and execute the other laws be insufficient for that purpose, Congress may extend and make them more effectual to those ends."

"If one of the States shall declare her independence, your action cannot depend upon the rightfulness of the cause upon which such a declaration is based," for the President does not have "the authority to recognize her independence or to absolve her from her Federal obligations." But if such a State should attempt secession, "in such an event I see no course for you but to go straight onward in the path you have hitherto trodden—that is to execute the laws to the defensive means placed in your hands and act generally upon the assumption that the present constitutional relations between the States and the Federal Government continue to exist, until a new code of laws shall be established by either force or law."

At the end he summarized in one sweep his whole position: "*The right of the General Government to preserve itself in its whole constitutional vigor, by repelling a direct and positive aggression upon its property or its officers, cannot be denied. But this is a totally different thing from an offensive war, to punish the people for the political misdeeds of their State Government.*"[13]

This was not a political document. It was a legal opinion, written by the President's constitutional legal adviser in his official capacity as Attorney-General. When Black denied to the Federal government the right to coerce a State, he was speaking in the language of jurisprudence. He was insisting that, legally, the coercion must be applied to the *individuals*, in rebellion and not to the *State* as a State. He was giving to the Federal government full power of suppressing any insurrection, however powerful, but was insisting that it must be done, not by casting the Constitution overboard, but by lawful means provided by that document for such crisis.

When, however, Buchanan desired to use this legal phraseology in his message to Congress, in saying that the United States could not "coerce a State by force of arms to remain in the Union," Black objected. A message to Congress was a political document, it would be published by the newspapers, and read by the public. "I told him that this expression would be read superficially and misunderstood. He did not think so—neither did other members of the Cabinet."[14]

Not only was Black right in forecasting the misunderstanding of this phrase when used in a political sense, but he himself was to be

[13] Black Papers, November 20, 1860; *Official Opinions of the Attorneys General*, IX, p. 517.

[14] F. A. Burr, Philadelphia *Weekly Press*, August 25, 1881; New York *Tribune*, August 20, 1883.

the chief victim. Neither Black nor Buchanan gave out to the press the official opinion of November 20, but Cass took upon himself the responsibility of having it published.[15] At once the radical press seized upon that part which denied the right of the Federal government to "coerce a State" and twisted it to their political ends. By separating it from the body of the opinion and by converting the technical, legal meaning of the phrase into its general and popular use, they made it appear that Black was an abettor of Secession. When the phrase was repeated in Buchanan's message to Congress, the blame for the President's espousal of so treasonable a doctrine was laid at the door of Black.[16] For twenty years—until the publication of his reminiscences by F. A. Burr in 1881—he was to live under the stigma of having been a traitor in high office.[17] Even Wells retained a distrust of him for many years.[18] Stanton's biographer devotes a whole chapter in making out Black to be a thorough renegade because of this opinion.[19] Unfortunately for him, however, there are two errors in his argument. His whole quarrel with the opinion was based upon his personal dislike of the view expressed—which, in fact, had nothing whatsoever to do with whether it was sound law or not. In the second place, he omitted telling us—or perhaps he did not know—that Black showed this opinion to Stanton himself before forwarding it to Buchanan; that Stanton suggested one slight alteration, which was made; and that Stanton "not only approved, but applauded enthusiastically," the final draft.[20]

That any public officer could have written such a document in the face of a national crisis, is a tribute to the government and the system of jurisprudence which produced such an official. Any Caesar or Catiline can use the excuse of open rebellion to justify the overthrow of instituted law. Thaddeus Stevens could trample the Constitution into the mud when he drove his measures of Reconstruction through, after the crisis had passed. "Who pleads the Constitution?" he taunted its defenders on the floor of Congress[21]—and they yielded that instrument to him to tear asunder.

Yet Black, faced by the greatest constitutional crisis ever imposed

[15] New York *Tribune*, August 20, 1883.

[16] New York *Evening Post*, December 10, 1860. New York *Tribune*, January 29, February 7, 20, 1861.

[17] When Black removed to York, Pa., in 1861, he was for many years exceedingly unpopular with most of the citizens of that city, who looked upon him as a "Copperhead." Not until near the end of his life did they come to understand his magnificent public service in the secession crisis and really soften toward him. Niles to the author, Jan. 10, 1930.

[18] *Diary of Gideon Wells*, Sept. 20, 1867.

[19] Gorham, *op. cit.*, I, pp. 94-105.

[20] Black Papers, end of 1869; C. F. Black, p. 275; Rhodes, *op. cit.*, III, p. 244; Clayton MSS.

[21] E. B. Callender, *Thaddeus Stevens*, p. 111.

upon an American public official, turned to that document for the weapons in its own defense. He gave to the Federal government full power to coerce an uprising against its authority, by punishing all *individuals* who partook of such an uprising. He denied only the right of the Federal government to wage an offensive war upon a *State*, as such, exactly as though it were a foreign nation. "This distinction between coercing a State and coercing the individual inhabitants of a State," said Curtis, ". . . is not a merely theoretical question. . . . Let it be supposed . . . that at the time when the Legislature of Massachusetts had in its contemplation to pass the laws which became known as 'liberty bills' and which put actual obstructions in the way of the extradition of fugitives from service, the President of the United States had stationed an army on Boston Common and had directed the commanding general to inform the Legislature that if they did not desist from that act of nullification he would shell the State House or would disperse them at the point of the bayonet. . . . Yet, if the President of the United States can properly apply coercion to one State to prevent her from adopting an ordinance of secession so-called, he can, with equal propriety, apply coercion to another State to prevent her from nullifying or attempting to nullify a particular provision of the Federal Constitution or the laws of the United States passed in pursuance of it."[22]

In truth, there is hardly room for argument upon any other ground. Hamilton, the greatest of all nationalists, admitted the impracticability of coercing a State.[23] Caleb Cushing, one of the greatest constitutional lawyers of his day, and Black's predecessor as Attorney-General, gave it his full legal support.[24] When Senator Wilson made a political attack upon it, Black invited him to get out of the political arena, to come to the legal issue at stake, and point out where, legally, it might be unsound or incorrect.[25] But this Wilson refused to do, a refusal which cannot be otherwise interpreted than that he could not find sufficient legal evidence with which to oppose it. Finally, this opinion has received as near the unanimous support of historical authorities as even Black could have wished.[26] We have here given some space to the support of this opinion, not because there is any question today upon that topic, but because of the ironic fact that the very act which, in historical judgment, elevated Black to the pinnacle of statesmanship in this trying period, is the identical act that brought down upon his head the bitterest of contemporary criticisms, the vilest abuse, open

[22] G. T. Curtis to the Philadelphia *Times*, August 20, 1883; quoted in Buchanan's *Works*, XI, pp. 44-45.

[23] *The Federalist*, No. 28, Hamilton ed., pp. 277-278.

[24] Cushing to Black, Black Papers, Dec. 11, 1860.

[25] *Galaxy*, February 1871, p. 258.

[26] See Rhodes, *op. cit.*, III, p. 143; Chadwick, *op. cit.*, p. 161. "As sound a jurist as ever advised a President," exclaimed Rhodes.

charges of being an abettor of Secession, a "Copperhead" of a low order.

Four days after he delivered this opinion to Buchanan, he wrote to his friend George W. Woodward,

> For myself, I value as highly as anybody the recollection that I once seemed to have some portion of the public confidence. But it will give me far more pride for the balance of my life to remember that I risked and lost it in a faithful support of principles which sooner or later will be acknowledged as necessary for the preservation of the noblest political system that the world ever saw.[27]

Unconsciously was he writing the epitaph of his political life.

Early in December Black amplified his position with a second paper upon the powers of the President. Since Buchanan was at this time drafting his message to Congress, it is possible that this second opinion was submitted in connection with the preparation of this message. "The Union is necessarily perpetual," said Black in this opinion. "No state can lawfully withdraw or be expelled from it. The Federal Constitution is as much a part of the Constitution of every State as if it had been textually inserted therein. The Federal Government is sovereign within its own sphere, and acts directly upon the individual citizens of every State. Within these limits its coercive power is ample to defend itself, its laws and its property. It can suppress insurrection, fight battles, conquer armies, disperse hostile combinations, and punish any or all of its enemies. It can meet, repel and subdue all those who rise against it. But it cannot obliterate a single Commonwealth from the map of the Union or declare indiscriminate war against all inhabitants of a section, confounding the innocent with the guilty."[28]

This document wears more of the air of a political document than of a legal one. The phrase "declare indiscriminate war against all inhabitants of a section, confounding the innocent with the guilty," while less concise than the legal phrase "coerce a State" which was used in the official opinion of November 20, was less open to popular misunderstanding. It was unfortunate that Buchanan chose to use the technical phraseology in his message to Congress.

Meanwhile Buchanan obviously was endeavoring to play the role of peacemaker. He was resorting to the tactics of Henry Clay, rather than of Andrew Jackson. He prided himself upon his statecraft. He had won his greatest recognition in public life as a diplomat at foreign courts. Of the approaching crisis he said, "I desire to stand between the factions like a daysman with my hand on the head of each, counselling peace."[29] There are some things to be said in defense of such

[27] Black Papers, November 24, 1860.

[28] F. A. Burr, Philadelphia *Weekly Press*, August 11, 1881; see also Joseph Holt in the *Weekly Press* of September 8, 1881, for confirmation of this view.

[29] F. A. Burr, *Philadelphia Press*, September 10, 1883.

a policy. The South was not a unit in favoring Secession. Although Breckinridge had carried all but two of the States which later formed the Confederate States, yet the combined vote against him (divided among the other three candidates) equaled 60% of the total vote.[30] And every vote against Breckinridge could be counted as a vote against Secession. The North, as we have seen, was sharply divided upon the question—with such powerful organs as Greeley's *Tribune* supporting Secession and denying the right of coercion. Diplomacy might yet achieve success where soldiery might fail.

Black had slight patience, with the crafts of diplomacy. Such tactics were foreign to his nature. Always about him was a note of the bugle and trumpet. One reads it in his letters; one hears it in his speeches; one sees it in his actions. At the first meeting which the Cabinet held upon the subject of Secession, he urged coercion of all individuals who might resist Federal authority.[31] After a Cabinet discussion over reinforcing Sumter, in which Black had earnestly urged immediate reinforcements, Howell Cobb called on him at the Attorney-General's office to discuss their pointed disagreements. Black said pointedly that he felt that some of Cobb's utterances were such as ought not to be made by any man who remained an official of the Federal government. Cobb disagreed. Finally Black closed the discussion by challenging Cobb to submit their differences to Buchanan. "You and I," said he, "can have no understanding on this subject but there is one man above us, and but one, who can settle this dispute. I will state my position upon the Secession movement in writing, and can do it in three lines. I will so state it and submit it to the President. If he does not agree with me, I will resign within five minutes. If he does agree with me, you should do the same, for there is certainly not room enough in the Cabinet for both of us while holding and expressing such diverse views."[32] Cobb was angry and felt insulted. Black disclaimed any personal insult but maintained his position. Cobb left the office. On December 8 he resigned from "a sense of duty to Georgia." He was the first official to leave the Cabinet.[33]

The resignation of Lewis Cass followed four days later. Cass gave as his reason one completely opposite from that of Cobb—namely that Buchanan was not in general vigorous enough in taking measures toward coercing Secession, and in particular that he had not reinforced the garrison in Charleston harbor.[34] Such a reason, re-

[30] *Tribune Almanac*, 1861, p. 64.

[31] Floyd's Diary; quoted in Pollard, *op. cit.*, p. 792.

[32] F. A. Burr, Philadelphia *Weekly Press* August 18, 1881; also August 25, 1881.

[33] *Harper's Weekly*, December 22, 1860.

[34] *Buchanan's Works*, XI, p. 68.

marked Buchanan in a memorandum written out on the date of receiving Cass's letter, was most remarkable in view of the fact that Cass had opposed his message to Congress upon the ground of its being not strong enough against the power of Congress to make war on a State.[35]

The next day Cass repented his hasty action and wanted to withdraw his resignation. Black urged Buchanan to let him do so, but Buchanan thought him a good riddance and refused to allow him to return.[36] No doubt there were reasons unstated which prompted Cass's resignation. He and Buchanan were never on the most friendly terms. Of him Buchanan wrote, that "most of the important dispatches which bear his name were written, or chiefly written, for him by Mr. Appleton, Judge Black, and myself. His original drafts were generally so prolix and so little to the point that they had to be written over again entirely." "When obliged to decide [questions] for himself, he called Mr. Cobb and Judge Black to his assistance."[37]

Black felt that Cass had covered his real reason with a false one, and wrote out for Buchanan a sharply rebuking letter to submit in accepting the resignation. But Buchanan, always the diplomat, took Black's draft and softened its outlines into a final reply.[38]

On December 17 Buchanan appointed Black to the office of Secretary of State left vacant by the departure of Cass. Upon that same day the convention of South Carolina met in the State House at Columbia to consider the ordinance of Secession. Upon that day, also, Greeley was announcing to the readers of the *Tribune* that "If seven or eight contiguous states shall present themselves authentically at Washington saying, 'We hate the Federal Union; we have withdrawn from it . . .' we could not stand up for coercion, for we do not believe it would be just."[39]

Three days later, at 1:15 P. M., the convention of South Carolina solemnly resolved that "We, the people of the State of South Carolina in convention assembled do declare and ordain and it is hereby declared and ordained that . . . the Union now subsisting between South Carolina and the other states, under the name of the 'United States of America,' is hereby dissolved."[40]

Cass had escaped the office in time to avoid the whirlwind.

[35] *Ibid.*, p. 59.

[36] Black to G. T. Curtis, *Buchanan's Works*, XI, p. 63. When Black also stated this to Buchanan, two years later, the latter replied that "It is not in accord with my recollections" (*Works*, XI, p. 361). But in a memorandum of Dec. 17, 1860, he had himself made a note of this desire of Cass (*Works*, XI, p. 67).

[37] *Buchanan's Works*, XI, p. 59.

[38] Black File, Buchanan Papers, December 15, 1860.

[39] New York *Tribune*, December 17, 1860.

[40] A. B. Hart, *American History as Told by Contemporaries*, IV, p. 185.

15

THE CABINET CRISIS

THE swiftly changing kaleidoscope of national events was reflected in the equally swift changes in the personnel of Buchanan's Cabinet. Already two men had gone, and three more were soon to go—a turnover of five members in a Cabinet of seven during a period of thirty-three days.

At Black's insistence, Stanton was elevated to the office of Attorney-General,[1] for Stanton, better than anyone else, was familiar with the cases now pending before the Supreme Court. The Treasury Department, vacated by Cobb, was filled by Philip F. Thomas of Maryland who lingered but a month, and finding himself out of step, followed the way of his predecessor.[2] At his resignation, John A. Dix of New York was appointed. Dix at once joined forces with Black, Stanton, and Holt and became one of the strong Union men of the Cabinet. "I do not recall a single instance in which there was a difference of opinion between us upon any important question," said Holt.[3] Jacob Thompson resigned on January 8. His assigned reason was because of the reinforcement of Charleston harbor.[4] But he could not have remained longer than twenty-four hours in any event. His State seceded from the Union the following day, and long before that event he had explained privately to the President that, while he was firmly opposed to the present movement toward Secession, yet he must follow whatever road his State might choose. The President respected his view. "When your State secedes," he said, "I will not insist upon your remaining."[5] Thompson's office was left vacant after his departure. Floyd resigned on December 29—but his is a long story and interwoven more deeply than the others with the swiftly approaching crisis. Let us follow it in detail.

By law, the Secretary of War was required to distribute to the States certain arms for the use of their militia. The South had not received its quota in 1860, and so on December 20 Floyd ordered a shipment to be sent from Pittsburgh to the Southern States. "It is, of course, possible that Floyd, acted in bad faith; but there is no proof of that,"

[1] Gorham, *op. cit.*, I, p. 121.

[2] *Buchanan's Works*, XI, p. 105.

[3] New York *Tribune*, August 20, 1883.

[4] *Buchanan's Works*, XI, p. 100.

[5] F. A. Burr, Philadelphia *Press*, September 17, 1883; Auchampaugh, *op. cit.*, p. 118.

said Black.[6] But, to say the least, the order was unwise. News of it reached the citizens of Pittsburgh simultaneously with that of the secession of South Carolina. Indignant, they protested and some of them resolved to prevent the shipment at all possible hazards. The news reached Black on Christmas Day. Late that night he dispatched a hasty note to Buchanan insisting that the matter must be "settled definitely, finally and forever early tomorrow morning." "*The arms will not be shipped*—they will be seized by the people probably."[7]

Buchanan revoked the order, and the arms were kept in Pittsburgh.[8]

Even before this order was revoked, however, Buchanan and Floyd had parted company upon quite a different matter. On December 22nd, Buchanan had learned of financial irregularities in the War Department. The firm of Russell, Majors and Waddell had been for many years delivering army supplies at the western posts. But with credit impaired from the financial panic of 1857, they were unable longer to continue this service without financial aid. To secure this aid, Floyd had taken bills for $870,000, drawn by this firm upon him as Secretary of War, in advance of their earnings, and exchanged these bills of exceedingly doubtful value for an equal amount of valid bonds held in trust by the Government for Indian tribes. These bonds had been purloined by a clerk from the Department of Interior, without the knowledge of Secretary Thompson.[9] At first it was naturally thought that Floyd had profited in the transaction, but Floyd in fact had not gained a cent by his conjuration. He was inexcusably irregular but not personally dishonest. He left the office so poor that he borrowed money to get out of the city.[10]

Buchanan determined to remove Floyd at once, and asked Black to go to him and request his resignation. But this Black declined to do. He was willing, he said, to do all that lay in his line of duty, but he considered this to be a matter entirely between the President and his Secretary of War and preferred not to interfere. Buchanan acquiesced, remarking that he would "find some one."[11] He then turned to Floyd's kinsman, Vice President Breckinridge who, on December 23, conveyed to Floyd the request for his resignation. Floyd heard the news with considerable feeling, but agreed to comply.[12]

Floyd lingered in the Cabinet, however, for some days; he was yet to appear in one more scene before departing.

The question of the Charleston forts was approaching a climax.

[6] C. F. Black, p. 266.

[7] Black File, Buchanan Papers, December 25, 1860.

[8] C. F. Black, p. 268.

[9] *Buchanan's Works*, XII, p. 164; 7 Wallace, p. 666.

[10] C. F. Black, p. 13. Written by Black's son, but undoubtedly expressing the father's knowledge.

[11] Black to Crawford; quoted in Crawford, *op. cit.*, p. 215.

[12] *Buchanan's Works*, XI, p. 164.

Events, both known and unknown to the administration, were moving to force a decision. On December 22, South Carolina—who was now, in her own eyes, an independent nation—dispatched a commission of three distinguished citizens to Washington. They were authorized by the Governor "to treat with the Government of the United States for the delivery of the forts, magazines, light-houses, and other real estate . . . within the limits of South Carolina and also for an apportionment of the public debt."[13]

They arrived in Washington on December 26 and, through Trescot the Assistant Secretary of State, arranged for an interview with the President on the following day at one o'clock.[14] In the meantime news of events, wholly unsuspected either by the President or the South Carolina commissioners, was arriving to startle and dismay both of them. But we must turn aside to view these events in their natural order.

Down in Charleston harbor was stationed a little force of eighty-four men and officers commanded by Major Robert Anderson. Anderson was a Southern man; his wife was Southern; his sympathies were Southern. To a friend at Washington he wrote, while he was in command of the Charleston harbor, that "my sympathies are in the matter of sectional controversy all with the South."[15] But his high sense of military duty preceded with him any personal feeling. His command was stationed at Fort Moultrie; but Moultrie was too weak to be defended if attacked, and was completely commanded by the far stronger Fort Sumter. Therefore, by what Black called "a beautiful stratagem" Anderson spiked the guns of Moultrie, on the night of December 26, and moved his entire command under the cover of darkness into Sumter. So closely did he guard his movements that not only were the authorities both at Washington and Charleston entirely unaware of his intentions, but even his own men were not informed of it until the movement was under way. After he was safely in Sumter, he notified the Adjutant General of his action.[16]

There was wild excitement in Washington at the news. Floyd telegraphed Anderson for a confirmation. Buchanan crushed a cigar in the palm of his hand and sat down heavily. According to Trescot, he exclaimed "My God, are my calamities (or misfortunes, I forget which) never to come singly! I call God to witness, that this is not only without but against my orders."[17]

Black heard the news as the Cabinet was assembling that morning

[13] *Official Records of the Union and Confederate Armies*, I, p. 111.

[14] Trescot was a native of South Carolina.

[15] Auchampaugh, *op. cit.*, p. 156.

[16] *Official Records*, I, p. 2: *Buchanan's Works*, XII, p. 159. Crawford, *op. cit.*, pp. 102-112. Crawford was one of the Sumter officers under Anderson.

[17] Crawford, *op. cit.*, p. 144.

—the 27th. "Good," he exclaimed, "I'm glad of it. It is in precise accordance with his orders." "It is not," said Floyd. "But it is," retorted Black. "I recollect the orders distinctly, word for word."[18]

Buchanan feared that Floyd was correct. Stanton's memory was not clear. So Black suggested that the orders be sent for and the dispute settled at once. Black was wholly correct. The instructions had been given Anderson by Major (later Major General) Buell in accordance with verbal order from the War Office. The astute Anderson had insisted upon having them set in writing, which Buell had done, at the same time filing a copy of them with the War Office. Both Buchanan and Floyd had signed their approval to it on December 21. They authorized Anderson to concentrate his force in any one of the forts he deemed most proper whenever he had "tangible evidence of a design to proceed to a hostile act."[19] Anderson had not only entrenched himself at Sumter; he had also entrenched himself at Washington.

Floyd, you will recall, already had been requested by Buchanan to resign his office. Four days had passed—and he had made no move to comply. Now was the chance to save his face by forcing an issue and resigning upon a point of honor. The Cabinet met a second time that day, in the evening. To the President and the Cabinet Floyd now read a paper in what Buchanan termed a "discourteous and excited tone, hitherto unknown," in which he declared that "it is evident now, from the action of the commander at Fort Moultrie, that the solemn pledges of this Government have been violated by Major Anderson" and that "one remedy only is left, and that is to withdraw the garrison from the harbor of Charleston altogether."[20] The refusal, which, of course, he knew would meet his demand was to be the point of honor upon which he could resign.

Black, however, would admit no point of honor in such an argument. He had that morning shown Floyd the copy of his own order delivered through Buell and approved by Floyd himself in writing after its delivery. He now listened to Floyd's words in amazement and indignation and upon him he turned in blazing wrath. "This," he said sternly, "is a question of fidelity to a solemn trust. There never was a moment in the history of England when a minister of the Crown could have proposed to surrender a military post which might be defended, *without bringing his head to the block!*"[21]

Buchanan thought the words were harsh, but he never denied their truth. Floyd grew intensely excited, for a moment almost uncontrolla-

[18] Black's written memorandum. Black Papers, end of 1861.

[19] *Official Records*, I, p. 89, Rhodes, *op. cit.*, III, p. 224.

[20] *Buchanan's Works*, XI, p. 166.

[21] Black's memorandum, Black Papers, end of 1861. See also F. A. Burr, Philadelphia *Weekly Press*, August 11, 1881; and testimony of Thomas and Holt in the *Weekly Press* for August 18 and September 8, 1881.

bly so, but in the blazing eyes of Black he found neither quailing nor apology.[22] He resigned from the Cabinet without the point of honor which he had anticipated. "Nothing has injured that administration," wrote Black to Buchanan shortly after the latter had retired from office, "so much as its over kindness" to Floyd.[23]

In the meantime the delegation from South Carolina was waiting to be received by the President—and Benjamin F. Butler had learned that its members were in the city. He at once evolved a Butlerian plan for disposing of them, and sought Black's aid and counsel in executing it. Buchanan, according to Butler, should allow them to appear in full confidence of being treated as envoys, but at the moment he had them in his power, he should say "Gentlemen, you are either ambassadors from a foreign state . . . or you are citizens of the United States giving aid and comfort to its declared enemies, which is treason," and thereupon seize and hold them for trial. Black did not hold the plan in so high esteem as Butler, but pointed out that to Buchanan alone must be left the manner of receiving the commissioners. Butler thereupon betook himself to Buchanan, who rejected the idea of seizing men who had come to him, in trust and without suspicion, as a violation of the unwritten code of ethics. Butler was disgusted.[24] His code involved no such scruples.

In truth, Buchanan was still hoping to limit the Secession movement to South Carolina alone. He was shaken by Anderson's movement to Sumter because he feared it might excite other cotton and border States into active sympathy with South Carolina.[25] Rightly or wrongly, he clung with consistency to his policy of conciliating rather than coercing, of depending upon diplomacy instead of force. Congress was engaged in drawing up plans for a compromise to settle this crisis as crises had been settled in 1820 and 1850, and Buchanan was playing for time until Congress was ready for action. The foundation of his plan was melting away, but he was not yet willing to yield it for another.

Meanwhile the commissioners of South Carolina were still waiting to be received. Buchanan refused to meet them as a commission from a sovereign state but granted them an interview on the 28th, recognizing them "only as private gentlemen." The original mission of these private gentlemen had been so violently disturbed by Anderson's *coup d'état* that they met Buchanan under great excitement, insisting "upon the immediate withdrawal of the Major and his troops, not only from Fort Sumter, but from the harbor of Charleston, as a *sine qua non* to any negotiation."[26]

[22] Thomas to Burr, Philadelphia *Weekly Press*, August 18, 1881.
[23] Black File, Buchanan Papers, March 11, 1861.
[24] *Ben Butler's Book*, p. 152.
[25] *Buchanan's Works*, XI, p. 159. [26] *Ibid.*, XII, p. 160.

This Buchanan refused to do and, after admitting failure in their first effort, the private gentlemen from South Carolina withdrew. On the following day, the 29th, they renewed their request in a letter which went over the ground formally, asserting that until Anderson's movement was explained the commission would be forced to suspend negotiations. They urged his withdrawal from Charleston in such a manner that Buchanan considered their language to be "an unmistakable threat of attacking Major Anderson if not yielded."[27]

Buchanan prepared an answer that day and read it to his Cabinet. Exactly what this paper contained is not known, for no draft of it is in existence;[28] but it provoked a sharp disagreement within the Cabinet. Toucey alone approved it. Thompson and Thomas felt that it yielded too little to the demands of the commissioners. Black, Holt, and Stanton opposed it as granting too much and as being entirely too unguarded in its language. The issue seems to have been more, however, than merely one of minor concessions and of language—it was rather one of whether Buchanan was to continue his policy of conciliation or to stand boldly against the whole tide of Secession, for it seems obvious that he was willing to remand Anderson to Moultrie and restore the status quo in Charleston harbor. He listened to the arguments of both sides, but made few if any comments of his own. No conclusion was reached, but Black retired with the feeling that the "President was inflexible" in his determination to submit the answer as he had read it.[29]

That night Black spent the most "miserable and restive night" of his life.[30] For more than twenty years he and Buchanan not only had been followers of the same political paths, but the closest of personal friends. Yet now it seemed that their ways must part. Through the night he wrestled with the problem, but by morning his decision was reached. No longer could he remain in the Cabinet.

It was Sunday, the 30th. Offices were closed, but Black drove to Toucey's home and informed him that, if the President's decision was unchanged, he would be compelled to resign. Black then sought out Stanton and informed him also of the decision. Stanton said that they would go or stay together. Meanwhile Toucey had carried the news to the White House, and the consultation between Black and Stanton was interrupted by a summons for Black to come at once to confer with the President. Black was loath to go. "I know," he said to Stanton, "the sort of appeal he will make to me, in the name of

[27] *Official Records*, I, p. 109; *Buchanan's Works*, XII, p. 161.

[28] F. A. Burr, Philadelphia *Weekly Press*, August 11, 1881; also *Press*, September 10, 1883; and Holt's letter to J. Buchanan Henry, *Buchanan's Works*, XI, p. 84.

[29] Black Memorandum, Black Papers, end of 1861.

[30] F. A. Burr, Philadelphia *Press*, September 10, 1883.

our sacred and long-standing friendship. To resist will be the most painful duty of my life."[31]

Stanton urged him to stand firm. Meanwhile a second messenger had reached him and Black turned his steps to the White House. He was not mistaken in the pressure to be put upon him. "Do you, too, talk of leaving me?" said the President soberly, and he went on to say that this was the worst news that he had yet heard, although "bad news was sadly frequent." Surely Judge Black would not desert him in the bitter hour. To have left him in the day of his power and prosperity would have been different, but now, in the moment of darkness and adversity, his friends "were few and sorely needed."

Painfully Black replied that he longed to stand by and defend the President to the end. "There is," he said, "no storm of popular indignation I would not breast by your side, no depth of misfortune into which I would not descend with you, provided you have a cause to defend. But your answer to the commissioners leaves you no cause; it sweeps the ground from under our feet; it places you where no man can stand with you, and where you cannot stand alone."[32]

Buchanan was a tenacious man. For four and fifty days he had clung to his dream of conciliation, clung to it against the opposition of the strongest members of his Cabinet, and clung to it even with the house tumbling about his ears. But now, with the sands of the old year running out and the loyal members of his Cabinet making ready to depart with it, he yielded at last and set himself to a change of policy. Without even a word of argument, he placed his proposed reply to the commissioners into Black's hands. "I cannot part with you," he said. "If you go, Holt and Stanton will leave. . . . Here, take this paper and modify it to suit yourself, but do it before the sun goes down."[33]

Black took the paper and hastened to his old office of the Attorney-General, where he was joined by Stanton. There, at one sitting, he wrote the following paper and Stanton copied it as rapidly as the sheets were thrown to him:[34]

MEMORANDUM FOR THE PRESIDENT ON THE SUBJECT OF THE PAPER DRAWN UP BY HIM IN REPLY TO THE COMMISSIONERS OF SOUTH CAROLINA

1. The first and the concluding paragraph both seem to acknowledge the right of South Carolina to be represented near this Govern-

[31] Black Memorandum, Black Papers, end of 1861; F. A. Burr, Philadelphia *Press*, September 10, 1883.

[32] Crawford, *op. cit.*, p. 152; Black Memorandum; F. A. Burr, Philadelphia *Press*, September 10, 1883.

[33] F. A. Burr, Philadelphia *Press*, September 10, 1883.

[34] The copy in Stanton's handwriting is now among the Black Papers in the Library of Congress. It has erroneously been placed at the end of the February 1861 collection. The original draft in Black's hand is in the Black File of Buchanan Papers, in the Historical Society of Pennsylvania, at the end of the 1860 collection. Both drafts are undated.

ment by diplomatic officers. That implies that she is an independent nation. . . . I think . . . that every word and sentence which implies that South Carolina is in an attitude which enables the President to "treat" or negotiate with her, or to receive her commissioners in the character of diplomatic ministers or agents ought to be stricken out and an explicit declaration substituted which would reassert the principles of the message. [i.e., message to Congress in which the right of Secession is denied.] . . .

2. I would strike out all expressions of regret that the commissioners are unwilling to proceed with negotiations, since it is very clear that there can be no negotiations with them, whether they are willing or not.

3. Above all things, it is objectionable to intimate a willingness to negotiate with the State of South Carolina about the possession of a military post which belongs to the United States. . . . The forts in Charleston Harbor belong to this Government—are its own, and can not be given up . . .

4. The words "coercing a state by force of arms to remain in the confederacy—a power which I do not believe the Constitution has conferred upon Congress" ought certainly not to be retained. They are too vague. . . . The power to defend the public property—to resist an assailing force . . . is *coercion*, and may very well be called "coercing a State by force of arms to remain in the Union." The President has always asserted his right of coercion to that extent. He merely denies the right of Congress to make offensive war upon a State of the Union as such might be made upon a foreign government.[35]

5. The implied assent of the President to the accusation which the commissioners make of a compact with South Carolina by which he was bound not to take whatever measures he saw fit for the defense of the forts, ought to be stricken out, and a flat denial of any such bargain, pledge, or agreement inserted . . .

6. The remotest expression of a doubt about Major Anderson's perfect propriety of behavior should be carefully avoided. He is not merely a gallant and meritorious officer who is entitled to a fair hearing before he is condemned. He has saved the country. . . . He has done everything that mortal man could to repair the fatal error which the Administration have committed in not sending down troops to hold *all* the forts. He has kept the strongest one. He still commands the harbor. We may still execute the laws if we try . . .

7. The idea that a wrong was committed against South Carolina by moving from Fort Moultrie to Fort Sumter ought to be repelled as firmly as may be consistent with a proper respect for the high character of the gentlemen who compose the South Carolina Commission. It is a strange assumption of right . . . to say that the United States

[35] Here again Black shows his discrimination between the legal use of the word "coercion" and its popular use. "There was entire consistency," said Rhodes, "between this memorandum of Black, Secretary of State, and the opinion of November 20, of Black, Attorney General. In the memorandum he appreciated and reflected the difference in meaning now attached to the word coercion from that implied in November." Rhodes, *op. cit.*, III, p. 233.

must remain in the weakest position they can find in the harbor. It is not a menace of South Carolina or of Charleston, or any menace at all; it is simply self-defense. If South Carolina does not attack Major Anderson, no human being will be injured . . .

These are the points on which I would advise that the paper be amended. I am aware that they are too radical to permit much hope of their adoption. If they are adopted, the whole paper will need to be recast.

But there is one thing not to be overlooked in this terrible crisis. I entreat the President to order the *Brooklyn* and the *Macedonian* to Charleston without the least delay, and in the meantime send a trusty messenger to Major Anderson to let him know that his Government will not desert him. The re-enforcement of troops from New York or Old Point Comfort should follow immediately.

If this be done at once all may yet be, not well, but comparatively safe. If not, I can see nothing before us but disaster and ruin to the country.

Here is a remarkable paper. In it we see Black—always the lawyer—laying down an unerring comprehension of the rights and duties of the Federal government toward the States, pointing the way in which national rights might be exerted without encroaching upon the rights of States. But he does not rest with a case at law. He rises to a high level of statesmanship and, with a grasp of the political aspects of the situation, he propounds a sagacious course of action—and all this arranged in cogent form and expressed in competent and vigorous language. It was delivered to Buchanan "before the sun went down," and using it as the basis, he drafted a radically changed reply to the commissioners of South Carolina. Upon the following day—the last day of the old year—the new reply was read to his Cabinet and delivered to the commissioners. "It has by no means the ring of Black's logic," said Rhodes, and he was right.[36] But there was no acknowledgment in it of the right of South Carolina to be represented at Washington by diplomatic officers, no expression of regret over their unwillingness to proceed with negotiations, no hint of any intention to negotiate about the possession of United States property in South Carolina; there was a flat denial that any compact had been made with that State forbidding Anderson to move to Sumter; and finally the unfortunate words about the lack of power to "coerce a State," were entirely omitted.[37]

Black had won. He had caused a shift of front in the policy of the administration. It may have been that Buchanan was right in adhering so rigidly to his hope of conciliation in the earlier days of the crisis. There is much to be said for his policy. But South Carolina was now out of the Union—out at least in her own eyes. She was arraying a

[36] Rhodes, *op. cit.*, III, p. 234.

[37] *Buchanan's Works*, XI, p. 79.

force with which openly to oppose the Federal possession of Charleston harbor if necessary. Had Anderson been returned to Moultrie it is not impossible that war might have started in January, instead of being delayed until the incoming administration was settled in office; for when the news of Floyd's resignation from the War Office reached the Senate, Wigfall of Texas telegraphed Charleston: "Holt succeeds Floyd. It means war. Cut off all supplies from Anderson and take Sumter soon as possible."[38] But Sumter could not be taken by the forces at the disposal of South Carolina in January. Moultrie, on the other hand, according to Anderson, could have been taken in from forty-eight to sixty hours.[39]

The effect of the new policy was at once apparent. It was an utterly different reply than that which the commissioners of South Carolina expected. It closed the door to all negotiations, made of their mission a failure, and their continuation in Washington useless. Smarting under the sense of complete failure, they penned an arrogant and insolent reply. The Cabinet heard it read with amazement and indignation. Taking his pen, Buchanan wrote across the manuscript that its nature was such that the "President . . . declines to receive it." It was returned to the private gentlemen from South Carolina, and they at once departed. Having gone part way, Buchanan now was willing to go the whole. "Let reinforcements now be sent," he said in reference to Charleston harbor. Trescot, who had known nothing of the cause for Buchanan's change of tactics, met Senator Hunter of Virginia who had returned at the moment from a final appeal to Buchanan to have Anderson returned to Moultrie. "Tell the Commissioners it is hopeless," he said. "The President has taken his ground. I can't repeat what has passed, but if you can get a telegram to Charleston, telegraph at once to your people to sink vessels in the channels of the harbor."[40]

To the uneasy friends of the union, the Christmas season had been a gloomy arctic night, but with the turn of the new year a positive light broke through the gloom. Word had filtered out, on January 1, that Anderson would not be returned to Moultrie. The news flashed across the North. To these friends of the Union it was indeed a happy New Year. Thousands breathed more easily, heads were up, and a surge of patriotism filled the hearts.[41]

But what of the man who had forced this change of policy? The part that he had played was not only unknown to the public, but even to the other members of the Cabinet, save to Toucey and Stanton. Thompson never suspected it until twenty-two years later, in 1882. "I noticed that it [the reply to the commissioners] had been

[38] *Official Records,* I, p. 252.
[39] *Ibid.,* I, p. 3.
[40] Trescot MSS; quoted in Crawford, *op. cit.,* p. 159.
[41] Rhodes, *op. cit.,* III, p. 236.

radically changed when I heard it read the last time," he stated, "and said so to the President. 'Yes,' he answered, 'I have modified it somewhat.' But I and my Southern colleagues never knew anything of the way in which the changes were made . . ."[42] Even Holt, warm friend and supporter of Black's policy, was given no hint that a crisis had threatened Black's presence in the Cabinet.[43] The radical press continued their execration of the man who had said that the Federal government had no power to "coerce a State."

[42] F. A. Burr, Philadelphia *Press*, September 17, 1883.

[43] Holt to J. Buchanan Henry, *Buchanan's Works*, XI, p. 86.

16

SECRETARY OF STATE

BLACK had urged that the man-of-war *Brooklyn* be used for the relief of Sumter and Buchanan had directed Scott to use this vessel. Scott, however, had unfortunately been convinced not only that the *Brooklyn* could not cross the bar at Charleston but that greater speed and secrecy would be insured by chartering the fast side-wheel merchant steamer *Star of the West*, then lying in New York. Therefore, upon the insistence of Scott and against the judgment of the President, this unarmed merchantman took aboard 200 men and four officers, with arms and ammunition, and at 9 P.M. of January 5 crossed the bar at Sandy Hook upon her errand of speed and secrecy.[1]

Speed the merchantman might have—but there was no such thing in official quarters as secrecy.

News of the "secret" expedition had appeared in one of the New York papers on the day of its departure. It was reprinted in the Washington *Constitution* on the 8th, and was even discovered by Anderson's officers in a Charleston paper on the same date. Thus while the *Star of the West*, unarmed, was speeding on its "secret" mission to Sumter, the Palmetto militia was feverishly preparing to receive her.[2]

The vessel arrived at 1:30 in the morning of the 9th, and hove to at the edge of the harbor. It was discovered at daybreak, and a masked battery from Morris Island, flying the Palmetto flag, opened fire upon it. Undaunted, the *Star of the West* steamed on toward Sumter. Ahead, between the vessel and Sumter, lay Moultrie; and as it approached that fort, its guns too were turned upon the helpless ship. There was no route to Sumter save under these guns of Moultrie—and this, the captain of the ship felt, his ship could not withstand. The *Star of the West*, therefore, put about and headed out to sea.[3]

From a military point of view, the only result of the expedition was to prove the unfitness of General Scott, at his extreme age, to remain as commander-in-chief of the army. The powerful twenty-two gun battery of the *Brooklyn* could have silenced both Morris Island and Moultrie,[4] but the merchantman was helpless. Politically, however, it was of highest significance, in that it offered an emphatic

[1] *Buchanan's Works*, XII, p. 172; *Official Records*, I, p. 9.
[2] Crawford, *op. cit.*, pp. 176, 180, 185.
[3] *Official Records*, I, p. 9.
[4] Chadwick, *op. cit.*, p. 231.

confirmation of the changing attitude of Buchanan, and removed the last Secessionist member of his Cabinet.

Anderson meanwhile had demanded of the Governor of South Carolina an explanation of his firing on the *Star of the West*, and after an exchange of letters, established a truce to refer the question of his future course of action to Washington.[5] The truce prevented an immediate dispatch of a second expedition.

Black was not content to let the subject rest. On January 16, he addressed General Scott a letter upon the whole subject of relief, seeking, as he said, "a little light" upon his own duty. The letter is so important that must be repeated substantially in full:

Dear General: The habitual frankness of your character, the deep interest you take in everything that concerns the public defense, your expressed desire that I should hear and understand your views—these reasons, together with an earnest wish to know my own duty and to do it, induce me to beg you for a little light, which perhaps you alone can shed, upon the present state of our affairs.

1. Is it the duty of the Government to re-enforce Major Anderson?

2. If yes, how soon is it necessary that those re-enforcements should be there?

3. What obstacles exist to prevent the sending of such re-enforcements at any time when it may be necessary to do so?

I trust you will not regard it as presumption in me if I give you the crude notions which I myself have already formed out of very imperfect materials. . . .

I. . . . Fort Sumter is invested on every side by the avowedly hostile forces of South Carolina. . . .

If the troops remain in Fort Sumter without any change in their condition, and the hostile attitude of South Carolina remains as it is now, the question of Major Anderson's surrender is one of time only. If he is not to be relieved, is it not entirely clear that he should be ordered to surrender at once? It having been determined that the latter order shall not be given, it follows that relief must be sent him at some time before it is too late to save him.

II. This brings me to the second question: When should the re-enforcements and provisions be sent? Can we justify ourselves in delaying the performance of that duty?

The authorities of South Carolina are improving every moment, and increasing their ability to prevent re-enforcement every hour, while every day that rises sees us with a power diminished to send in the requisite relief. I think it certain that Major Anderson could be put in possession of all the defensive powers he needs with very little risk to this Government, if the efforts were made immediately; but it is impossible to predict how much blood or money it may cost if it be postponed for two or three months. . . .

The anxiety which an American citizen must feel about any future

[5] *Official Records,* I, pp. 134, 135, 140.

event which may affect the existence of the country, is not less if he expects it to occur on the 5th of March than it would be if he knew it was going to happen on the 3rd.

III. I am persuaded that the difficulty of relieving Major Anderson has been very much magnified in the minds of some persons. . . . A vessel going in where the *Star of the West* went will not be within the reach of the battery's guns longer than from six to ten minutes. The number of shots that could be fired upon her in that time may be easily calculated, and I think the chances of her being seriously injured can be demonstrated, by simple arithmetic, to be very small. . . .

I am convinced that a pirate, or a slaver, or a smuggler, who could be assured of making five hundred dollars by going into the harbor in the face of all the dangers which now threaten a vessel bearing the American flag, would laugh them to scorn, and to one of our naval officers who has the average of daring, "the danger's self were lure alone!"

There really seems to me nothing in the way that ought to stop us except the guns of Fort Moultrie. . . . Would it not be an act of pure self-defense on the part of Major Anderson to silence Fort Moultrie, if it be necessary to do so, for the purpose of insuring the safety of a vessel whose arrival at Fort Sumter is necessary for his protection, and could he not do it effectually? . . . But suppose it impossible for an unarmed vessel to pass the battery, what is the difficulty of sending the *Brooklyn* or the *Macedonian* in? I have never heard it alleged that the latter could not cross the bar, and I think if the fact had been so it would have been mentioned in my hearing before this time. It will turn out upon investigation, after all that has been said and sung about the *Brooklyn*, that there is water enough there for her. She draws ordinarily only sixteen and one-half feet, and her draught can be reduced eighteen inches by putting her upon an even keel. The shallowest place will give her eighteen feet of water at high tide. In point of fact she has crossed that bar more than once. . . .

I feel confident that you will excuse me for making this communication. I have some responsibilities of my own to meet, and I can discharge them only when I understand the subject to which they relate. . . . If you would rather answer orally than make a written reply, I will meet you either at your own quarters or here in the State Department, as may best suit your convenience.

I am, most respectfully yours, &c,

J. S. Black.[6]

Crawford, who was with Anderson at Sumter and later arose to the rank of Major General, declared this to be an "able grasp of the military situation."[7] In truth, this letter expresses views which Black had formed after the most exhaustive efforts to secure the facts which Scott

[6] Black Papers, January 16, 1861; *Official Records*, I, p. 140.

[7] Crawford, *op. cit.*, p. 239.

ought to have had at his finger tips. Black and Stanton had worked together upon the problem, and their search had led them even to consult the most expert of pilots in New York who were familiar with Charleston harbor. These pilots had assured them that any vessel of the size of the *Brooklyn* could be taken into that harbor without the slightest danger of grounding."[8] Scott, however, had thought otherwise.

Scott endorsed this letter to the effect that it arrived "at too late an hour and in the midst of too perplexing engagements to attend to it up to that day," but that he would "seek Mr. Black, and repeat his efforts until he has had the pleasure of finding him." His ardor soon cooled, however. Shortly afterward he met Black upon the street, and complimented him heartily upon the letter which, he said, was worthy of a Field-Marshal. "Judge Black," he added, "where did you get your military education?" Retorted Black, "I was first lieutenant of the Bloody Mountain Cavalry in Somerset County."[9]

Three weeks later they again met, this time at a dinner. Scott once more discoursed upon how interesting and learned the letter was—and in the end did nothing whatsoever either about the letter or about reënforcing Sumter.[10]

Other duties had been pressing upon Black. On January 8 Buchanan had submitted a special message to Congress on the state of the nation, including with it a report of the correspondence with the South Carolina commissioners. He called upon Black to draft the message for him, as was often his custom in such matters. In his draft of this document, Black seized upon the occasion to define properly the power of Federal government in relation to the States, much as he had set it forth in his memorandum of December 30 to Buchanan. Congress had been weighing proposals of compromises to terminate the crisis peacefully but, after the manner of legislative bodies, their progress was leisurely and irregular. One senses a loss of patience in Black's mind over their delays. "Action, prompt action, is required," he wrote. "A delay in Congress to prescribe or to recommend a distinct and practical proposition for conciliation may drive us to a point from which it will be almost impossible to recede."[11]

[8] Black Papers, January 10, 1861.

[9] Crawford, *op. cit.*, p. 240.

[10] F. A. Burr, Philadelphia *Press*, August 11, 1881.

[11] Black Papers, January 8, 1861. A comparison of the original Black draft with the final message of Buchanan shows that the first third of the final message (down to the end of the italics in the second paragraph in *Buchanan's Works*, XI, p. 96) is taken verbatim from Black's draft. About half of the remainder of the paragraphs, down to the taking up of the correspondence with the South Carolina commissioners, are also taken verbatim from the Black draft. The material covering the correspondence with the commissioners is entirely Buchanan's own.

But Congress took no action, prompt or otherwise. In truth, of all the supine failures during this crisis, Congress stands alone above others. Its impotent wrangling cannot but remind one of the like impotency of the Polish diet before the eighteenth-century dismemberment of that unhappy nation.

The run-sheep-run historians, of course, point their fingers at Buchanan alone. It was, for many years, the popular and fashionable thing to do in historical society. "Oh, for one hour of Andrew Jackson!" became the watchword of certain of these savants. In truth, LeBon and Ross, Martin and Allport—students of the mass mind—are of more value to us in understanding this era of history than are Nicolay and Hay, Henry Wilson and Lodge—and even Rhodes, master historian that he is, might have learned much from them. Louis XIV sneered at the mob: *"L'Etat? C'est moi."* But that sneer cost the hapless Louis XVI his royal head. Andrew Jackson pursed his lips and exclaimed, "The Union. It must be preserved!" and South Carolina backed down. But the South Carolina of 1860 was not the South Carolina of 1832. Then she stood alone; now she stood with a united section behind her. True, people of the South of 1860 wanted no war. They had cast a 60% vote against Secession in November of that year. But they had, they felt, endured much. They saw neither peace nor security with the abolitionist banner flying over the White House, and they regarded the election of Lincoln as the first step toward that control. They were resolved now for action. They were grimly in earnest.

When Lincoln issued his call for volunteers in April 1861, Virginia, North Carolina, Tennessee and Arkansas went out of the Union and into the Confederacy. Had Buchanan lifted up the armed forces of the nation against South Carolina in December, that State would have had ten sister States by her side over night. This was no hot tempered flare-up as in 1832. It was a cold and deliberate business. Buchanan knew it. Black knew it. In every letter and every document from his hand upon this question, one sees that one of the driving incentives in him for urging the adequate protection of government property was to prevent any open assault of armed forces between the seceding and Union forces until some compromise might be brought about.

Yet Congress did not act. It debated. Certainly Buchanan's own actions during this period are not all that could have been asked. Wisdom, however, is easy after the event, and in this sort of wisdom much ink has been spilled. But the wisdom of Congress was spent in doing nothing. When Jackson faced a crisis in his dealing with the lone State of South Carolina, Congress gave him a Force Bill—and attached to it a Tariff Compromise. The Force Bill had expired in 1834. When Buchanan faced a crisis against a whole section of the Union, Congress introduced four bills into its sessions. One of them died of abortion. The others died after only a weak squawk. When he pointed out the inadequacy of the Act of 1795 for coping with the crisis, Congress passed the desired bill—on July 29, 1861, four months after he was out of office. When the Charleston collector resigned, he at once nominated Peter McIntyre, of Pennsylvania, for the position. It was at least a gesture toward enforcing the law, but the Senate never acted upon the nomination.[12] The radicals upon both sides had gone beyond any hope of compromise.

Black's view of both extremists was well expressed in a letter of January 17 to A. V. Parsons:

> It undoubtedly would be a great party move as between Democrats and Black Republicans to let the latter have a civil war of their own making. It would also be poetical as well as political justice to let them reap the whirlwind which must grow out of the storm they sowed. But . . . is not the business altogether beyond party considerations? For South Carolina compels us to choose between the destruction of the Government and some kind of defense. . . . I am not in favor of war, but I can not resist the conviction that when war is made against us a moderate self-defense is righteous and proper. Coercion—well, I would not care about coercing South Carolina if she would agree not to coerce us. But she kicks, cuffs, abuses, spits upon us, commits all kinds of outrages against our rights, and then cries out that she is coerced if we propose to hide our diminished heads under a shelter which may protect us a little better for the future.
>
> I agree with you that we ought not to make a civil war. Do you agree with me in the opinion that we are bound to defend ourselves from an unjust and illegal attack? Whatever your answer may be, it cannot prevent me from being, Your friend, J. S. Black.[13]

In the meantime the Gulf States were falling away from the Union as autumn leaves—Mississippi on the 9th of January, Florida on the 10th, Alabama on the 11th, Georgia on the 19th. Louisiana and Texas were soon to follow. In the United States Senate there came, on January 21, a day of awful import. It was the day agreed upon by the Senators of the seceding States to make their official farewell. The Senators of South Carolina had not appeared at the opening of Congress. None of the Senators of the other States had yet departed. This day, therefore, was to witness a scene never before experienced in American annals—the peaceful withdrawal, under the contention of exercising a constitutional right, of the representatives of States which

[12] See *Buchanan's Works*, XI, pp. 134-141 for a summary of this inaction. For the student who desires to consult abbreviated direct sources, the *American Annual Cyclopedia* of 1861, pp. 166-225, gives extracts collected from the *Congressional Globe* of sufficient extent to follow the whole impotent trend of Congress upon this crisis.

[13] C. F. Black, p. 13.

had dissolved their allegiance to the Union. The hour arrived. The galleries of the Senate were packed with trembling and excited spectators. "Everywhere," said the wife of one of the seceding Senators—who was herself in the galleries—"the greeting or gaze of absorbed, unrecognizing men and women was serious and full of trouble."[14]

Senator David L. Yulee of Florida led off. To the tense galleries and a hushed Senate, he announced the secession of his State from the Union and of his withdrawal from the Senate "in willing loyalty to the mandate of my State."

He was followed by Mallory of Florida. "In thus severing our connection with sister states," said Mallory, "we desire to go in peace." But "if folly, wickedness and pride shall preclude the hope of peace . . . we stand forth a united people to grapple with and to conquer."

Clement C. Clay of Alabama was next. "I shall return, like a true and loyal son," he said in speaking of his State, "to defend her honor, maintain her rights, and share her fate." The last phrase was prophetic—for we shall meet Clay again in those bitter years of sharing her fate. "It seemed that the blood within me congealed," said his wife, as she heard his voice.

Fitzpatrick was next. Then Jefferson Davis of Mississippi. The tension in the galleries was increasing. "I rise, Mr. President," said Davis in his clear voice, "for the purpose of announcing to the Senate that the . . . State of Mississippi, by solemn ordinance of her people in convention assembled, has declared her separation from the United States. Under these circumstances, of course, my functions are terminated here . . ." And after detailing the reasons for her action, Davis rose to his valedictory: "Whatever offence I have given [to colleagues of the Senate] . . . I have, Senators, in this hour of our parting, to offer you my apology. . . . I go hence unencumbered of the remembrance of any injury received."[15]

"As each Senator, speaking for his State, concluded his solemn renunciation of allegiance to the United States," said an eye witness, "women grew hysterical and waved their handkerchiefs. . . . Men wept and embraced each other mournfully. At times the murmurs among the onlookers grew so deep that the Sergeant-at-Arms was ordered to clear the galleries; and, as each speaker took up his portfolio and gravely left the Senate Chamber, sympathetic shouts rang from the assemblage above. . . . There was everywhere a feeling of suspense, as if, visibly, the pillars of the temple were being withdrawn."[16]

At the time of the enaction of this scene in the Senate, Black was confined to his home by illness. The excessive strain and labor had

[14] Mrs. Clement C. Clay of Alabama, *A Belle of the Fifties*, p. 147.
[15] Appleton's *Annual American Cyclopedia*, 1861, pp. 195-199.
[16] Clay, *op. cit.*, p. 147.

told upon him, and his health was lower at this time than at any other time of his life until after he had passed seventy years of age. But even though confined by illness his restless mind was still working on the affairs of state. He was concerned for the safety of the national capital—for he foresaw that, if by some bold stroke, the seceding states should seize the now defenseless city, the Federal government would be permanently if not irreparably crippled. Therefore, on the day immediately following the withdrawal of the Senators of seceding States, he addressed a note to the President upon the subject. "Of course I shall not be at the Cabinet meeting," he said, "but the deep interest I feel in the result of your deliberations induces me to write this note, not to be laid before the heads of Departments, but for your own eye alone. . . . You must be aware that the possession of this city is absolutely essential to the ultimate designs of the secessionists. They can establish a Southern Confederacy with the Capital of the Union in their hands. . . . If they *can* take it and *do not* take it they are fools. Knowing them as I do to be men of ability and practical good sense . . . I take it for granted that they have their eye fixed upon Washington . . ."

After detailing the reasons why he believed this to be so, he added an urgent request to put the city in a state of defense. "Shall we be prepared for the worst, or leave the public interests unguarded so that the 'logic of events' may demonstrate our folly? Preparations can do no possible harm in any event and in the event which to me seems most likely it is the country's only chance of salvation . . ."

Other problems too were disturbing him. "I understand that the Secretary of Navy has promised the Secessionists that he will withdraw the ships from the Florida and Alabama harbors. I hope and believe that he has no authority from you to make such a promise; and if he has done it of his own head, I am sure he will receive a signal rebuke. You know how much I honor and respect Toucey, but I confess I find it a little difficult to forgive him for letting it be understood that the *Brooklyn* could not get into the harbor of Charleston; and the order which he gave to that ship, by which the commander felt himself compelled, after he was in sight of Fort Sumter, not to go in, is making this Government the laughter and derision of the world."

Black was still concerned over the relief of Anderson. "I hope it will soon be decided what our policy is to be, with reference to the relief of Major Anderson. . . . The South Carolinians are increasing their means of resistance every day, and this increase may be such as to make delay fatal to his safety . . ."

The general lack of aggressiveness of the administration worried him most, and at the end of his letter he struck a high note upon this theme. "In the forty days and forty nights yet remaining to this administration, responsibilities may be crowded greater than those which are usually incident to four years in more quiet times. I solemnly believe that you can hold this revolution in check, and so completely put the calculations of its leaders out of joint that it will subside after a time into peace and harmony. On the other hand, by leaving the Government an easy prey, the spoilers will be tempted beyond their power of resistance, and they will get such an advantage as will bring upon the country a whole iliad of woe. The short official race which yet remains to us, must be run before a cloud of witnesses, and to win we must cast aside every weight, and the sin of statecraft which doth so easily beset us, and look simply upon our duty and the performance of it as the only prize of our high calling."[17]

But the pace of the administration was not to be hastened by a mere letter from the sickroom, and the time dragged its weary way unto the end. On the matter of putting the capital in a state of adequate defense, however, Black continued to be insistent. Four days later he again addressed a letter to Buchanan on this subject, and secured to his letter the signatures of both Dix and Stanton, urging that Holt, the Secretary of War, be authorized to order a company of light artillery from West Point to Washington. Holt and Scott both joined in the plea.[18]

Buchanan finally brought a force of 650 troops into Washington, whereupon the House of Representatives passed a resolution inquiring of him "the reasons that have induced him to assemble so large a number of troops in this city." Even further, they appointed a select committee which duly investigated and reported back to the House that "the evidence produced before them" did not prove the existence of any organization that intended an "attack upon the Capitol or any of the public property here." Buchanan was accused by some members of Congress of being prompted by cowardice, by others of acting in the spirit of despotism. Holt was defamed in his own state.[19]

Black's duties as Secretary of State during the period of December 1860 until 1861 were little different than if he had continued in the office of Attorney-General, save that he was relieved of any actual appearance before the Supreme Court. All business of the administration was centered upon the crisis of Secession. The problem of foreign affairs was very much in the background. His last official act as Secretary of State was concerned with the recognition of the seceding States by foreign countries. It was a dispatch of February 28, 1861—ten days after the inauguration of Jefferson Davis as President of the Confederate States—sent to all of the American representatives at foreign governments, instructing them, "in the event of such an effort

[17] Black Papers, January 22, 1861.

[18] Black File, Buchanan Papers, January 26, 1861.

[19] See Buchanan's correspondence with the House on this subject, and also Holt's correspondence with Buchanan, *Buchanan's Works,* XI, pp. 152, 154.

being made" by the Confederate States to obtain recognition, "to use proper and necessary means to prevent its success," and to warn foreign governments that "if the independence of the Confederated States should be acknowledged by the great powers of Europe it would tend to disturb the friendly relations . . . now existing between those powers and the United States."[20]

[20] Black Papers, February 28, 1861.

17

REJECTION OF THE SUPREME COURT NOMINATION

SINCE the Dred Scott decision the Supreme Court had been under intensely bitter and partisan fire. Some of it was sincere, some of it was supported by a willful and deliberate misstatement of fact.[1] Regardless of source, however, it kept the Supreme Court more than usual in the public eye.

Therefore, when Justice Peter V. Daniel died on May 30, 1860, there was much speculation and interest upon his successor. His death had left the Court evenly divided between Northern and Southern members, with four from each section. Naturally the South wanted this vacancy, caused by the death of a Southern member, to be filled by another member from the South—for with the odds of population against them, that section was now looking to the Supreme Court as its last line of defense.

Meanwhile, from June to December, Buchanan made no move toward indicating a successor to Daniel. The December term of Court opened with eight justices, instead of nine, upon the bench. Congress convened, but no name was submitted to the Senate for its approval. The reason for the unexpected delay caused some comment at the time, but it is now well established.

Buchanan had determined to appoint Black to the Supreme Court. There seemed good reason, however, to believe that, by waiting a few months, he could make him the Chief Justice instead of an Associate Justice. Roger B. Taney, who then held the office of Chief Justice, was approaching his eighty-fourth year and for some years had been in feeble health.[2] He was a Democrat of the same staunch States Rights school as Buchanan, and the rumor had made its run in official quarters that he would resign in time to allow Buchanan to name his successor in office. Therefore, Buchanan withheld Black's name until

[1] The hostile press, for example, led millions of readers to believe that Taney said in the Dred Scott decision that the negro "had no rights which the white man was bound to respect." Actually Taney said that *before the adoption of the Constitution*, negroes (both North and South) "had no rights which the white man was bound to respect." Warren, *op cit.*, III, p. 26, says that *The Independent* of April 3, 1886, apologized for this falsification. There was no issue of that date, but one of April 1st. I find no apology in that issue.

[2] Even three years previously, Judge Curtis had written to his brother that Taney "grows more feeble in body" and "is not able to write much" although he "retains his alacrity and force of mind wonderfully." B. R. Curtis, *The Life and Writings of Benjamin R. Curtis*, I, p. 193.

Taney should choose to submit his resignation. The decision of Buchanan to make Black Chief Justice seems to have become the common knowledge of their intimate friends. As the day approached for the opening of the December term of Court, Black received several letters, stating that when they reached him he would, of course, be Chief Justice. Even his son-in-law, James F. Shunk, wrote him a letter from California concerning official business in the Attorney-General's office and noted upon it that, since he would be upon the Supreme Court Bench before the letter would reach him, to please forward it at once to his successor in the Attorney-General's office.[3]

But December 3rd came and passed. The Supreme Court opened—and Taney had not resigned. George W. Woodward of the Pennsylvania Supreme Court, who was a close friend of both Black and Buchanan, grew impatient. A week after the opening of court, he wrote to Black: "I expected you would be, before this time, Chief Justice. . . . What means the delay?"[4] Apparently the reason for the delay was unknown, even to Buchanan, for December passed, then January. Still he waited, but Taney gave no hint of resigning. Finally, on February 5, 1861, Buchanan sent Black's appointment to the Senate as Associate Justice of the Supreme Court to the vacancy caused by the death of Judge Daniel.

Of all times in which the appointment might have been made, this was the most singularly unfortunate, for the strength of the Democratic party in Congress had wasted away. Twelve Southern Senators, who might have been depended upon to support the administration, had withdrawn from the Senate. The remainder had been antagonized by Black's militant opposition to Secession. The wound which Black had inflicted on Douglas in the Popular Sovereignty controversy had not healed, and the Douglas Democrats felt no enthusiasm for supporting Buchanan's swordsman in that controversy. But the bitterest opposition came from the Republicans. The radical Republicans were so utterly hostile to the Supreme Court that they would have opposed the appointment of any Democrat under any conditions. The conservative Republicans were determined that no important appointments of any kind should come out of the Buchanan administration during its closing days, since, if they could block such appointments, the offices would be left for the incoming Republican administration to fill. Besides, the Democrats had in 1853 turned down two Whig appointments to the Federal courts made during the closing days of the Fillmore administration. Now, the Republicans insisted, they could take their own political medicine.[5]

It was a hostile Senate, therefore, which received the notice of this

[3] See Black Papers, November, 1860.

[4] Black Papers, December 10, 1860.

[5] C. F. Black, p. 24; Warren, *op. cit.*, III, p. 86.

appointment. The issue hung fire in executive sessions for sixteen days. But if the Senate was hostile, the abolitionist press was bitter and venomous. John W. Forney, in the Philadelphia *Press*, charged that Black had shown a want of knowledge in the law throughout his career upon the Supreme Bench of Pennsylvania.[6] Forney, it will be remembered, had supported Black's election to that court in 1851 and had supported his reëlection in 1854. Now, after losing state control of the party, he was in this wise taking his revenge. The New York *Tribune*, however, led the assault, at least in viciousness, for Forney at his best was never a match for the tart and fractious Greeley. Greeley's Washington correspondent had opened the attack with a news dispatch. "Judge Black's nomination made a decided stir in the executive chamber," he wrote. "It was not referred to the Judiciary Committee. . . . There is a decided majority against the confirmation . . . if pressed to a vote he must be rejected. The President was informed of this fact after a careful canvass of the Senate last week, and much surprise is excited that he should expose a friend to unnecessary mortification." Thereupon the correspondent launched into an argument against any such appointment coming out of the Buchanan administration during its closing days.[7]

Buchanan, however, did not withdraw the nomination. Instead he made a personal appeal to the Democratic Senators to secure its confirmation.[8] When this word reached Greeley, he unleashed upon Black one of those acrimonious, ill-tempered attacks which has made his name famous. In Greeley's eyes, there was nothing to be found in Black that was either honest or able. He attacked Black's policy in the California land claims as "doing as much mischief as rarely falls to the lot of one executive officer to inflict upon his fellow citizens," and as being characterized "with an audacity or insensibility to shame almost beyond parallel." He accused Black of serving as a catspaw for Buchanan "in connection with the notable endeavors of Mr. Buchanan to buy Mr. Forney and his newspaper . . . engaged in the pleasing task of negotiating a bargain for the soul and brain of a public writer." He denied that Black possessed the judicial qualities, the vigorous intellect, or the calm, dignified manner required of such an office. Indeed he thought that "Mr. Black . . . most felicitously describes by contrast, all that a Judge should be." He denounced the appointment as an attempt "to provide for Mr. Buchanan's Attorney-General and Secretary-of-all-work the comfortable retiring pension and good service sinecure of a seat on the Supreme Bench," and relentlessly continued that "in all the extensive range of his most unhappy selections for office, Mr. Buchanan has never hit upon a single

[6] Press clipping, Clayton MSS.
[7] New York *Tribune*, February 7, 1861.
[8] *Ibid.*, February 18, 1861.

nomination more eminently unfit to be made than this one." Regardless of all of these disqualifications for office, however—and here, one suspects, Greeley rises to the real basis of his opposition—he would oppose Black even if he united "the virtues of a Marshall" with "the learning of a Story," because he was not a Republican.[9]

Such was the temper of the abolitionist opposition. It was reflected among the radical members of the Senate. Buchanan, however, felt that he had at last arranged the Senate to secure the confirmation, and on February 21 the Senate went into a turbulent and stormy executive session. Senator Breckinridge left the room and was absent at the final voting. The Senate decided in the end, by a vote of 26 to 25, for "not taking up the nomination of Judge."[10] Technically, therefore, the nomination was neither confirmed nor rejected. In actuality, it was rejected.

If Black was angered by Greeley's unjust attack upon him, or was mortified by the rejection of his appointment by the Senate, he gave no discoverable sign. The administration had but eleven days of life remaining to it, and there was some relief to be gained from escaping from the excessive strain that had been laid upon him. He had been stricken once with rheumatism during the winter and once with pneumonia. His daughter recorded "those anxious days and sleepless nights" which he had spent during the crisis of Secession, and noted that "his picture taken just after he left the Cabinet shows a care-worn, sad, thin face, not recognizable by those who knew him in his later years of prosperity and happiness."[11]

At ten o'clock upon the morning of March 4, while the crowds were assembling before the Capitol to witness the inauguration of the new President, the Cabinet of the departing President assembled in the President's room of the Capitol for their last official service—to assist in examining whatever bills the expiring Congress might present for approval. At the hour of twelve they arose and departed. A new administration had come into power. The king was dead; long live the king. That evening they gathered at a private residence for a personal farewell.[12]

Black had gone out of office with "clean hands and empty." Yet he was to walk in the shadow of misunderstanding and to hear the maudlin tones of political abuse for two decades and more. In the effort to preserve the Union, Black, Stanton, Holt, and Dix had stood shoulder to shoulder without a single disagreement among them.[13] Yet in the years following—when the abuse of Buchanan became a

[9] *Ibid.*, February 20, 1861.

[10] *Harper's Weekly*, March 2, 1861; New York *Tribune*, February 22, 1861.

[11] Clayton, p. 115.

[12] See Buchanan's memorandum, *Buchanan's Works*, XI, p. 156.

[13] Holt's testimony, New York *Tribune*, August 20, 1883.

patriotic act—Stanton, Holt, and Dix were upheld as saviors of the administration while Black was painted as a traitor. Stanton, Holt, and Dix had joined the Republican party; Black had remained a Democrat. Stanton, of course, joined the maligners, but Holt and Dix refused to lend their voices to the clamor. They remained silent. But Black drew his sword in open defense of Buchanan. He had disagreed with Buchanan over many points over the details of his policy, and at one time their differences had nearly reached an open rupture; but he had agreed with the broader scope of the policy—as had Stanton, Holt, and Dix.[14] Therefore, rather than allow his loyalty to that policy to be misunderstood, he kept hidden even the facts of his disagreements over details—and kept his sword unsheathed in Buchanan's defense.

Upon him poured all the green fury of which only a war-mad people are capable.

But in the end, his vindication was to be complete and permanent. Forney's newspaper in Philadelphia, once his bitter denouncer, was to publish the records of that vindication. Even the New York *Tribune* was to recant its bitter attacks upon him, and the pen of Whitelaw Reid, successor to Greeley, was to extol his services during the crisis of disunion and to write, as its final opinion, that his part in this crisis was "a patriotic service which will not be forgotten."[15] But of these events we shall treat in their proper sequence.

March fourth of 1861 marked the second epoch of Black's life, as March sixth of 1857 had marked the first. Its run was reversed from the normal course of public men. Its earlier part was spent in public office; its later part, as a private citizen. For nineteen years he had served in high judicial and executive places. Now, at fifty-one, his career in public office was over and he was to return to the private life which, in most careers, precedes the holding of such high offices. Paradoxically again, his greatest public service was to be done in private life. As an attorney and writer, as a defender of minority causes and inviolate personal rights of man, he was to leave a greater stamp upon the political history of the nation than he ever had done in public office.

[14] See Holt's testimony, *Buchanan's Works,* XI, p. 87.

[15] New York *Tribune,* August 20, 1883.

18

THE NADIR OF PERSONAL AND POLITICAL FORTUNES

BLACK went out of office in 1861 as a member of a defeated and discredited party. But to him the Republican triumph of 1860 was an "unrelieved evil." He "knew the abolitionists to be the avowed enemies of the Constitution and the Union," and feared that the "Republicans would necessarily be corrupted by their alliance with them." As he saw the march of these combined forces upon the capital, he felt "that the constitutional liberties of the country were in as much peril as Rome was when the Gauls were pouring over the broken defenses of the city."[1] The dangers of disunion were imminent. He saw little hope of Lincoln reconciling the South where Buchanan had failed. He left office with a grave foreboding of the future and a sense of the coming horror of war.

Anxieties of a personal nature were likewise pressing down upon him. His health was upon the verge of breakdown. Gravest of all at the moment, however, were his financial worries; for through unfortunate investments he had lost every penny of the money which he had accumulated during a lifetime of saving. Now, at fifty-one, he was out of public office for the first time in nineteen years; thrown back upon the private practice of law; exceedingly poor in health; stripped of a lifetime of savings and, even worse, several thousand dollars in debt, with a wife and five children upon his hands.

During his early private practice and his public career, Black had amassed the modest savings of about $27,000. This was his entire fortune. When he removed to Washington he had sold the house in Somerset which had been his home for the twenty years preceding,[2] and the money obtained from this sale, together with the remainder of his fortune, was placed in two types of investments. Six thousand dollars was invested, through a relative in Baltimore, in Patapsco bonds.[3] The remainder, approximately $21,000, had been invested with a brother-in-law, Ross Forward of Somerset, in a coal and iron land project. The latter does not seem to have been an out-and-out lump investment on the part of Black, but rather his generous response to Forward's urgent pleas for additional money which his business demanded. It began with the endorsing of notes which Forward

[1] Open letter to New York *Herald*, Clayton MSS.
[2] Black Papers, May 5, 1857.
[3] P. H. Sullivan to Black, Black Papers, May 27, 1859 and August 9, 1859.

had made at banks—and then paying notes when the latter was unable to take them up.[4] The financial panic of 1857 seems to have caught Forward in a stage of overexpansion, and he was unable to ride the storm. For two years, however, Black among others carried along his business by pouring in money. By 1859 he had put in nearly $10,000. In May of that year Forward asked for another thousand. Apparently Black demurred, for upon June 2, Forward besieged him with a second letter. "If you have any bonds of compassion . . . ," he urged, "send me that money . . . I am straightened for the means to keep the hundred hungry mouths filled that are looking to me for their daily rations in return for their labor here."[5] But the need had grown from one thousand dollars to two thousand, and Black that day sent him a draft for the full amount.[6] This pouring of water into sand came to an end in October when Forward's business collapsed and his creditors entered judgments for the payment of his debts.[7]

For years not a cent was recovered from the entire investment. Suits at law, counter suits, and injunctions were filed and cross-filed for the next twenty-odd years, and Black in writing his final will in 1883 noted that his Somerset affairs were still in confusion.[8] The last report of the trustees of his estate, made in 1897, shows that no substantial amounts were realized from this entanglement after his death.[9]

The strain of trying to save his brother-in-law from financial collapse had forced Black in turn to borrow money for personal expenses. From Stanton he obtained $2,000,[10] from Buchanan another $2,000.[11]

He went out of office, therefore, in March of 1861 with no practice of law to fall back upon, with the bulk of his private fortune gone, and with debts of $4,000 over his head. But the end had not yet been written. Before that month had passed, he was notified that Patapsco bonds, in which the small remainder of his fortune was invested, had suspended all payment of interest.[12] He was forced to turn his hand to the immediate earning of money. On March 11 he wrote from

[4] Black Papers, No. 47,388, undated, lists a $2,000 note which Black was called upon to pay.

[5] Black Papers, May 17 and June 2, 1859.

[6] Forward's note, Black Papers, June 6, 1859.

[7] D. Weyand to Black, Black Papers, October 5, 1859, and November 7, 1859.

[8] The Black Will, Will Book C. C. No. 3, pp. 346-351, York (Pa.) County Court House.

[9] Trustees' Report, June 2, 1897, on Black Estate. York (Pa.) County Court House. On August 23, 1861, a statement of settlement shows the authorization of payment of 55.2 cents on the dollar of this property. Presumably it was paid. See Black Papers of that date.

[10] Black Papers, Note of November 17, 1859. See also June 27, 1861 and March 31, 1862 for partial repayments of this loan.

[11] Black to Buchanan, *Buchanan's Works*, XI, p. 200.

[12] P. H. Sullivan to Black, Black Papers, March-April, 1861.

Washington to Buchanan (who had now retired to his estates at Wheatlands): "I shall get a respectable, perhaps a heavy practice at Washington if I try. I will manage it if possible so as not to lose my rights as a citizen of Pennsylvania."[13]

This expressed a hope rather than an expectation, for the old fears which had haunted him when, as a youth, he first took up the study of law and again in the early days of legal practice, now once more disturbed him. It is a remarkable commentary upon his character that he should have been so innocent of the prestige which his service as Chief Justice of Pennsylvania and Attorney-General of the United States had brought to his name. In actuality, although he hoped for a "heavy practice," he was not sure even of a "respectable" one. In his heart he really feared that he could not make a living at the bar, and so discouraged was he over the prospect that his depression infected even his family.[14] He remained in Washington during the month of March,[15] but in April he returned to Somerset with his son Chauncey, and there the latter was admitted to the Somerset bar.[16] Early in June he was back in Washington, but later in the month he returned to Somerset. His whole plans for the future seemed unsettled. There is some reason to believe that for a while he seriously considered returning to Somerset and starting over again in this small community where he had made his first start more than thirty years before. For a while he also considered an offer to edit an abridged edition of the Pennsylvania law reports, condensing the one hundred volumes of complete reports into fifteen. Buchanan had laid before him still another offer. Smarting under the political attacks which were being made upon his administration, he offered to engage Black to write a complete biography of his public life embodying a detailed explanation of his Presidential administration. This Black was willing to do,[17] but the plan eventually fell through.

In the end, he regarded himself fortunate to secure the position of Reporter to the United States Supreme Court. The entire history of that Court offers no parallel to this. For nearly four years, Black appeared before that tribunal as Attorney-General of the United States. Less than a year previous, he had looked forward with confidence to becoming its Chief Justice. Six months previous he had missed confirmation as an Associate Justice by a single vote in the Senate. Now he stood be-

[13] Black File, Buchanan Papers, March 11, 1861.

[14] Clayton, p. 118.

[15] Stanton's letters to Buchanan, *Buchanan's Works,* XI, pp. 164, 170.

[16] Black Papers, April 26, 1861. Chauncey Black was at this time 22 years old; he had been a student in the University of Georgia Law School. See Black Papers, Nov. 6, 1860.

[17] Black fully discussed these projects for "maintaining my family" in a letter to Buchanan treating upon the proposed biography. Black File, Buchanan Papers, June, 1861.

fore that body in the humble position of court reporter. The salary was modest,[18] but at least it kept him in the profession of law and offered a possibility of building a practice upon the side. What his own feelings were at this descent can only be conjectured, but a letter from Buchanan well expressed the situation: "I was rejoiced to learn you had been appointed Reporter to the Supreme Court. Although you have descended from your former elevation, yet the office is respectable."[19]

The relationship between Black and Buchanan following their retirement from office might be paraphrased as that of David and Jonathan. They saw the issues of the Civil War in a different light. They vigorously disagreed upon many phases of politics and upon their evaluation of many acts of the Buchanan administration. They were at times upon the verge of breaking. But their innermost admiration for each other weathered all storms and they continued through all vicissitudes to remain close friends. Although Buchanan was seventy at his retirement, he lived to see Lee's army threaten the capture of his estate at Wheatlands during the Gettysburg campaign, lived to see the end of the bitter struggle, the assassination of Lincoln, and the beginning of the tragic era of Reconstruction. He died in 1868.

He was deeply hurt by the wanton attacks against his administration and sought for a means to lay his defense before the public. In May following his retirement in March, he laid an offer before Black to prepare "a true and fair historical account" of his public life and especially that part of it which he spent as President. Black's detailed reply to that offer, written in June 1861, gives an intimate picture of the relations then existing between them.

I have thought carefully over the matter of which we spoke at Wheatlands when I was there (he wrote). I think you owe it to your friends and to your country to give them a full and clear vindication of your conduct and character. If this be not done, you will continue to be slandered for half a century to come. In the mean time nothing is easier than a perfect defence of every important measure which you ever adopted or carried out—nothing plainer than the task of putting the responsibility where it properly belongs for every misfortune which the country had fallen into. Nevertheless, it will be a work of much labor and time—that is, if it be done well, as it ought to be. Any one could soon and easily get up a compilation of documents and letters with such a statement of facts as might be necessary merely to connect them. But . . . nobody would read it. It should be a compact narrative of what occurred in Congress, in the executive departments, in the country at large; readable, attractive, and interesting to all—comprehensive in its scope, accurate in its detail, vigorous enough

[18] Including the sale of the United States Reports, it seems to have been less than $3,000 a year.

[19] Black File, Buchanan Papers, Jan. 6, 1862.

to be convincing, and yet impartial enough to prevent the authority of it from being impugned.

> Though deep yet clear, though gentle yet not dull,
> Strong without rage, without o'erflowing full.

If such a thing could be reproduced, no matter when, it would be the standard authority for everything that concerns your times and particularly for what concerns yourself . . .

But who is to do this?—I certainly do not pretend that I have the qualities which would enable me to execute the plan of which I have given this imperfect outline . . . I feel deeply interested in the subject, to be sure, and think it the best chance for making a literary reputation that I have ever seen or thought of. But I cannot afford to indulge in such ambition; or indeed in ambition of any kind except that of maintaining my family.

It will take years to accomplish the work . . . this will require so long for its completion that one of the objects—an early vindication of your character—will be defeated. But that is provided for in my programme. I propose to prepare that portion of it which may now be needed, at once, and print it whenever it is deemed desirable to do so in any form that may be thought necessary. But I will not consent to publish the whole as a whole until I have time to give it as perfect a form as I can.

You know the reasons which compel me to treat this as a matter of business, which otherwise would be a mere labor of love. Now, therefore, let me speak of it as business.

You have my note for $2000. Let that stand, and I will pay you the interest on it during your life. But let me have $1500—now or at any time during the present year—and at your death remit me the $2000 debt, and give to my family $3500.

If you agree to this I will immediately move to York or Lancaster, and during the present summer and next winter devote most of my time to the business with all the aid I can command. . . .

We must for obvious reasons be distinctly understood that I am not acting as your mere amanuensis or servant—that it is not an autobiography, but a thing for which I am responsible in my proper person. I am therefore to be the judge of what shall go in and what shall be left out, and to express my own views and opinions. Of course you can have no doubts about my willingness to do you justice. The great danger would be the contrary—that is, that I would do you more than justice . . .

If you approve . . . a single line to that effect will reach me at Washington and I will conduct myself accordingly . . .[20]

Buchanan agreed to his terms and Black accordingly prepared to undertake the biography. His first task was to find a suitable location in which to live. He wished to retain his citizenship in Pennsylvania and therefore his choice of cities was restricted to that state. He must

[20] Black File, Buchanan Papers, June 1861.

be near enough to Buchanan's Wheatlands estates, near Lancaster, to allow frequent consultations. At the same time he had not yet given up the hope of ultimately establishing himself in the practice of law and therefore he wanted a location accessible to Washington and to Philadelphia. His choice was for these reasons narrowed to two small cities of Pennsylvania, bearing the historic names of Lancaster and York—"the rival claims of the White Rose and the Red," as he wrote his wife upon the subject. The White Rose won and he settled in York, partly because it was the town in which his mother had been born, but more perhaps because he found there a suitable house at a reasonable rent and because his son Chauncey had found an opening to start the practice of law.[21]

The city, in general, did not receive him kindly. The war was on. The battle of Bull Run had just been lost. The term "Copperhead" had been coined and it was fresh upon the lips of the new war patriots. Any man who was a friend of Buchanan must surely be a Copperhead. There were of course friends, who were warmer and the more staunch because of this general unfriendliness. The Democratic paper of the city was his unwavering and militant defender. His home was a rallying place for friends and admirers. As for the aloofness of the city in general, it mattered little to Black himself. He went his way unperturbed. His knee was too sturdy and his head too high to bow before any storm of public abuse. But in the end York, like the nation, softened and claimed him as its own.[22]

Upon moving to York, he at once began the biography of Buchanan, but the project was never completed, for the two men could not agree over many phases of its treatment. Black looked upon Lincoln's manner of prosecuting the Civil War as a direct overthrow of the Constitution. In his view, the Federal government must act "upon individuals, not upon States." Therefore the force that sustains Federal laws, "must be directed against the force that opposes them," and since "individual insurgents were personally responsible for any insurrection, not the State in its corporate capacity," he "repudiated utterly the whole idea that war can be declared . . . against a State . . . merely because some persons within the State had done or threatened to do certain things inconsistent with their Federal obligations. . . . Innocent people—those who were in no way concerned with the rising—were as much entitled to the protection of the Federal government as if they lived in any other State, and in fact had a stronger claim to it, for they might need it much more."

This was no mere splitting of legal hairs. "Mr. Lincoln four months after his inauguration," said Black, "declared in a message to Congress

[21] Clayton, p. 111; Black letters to Buchanan, Black File, Buchanan Papers, March 11 and July 8, 1861.

[22] Niles to the author, January 10, 1930.

that there was not a majority for secession in any State except, perhaps, South Carolina. Yet war was made upon the States and the innocent were confounded with the guilty—the friends of the United States were compelled, in self defence, to unite with the enemies, and now, instead of dealing with a tenth of the people, we have a deadly and terrible conflict with all of them."[23]

Buchanan, upon the other hand, addressed an open letter to the citizens of Chester and Lancaster Counties in September approving Lincoln's entire plan of war. At once Black wrote him,

> Your letter . . . surprises me a little. Those are no doubt your true sentiments, and you had a right to express them. But your endorsement of Lincoln's policy will be a very serious drawback upon the defence of your own. It is in vain to think that the two administrations can be made consistent. The fire upon the *Star of the West* was as bad as the fire on Fort Sumter; and the taking of Moultrie and Pinckney was worse than either. You know what I thought of these events at the time they occurred. If this war is right and politic and wise and constitutional, I cannot but think you ought to have made it. I am willing to vindicate the last administration to the best of my ability, and I will do it; but I can't do it on the ground which you now occupy, and therefore I cannot conscientiously ask you to pay anything for the work.
>
> My affection for you has moulted no feather. No difference of opinion shall diminish our friendship if I can help it. It is simply a consideration of duty to you as well as myself which obliges me to decline receiving anything from you. When you come over here on Thursday I will show you my manuscript; from which, slovenly as it is, you will see the radical difference of our views, and understand how wrong it would be to make you in any manner responsible either in pocket or in character for what I may write on that theme.[24]

Their views upon the subject could not be reconciled, and Black gave up the project. To his niece, Buchanan wrote on November 6th: "Judge Black came here yesterday . . . I presume the Biography is all over. I shall now depend on myself with God's assistance."[25]

Again, on November 13th, he wrote her: "Judge Black . . . went to Washington on Monday last. I shall be prepared, I think, before the meeting of Congress without his aid."[26]

Although Black had withdrawn from the writing of Buchanan's defense, his interest in the work remained, and the two were in frequent correspondence concerning it. There were, however, many points of disagreement upon the subject. Buchanan was still anxious to lay his

[23] Black expressed this view at many different times. The above quotations are from a speech in Philadelphia, October 24, 1864. Clayton MSS.

[24] Black Papers, October 5, 1861.

[25] *Buchanan's Works,* XI, p. 226.

[26] *Ibid.,* p. 229.

defense at once before the public. Black felt that, with the country in a state of war hysteria, the publication of any defense would be wholly useless and the opportunity for its timely and effectual appearance would be spoiled. "You speak of laying facts before the public," he wrote. "I fear you forget that *there is no public.* There is nothing left in this country but a '*government.*' " For that reason he contended that it would be better to "let your vindication await the revival of the laws and the restoration of the popular mind to its wholesome normal conditions. I know that in the mean time you must suffer annoyances, submit to misconstruction, and be the victim of many malicious slanders. . . . But better that than worse . . . The tribunal that condemned you against evidence will drown your defence with the sound of its drums . . .

"It is not to be denied that we all committed some errors. I am sure I did, and I think you did. I am quite willing that these shall be blazoned to the world and that the whole truth shall be made known for the sake of showing exactly how it was and by whom the present calamities were brought on the country. But at this moment the time is out of joint."[27]

The friendship of the two men had reached thin ice. Referring to a previous letter of Buchanan, Black wrote him in reply: "It grieved me to perceive a tone of melancholy running through it. You have in my opinion no cause for low spirits." Thereupon Buchanan retorted by the next mail, "I am happy to say you are entirely mistaken in supposing that I suffer from low spirits. I am astonished at my own health and spirits and the zest with which I enjoy the calm pleasures with which Providence has blessed me." After wrestling with the form and manner of Buchanan's defense, without reaching agreement, Black at last wrote Buchanan: "I am afraid that your views and mine are so far out of accord that you will never approve mine," whereupon the latter retorted: "I am not at all astonished. . . . My policy was well matured, at least to myself . . . I never consciously swerved . . . I would not, if I could, alter this policy in any particular."[28]

Yet at the bottom, neither man was willing to part with the other. Buchanan, after taking issue upon substantially every statement contained in Black's letter, closed with a hesitating proffer of continued friendship. "I presume I need scarcely invite you to pay me a visit," he wrote. "This I promise, however, that if you will come and bring Mrs. Black along, I shall not introduce any subject which will give you pain, or on which we can possibly differ."[29] Black was not wanting in willingness to continue their friendship. At the moment he was

[27] Black File, Buchanan Papers, March 1, 1862.

[28] Black File, Buchanan Papers, Black letter of March 1, Buchanan letter of March 4, 1862.

[29] *Ibid.*

tied up in the Supreme Court, but upon the instant the court term had ended, he replied: "The court adjourned today. . . . As soon as I get through some work it has left me, I shall go home. I will not be at York more than a day or two without going to see you."[30]

Presumably the visit was made. Certainly the test of friendship in some manner passed the crisis. They continued to have vigorous disagreements upon many topics, to be sure, but there was never a wavering in personal affection. Their correspondence was frequent and regular. Black's visits to Wheatlands became a feature in Buchanan's life. To Toucey, he wrote of Black, "He is just as agreeable as ever."[31] When Thurlow Weed made his false charge that Stanton had bulldozed and dictated to Buchanan while a member of his Cabinet, thereby opening his "bleary eyes," Buchanan felt injured that every member of his former Cabinet did not at once publicly deny the charge.[32] Some of them, he felt, were led by the desire not to oppose Weed, who stood high with the new administration. "I except Judge Black," he added. "I believe his heart is in the right place; and his conduct has proceeded from constitutional timidity, and not from any want of regard from myself."[33] In fact, Black had not for a long time even seen a copy of the story. Later he labeled it as "wholly fictitious."[34] He was not greatly concerned, however, over the manufacture of political falsehoods which seems to have been plied as a trade by a part of the radical press, not even when the New York *Evening Post* circulated a sensational story purporting to tell how Black had gained the nomination for Buchanan in 1856. The Democratic Convention at Cincinnati was deadlocked, according to this story, until Black took the floor and in a rousing speech denounced the abolitionists and Republicans, and wound up by promising that if Buchanan was nominated and elected President and a Republican should be chosen as his successor, he would not interfere with Secession, should any states desire to do so. After this guarantee, Buchanan was nominated on the next ballot.[35]

The *Tribune*, of course, repeated the charge and the story gained wide circulation. At first Black never troubled himself even to answer it. Buchanan, however, at once came to Black's defense with a letter of denial to the editor of the *Evening Post*,[36] and when specifically called upon for his version of the story, Black wired this devastating answer: "I was not at Cincinnati in 1856, or at any other time in my life."[37]

[30] Black File, Buchanan Papers, March 25, 1862.
[31] *Buchanan's Works*, XI, p. 362.
[32] See *supra*, p. 74 for the details of this story.
[33] *Buchanan's Works*, XI, p. 272.
[34] Letters to Augustus Schell for publication. Black Papers, August 6, 1863.
[35] *Evening Post;* quoted in the New York *Tribune* May 10, 1865.
[36] *Buchanan's Works*, XI, p. 388.
[37] Black File, Buchanan Papers, May 13, 1865.

The falsehood thereupon collapsed in midair.

Thus the friendship of the two men continued. However vigorous might be their political disagreements, they stood united before all critics, and the personal ties between them remained warm. Buchanan died, still smarting under a sense of public injustice, but Black's tongue and pen remained loyal and vigorous in defense of Buchanan's life and of his administration.

Toward the Civil War Black gave lip service, but it cannot be said that he approved of the war as a matter of principle, nor did he sanction the particular mode of conducting it. Declaring war upon States, he felt, was in complete violation of the Constitution. Individuals in the Southern States were responsible for the insurrection—and force should be applied upon individuals as such.

Nevertheless he seems to have had some personal influence with officials of the Lincoln administration. His papers contain a flood of letters that had poured in upon him, begging his influence to enable applicants to secure appointments to government office. There are also a few letters of appreciation from successful applicants, thanking him for his influence.

For a while he maintained friendly relations with Stanton. The latter, at the moment of his appointment as Secretary of War under Lincoln, wrote Black:

> I have just received your note and would answer it by calling to see you but have a bad cold and dare not go out. . . . As to the appointment referred to you may say to your friend Mr. Pierson that if I go in to the war office and have any clerkship in my gift, your friend shall have it. As the Senate has not yet acted on the nomination and there may be a fight of some days over the Minister to Russia[38] I can say nothing more now.

Yet already there was the beginning of a rift between these two men. "I do not like," continued Stanton, "your *disclaimer* of *this* administration if I go in it." A glimmer of the old friendship still remained, however, and Stanton could add, "no one can ever have more influence with me than yourself."[39]

Gradually, however, the two men grew wider apart. Inevitably so. Stanton's activities were revealing him as a strange personage "whose amazing record of duplicity," said Dunning, "strongly suggests the vagaries of an opium-eater."[40] Yet a trace of friendship still remained. In an argument before the Supreme Court during the spring of 1864, Black threw in an aside which revealed his puzzled opinion of Stanton

[38] This refers to Simon Cameron, whom Lincoln had just deposed as Secretary of War by appointing him to Minister of Russia.

[39] Black Papers. By error this letter is placed at the end of the 1857 collection. See No. 50,902.

[40] W. A. Dunning, *Reconstruction*, p. 91.

at the time. "I happen to know that gentleman as a lawyer very well. In some other respects, it is possible he may be beyond my depth; but, in his professional character, I know him as well as one man can be known to another."[41]

The final break between them came over the so-called Canadian Mission. Jacob Thompson, former colleague of Black and Stanton in the Buchanan Cabinet, had been sent upon some mission to Canada by the Confederate government. Black decided to visit Thompson, "impelled mainly by motives," he said, "arising out of our past intimacy and long personal friendship." He spoke to Stanton of the intended visit and the latter, it seems, expressed his approbation of the visit. After his return from Canada, Black sent to Stanton an account of his conversations with Thompson.

"I made him understand at the beginning," he wrote, "that I had changed no political opinion . . . That the Federal Constitution was still my standard of political orthodoxy; that I desired, above all things, a peace which would leave the States united and at the same time secure all of them their just rights. I told him that though I was not in any sense, an agent of the Federal Government, yet if I learned from him any fact which it was important for the public authorities to know, I would regard it as my duty to communicate it to some member of the administration in Washington."[42]

Following that, the two men talked peace candidly; Thompson expressed the view that the South wanted peace, but was convinced that the war was carried on for complete subjugation, that surrender would mean universal confiscation of lands, spoliation of goods, military execution of the best men and arrest or banishment of the others. Free speech and personal liberty would be at an end, and wars must break out again until the end "could only be seen through a long vista of blood, conflagration, terror, and tears."[42a]

The two men, talking as private citizens only, saw only two outcomes: Either the war must go on until the Southern armies were totally annihilated; or to the South must be conceded the right of self-government "on all subjects as fully as they had that right under the federal Constitution." That is, the South would return to the Union under the guarantee of their constitutional rights. On this basis, Black summarized his letter to Stanton by saying, "I do not presume to advise you, but if I were in your place I would advise the President to suspend hostilities for three or six months and commence negotiations in good earnest, unless he has irrevocably made up his mind to fight it out on the emancipation issue."[43]

[41] C. F. Black, p. 453.
[42] Black Papers, August 24, 1864.
[42a] *Ibid.*
[43] *Ibid.*

Stanton was peevish toward the whole affair. "I am not disposed to give the President the advice you recommend," he wrote, and added, "It seems a little curious, the pains you have taken to connect your visit to Thompson with my 'wish' and my 'approbation.' "[44]

To this Black vigorously retorted that he had never "asked" Stanton about visiting Thompson, he had told him that he "*was going*," that he had mentioned it by accident to Stanton, whereupon the latter "instantly and very unequivocably" expressed his wish that Black should go. "You repeated it not less than three times." Besides, Black continued, why did it matter? He had not gone to Canada as an agent, he had asked for no credentials. "Surely you can not suppose that I wanted to be an agent of yours." Vigorously also he defended his wish for an armistice. For if the war went on until the South was crushed, he feared the Constitution would be overthrown.[45]

Behind this wish for an armistice and a settlement of the war without victory to either side, was Black's eternal fear that a complete victory at the North would place the abolitionists in full control. To him that control had become the greatest menace to the Constitution. We shall meet again this fear in the days of Reconstruction, when control by the abolitionists had been realized.

But Stanton had gone over to the radical—the abolition—wing of the Republican party. The views of the two men were now completely irreconcilable.

The Democratic party had been defeated in 1860, and during the war it came to be thoroughly discredited. The ante-bellum South had been evenly divided between the Whigs and Democrats, but Republican politicians skillfully made it appear that the Democratic doctrine was the doctrine of Secession. The phrase "every soldier killed in defending the Union, was shot by a Democrat" became an effective slogan, in stamping this impression upon the public mind.[46] The fact that Grant, McClellan, Hancock, and other famous generals in defense of the Union had been Democrats at the outbreak of the war, and that many if not all of them remained so during the war, was forgotten. The "Copperhead" activities of Vallandingham and his associates were perhaps the final straw in the discrediting of the Democrats as a "Secession party."

Nevertheless, the year 1864 saw Black in a strenuous campaign to elect McClellan, the Democratic nominee, over Lincoln. Invitations poured in upon him begging his aid as a speaker, both in the national and local elections of Pennsylvania. When the elections in that state were over, on October 11th, the Democracy of Maryland demanded his aid.

[44] Black Papers, August 31, 1864.

[45] Black Papers, September 3, 1864.

[46] See New York *Tribune*, and Philadelphia *Press* during the campaign of 1864.

He was fearless, and even reckless, in his attack upon the Republican administration. At Pittsburgh he made a speech "of greater severity and power" against the conduct of the war, said Buchanan, "than any delivered throughout the campaign."[47]

On the eve of the elections, however, he made his greatest effort of the campaign, at Philadelphia. The ultimate control of the Republican party by the abolitionists was the theme of his address. "John Hampden did not differ so much from Charles I, nor William Tell from Gessler, nor the Congress of 1776 from the ministry of George III—nay; the most orderly, humane and anti-revolutionary Frenchman that inhabited Paris in 1789, could not have differed from Robespierre about the use of the guillotine, more entirely than we differ from the abolitionists concerning the whole purpose and object of the Federal Government."

He followed with a bill of particulars: Destruction of States, negro equality, suppression of free speech, "higher laws." All of these were favored by abolitionists, and, in his view, endangered the Constitution. Virginia, torn into two parts against her will, or at least by the expression of consent from only one-tenth of her people. Maryland, Indiana, Pennsylvania—where "companies, battalions, and regiments of Federal soldiers, without pretense of right poured their votes into the ballot box to overwhelm the true voice of the people." Free speech—"abolitionism has suppressed two hundred and fifty newspapers (I think that is the number) by arbitrary orders, executed at the point of the bayonet, or by mobs, hissed on to their brutal work by the general approbation of the whole party."

As to prosecuting the war, "I am not only no believer in the right of Secession, but I go further than even an Abolitionist would ask me to go. I deny the right of revolution." But he refused to sanction a "higher law," or the doctrine of "irrepressible conflict," or of overthrow of the States. A war must be for the restoration of the Constitution, and "a war for this purpose . . . under General McClellan, would be conducted" for such an object.[48]

But Atlanta had fallen into Sherman's hands, news from the front was more encouraging than at any previous time of the war. The nation decided not to "swap horses in the middle of a stream." The Democratic party suffered the greatest defeat in its long and checkered history as a party.

[47] Buchanan to Toucey, May 13, 1864, *Buchanan's Works*, XI, p. 362.

[48] Delivered October 24, 1864, Clayton MSS.

19

CALIFORNIA LAND CASES

BLACK'S first appearance before the Supreme Court as Attorney-General had been in a case involving Mexican land grants in California—and his first appearance before that court after the return to private life was in the same capacity. As we have seen,[1] when the United States took over California from Mexico, more than 800 claims for land, totaling nearly 20,000 square miles in area, were presented to the American government for confirmation. Most of these claims were valid; but many of them—especially the larger claims, those to mineral lands, and to sites occupied by cities—proved to be fraudulent. In order to determine the final justice of any claim, Congress, by a special act, authorized either the government or the claimants to take an appeal to the Supreme Court of the United States and, under this act, ninety-nine of the most valuable claims were so appealed. They formed an enormous proportion of the business of that court during the decade between 1855 and 1865.

Black, as Attorney-General, had undertaken a vigorous prosecution of those cases which were believed to be fraudulent. He had made a study of Mexican land laws and of the Spanish language. He was, therefore, in a position of peculiar and commanding authority upon this type of case. As early as November 1860, his son-in-law, James F. Shunk, had written him from California regarding the desire of the agents of John C. Frémont to retain him as a counsel. "They propose to engage your services *permanently*," wrote Shunk, "expecting to invoke your aid *whenever* and *wherever* it may be necessary in the future to maintain the legal rights of Frémont. They wish you to fix the amount of your *retainer* and advise me of it by the *return Pony* [express]—they will then pay it to me and I will receipt for it. They are disposed to be liberal and fair."[2] Later Shunk wrote "I have seen Palmer [agent for Frémont]. He agrees to your terms." Being on the ground in California, Shunk grasped the possibilities for a thriving law practice in these land claims, and pressed the matter upon Black's attention. "I think that if you and I form a partnership," he wrote, "that we can get a great deal of California business . . . I saving you all the vile drudgery of the profession, and you giving to the cases your experience, knowledge, and influence."[3] But Black's

[1] See *supra*, Chapter 10.
[2] Black Papers, November 14, 1860.
[3] Black Papers, January 21, 1861.

despondency over earning a living at law, and his eventual acceptance of the position as Reporter to the Supreme Court, would indicate that he did not share Shunk's enthusiasm over the outlook.

Shunk, however, being in California, realized the enormous prestige which Black's name carried among the settlers. He therefore went ahead with his arrangements and engaged a San Francisco attorney, one J. B. Williams, to serve as solicitor to handle the California end of the business. In the spring of 1862, Shunk returned to Washington. The firm of "Black and Shunk" was formed, subject to the approval of California claimants.[4]

When the December term of court opened, Williams and Shunk had, between them, secured for Black retainers in two of the California cases on the docket.[5] Before the end of the term half a dozen others had been added.

Each of these first two cases involved land claims which had been confirmed to the claimants by the District Court of California, but had been appealed to the Supreme Court by the government. There were other persons than the government and the claimants, however, who were concerned with the outcome. Hundreds of American settlers had purchased from the government the land now involved in these claims. Should the Supreme Court uphold the decision of the District Courts in sustaining these claims, the settlers would be evicted from their land and property. They had, therefore, organized for protection and, through Williams and Shunk, engaged Black to represent their rights before the Supreme Court. To them the outcome was a matter of grave concern.

The first of these cases was known as the Morehead case.[6] It was argued before the Supreme Court upon December 24, 1861. Shunk appeared with Black for the settlers. For the claimants were Edwin M. Stanton and Thomas Sunderland.[7]

The case involved a claim of some 57,000 acres of land on the Sacramento River purported to have been granted to one William Knight, a roving adventurer.

According to Mexican law, an *expediente*, or full set of papers conferring a land grant, consisted of six series of papers—(1) a petition for the land with a map attached thereto; (2) a "marginal decree," written and signed upon the margin of this petition by the Governor, granting it; (3) an "order of reference" to the proper official for in-

[4] Williams to Black and Shunk, October 23, 1861.

[5] Black Papers, Williams to Black, October 23, 1861; Gaddis to Black, November 25, 1861.

[6] Officially known as *U. S.* vs. *Knight's Administration.* The report of this case is found in 1 Black, p. 227, from which the account here given is taken.

[7] Sunderland was from California. He and Shunk were young lawyers, making their first appearance before the Supreme Court, and the bulk of the argument fell to Stanton and Black.

formation as to whether the land is available for grant; (4) the *informe*, or reply of that officer; (5) the official decree of concession; and (6) finally a copy or duplicate of the grant. A copy of such an *expediente* should be in the possession of the claimant and a record of it should be in the official archives of the government.[8]

But Knight's title lacked three of these, namely the map, the order of reference, and the copy of the grant. These were claimed to have been lost while Knight was escaping from Indians in 1847.

Sunderland and Stanton argued that the signatures to Knight's papers were genuine, and that the *expediente* had been found in the Mexican archives and indexed by an American clerk, Hartnell, who was a man of high integrity and an accomplished Spanish scholar. Here indeed was the significant issue of the whole case. If the Hartnell Index should be accepted by the Supreme Court, it would set up an entirely new basis for validating Mexican claims and would result in evicting thousands of American settlers from their homes.

Black, therefore, attempted once and for all to destroy the validity of the Hartnell Index. "The papers indexed by Hartnell are not records," he said: "It is true that they are now in the Surveyor General's office, and may have been there as early as 1848, when Mr. Hartnell finished making his Index. That shows only that they were not forged since 1848." They were not, nor do they pretend to be the official *records*. They were merely "loose papers, . . . found lying on the floor of the custom-house at Monterey and piled up against a wall, which were by Mr. Hartnell placed among the records of the office." "The mere fact that a loose paper is found in a public office does not give to that paper the dignity or entitle it to the faith of a public record without some evidence . . . to show that it is properly a part of the records." It had been proved that "many false papers were placed among" these records "for their fraudulent ends," until it was impossible "to tell whether a loose paper found in the Surveyor General's office comes from the sweepings of the custom-house floor, from the documents openly deposited by private persons, or from the felonious droppings of those who fabricated them. Limantour's papers were found in a public office as well as papers of dozens of other men, "who have been gibbeted in the face of the world as fabricators of false titles."

Having cast this grave doubt upon the reliability of Hartnell's Index, Black turned to the final and clinching argument. The only catalogue of genuine *expedientes* was the Jimeno Index, "made before the conquest, by Mexican officers, who had the means of knowing, and did know the true from the false." This, of course, Mr. Stanton must well know, for he himself had discovered and collected this Index. And

[8] Justice Nathan Clifford, see 1 Black, p. 245.

the Jimeno Index showed no title to Knight. This, Mr. Stanton must admit, was fatally damaging to the Knight claim. Finally, he could not agree with Mr. Stanton, even upon the high qualifications of Mr. Hartnell. "Mr. Hartnell could read and write and speak Spanish. That was his sole qualification. He knew nothing of Mexican laws or records. He was wholly without experience." He had incorporated too many papers, already proved to be fabricated, to allow any reliance upon his judgment.

The Supreme Court handed down its decision upon January 27, 1862. That court agreed with Black that there were "fatal defects" in the claim. It therefore reversed the decision of the lower court and rejected the grant. The opinion not only followed with surprising closeness the lines of argument laid down by Black, but even took all save one of its citations to previous decisions from his argument. Of greatest importance, however, was its overthrow for once and all of the Hartnell Index. Fraudulent claims must henceforth seek elsewhere for refuge.[9]

For a brief moment, the settlers were jubilant, then came the word that the Knight heirs were making a final desperate attempt to reopen the whole case, for the taking of new testimony in the lower court. This would mean another trial in the District Court and doubtless another appeal to the Supreme Court. They were again thrown into suspense.[10] On February 20 Reverdy Johnson, veteran practitioner before the Supreme Court, moved before that body for a reopening. This Black opposed—and the court agreed with him, denying the petition.[11] The case was over.

Already half a dozen other important land cases had been pressed upon Black, but following this legal victory he was flooded by claimants and settlers begging his services. Some of them brought him cases already settled five years before, begging him to secure a rehearing and offering staggering fees in event of a successful establishment of these claims. These latter cases, of course, he rejected but within a few months he had enough cases on hand to engage him for several years.

The second land case in which Black appeared concerned the claim of a former Mexican General, one Don Maria Guadalupe Vallejo, for 162 square miles of land. As in the previous case, Black appeared for the settlers who were resisting this claim. Vallejo's claim lay along San Francisco Bay and included the town of Vallejo, the city of Bernicia, the United States Navy Yard, and the depot of the Pacific Steamship Company. It included about 100,000 acres of land and was of enormous value.

[9] *Ibid.*

[10] See Williams letters to Black, Black Papers, February, 1862.

[11] 1 Black, p. 488.

This case, even more than the previous one, revealed Black's skill and knowledge of the Mexican law involved. Vallejo claimed two grants in this tract of land. One was a "colonization grant," dated March 15, 1843, made out in the usual form, signed by Micheltorena, then Governor of California, and by one Arce, who was secretary to the Governor. The other grant purported to be a purchase made by Vallejo from the Governor of California on June 19, 1844. There was also a certificate purporting to be from the Departmental Assembly of California attesting that both of these grants had been approved by that body.[12]

In arguing this case, Black again went to the issue of the official record. The Jimeno Index—the ultimate authority for all grants—showed no record of either of these grants. Even worse, the original journals of the Departmental Assembly showed that there had never been an approval of either grant; the "certificate" to this effect must therefore have been forged. Added to that, the signatures of Micheltorena and of his secretary, Arce, had never been proved; and when the United States tried to call Arce, who was within the court jurisdiction, the motion was successfully resisted by the claimant. The most logical reason would seem to be that the truth would overthrow the case.

This perhaps would have been enough, but Black then took the Mexican laws upon land grants, showing that these were covered in two acts—those of 1824 and of 1828. One of Vallejo's grants purported to be derived from a purchase of land through the Governor of California. Yet these laws allow no Governor to sell an inch of land. Another grant claimed to have been taken as a "colonization grant." It was along the shores of San Francisco Bay. Yet the Mexican laws prohibited any colonization grants within ten leagues of the seacoast.

The lower court, however, had cited as its authority for the Governor's power to make these grants a certain Spanish text, *Leyes Vigentes*. This work Black produced in court, opened it to the page cited, and translated it. It was an old decree of the Spanish Cortes, in 1813. This, Black showed, had no bearing in the first instance upon any but crown lands. Added to that, it had been repealed by the Mexican act of 1824.

In vain did Reverdy Johnson, on the other side, contend against this invincible exposition of Mexican law. The Supreme Court reversed the decision of the lower court, rejected both claims "for want of power in the Governor" to make them.[13]

Five days later Black again appeared for the settlers against the claim of Neleigh for fifty-four square miles of land, which he claimed to have bought from one José Castro. With him, as junior counsel,

[12] *Ibid.*, p. 541.

[13] *Ibid.*, p. 550.

was Shunk. Again Reverdy Johnson appeared for the claimants, with R. H. Gillett as the junior counsel. It was a repetition of the two previous cases. There was no record of the grant or, as Black put it, here was a "naked grant, without an expediente . . . without record evidence of any kind to show that it was ever issued or even applied for." Added to that, upon the date of the pretended grant, Castro was in open war against the Governor whose name was signed to the grant. Worse, the forgers had erred in their knowledge of Mexican law in drafting the papers. It was signed by Pio Pico as "Constitutional Governor of the Department of the Californias," and dated April 4, 1846, whereas Pico was merely the "Governor *ad interim*," until the 18th of that month and had signed no papers before that date, theretofore discovered, except by the latter title. Worst of all, however, was the fact that the fluent falsifier, José M. Moreno, whose name appeared as secretary to the Governor upon these papers, was shown not to have been serving as secretary on this date.

Again the Supreme Court ruled that the error in stating Pico's title as Governor, and the signature of the untrustworthy Moreno, were proof of fraud. The decision of the lower court was reversed and the claim rejected.[14]

These claims totaled more than 300 square miles of land. All were defeated. Upon the other hand, two small claims had been appealed during Black's incumbency as Attorney-General, which the new Attorney-General, Edward Bates, called upon Black to argue. One was a third Vallejo claim for six square miles of land. The other was a claim for fifty acres based upon an Indian grant.[15] Both of these claims the Supreme Court held to be valid.

During the next term of court Black appeared for the settlers against the famous "Tomales" claim for sixteen square miles of land. Again the Supreme Court reversed the lower court, and rejected the claim.[16]

During the term of court beginning December 1863, he appeared in five more of these cases. Four of them were mere ordinary cases, as land cases went. One was the Romero claim, for an amount unstated.[17] Another was the Malarin claim, involving eighteen square miles of land;[18] a third was the Halleck claim for seventy-two square miles of land;[19] and the fourth was the Estudillo claim for an amount unstated.[20] In each of these cases, save the Malarin case, Black appeared for the settlers. In this one he represented the Malarin interests. In all four cases, the Supreme Court decided in favor of his clients.

[14] *Ibid.*, p. 298.
[15] *Ibid.*, pp. 283, 267.
[16] Officially known as *U. S.* vs. *Galbraith*. 2 Black, p. 394.
[17] 1 Wallace, p. 721.
[18] *Ibid.*, p. 282.
[19] *Ibid.*, p. 440.
[20] *Ibid.*, p. 710

But the most famous of all the California land cases ever argued before the Supreme Court was the Fossat, or New Almaden Quicksilver Mine case. It involved a long series of litigations in the District Court of California, together with four appeals to the Supreme Court, over a period of twelve years, for possession of the most productive quicksilver mine in the world. The mine was located fifteen miles south of San Francisco Bay and was known as the New Almaden, after the famous Almaden quicksilver mine of Spain. It was valued at from $20,000,000 to $25,000,000. In 1865 its yield was more than 47,000 flasks of quicksilver, at 76½ pounds to the flask. As late as 1881 it was still yielding 26,000 flasks of the total world yield of 115,000.[21] It was the greatest mining prize of California, and litigants were not lacking to lay claim to it.

The beginning of the dispute went back to 1842, before the discovery of the mine. Two Mexicans, by the names of Larios and Berreyesa, each had secured a grant of one square league of land from the Mexican government. Their lands adjoined and a dispute arose over the boundary between them. This dispute was settled by the Mexican government, but there was no official survey used in the markings, and the language used in describing the boundaries was susceptible to more than one interpretation.[22]

There also arose a third claimant, one Castillero, who claimed not only to have discovered the mine in 1845 but to be entitled to two square leagues of land around it, thus swallowing up both of the other claimants. On the strength of this claim Castillero formed a company and began taking the ore from the mine, removing altogether some $8,000,000 before being stopped by a Federal injunction. This injunction was secured in 1858 by Stanton, by order of Black as Attorney-General. Stanton produced before the California District Court some forty letters from the Castillero conspirators, written from six months to three years after California was ceded to the United States. In them the California conspirator had notified his Mexican co-worker just what perjured documents the latter must secure in Mexico in order to manufacture a title to the mine.[23]

Defeated in the courts, the Castillero interests turned to political intrigue, getting from the Legislature of California a resolution instructing the California Senators and Congressmen to "use their best endeavors" to validate this fraudulent claim. But Black, as Attorney-General, quashed their efforts with the decree that a court had issued the injunction and hence only a court could dissolve it.[24]

An official survey was made in 1860 which located the mine upon

[21] Bancroft, *op. cit.*, VI, p. 525; VII, p. 657.
[22] 2 Wallace, p. 649.
[23] Gorham, *Edwin M. Stanton*, I, p. 69.
[24] Report to the President on the California Resolutions. Clayton MSS.

the Larios grant (now owned by Charles Fossat). But the issue was still unsettled as to whether title to the mine went with the land. So stood the situation when Black retired from public office.

Two startling developments followed shortly. First, the Berreyesa claimants appealed and won from the courts the order for a new survey. This survey changed the line so that the mine now was on the Berreyesa land instead of on Fossat's. Second, the Castillero claimants finally got the District Court to dissolve the injunction and to decree that, regardless of whose land the mine was on, the mine itself belonged to Castillero. Fossat was now left out on both counts.[25]

At this state of affairs, the Fossat interests secured Black as counsel to represent their interests;[26] and for the next four years the files of Black's papers are strewn with long and anxious letters between the clients and their counsel. The suspense at times was so great that even the private stockholders besieged Black with letters of inquiry—to say nothing of anxious traders on the stock market who begged to know, privately, if he would win the case and, if he did, how much the quicksilver stock would rise on the market.[27]

Black's first move as counsel for Fossat was to dispose of the Castillero claim. Appeal was taken from the decision of the District Court, awarding the mine to Castillero, to the Supreme Court. There the case came up for hearing upon January 30, 1863. A more brilliant counsel for both sides could not have been imagined. For Castillero appeared the veteran, Reverdy Johnson, the brilliant Charles O'Conor of New York, and several lesser known members of the bar. With Black appeared the new Attorney-General, Edward Bates, Edwin M. Stanton, and Benjamin R. Curtis, a former justice of the Supreme Court.

The Supreme Court rendered its decision upon March 10, rejecting both the mining claim and the land claim of the Castillero interests. The letters of the conspirators, planning the details of buying the forged documents in Mexico, was the final blow to the Castillero cause. "Comments upon these extraordinary documents are unnecessary," said Judge Clifford in rendering the decision, "as they . . . afford a demonstration that those in possession of the mine, holding it under conveyances from the claimant, knew full well that he had no title."[28]

The first hurdle had now been passed. One of the claimants to the mine was forever disposed of. But the District Court of California had decided that the land upon which the New Almaden mine was located belonged to Berreyesa. Appeal was accordingly taken from that decree to the Supreme Court. It came up for hearing in February

[25] 2 Black, p. 17.
[26] Bond to Black, Black Papers, November 25, 1861.
[27] See Peirce to Black, Feb. 17, 1864, for one of these letters.
[28] 2 Black, p. 17.

1864. J. B. Williams came east from California to argue the case for the Berreyesa interests. Williams, it will be remembered, was the San Francisco attorney who had been handling the California end of Black's practice since 1861. With him was J. M. Carlisle. Black had secured Caleb Cushing to aid him as counsel for the Fossat interests.[29]

The contest once again assumed a three-sided aspect. Stanton, during his short term as Attorney-General, had accepted the Fossat and Berreyesa grants as conclusive and had abandoned all claim of the United States to the mine. But Edward Bates, who succeeded Stanton on March 4, 1861, had revoked this decision and had undertaken to dispute both claims, thereby securing possession of the mines for the United States Government.[30] Therefore Bates, with J. A. Wills, appeared before the court in behalf of this effort.

The case was a record one for length. The testimony filled 8,000 printed pages. The briefs of the opposing counsels filled 1,700 pages more. The arguments consumed nine days. Black made the final argument, condensing the points of all this mass of testimony into an eight-hour speech.[31]

This speech is remarkable in at least one respect. Although it was discussing a claim that had confounded the courts by its technical nature for more than a decade, yet the speech itself was so free from involved and technical language that any normally intelligent youth of twenty can read and grasp without difficulty every point it contains. The original Mexican grants had defined the boundaries in terms of land marks upon the terrain. Black himself had never been in California, yet his description of this terrain is so vivid that any reader can form a perfect picture of the whole scene. "This land lies about fifteen miles south from the southern end of the Bay of San Francisco," he began. "In going from the bay to the land in controversy, if you follow the principal watercourses, you rise gradually at the rate of about seventy-five or one hundred feet to the mile; but if you want to go directly over the country, the way the crow flies, you must cross a succession of hills and hollows," and he took the court with him in imagination over that country, pointing out the landmarks, and building for the members of the court a clear picture of the whole country.

"Somewhere in the valley," he continued, ". . . lies a league of land which the government of Mexico granted to Justo Larios. [Now owned by Fossat.] That much is admitted to be true." The only ques-

[29] Cushing was Black's predecessor as Attorney-General. The Fossat interests, for some reason, had strongly objected to his employment. But Black knew him to be an exceedingly able lawyer, and upon his insistence they yielded. See Black Papers, Eldridge to Black, Dec. 23, 1862.

[30] C. F. Black, p. 453.

[31] F. A. Burr, Philadelphia *Press*, August 20, 1883.

tion was where the boundaries of this land were run. Perhaps the only technical part of the whole speech was the describing of those boundaries under the terms of the original grant. "The grant itself describes the location of the land granted. On the south it is "*colindante con la Sierra.*" This word *colindante* has as clear and plain a signification in the Spanish language as any word in any language can have. It is translated by the two Latin words *adjacens* and *contiguus*, which signify *lying next to, touching with.* The etymology of the Spanish word itself shows very clearly what it means. *Linde, lindano, lindero,* are synonymous terms, and mean always a landmark, a boundary. *Co* is the Latin *cum* and the English 'with.' *Colindante* signifies *coterminous, adjoining.* . . . If Justo Larios had a league of land *colindante* with the mountain, then his land begins where the mountain ceases, and the mountain ceases where his land begins."[32]

And so through the whole argument. The description of every boundary was taken from the original grant, clearly explained, and located upon that picture of the terrain which had been so vividly painted in the minds of members of the court. All seems so exceedingly simple to a reader of the speech, that it is hard to imagine why any dispute should ever have arisen over the boundary, or how the lower court could have decided that the mine lay upon any land other than Fossat's.

When Black had finished, there was no doubt in the minds of the court. They reversed the decree of the lower court and ordered the original survey to be accepted as the correct one.[33] After twelve years of litigation, the dispute was over. The mine belonged to Fossat.

Two others of the most famous land cases ought to be mentioned. One concerned the location of the famous Sutter grant for eleven square leagues of land. The grant to this land was confirmed, and the only issue raised was concerning its location. Sutter was a man of loose business habits, and had sold more land than he owned. Each of his purchasers was concerned to see that his own land should be included in the final location of the grant. Black appeared for the citizens in and around the city of Sacramento who desired to have all of that territory excluded from the Sutter grant. In this effort, however, he was but partly successful, and of the three possible locations the Supreme Court chose the middle ground, alloting one-fifth of Sutter's land in and around the city of Sacramento.[34]

The other case concerned the famous New Idria Quicksilver Mine. This was often known as the McGarrahan claim. The mine stood next to the New Almaden in value and had even a longer history of litigation. Through the fraud of a United States District Attorney who had

[32] C. F. Black, p. 438.
[33] 2 Wallace, p. 649.
[34] *Ibid.*, p. 562.

an interest in the claim, the title in the mine was confirmed to one Gomez, sold by him to McGarrahan, and the right to take an appeal was dismissed. Other claimants seeking to oust the McGarrahan interests then engaged Black to secure an appeal to the Supreme Court. This was by no means an easy thing to do, since the right to appeal following the decision of the lower court had been waived; but after a sharp conflict with the McGarrahan lawyers, an order was secured from the lower court for an appeal. The McGarrahan lawyers then took the issue to the Supreme Court, resisting the right to take the appeal after once waived, but Black successfully contested their opposition, and the Supreme Court granted the appeal.[35]

The case came up "on its merits" in March of 1866. The decree of the lower court was reversed and the Supreme Court proclaimed the McGarrahan claim to be tainted with fraud.[36]

McGarrahan, now defeated in the courts, continued to press his claim. For twelve years or more he vexed every Congress with his appeals and filled the legislative halls with his clamor. Black appeared against him before a Committee of Congress in 1870[37] and again before the Senate Committee on Public Lands in 1878, until McGarrahan came to look upon Black as the author of his troubles. Before the Senate Committee Black branded McGarrahan with his partner Ord as "a brace of knaves as sorry as one fraud ever yoked together," and disposed permanently of that adventurer's claim by tracing the merits and history of the case back to 1857, showing that at every step of the way it was tainted with fraud and bribery.[38]

Unquestionably was Black's handling of these California land cases one of the most remarkably successful series of litigations ever carried on by any American lawyer at any time. In 1861 he had turned his hand to the private practice of law for the first time in nineteen years, for the first time since he was thirty-two years of age. He began this new career filled with doubt and despondency, with grave fears that he could not really succeed in the law. Yet within the four years between 1861 and 1865 he came before the Supreme Court not less than sixteen times in cases involving staggering amounts of wealth. In thirteen of these cases he was completely victorious. In one, the Sutter case, he was partially so. Only two cases were lost. Even these were of minor importance—one being for but fifty acres of land—in which he appeared only at the request of the new Attorney-General.[39] Not one important case was lost. Yet eight of these thirteen cases which he won required the Supreme Court to reverse decisions of the lower court.

[35] 1 Wallace, p. 690.

[36] 3 Wallace, p. 752.

[37] Black Papers, March 23, 1870.

[38] Clayton MSS.

[39] The Wilson claim, 1 Black p. 267; and a second Vallejo claim, 1 Black p. 541.

Even this does not mark the full extent of Black's success in handling these cases, for his correspondence through the years 1863 to 1865 shows him to have been engaged in at least eight other cases, in which he seems to have successfully settled every one. They were cases in which land claimants won their suits in the lower courts, but in which an appeal had been taken by the government to the Supreme Court. The claimants engaged Black to secure a dismissal of the appeal if possible, and, if that was not possible, to argue the case before the Supreme Court. Not one of these cases ever was argued before the Supreme Court. Presumably, therefore, they were dismissed, and the claimants left in possession of the land.[40]

The fees which he received for handling these cases were not out of proportion to the customary fees of that time, yet because of the tremendous amounts of property involved they ran into large figures. Black never haggled over fees. Indeed he seldom even settled upon a fee in advance unless the client himself offered a set fee in engaging his services. As for drawing up a contract for stipulating a certain fee, it is doubtful if he ever did such a thing in his life. He kept no record, or even a memorandum, of the fees that were due him, and sometimes could not remember the amount of one even after it had been agreed upon. For that reason, it is impossible in most cases to determine exactly how much he did receive for handling these land cases of California, except where the arrangements were made through Williams of San Francisco, who always stipulated a specific fee in each case and notified Black of the amount.

Through Black's papers are strewn scores of small payments, ranging from $250 to $1,000, in part payments upon these fees. They tell nothing except that the total runs into enormous figures. But in a few cases it is possible to fix upon the full and definite amount. For one of the cases settled out of court, the "Juares case," he received not less than $4,000.[41] For the Sutter and the Gailbraith cases, the fee was $10,000 in each case.[42] For the New Idria Quicksilver Mine case, it was $11,000. In this case Black's clients seem to have taken a deliberate advantage of his unbusinesslike treatment of fees. They brought him a desperate case in the first instance, offering him a retaining fee of $5,000 to take the case, and a contingent fee of $5,000 if he could get the case appealed to the Supreme Court. He secured the appeal. Then they asked him to argue the case for them, saying nothing about a fee for the argument. This argument, of course, should have com-

[40] See Black Papers, Dec. 19, 1864, and Feb. 12, 1865 for letters upon some of these cases. A question arose before the Supreme Court as to whether one of these suits, on the Castro claim, had been properly dismissed. That court decided that the dismissal was proper and that no reopening of it was possible. 3 Wallace, p. 48.

[41] Black Papers, Dec. 19, 1864; and Sept. 29, 1865.

[42] Black Papers, Oct. 23, 1861, and July 11, 1863.

manded at least as high a fee as that for gaining the appeal. But when he had argued and won the case, his clients sent him a check for only $1,000. Having made no agreement with them, he said nothing, although he felt that the amount was rather negligible in view of his services.[43] For handling the important Morehead, or Knight case, he was paid $15,000.[44] These payments, it should be added, were made in gold coin. The importance of this fact is seen when one remembers that during the Civil War period of our history, gold was at a premium. Some of the drafts in payment show that gold at the time stood at 190½.[45]

But the crowning fee for all of the California land cases, and the largest single fee that Black ever received during his life, was in the Fossat or New Almaden Quicksilver Mine case. The amount was $180,000. This is the largest known fee ever paid an attorney for handling a single case during this period of American history.[46]

Four years before, Black had lost the savings of a lifetime, and had gone out of office not only penniless, but in debt. At fifty-one, he had been forced to start his economic life anew. To relieve the immediate pressure of pecuniary needs, he had even accepted the modest retainer as Reporter of the Supreme Court. Certainly it was not an office for a man of his mental stature. Yet he kept this office for three years, even reporting eight of his own arguments before the Supreme Court, until heavy practice forced him to resign,[47] leaving two volumes of Reports which, as Klingelsmith has well said, was "a record of mechanical work well done by a master hand."[48]

In the short space of four years he had earned a fortune ten times greater than the one he had lost. Never again was he to know the pres-

[43] Black Papers, March 23, 1870.

[44] Black Papers, January 4, 1862.

[45] Black Papers, June 2, 1864.

[46] The total fee for this case, has been variously stated at from $120,000 to $300,000. Two lines of evidence seem to fix the above figure as the correct one. (1) The author is assured by Judge H. C. Niles that he recalls distinctly the following details: That Black had made no written agreement regarding the fee, but that his son Chauncey had kept a memorandum of the verbal agreement; that when the Fossat claimants tried to escape full payment, Chauncey produced his written memorandum and on that basis obtained the full amount, which was $180,000. (2) Judge W. F. Bay Stewart assures the author that he recalls Black having in his possession one check for $100,000 as a part payment on this fee. Then, among the Black papers, the author found evidence of three other payments, two of $10,000 each and one of $55,000. This totals $175,000. But there was also mention of a retaining fee, of which the amount was unstated. On a case of this magnitude, it could not have been less than $5,000—making a total of $180,000.

[47] His resignation is dated March 21, 1864, two weeks after the conclusion of the New Almaden quicksilver argument. See Black Papers of that date.

[48] M. Klingelsmith, in W. D. Lewis, *Great American Lawyers*, VI. p. 48. The volume of reports referred to are 1 and 2 Black, so often cited in this chapter.

sure of financial want. His earnings to the end of his life were amazingly large, yet he never became a wealthy man. He had no taste for the accumulation of money. A modest competence satisfied his ambition. "The rest of the golden shower was neglected," wrote his son. "He would scarcely stoop to pick it up, or, when he did, he gave it away, or let it run through his hands like water. He never kept a book or an account of any description; never invested a dollar on speculation. . . . He lost large sums by indulgence of clients who were neither entitled to his charity nor in need of it, and he was swindled out of much more by clients and others who dishonestly availed themselves of his known simplicity and easiness in matters of this kind."[49]

Not all of the golden shower, however, could run through his hands. He bought a house in York[50] and moved from the humble home where he formerly had lived. He bought also a farm from his old friend Buchanan.[51] Finally, by piecemeal and regardless of the prices, he acquired 200 acres of land, just south of York. It was poor farming land, but it topped the highest knob in the county and gave a twenty-mile view of the winding Codorus valley.[52] Close to the soil he had been born. Close to it he had lived during most of his life. Now that the means was at hand, he was longing to return.

Yet golden showers, homes, and farms, were but forces incidental. Of greatest, and lasting, significance was the fact that through them he was relieved from the menial worries of life. He had reached as high a plane of independence as one can expect to attain. He held no political ambitions to promote or to endure defeat. Freedom was his, as completely as any life may possess it.

As he was attaining this level of freedom, the Civil War had drawn to an end. Grant had offered to Lee his soldier's hand at Appomattox. Lincoln had said, "Let the band play Dixie. It is ours now." But Lincoln was gone—and the Radicals were drawing together in Washington with indecent haste to wreak vengeance upon the prostrate South. The Constitution; in the hands of its avowed friends, never was in so great a danger as now. Its defenders were mute. Some of them were suckled with greed. Others were silenced with fear. One man, however, gazing toward the Capital from across the Codorus valley, was not mute. He could not be tempted with plunder, neither could he be silenced by fear.

[49] C. F. Black, p. 25.

[50] Black Papers, March 23, 30, 1864.

[51] Etnier Collection, Black Papers, 1863. Also Black Papers Library of Congress, June 8 and 16, 1863.

[52] Clayton, p. 139.

20

EX PARTE MILLIGAN

THE Civil War had been conducted with a sinister neglect of guarantees in the Bill of Rights, especially those of a "free and public trial" to all accused persons "by an impartial jury." Thomas Jefferson, writing from the American Embassy at Paris in 1788, had foreseen the danger of omitting such guarantees from the original Constitution. "It astonishes me," he exclaimed, "to find . . ." Americans "contented to live under a system which leaves their governors the power of taking from them trial by jury in civil cases, freedom of religion, freedom of the press, freedom of commerce, the habeas corpus laws, and of yoking them with a standing army."[1]

The American people, however, were far from contented with this prospect and the Constitution was ratified only after assurance was given that these guarantees would at once be perpetuated through constitutional Amendments. So rigidly were these rights fastened into the Constitution by these Amendments that, according to the decision of John Marshall, the opinions of Story and of Taney, not to mention English precedent for two centuries, the suspension of habeas corpus, even temporarily in times of great crisis, could be done only through an Act of Congress.

Yet in defiance of decisions, precedent, and Constitution, habeas corpus *was* suspended shortly after the outbreak of the Civil War by executive proclamation, and it remained suspended unto the end. Arrested victims were charged with no offense, but merely confined to jail as "prisoners of state." How many were so imprisoned can never be known, but it has been conservatively estimated at about 38,000.[2] Late in the war Congress legalized the suspension of habeas corpus, but required that a list of persons so detained must be furnished Federal judges. These judges were authorized to discharge all unindicted prisoners within twenty days after the next session of the grand jury.[3] But the law was ignored and the victims languished in jail.

Lincoln's own personal kindness and mercy would, of course, have mitigated the harshness of this act, had not the execution of this policy fell to Seward and Stanton. In their hands there was no softening of its features. Rhodes gravely records "the despotic power so notice-

[1] *Writings of Jefferson*, Ford ed., V, p. 3.

[2] Professor Howard W. Caldwell, to the author, 1920.

[3] *Statutes at Large*, XII, p. 755; Act of March 3, 1863.

able in the proceedings of Seward and Stanton . . ."[4] and notes that even Jefferson Davis, with his government toppling about his ears, never arrogated such a power.[5] The procedure of Seward and Stanton was, for them, delightfully simple. A letter, or order, or even a simple telegram was all that was needed. It was but one step from illegal arrests to illegal trials, and it is with one of these illegal trials that we are here concerned. Lambdin P. Milligan, together with two other men, Bowles and Horsey, were arrested by order of the commanding general of Indiana upon October 5, 1864. Sixteen days later —in the city of Indianapolis where the civil courts were open—they were tried before a military commission upon charges of conspiracy, of aiding the enemy, of inciting insurrection, of disloyal practices, and of "a violation of the laws of war." They were found guilty and sentenced to death by hanging. The date for the hanging was set for May 19, 1865.[6] Nine days before that scheduled event the New York *Tribune* announced in its headlines: "Traitors to be Hanged."[7]

But upon that same day, Milligan filed a petition in the United States Circuit Court to be discharged. He recited the facts necessary, under the act of Congress of March 3, 1863, to warrant the discharge, namely that he had been held more than twenty days after the grand jury had adjourned and that no indictment had been made against him. In other words, he ignored the whole proceedings of the military commission as void, and demanded his rights under the Act of Congress. The Circuit Court recoiled from its plain duty. Yet it dared not deny the petition. Instead its members divided, and certified three questions to the Supreme Court for a final ruling: 1. Was Milligan entitled to a writ of habeas corpus? 2. Ought he to be discharged? 3. Had the military commission the jurisdiction legally to try and sentence him.[8]

Meanwhile, of course, a stay of sentence had been granted to all three of the convicted men until a final ruling could be made, and attorneys girded themselves for this, the greatest conflict over personal liberty that ever has been waged before the American Supreme Court.

Inevitably Black was chosen to head the counsel for Milligan. His overshadowing reputation at the bar, together with his pronounced views upon constitutional rights, brought the case to him as a matter of course. With him it was a service of gratuity, willingly given. He took the case without fee or hope of fee,[9] and gave to it without stint of time or labor. He was aided by two other lawyers famous before

[4] Rhodes, *op. cit.*, V, p. 457.
[5] *Ibid.*, p. 470.
[6] 4 Wallace, p. 6.
[7] New York *Tribune*, May 10, 1865.
[8] 4 Wallace, p. 8.
[9] C. F. Black, p. 27.

the bar, J. E. McDonald and David Dudley Field. There also was with him a young man of rising prominence who, by turns, had been a school teacher, a Major General in the army, and was now sitting in Congress. He had never argued a case at law in his life, not even before a justice of the peace, but he commands our attention, not only because of himself, but because of the long and lasting friendship which was developing between him and Black, one that was to have a great influence upon the lives of both.

The man was James A. Garfield. In 1853 he had made the acquaintance of Black's son Chauncey, while both of them were attending the Eclectic Institute in Ohio. Nine years later, while in Washington, Garfield met Chauncey Black upon the street, and through him became acquainted with his father.[10] Thereupon began one of the most unique of friendships among public men. Black was twenty-one years the elder. He was an intense and radical Democrat. Garfield was a thorough Republican. Upon the surface, the only common tie between them was the fact that both were members of the same church—the Disciples of Christ, "first called Christians at Antioch." But their minds struck flint upon the same topics, often even in politics. Each respected the great ability of the other and there grew up between them deep friendship, until after a long separation Garfield could write to Black, "For many months I have been hungry for the sight of you."[11]

Garfield in Congress had resisted some attempts to extend the power of military commissions to try civilians, so to him Black now came with the details of the Milligan case. But let us take the account from Garfield's own hand:

> Here Black came to me, he had seen what I had said in Congress, and asked me if I was willing to say that in an argument in the Supreme Court. "Well," I said, "it depends upon your case altogether." He sent me the facts in the case—the record. I read it over and said, "I believe in that doctrine." Said he, "Young man, you know it is a perilous thing for a young Republican in Congress to say that, and I don't want you to injure yourself." Said I, "It don't make any difference. I believe in English liberty and English law. But," said I, "Mr. Black I am not a practitioner in the Supreme Court and I never tried a case in my life anywhere." Said he, "How long ago were you admitted to the bar?" "Just about six years ago." "That will do," said he. I had been admitted to the Supreme Court of my state enough years to come under the rules of the Supreme Court.
>
> I was admitted to the Supreme Court and immediately entered upon this case. . . . The day before the trial was to come off in the court, all of the counsel got together for consultation at Washington to de-

[10] T. C. Smith, *Life and Letters of James Abram Garfield,* p. 825.

[11] Black Papers, October 27. 1873.

termine upon the course of the case and when we got together Judge Black said, "Well, we will hear from the youngest member in the case first. What do you intend to do?"

Well, there were the very foremost lawyers in the land and I had to put myself forward before them and show my hand. I took my points and stated succinctly the line of my argument and when I got through they said with one accord "Don't you change a line or word of that." The next day I went in and spoke two hours before the Supreme Court.[12]

Upon the other side of this case were three attorneys, likewise of outstanding prominence. Two of them—James Speed and Henry Stanbery—were government officials and as such were compelled to represent the government in the case. Stanbery, at least, later proved his soundness as a constitutional lawyer in passing upon the Reconstruction Acts as unconstitutional and in defending Andrew Johnson in the impeachment trial. In the Milligan case, he argued only the technical question of jurisdiction. Seemingly neither he nor Speed had any stomach for an open assault upon the Constitution. That unpalatable task was left to Benjamin F. Butler, "special counsel of the United States" in this case.

Butler is deserving of our attention. He had served as a Major General of volunteers during the Civil War. His military knowledge was negligible, but he possessed a flair for publicity. Even in the days when Grant's name was at its zenith, Butler's name would somehow gain the top heads of the newspapers and leave to Grant the lower items. For a time he had commanded the city of New Orleans. There he gained too much publicity, even for his taste. The ladies of that city said that he stole their silverware. Their descendents still insist upon it. But any historian will put this down as a newspaper war story —until he makes the acquaintance of Butler. Then he will overlook the spoons as a negligible item among the others. Butler made a requisition upon a New Orleans bank for $80,000 in gold. After the war the bank employed an attorney to bring suit for this money on the ground that Butler had never turned it over to the government. It was an odious stain upon his name, yet Butler did not allow the suit to come into court. He paid the full amount back to the bank out of his pocket, making the jocular remark that his constituents would "think me a fool" for not having stolen ten times that amount.[13]

Later he was transferred to Virginia. Here Grant entrusted to him the important task of capturing Petersburg, but he ran afoul of Pickett's division which, though outnumbered, drove him out of that war zone and locked him up safe from harm. Grant, disgusted, wired

[12] Garfield's notes of 1880; quoted in Smith, *Garfield*, p. 826.

[13] G. F. Hoar, *Autobiography of Seventy Years*, I, p. 343.

to Lincoln: "Pickett has bottled up Butler at Petersburg."[14] Butler, smarting under the sting, wreaked a Butlerian revenge. Pickett's home was within his reach, although far removed from the line of battle. Butler's troops looted it, used it awhile for artillery target practice, then burned what was left of it to the ground.[15]

Having thus served his country in time of war, Butler had now returned to champion her in the era of peace. He had a well formed opinion of the value of military commissions. They were convenient things to have at hand when a conviction was desired of persons whom juries were liable to acquit. To Andrew Johnson he went with his plan for disposing of Jefferson Davis. If Johnson would put him, Butler, at the head of a military commission and turn Davis over to this commission for trial, Butler would guarantee at least one vote for conviction in advance of the trial.[16] Johnson, for peculiar reasons of his own, did not approve of the plan.

Such was the background of the man who now, as special counsel of the United States, came forward as defender of the right of major generals to set aside the Sixth Amendment at their pleasure, and to try civilians by courts martial instead of allowing a "public trial by an impartial jury." A demagogue of Butler's type, however, never creates a storm. He merely rides the waves. And the waves of political passion at the time were rolling high. One Senator and three Congressmen from Indiana had protested against any commutation of Milligan's sentence by the military commission.[17] Congress, at this very moment, was debating whether military control should not be continued—even though a year had now passed since the close of the Civil War.[18] The public mind was inflamed into acute distemper against any restrictions upon popular wrath. "Vengeance is mine, saith the Lord," but the lord of might had been mistaken for the Lord of Hosts. With far better reason could the shade of John Marshall then have uttered the words which his lips had phrased in 1832; "I yield slowly and reluctantly to the conviction that our Constitution cannot last."[19]

One barrier stood between the Bill of Rights and the abyss—the Supreme Court.

The argument in the Milligan case covered the week of March 6 to 13, 1866. Stanbery opened the case for the Government. He argued the question of jurisdiction, claiming that the Supreme Court held no jurisdiction whatever in the case. The pillars of his argument were two. First, that under the original Act of Congress, passed April 29, 1802,

[14] *Grant's Memoirs,* II, p. 75, denies intending any open reproach toward Butler by this telegram.

[15] G. E. Pickett, *Soldier of the South,* p. 105.

[16] *Ben Butler's Book,* p. 915.

[17] Rhodes, *op. cit.,* V, p. 328.

[18] Warren, *op. cit.,* III, p. 147.

[19] A. J. Beveridge, *The Life of John Marshall,* IV, p. 559.

providing for the certification of disagreeing opinions of judges in lower courts, the words "for the purpose of inquiry into the *cause* of commitment" were used. But Milligan had no "cause," he had only a "case." Second, Milligan "having been sentenced to hang on the 19th of May, the presumption is that he was hanged on that day," and so "we are discussing a question relating to the liberty of a dead man."[20]

Speed and Butler argued the question upon its merits. Their arguments rested the case chiefly on Lincoln's proclamation suspending habeas corpus and on the Act of Congress in 1863. Butler disposed of the constitutional amendment prohibiting the trial of civilians by military commissions, by arguing that such enactments "were silent amid arms"—that is, were suspended during time of war.[21] Butler's military and political reputation drew eager attention to his argument, not only by spectators and opposing counsel, but "even by their honors on the bench," but within ten minutes after he began the novelty was gone and interest had collapsed. "The Judges sat quietly back in their chairs, and the monotonous jar of Butler's voice tired the patience of the spectators. . . . The case was too big for him."[22]

In behalf of Milligan, David Dudley Field handled chiefly the question of jurisdiction. Garfield took up the question, "Had the military commission jurisdiction legally to try and sentence" Milligan? He examined the Constitution, the acts of Congress and previous precedents of law.[23]

Black then arose to close the case for the Milligan counsel. He was about to make the greatest argument of his life. Perhaps, as many have claimed, it was "indisputably the most remarkable forensic effort" ever made before the Supreme Court.[24] Certainly living members of that court had never heard its equal, nor ever heard it again. He appeared "like one of King John's angry barons," exclaimed Senator Edgar Cowan, "who had re-appeared upon the earth to punish a violation of the Magna Charta and the Bill of Rights with his mace.[25] For more than two hours he stood before the court, "without a solitary note of reading from a book, and yet he presented an array of law, fact and argument, with such remarkable force and eloquence as startled and bewildered those who listened to him."[26] All of the quibbling that had been carried on over the question of jurisdiction, over Proclamations of the President and Acts of Congress, dwindled, as he spoke, below the margin of sight. They were transient things and petty. He lifted the case to higher ground, made Freedom his client,

[20] 4 Wallace, p. 10.
[21] *Ibid.*, p. 15.
[22] Washington Correspondent, Boston *Post*, Clayton MSS.
[23] 4 Wallace, p. 42.
[24] Levi Maish; quoted in Clayton, p. 131.
[25] Black Papers, April 11, 1884.
[26] Levi Maish; quoted in Clayton, p. 131.

made the great cause of Constitutional Liberty hang by the slender thread of Milligan's life. But let him speak for himself:

"May it please your Honors: I am not afraid that you will underrate the importance of this case. It concerns the rights of the whole people. Such questions have generally been settled by arms. But since the beginning of the world no battle has ever been lost or won upon which the liberties of a nation were so distinctly staked as they are on the result of this argument. The pen that writes the judgment of the court will be mightier for good or evil than any sword that ever was wielded by mortal arm."

"The case before you presents but a single point, and that an exceedingly plain one. . . . My clients were dragged before this strange tribunal, and after a proceeding, which it would be mere mockery to call a trial, they were ordered to be hung. The charge against them was put into writing and is found on this record, but you will not be able to decipher its meaning," for it had no meaning. They were charged "with some offense unknown to the laws" by a military officer who made it a capital offense "by legislation of his own."

With this stripping away of extraneous matter, he exposed the real issue. "Let us come at once to the simple question . . . Had the commissioners jurisdiction—were they invested with legal authority to try" Milligan and put him to death? "We answer, No."

At the beginning he forewarned the court that "I shall necessarily refer to the mere rudiments of constitutional law . . . common topics of history . . . plain rules of justice," and for this he apologized in advance. "I beg your honors to believe that this is not done because I think that the court . . . is less familiar with these things than I am . . . but simply and only because . . . there is absolutely no other way of dealing with it. If the fundamental principles of American liberty are attacked, and we are driven behind the inner walls of the Constitution to defend them, we can repel the assault only with those same old weapons which our ancestors used a hundred years ago. You must not think the worse of our armor because it happens to be old-fashioned and looks a little rusty from long disuse."

He then traced the rise of the jury system—through Tacitus . . . Alfred . . . the Magna Charta, through upheavals in which blood had been spilled in its defense. It was not "an infallible mode" of justice. "Like everything human, it has its imperfections," but it was "the best protection for innocence" yet discovered.

From trial by jury, he turned to trial by military commissions, and here his sentences ring with the clink of steel. There is a martial music in his words. He is fencing to the sound of fifes and drums. "Many times," he said, "the attempt was made to stretch the royal authority far enough to justify military trials; but it never had more than temporary success. Five hundred years ago Edward II closed up a great rebellion by taking the life of its leader, the Earl of Lancaster, after trying him before a military court. Eight years later that same king, together with his lords and commons in Parliament assembled, acknowledged with shame and sorrow that the execution of Lancaster was a mere murder, because the courts were open and he might have had a fair trial. Queen Elizabeth, for sundry reasons affecting the safety of the State, ordered that certain offenders not of her army should be tried according to the law martial. But she heard the storm of popular vengeance rising, and, haughty, imperious, self-willed as she was, she yielded the point. . . . Strafford, as Lord-Lieutenant of Ireland, tried the Viscount Stormont before a military commission. When impeached for it, he pleaded in vain that Ireland was in a state of insurrection, that Stormont was a traitor, and the army would be undone if it could not defend itself without appealing to the civil courts. The Parliament was deaf; the king himself could not save him; he was condemned to suffer death as a traitor and murderer. Charles I issued commissions to divers officers for the trial of his enemies according to the course of military law. If rebellion ever was an excuse for such an act, he could surely have pleaded it; for there was scarcely a spot in his kingdom, from sea to sea, where royal authority was not disputed by somebody. Yet the Parliament demanded their petition of right, and the king was obliged to concede that all of his commissions were illegal."

"The truth is, that no authority exists anywhere in the world for the doctrine of the Attorney-General. No judge or jurist . . . sustains him. . . . Every elementary writer from Coke to Wharton is against him. . . . No book can be found in any library to justify. . . . When I say no book, I mean, of course, no book of acknowledged authority. I do not deny that hireling clergy have often been found to disgrace the pulpit . . . that court sycophants and party hacks have written many pamphlets, and perhaps large volumes. . . . Those butchers' dogs, that feed upon garbage and fatten upon the offal of the shambles, are always ready to bark at whatever interferes with the trade of their master."

From the authority of great writers, he went direct to the Constitution itself—disdaining even to touch, in passing, upon the Acts of Congress and Proclamations of the President evoked by the opposing counsel. From three distinct places in that Charter he lifted exact and specific guarantees of trial by jury to all citizens, except only "in cases arising in the land and naval forces, or in the militia when in actual service in time of war or public danger." To this exception he then gave attention.

"The learned counsel on the other side will not assert that there was war at Indianapolis in 1864, for they have read *Coke's Institute*, and Judge Crier's opinion in the *prize cases*, and of course they know it to be a settled rule that war cannot be said to exist where the civil courts are open. This, therefore, must be their position: That . . . if there was a war anywhere else, to which the United States was a party, the technical effect of such was to take the jurisdiction away from the civil courts and transfer it to the army officers."

At this point, General Butler—seeing the lifeblood being crushed out of his case—attempted to save it. "We do not take that position," he objected. Black shot him a piercing glance, and turning again to the court, broke his lance with these words: "I do not wonder to see them recoil from their own doctrine when it is held up to their eyes. But . . . What else can they say? They will admit that the Constitution is not altogether without meaning. . . . If no war existed they would not deny the exclusive jurisdiction of the civil courts in criminal cases. How, then, did the military get jurisdiction in Indiana? . . . Military jurisdiction comes . . . in Indiana only as the legal result of a war that is going on in Mississippi. . . . The opposing argument, when turned into plain English, means this, and only this: That when the Constitution is attacked upon one side, its official guardians may assail it upon the other; when rebellion strikes it in the face, they may take advantage of the blindness, produced by the blow, to sneak behind it and stab it in the back."

Having thus silenced Butler, Black now turned his attention to Attorney-General Speed. "Ask the Attorney General," he said to the court, "what rules apply to military commissions in the exercise of their authority over civilians. Come Mr. Attorney General, 'gird up thy loins now like a man; I will demand of thee, and thou shalt declare unto me if thou hast understanding.' How is a military commission organized? What shall be the number and rank of its members? What offences come within its jurisdiction? What is the code of its procedure? . . . What is the nature of their punishment? . . . In addition to strangling their victim, may they also deny him the last consolations of religion, and refuse his family the melancholy privilege of giving him a decent grave?"

The Attorney-General had witnessed Butler's retirement. He offered no answer. Turning to the court, Black disposed of him with one merciful thrust. "To none of these questions can the Attorney-General make a reply, for there is no law upon the question. He will not attempt to 'darken counsel by words without knowledge,' and therefore, like Job, he can only lay his hand upon his mouth and keep silence."

Black was now approaching the end to his argument. He had one more coating of obliquity to lay upon military commissions. He had finished with his legal exposition of the subject. He now turned to its broader, moral aspect. "Nero accused Peter and Paul of spreading a 'pestilent superstition' " he said, "which they called the Gospel. He heard their defense in person, and sent them to the cross. . . . Herod saw fit, for good political reasons, closely affecting the permanence of his reign in Judea, to punish certain *possible* traitors in Bethlehem by anticipation. This required the death of all the children in that city under two years of age. He issued his 'general order'; and his provost-marshal carried it out."

But neither to history nor the Bible did Black turn for the crowning illustration of his speech. Out of Shakespeare—his constant companion of literature—he lifted an example already known to every member of the court, and written deep into subconscious impressions. "Macbeth," he said, "understood the whole philosophy of the subject. He was an unlimited monarch. His power to punish for any offense or for no offense at all was as broad as that which the Attorney-General claims for himself. . . . But he was more cautious how he used it. He had a dangerous rival. . . . The necessity to get rid of him was plain enough, but he could not afford to shock the moral sense of the world by pleading political necessity for a murder. He must—

Mask the business from the common eye.

"Accordingly he sent for two enterprising gentlemen, whom he took into his service upon liberal pay—'made love to their assistance'—and got them to deal with the accused party. He acted as his own Judge Advocate. . . . The commission thus organized in Banquo's case sat upon him that very night, at a convenient place beside the road where it was known he would be traveling; and they did precisely what the Attorney-General says the military officers may do in this country—they *took* and *killed* him, because their employer at the head of the government wanted it done, and paid them for doing it out of the public treasury."

At this point a spectator rushed from the room. He was a stranger from Kentucky who had been on his way to hear his Congressman address the House, but missed the way and got into the Supreme Court room. He saw Black's towering figure striding back and forth before the court. He listened while the speaker swept on through Herod, Nero, and Macbeth. He sensed the approaching climax, rushed out of the room, across into the hall of the House of Representatives, past the doorkeeper, down the aisle to the place where his friend stood addressing the House, plucked him by the coat tail, and said in a voice that could be heard a dozen seats away: "Wind her up, Bill! Wind her up, and come over here and listen to old Jerry Black giving 'em hell."[27]

While this little diversion was disrupting proceedings of the House, the speaker over in the Supreme Court room had swept through to the close of his argument. Swiftly now he drew the threads together. Military commissions "will always be organized to convict, and the conviction will follow the accusation as surely as night follows the day.

[27] Clayton, p. 132; Clayton MSS.

. . . Plied on as it may by the arts of a malignant priesthood, and urged on by the madness of a raving crowd, it will be worse than the popish plot, or the French revolution—it will be a combination of both, with Fouquier-Tinville on the bench, and Titus Oakes in the witness's box. . . . You alone can 'deliver us from the body of this death.' To that fearful extent is the destiny of this nation in your hands."[28]

He had finished. "Never," said 'Sunset' Cox, "had the question of personal liberty been so thoroughly discussed, from the time of the Magna Charta down."[29] The fate of trial by jury was now in the hands of the nine men whose opinion, Black had said, "would be mightier for good or for evil than any sword that ever was wielded by mortal arm."

Before reviewing that decision, let us look for a moment at these men who sat upon the Supreme Court. Only three remained who had been members when the Dred Scott decision was rendered—Wayne, Nelson, and Grier. James M. Wayne was the senior member of the court, having been appointed by Jackson in 1835. Next in order were Samuel Nelson, appointed by Tyler in 1845; and Robert C. Grier, appointed by Polk in 1846. With them was one other pre-war judge, Nathan Clifford, appointed by Buchanan in 1858. Taney was dead and Salmon P. Chase now sat as Chief Justice. With him were four other Lincoln appointees—David Davis, Noah Swayne, Samuel F. Miller, and Stephen J. Field.[30] The Lincoln appointments, therefore, were in the majority. The Supreme Court for five years had been wholly free from the partisan attacks so constant during the decade before the Civil War. But the era of judicial calm was drawing to its close.

In the remarkably short space of three weeks, upon April 3, 1866, that court rendered its decision. The decision declared that Milligan and his associates had been illegally tried and convicted. They were ordered, therefore, to be discharged. The court did not, at this time, deliver its full opinion upon the subject, but made merely an announcement of its judgment. The full opinion, setting forth its reasoning, was reserved until the fall term of court.

The President and the Radical Reconstructionists at once caught the sweeping significance of the decision,[31] but the press and the public missed it until the formal opinion was released to the press upon December 17, 1866.[32] In brief, that opinion consisted of two judgments. Unanimously the Supreme Court held that all military commissions authorized by the President to try civilians in areas where civil courts were open were illegal. A majority of the court went even further.

[28] The full copy of this speech appears in practically every collection of forensic speeches since that date. It appears in C. F. Black, p. 510.

[29] S. S. Cox, *Three Decades of Federal Legislation*, p. 280. Cox was a Congressman from Ohio.

[30] 4 Wallace, preface.

[31] *Welles's Diary*, April 6, 1866.

[32] *National Intelligencer*, December 18, 1866.

They took the occasion to state that neither the President nor Congress possessed the power ever to legalize military commissions, except in the actual theatre of war, where civil courts were not open. This, of course, had been Black's whole case. Milligan, as a man, was a mere incident. But as a cause, he represented a *Petition of Right* in the nineteenth century. He was an instrument to be used for the restoration of the Constitution; and the Supreme Court had gone the whole way in sustaining Black's view. Its decision also was remarkable in another way. It was written for the court by Lincoln's old personal friend, David Davis—once the judge of that famous circuit in Illinois.[33]

In effect, the decision meant that, in the North at least, the reign of military law was over. The Constitution was restored.

So long has this famous decision been recognized as a bulwark of liberty, a landmark in jurisprudence, that it is difficult in this day to understand the bitterness of the abuse, the intensity of the wrath, which it brought down upon the Supreme Court. Not even the Dred Scott decision itself was more violently assailed. One can understand the abuse only by keeping in mind that the after-effects of war hysteria still prevailed. National nerves were still shaky.

Wendell Phillips became so excited that he proposed the abolition of the court, out of hand, for "the nation must be saved," he exclaimed, "no matter what or how venerable the foe whose existence goes down before that necessity."[34]

Thaddeus Stevens, speaking solemnly and deliberately upon the floor of Congress, said "That decision, although in terms perhaps not as infamous as the Dred Scott decision, is yet far more dangerous in its operation."[35]

The *Independent*—always political beneath its religious veneer—gave vent to feelings spread into more than a column and a half. "We . . . regard it as the most dangerous opinion ever pronounced by that tribunal," this organ said. "It unheaves the foundations of a large share of the war legislation of three congresses. . . . It nullifies innumerable military orders."[36]

Harper's Weekly raged that "like the Dred Scott decision, it is not a judicial opinion—it is a political act," and it proposed—as a legal, constitutional remedy—to "swamp" the court by padding it with judges enough to outvote those already members.[37]

Even the then conservative *Nation*—which carried by all odds the most thorough and temperate discussion of any national periodical—lent its weight to the criticism. It agreed with the court that Milligan

[33] 4 Wallace, p. 107.
[34] A. B. Hart, *Life of Salmon Portland Chase*, p. 346.
[35] *Congressional Globe*, January 3, 1867, p. 251.
[36] The *Independent*, January 10, 1867.
[37] *Harper's Weekly*, January 19, 1867.

should have been freed, but it deplored the "discussions of political questions not necessarily involved."[38]

Among the newspapers, the New York *Times* recognized "an old foe with a new face,"[39] while John W. Forney's Washington *Chronicle*—now a semi-official Republican organ—asserted that the decision could not "fail to shock the sensibilities and provoke the severe rebuke of loyal men everywhere."[40]

There were, of course, those who dared to defend the decision. Leading among these was the Washington *National Intelligencer*, which again and again carried bold arguments in its defense. Its competitor, Forney's *Chronicle*, called this "The exaltation of the rebel *Intelligencer*," but undaunted, that organ opened its editorials of the new year with a whole column of praise for the Supreme Court.[41] But views like this were in the minority. War upon the Supreme Court had begun anew.

[38] The *Nation*, January 10, 1867.

[39] New York *Times*, January 3, 1867.

[40] Washington *Chronicle*, December 19, 1866.

[41] Washington *National Intelligencer*, Jan. 1, 1867. See also Dec. 20, 25, 27, 28, 31, 1866 and Jan. 3, 11, 15, 17, 1867 for other editorial defences.

21

CONFEDERATE PRISONERS

FOLLOWING the assassination of Lincoln, wild rumors arose that the plot had been instigated by the Confederate leaders. Who would dare to defend Jefferson Davis and his fellow Confederates upon such a charge? It was not a popular cause. Three days after Davis was settled in prison, George W. Woodward wrote to Black, "I think you ought to take a hand in the defense."[1] Charles O'Conor, the brilliant Irishman from New York, addressed Black ten days later. Already he had written Davis in jail and offered his services. "I think you ought to have tendered your services," he added. "You are infinitely better able to sustain the argument than I am; and, even now you ought to volunteer."[2]

Jacob Thompson, in Halifax escaping to England, also urged Black to join in Davis's defense. "Fix your fee for services at whatever standard you may think is right, and I will see that it is paid," he said. "But you must appear in this trial." As for himself, Thompson added "I am proscribed. I have no home or country." He denied as wholly absurd the charge, and the $25,000 reward, for his capture as a conspirator to Lincoln's assassination. He did not, however, yet know that his bitter enemy, Joseph Holt, was the instigator of the reward.[3]

Black offered his services, without charge, for the defense of Davis and Clay. To Mrs. Clay he wrote that "I hasten to assure you that I will do all that in me lies to secure justice in Mr. Clay's case. I have written to the President, Secretary of War, and Mr. Davis."[4] Through the summer of 1865, Black and O'Conor were in long and serious correspondence upon the mode of defense. The ex-Confederates were confined to prison, yet no charges were preferred against them, nor could it be ascertained whether they would be granted a trial in civil courts or whether they were to be sent before a military commission.

Finally in November, Mrs. Clay, the famous and beautiful wife of the imprisoned ex-Confederate, came to Washington. Here she met Black in person for the first time. He proved "a bulwark of sympathy that thereafter never failed." In passing, she left her impressions of Black at this first meeting. They are worthy of record. "He was a

[1] Black Papers, May 28, 1865.
[2] Black Papers, June 7, 1865.
[3] Black Papers, July 6, 1865.
[4] Mrs. C. C. Clay, *A Belle of the Fifties*, p. 292.

peculiar man in appearance," she said, "with shaggy brows, deep-set eyes, and cavernous mouth, out of which invincible arguments rolled that made men listen. This feature was large when he spoke, but when he laughed the top of his head fell back like a box cover, and looked as if it must drop over the other way."[5]

He took general charge of her activities, "gave his time and advice unstintedly." Mrs. Clay executed the details as only a skillful and lovely woman could. From Johnson, to Stanton, to Holt, to Grant, she appealed by turns. As Black had forwarned her, Johnson pushed the responsibility upon Stanton, and Stanton gave her encouraging assurances—but no action. Holt, although he once was a personal friend of hers, refused even to see her. Grant acted every inch the soldier. Not yet had his ear been poisoned by the venom of Radicals. "If it were in my power, Mrs. Clay, I would tomorrow open every prison in the length and breadth of the land. I would release every prisoner unless —(after a pause) unless Mr. Davis might be detained awhile to satisfy public clamour." And he wrote to Johnson in her behalf.[6]

In the end Johnson yielded, and Clay was freed, in April of 1866. At the news, Black at once wrote to Mrs. Clay.

> Tell your great and good husband I could do nothing for him, because his magnificent wife left nobody else a chance to serve him! I would have been proud to have some share in his defense, but circumstances have denied me the honour. I rejoice none the less in his happy deliverance. . . . Your note of yesterday evening literally took my breath away. After you had done so much for yourself and I had done so little, nay, less than nothing, you address me as if I had been your benefactor merely because I rejoiced in your success.[7]

Davis languished in jail for another year. In all probability he would have been tried, but every charge against him and every proposed method of trial in a civil court that the government could suggest was rejected by the best legal minds of the country either as unconstitutional, or impossible of conviction. Meanwhile he was being held in denial of the right of habeas corpus. For a time his legs had been riveted in heavy irons. His health was slowly ebbing, and the army physician in charge gave warning that if he was kept in close confinement death was certain. Stories of his harsh treatment crept out, and the collapse of the charge of conspiring to assassinate Lincoln caused a reaction in his favor among leaders at the North.[8] His death in jail would embarrass the government.

At least he was granted bail. The amount was fixed at $100,000 —a high figure and worthy of a rebel ex-President. But the bail was

[5] *Ibid.*, p. 310.
[6] *Ibid.*, pp. 300-316.
[7] *Ibid.*, p. 376.
[8] See New York *Tribune*, June 17, 1866.

easily arranged. With a magnificent gesture that quixotic old abolitionist, Horace Greeley, came forward and signed his name at the head of the sureties. Davis was released from jail in May of 1867 after two years of confinement.[9]

To Black came also numerous appeals to secure reimbursement for property stolen or confiscated by Federal armies during the war. Myra Clark Gaines of New Orleans engaged him to present her claim for several hundred thousand dollars worth of property destroyed.[10] A Mrs. Pugh urged him to look after her claim for 160,000 cords of wood, which had been burned by General Thomas on Paw Paw Island, just below Vicksburg.[11]

Jacob Thompson, still proscribed and without a home, wrote to Black telling of the confiscation of 199 bales of cotton belonging to his wife, of "61 mules, 10 horses, 133 sheep, 264 or more fatted hogs, 80 head of cattle, more than 50,000 bushels of corn, leaving out of account the burning of my homestead which was worth $40,000 and my residence on my plantation and my smoke-house containing about 16,000 pounds of bacon,"—all belonging to himself. "My mother-in-law is now with me," he continued. "When the Federal Army came to Oxford, Mississippi, she lived alone on her plantation with her negroes. By an order of an officer, or pretended officer, her house was literally stripped of all her furniture worth $8,000 to $10,000. She was robbed of $1,600, a portion of it in gold. At least 5,000 bushels of corn was taken and hauled away. . . . She was then about 65 years old and could have been accused of no disloyalty. Her only crime, as alleged at the time, was that she had more than was necessary for her." The proof of all of this could be made clear and easy. Could any indemnity be obtained?[12]

But war indemnities were hard to collect. Upon the Gaines claim Black secured a settlement.[13] On the other claims apparently no indemnity was ever secured.

[9] Mrs. V. H. Davis, *Jefferson Davis,* II, pp. 772-788.

[10] Black Papers, November 20, 1875.

[11] Black Papers, 1874.

[12] Black Papers, July 24, 1868.

[13] *Sen. Report,* p. 641, 44 Cong., 1st Sess; also Gaines Note in the Black estate, 1883, York Co. Court House.

22

STEAMROLLING THE CONSTITUTION

FROM the beginning of Reconstruction to the end, Black played a singular and dynamic role. He drafted the message of the President for the veto of the Reconstruction Bill. He drafted the third annual message of the President to Congress attacking its operation. He assaulted it repeatedly in the courts. In the closing act of this tragic period, the curtain fell with the ringing words of his philippic before the Electoral Commission of 1876 still resounding in the press. Therefore, to understand the significance of Black's relations to these events, we must turn our attention for the moment to this Reconstruction policy, as it was formulated and developed by the Radical Congress of 1867.

When the State of Tennessee seceded from the Union in 1861, and Andrew Johnson elected to remain in the United States Senate, a Senator without a State, his presence was gladly welcomed in that body. The Civil War was fought to prove that no State had seceded—or ever could secede from the Union. Johnson, therefore, still was representing the State of Tennessee. In 1864, when the Republican party coveted the votes of loyal Democrats to remain in power, they added the name of Andrew Johnson to their ticket. The fact that Johnson's native State of Tennessee claimed to have dissolved its ties with the Union offered no embarrassment whatever to putting him on the ticket. Tennessee was still in the Union, could not get out, and a native of Tennessee was still a citizen of the United States. Greeley hailed this choice of a Vice President as a happy omen. "His nomination is a pledge to the Unionists of the seceded states," he said, "that they at least are not deemed outcasts from the pale of our nationality . . . that their long suffering devotion to the national cause is appreciated and will not be forgotten."[1]

Then came the election. Most Southern states, of course, cast no vote. But in two of these states—Louisiana and Tennessee—the Union element under Lincoln's "Restored Governments" cast their vote for President and sent the returns to Congress. The war was fought to prove that Louisiana and Tennessee were still in the Union, and under the Twelfth Amendment to the Constitution the vote of every State must be counted. Yet after the election was over and the Radicals in Congress saw that the votes of these two states were not needed to

[1] New York *Tribune*, June 9, 1864.

retain them in power, that body solemnly resolved that the electoral votes of these states which "rebelled" should not be counted.[2] "It is difficult to see," comments John W. Burgess, a leading authority upon Reconstruction and the Constitution, "how the Republicans could have consistently rejected the vote of Tennessee after having nominated and elected a citizen of Tennessee as Vice President of the United States."[3] "Why was it difficult?" retorted a biographer of Johnson. "There was only the Constitution in the way, and what was that?"[4]

This Act of Congress stands out as one of the extreme significance. It marks the setting of the Reconstruction policy of the Radicals.

It also ended the reign of the Constitution during Reconstruction. Henceforth it was Thaddeus Stevens, not the Constitution, to whom Congress paid homage. Before Stevens we must pause for a moment. To understand him is to understand the whole dementia of the Radical Congress. He was a Congressman from Pennsylvania and a resident of Buchanan's home city of Lancaster. Earlier in life he had acquired a fanatical obsession against the Masonic order and had dedicated himself in a crusade to outlaw it from America.[5] later this obsession was transferred to slavery, and the venom in his nature turned greener with age. He was now seventy-four. He had a club foot and a head as bald as ivory. The latter was covered with a massive brown wig, but Stevens was not averse to removing it and to displaying a gleaming head coupled with a sardonic grin. James G. Blaine said of him that he had the reputation of being "somewhat unscrupulous as to his political methods, somewhat careless in his personal conduct, somewhat lax in personal morals."[6] All of this—and more—was written in his face. His skin was a drawn parchment, bluish white. The gall of bitterness that saturated his life had twisted his features into cruel lines. Malice is written into every seam. The effect was intensified by the thick, protruding underlip.

He believed in the absolute equality of the negro race. Unlike many others who professed to this creed, Stevens practised it, for he was a realist to the core. He was never married, yet for many years he lived with a mulatto woman. Nominally, she was his housekeeper. Actually, it appeared to visitors to his home that she was more than a housekeeper. A newspaper of his home city commented: "Nobody doubts that Thaddeus Stevens has always been in favor of negro equality and here, where his domestic arrangements are so well known, his practical recognition of his pet theory is perfectly well under-

[2] *Cong. Globe*, 38 Congress, 2nd Sess., p. 618. The resolution was passed on February 6, 1865.

[3] J. W. Burgess, *Reconstruction and the Constitution*, p. 23.

[4] P. L. Stryker, *Andrew Johnson*, p. 162.

[5] J. A. Woodburn, *Life of Thaddeus Stevens*, pp. 13-27.

[6] Blaine, *Twenty Years*, I, p. 325.

stood." This was a plain inference, but the editor of this paper did not stop with inferences, however plain. He labeled a spade by its name. Referring to this mulatto housekeeper, he said, "Even by his own party friends she is constantly spoken of as Mrs. Stevens, though we fancy that no rite of Mother Church ever gave her a right to it."[7]

The charge was broadcast over the nation. It was repeated at various times. Either the accusation was true, or it was the most glaring of libels. Stevens, in his earlier life, had prosecuted a newspaper for a libel against him, and convicted the editor. But against this charge he offered no defense, either in behalf of his own character or to protect the name of a woman whose reputation, in his philosophy of life, could not be less important because she was black. They continued to live under the same roof. She was at his bedside at his death. She was left a life annuity in his will.[8]

He ruled the House with an iron hand. Many of his colleagues hated him. Most of them feared him. His power, like his visage, was sinister. Among the Radical Republicans at first he found a few members who felt slight twinges at trampling upon the Constitution. But Stevens made short work of them. "Who pleads the Constitution?" he sneered.[9] In the end no Radical in the House dared to plead it. At least one of his followers discovered a conscience which disturbed him at times. "Conscience indeed," jeered Stevens. "Throw conscience to the devil and stand by your party."[10]

It was a characteristic statement. For Stevens was bitter, venomous, sinister, and ruthless—but he was not underhanded. He played his cards above the table. He believed that the voting majority of the American public could be reached by an open appeal to base motives. We shall see presently that he was not mistaken. The purists of his party might gloss his scheme in colors of charity and justice—but Stevens, at least, pitched his appeal at its true level, mean and base, but impelling.

On December 18, 1865, he addressed the House, or rather through the House he addressed the Republicans of the nation. Unto the top of an exceeding high mountain he took them, and showed them all of the rewards of the flesh and the lust of it—if they would follow him and grant to the millions of densely ignorant negroes the right of suffrage. What were these rewards of the flesh? None less than to "secure perpetual ascendency" to the Republican party. Give the illiterate negro the ballot—and the Carpetbaggers in the South would do the rest. "Aided by the blacks," they would "divide the representation" of the Southern white vote and "thus continue the Republican ascendency."

[7] *Lancaster Intelligencer*, July 6, 1867.
[8] Woodburn, *op. cit.*, p. 588.
[9] E. B. Callender, *Thaddeus Stevens*, p. 111.
[10] *Lancaster Intelligencer*, Jan. 17, 1866 (quoted from Philadelphia *Ledger*).

This master politician played also upon the political fears of this party. Refuse to give the negro the ballot, then what? A most horrible calamity would follow. The Democratic party would at once control the South. At the next national election Democrats from the North and South would unite and again control the nation.[11] This, of course, was unthinkable.

Black once said of Stevens, "his mind, so far as any sense of obligation to his God was concerned, was a howling wilderness."[12] But however devoid Stevens might be of obligations or personal morals, he was not deceitful. Nor was he mistaken in his judgment of the public mind. His mingled play upon avarice and fear became a leaven to ferment in the public mind.

What of the public mind to which the abolitionists were appealing? A great war had just ended. Like all wars, it had been fought in the minds of the people and was still being fought after the guns were silent upon the field of battle. Dreams and delusions may afflict a million people as well as one. Obsessions of paranoia may haunt a nation as well as an individual. In normal times, the gnawing desires of the savage within us are suppressed and we assume the veneer of civilization. But the hysteria of war strips this veneer of restraint from human behavior, and leaves in command the raw urges of the wild. A crowd or a nation so afflicted mistakes its delusions and its passions for the Voice of God. It forsakes reason—for reason is the hard-earned product of civilization. It deserts its great leaders, its Mirabeaus and its Lincolns, and descends to its Robespierres, its Wendell Phillipses, its Thaddeus Stevenses.

Only one result was possible. The Radical wing of the Republican party—dominated by the abolitionists—was swept into complete control of both Houses of Congress by the election of 1866. The figure of Stevens now cast its sinister and elongated shadow across the history of the nation. In swift succession two Acts of Congress laid prostrate the Southern States. The first Act of March 2, 1867, abolished all governments in the South and converted these States into "military districts" to be ruled by generals of the army. These generals were given the option of allowing "local civil tribunals" to handle judicial affairs, or of suppressing all courts and instituting trial by military commissions. Martial law was to remain in the South until new civil governments were organized. These reconstructed governments must disfranchise the Confederate leaders, they must give full suffrage to the negroes, they must ratify the Fourteenth Amendment—which was not yet a part of the Constitution—and finally they must submit their State constitutions to Congress "for examination and approval."[13]

[11] *Cong. Globe,* 39 Cong., 1st sess., p. 74.
[12] Hensel, p. 196.
[13] *Statutes at Large,* XIV, p. 428.

The second Act was passed three weeks later, on March 23. It provided for the details of carrying the former law into effect.[14] "There was hardly a line in the entire bill," exclaimed Burgess in writing of the first Act, "which would stand the test of the Constitution.[15] In defiance of the Constitution and of the Supreme Court interpretation of that document in the Milligan decision, this bill suspended habeas corpus in eleven States of the Union, and instituted martial law. More sinister, if possible, was its demand that these "reconstructed" States must ratify the Fourteenth Amendment before being restored to statehood. This Amendment was not a part of the Constitution, and each State had a right to cast its vote upon it in the light of its own free will. But here the will of Congress—rather of the abolitionists—was made fiat. They had determined to change the Constitution, and they demanded the right to cast the vote of eleven States, as part price of relieving those States from the unconstitutional yoke of subjection. "Stevens's Reconstruction Acts . . ." exclaimed Rhodes, "were an attack upon civilization."[16]

Both of these Acts were vetoed by Andrew Johnson. In writing of these vetoes, Burgess comments that they are "masterpieces of political logic, constitutional interpretation, and official style." So impressed is he by these splendid qualities that he added, "If not written by Mr. Seward, they must have been edited and revised by him."

Burgess was correct in his surmise that Johnson had not drafted the text of the vetoes. But he was mistaken in the man who did. It was not Seward, but Jeremiah Black, whom Johnson called upon for the task.[17]

The political views of these two men, Black and Johnson, had much in common. During the crisis of Secession in 1861 their opinions, as Black stated it, "happened to coincide . . . exactly. . . . We had some little conversation at that time, and probably took some little fancy for one another, in consequence of our agreement of opinion."[18]

After the war broke out, the two men saw little of each other, for Johnson was in Tennessee serving as military governor. When Johnson became President, Black did not approach him for three or four months, until at last a mutual friend induced him to believe that Johnson would be glad to renew their acquaintance.[19] But from that time until the impeachment of Johnson, the two men were in close harmony and consultation upon affairs of Reconstruction.

[14] *Statutes at Large,* XV, p. 2.

[15] Burgess, *op. cit.,* p. 113.

[16] Rhodes, *op. cit.,* VI, p. 35.

[17] *Welles's Diary,* Feb. 27 and March 1, 1867. The original Black draft is now among the Johnson Papers, Library of Congress.

[18] Testimony before House Judiciary Com., *Rep.* 7, 40 Cong., 1st Sess., p. 273.

[19] *Ibid.*

After the Radicals had captured control of the Fortieth Congress, Black wrote to Johnson: "I am perfectly sure that the public mind of the Nation has not yet gotten possession of the facts or the principles upon which your controversy with Congress depends. . . . I have thought it over somewhat carefully; and I am convinced that you ought to make a solemn appeal to the constituent body which is the ultimate arbiter between you and your adversaries. . . . It will put your whole case on record at once and if properly made up it will be unanswerable." Black was not without experience in pamphleteering, and he urged Johnson to make a "written address to the people of the United States." He went further. He offered his assistance in preparing such an address, on condition that Johnson would treat it as a "confidential secret—not to be known even to the members of your Cabinet."[20]

This would have been an ideal pairing in a joint cause. Johnson's name would have given to the document all of the prestige of the nation's Chief Executive. Black's knowledge of constitutional law and his literary skill would have laid Johnson's case before the public, buttressed by legal defenses and phrased in language to command popular attention. But the "solemn appeal" was never made in the form proposed by Black, for already the Reconstruction Bill was pending in Congress and within a month it was laid before Johnson for action. Of course he would veto it, and of course Congress would pass it over his veto, but the "preparation of the veto," said Dunning, "would afford an admirable field for Black's constitutional learning and literary gifts," and a fitting medium for the solemn appeal over Congress to the people.[21]

Black, therefore, prepared the veto message of March 2 for Johnson. A comparison of the original Black manuscript, now among the Johnson Papers, with the message sent in shows that Johnson incorporated three-fourths of Black's draft without any change whatever.

But Black's part in the affair was not kept secret. His unique style of writing was too distinctive to remain unrecognized by those who knew it, especially when appearing above the signature of Johnson. Throughout the message were strewn the trade-marks. There were his proud words and phrases—"genius of the American people," "the unspeakable blessings of local self government"; and that most frequent of all phrases he ever used, taken from Jefferson: "the sheet anchor of our safety abroad and our people at home."[22]

There also were his favorite weapons of the anvil and hammer, mercilessly pounding the legal life out of this misshapen law cast in

[20] Johnson Papers, January 22, 1867.

[21] W. A. Dunning, "More Light on Andrew Johnson," *Am. Hist. Rev.*, XI, 1906, p. 585.

[22] J. D. Richardson, *Messages and Papers of the Presidents*, VI, p. 508.

the image of Stevens. In denouncing its unconstitutionality, he adduced the historical reasoning that so often marked his discourses: "The Parliament of England, exercising the omnipotent power which it claimed, was accustomed to pass bills of attainder. . . . The fathers of our country determined that no such should occur here. They withheld the power from Congress and this forbade its exercise by that body, and they provided in the Constitution that no State should pass any bill of attainder. . . . Nevertheless, here is a bill of attainder against 9,000,000 at once. It is based upon an accusation so vague as to be scarcely intelligible and found to be true upon no credible evidence. Not one of the 9,000,000 was heard in his own defense."[23] In that passage, one hears again Black's Milligan argument.

Within ten days Congress had scented Black's hand upon the veto message and used the knowledge to torment him, and if possible, to discredit Johnson as its signer. Exactly who made the discovery is not known, but John W. Forney, Black's erstwhile political friend, now lackey for the Radicals as Secretary of the Senate, offers the most plausible source of recognition. At any rate the Judiciary Committee of the House, already "inquiring into the official conduct of Andrew Johnson" for impeachment thunder, haled Black before it for questioning. Let us have the story from his own account. To Johnson he wrote. "Those low down devils on the Judiciary Committee summoned me up and notwithstanding my protest compelled me to testify concerning the last veto. I mentioned to Mr. Stanbery what I felt obliged to reveal. I told him too beforehand what I would have to say and he agreed with me that there was no escape."[24] Black indeed spent a most uncomfortable half-hour before this Committee. When asked point-blank if he had prepared or had any part in the preparation of the veto message, he objected to answering. "You have the power to compel an answer under penalties which I cannot resist," he argued. "If, therefore, you insist . . . I suppose I am bound to answer but I submit to the Committee that you ought not to press that question." The Committee, after consultation, determined to require him to answer it.

But Black refused to go beyond the legal limit of the law. "If the question relates to this paper as a whole, then I answer 'no,' " although he admitted that some portions of the paper were "suggested by me."

The Committee, however, persisted. They produced a printed copy of the veto message, demanding to know what parts were prepared by him. This Black refused to answer, except in a general way, claiming that he had had no *carte blanche* to write the veto message, that his opinions and the President's "perfectly agreed" in so many points

[23] *Ibid.*, p. 507.

[24] Johnson Papers, no date but annotated "[Mar. 23, 1867] (Sic.)."

that he could not risk testimony upon parts which expressed his views, but which the President might have drafted in its exact wording.

The Committee then resorted to other tactics. "Can you," they inquired, "point out any parts of the message which did not originate with you?" "Yes," said Black at once, "here is a paragraph which did not originate with me, and yet it is expressed in exactly my language."

Upon the whole, however, the published report is entertaining reading. Black not only made the best of his situation, but delivered a few telling side-blows in return. "If I had written the message" (i.e., in full) he shot, when this question was put, "it would have been a much more objectionable document to the majority in Congress than it is." Again, when they laid before him a copy of the veto message, he pointed to the paragraph on trial by jury. "That one is partly mine. I have a weakness for that portion of the Constitution. I never did . . . speak of a violation of" it "without a certain amount of boiling and indignation."[25]

Not only did the Committee learn the utmost minimum of information from him, but upon the very day he appeared before them—March 14th—"the unterrified and indefatigable victim," as Dunning put it, was engaged in drawing up plans for the veto of the second Reconstruction Bill. This he sent to Johnson with the letter, quoted above, describing "the low down devils" who had compelled him to testify. As to his draft of his veto on the second Bill, he added: "I have drawn up a paper which I submit. It is transcribed by a perfectly confidential person—a member of my own family."[26]

Less of this draft, however, was used by Johnson than of the former one, although he relied upon parts of it in his final message.[27] Possibly Johnson was wary for the moment of further Committee investigations.

Nevertheless he continued to consult often and earnestly with Black. "Jere Black is spending much time with the President of late . . ." complained Welles, the chronicler of Johnson's Cabinet, a few months later. "He has legal ability and is a politician of more than ordinary power, but I distrust that class of politicians who really promoted rebellion when they declared themselves paralyzed and unable to coerce a State."[28] Welles, however, struggled to be just, even to an outsider usurping what he felt to be his own rightful place. Although regretting that Black "is so much consulted and deferred to," he admitted that Black nevertheless had "a good deal of sagacity and shrewdness."[29]

Others, however, were less temperate in their judgment of relations between Black and Johnson. Radical newspapers complained of men

[25] *House Com. Rep.* 7, 40 Cong., 1st Sess., pp. 271-273.
[26] Johnson Papers, annotated, "[Mar. 23, 1867] (Sic.)."
[27] Dunning, *Am. Hist. Rev.*, XI, 1906, p. 587.
[28] *Welles's Diary*, September 20, 1867.
[29] *Ibid.*

who were "poisoning the ear of the President with their fatal advice," and that "Jeremiah Black, the evil genius of Buchanan's government, is even now weaving his snares at the White House and urging its occupant on to violent courses."[30]

Johnson was impervious to these criticisms and, as the time approached for the next annual message, he again called upon Black to draft the message. From York, Black answered him: "I have received a notice which requires my presence at Pittsburg and I *must* go there before I return to Washington. In the mean time I am doing all that I ought to and you will not be disappointed in any expectations you have formed. I will do all that I said and do it in good time."[31] Black kept his promise and furnished Johnson with a proposed draft of the message. Black's manuscript corresponds with great exactness to the first half and more of the message which Johnson sent to Congress upon December 3rd. That is, Black formulated the message down to that part of the document which was sent in by the various departments.[32]

How different in rhythm and language was the third annual message of Johnson from his first one. That one had been drafted by George Bancroft, the historian, and in it one reads such liquid sentences as the following: (pertaining to Washington's first Inaugural Address) "More than seventy-six years have glided away since these words were spoken; and the United States have passed through severer trials than were foreseen . . . and now . . . with our Union purified by sorrows and strengthened by conflict . . ."[33] That was Bancroft.

Now hear Black, laying heavy blows upon the Reconstruction Acts: "It binds them hand and foot in absolute slavery. . . . It tramples down those rights in which the essence of liberty consists. . . . It denies habeas corpus and the trial by jury. Personal freedom, property, and life, if assailed by the passion, the prejudice, or the rapacity of the ruler, have no security whatever. It has the effect of a bill of attainder . . . upon whole masses, including the millions who inhabit the subject states, and even their unborn children."[34] When read aloud, the two passages compare much after the manner of a concerto of Mendelssohn with the anvil chorus from *Il Trovatore.*

So it sounded to the ears of others. John W. Forney was still Secretary of the Senate. Two days after the message was read to Congress, one of Forney's newspapers, the Philadelphia *Daily Chronicle,* pub-

[30] E. C. Wilson to Black, Black Papers, Sept. 9, 1867, enclosed this clipping from a Meadville paper stating that it was typical of many he had seen.

[31] Johnson Papers, October 22, 1867.

[32] Dunning, *op. cit.,* p. 587.

[33] Richardson, *op. cit.,* VI, p. 353. Stryker claims that Bancroft did not draft this message for Johnson. Unfortunately for his claim, the original draft in Bancroft's own hand is still in the Library of Congress.

[34] *Ibid.,* p. 563.

lished a letter from its "Washington correspondent" accusing Black of having written the message. "With some of the style of that eminent dialectician," said this correspondent, "I have had little difficulty in tracing alike his venom and his logic in the argument which Andrew Johnson has adopted as his own."[35]

The Judiciary Committee of Congress, however, already had amassed 1200 pages of "evidence" against Johnson. It did not again summon Black to answer for his handiwork in the message.

Although rumors throughout this period were persistent that Seward would soon resign from Johnson's Cabinet,[36] Seward remained to the last day of the term. F. A. Burr, a political writer whose career led to an intimate acquaintance with many public men, stated that he had it upon private and high authority that Seward's reason for not resigning was that he learned that Johnson intended to put Black in his place.[37]

But Black would have ill fitted the Cabinet, for cabinets and presidents, like the Constitution, had small place in the new order of things. It was the day of Congress, of the abolitionist wing of Congress, of major generals and military commissions.

[35] Philadelphia *Daily Chronicle*, Dec. 5, 1867, quoted in Dunning, *op. cit.*, p. 587.

[36] Cf. *Welles's Diary*, Aug. 26, and Sept. 20, 1867.

[37] F. A. Burr, Philadelphia *Press*, August 20, 1883.

23

EX PARTE McCARDLE

THE Milligan case had ended military rule in the North. Black attempted, in the McCardle case, to end it in the South. Two previous efforts had been made to bring the Reconstruction Acts before the Supreme Court for review. One endeavored to enjoin the President from enforcing them on the grounds that they were unconstitutional,[1] but the Supreme Court held that it had no jurisdiction to enjoin the President in his performance of official duties. The second attempted to restrain Grant and Stanton, as General of the Army and Secretary of War, from executing the provisions of the acts,[2] but again the Supreme Court refused the injunction, stating that since only political rights and not property or personal rights were involved, it had no jurisdiction. Such a doctrine was by no means new, yet Democrats throughout the country felt that the court was evading its plain duty. "What is to become of the Supreme Court . . .?" wrote Buchanan, now an old man of seventy-six, from his home at Wheatlands. "I cannot help thinking we have fallen on evil times."[3]

Black had taken no hand in either of these cases. One cannot help but wish that he had. Courts are more sensitive to argument than are legislative bodies or the general public. Even John Marshall once reversed a decision of the Supreme Court and apologized for the previous error by explaining that in the former case it had not been "argued by counsel"—a factor which he deemed of exceeding importance in rendering final judgment. Washburn, in his *Judicial History of Massachusetts*, when treating of trials for witchcraft in that state, presses the point that such abuses could not have occurred had there been an enlightened bar whose services could have been enlisted in favor of the accused.[4]

Black had made the cause of liberty hang by so slender a thread as Milligan's life. He literally had startled all who heard that argument by his arraignment of the mailed fist of military despotism.[5] Had he argued here in behalf of nine million people, instead of one, the Supreme Court must certainly have been moved again by his relent-

[1] *Mississippi* vs. *Johnson*, 4 Wallace, p. 475.

[2] *Georgia* vs. *Stanton*, 6 Wallace, p. 50.

[3] *Buchanan's Works*, XI, p. 446.

[4] See *Cong. Rec.* 44 Cong., 1st Sess., part 7, p. 320.

[5] Levi Maish, quoted in Clayton, p. 131.

less logic, by his welding the rude Latin of Magna Carta to the institutional liberties of his own day, by his anvil chorus upon the motives of self-preservation. Perhaps they would again have seen the issue as he viewed it. Certainly they would have been given a greater occasion to pause before delivering judgment. This is not mere idle speculation. The faithful Welles, who certainly was not a friend of Black, chronicled indirectly the same reaction. Before the decision of the Supreme Court had been announced, he set down in his diary his fears of the outcome. Of Charles O'Conor, who argued the appeal for the injunction against Stanton, Welles wrote that he was "evidently more of a lawyer than a statesman, studies law more than Constitution, cases more than government principles. Nothing will be got from the Court, I apprehend. . . . Why O'Conor and his associates make no use of the recent decision of the Court in Milligan's case, I don't understand. Congress under color of law cannot invest brigadiers with power to abolish jury trial or to suspend the privilege of habeas corpus in time of peace."[6]

O'Conor was a lawyer of unquestioned brilliancy, and in some phases of the law he may have had no equal at the American bar. But neither he nor any other living man was the peer of Black in the power of historical argument—the power to make the struggle for human rights since the day of the Magna Carta live again in the present; to reveal liberty as a heritage won at terrific costs upon bloody fields, as a trust delivered unto his generation, and to be transmitted to posterity whatever the price. It was precisely upon the point that no personal or property rights were involved, but only political rights, that the Supreme Court reasoned it had no jurisdiction in the case.[7]

Black was soon to have his day in court, however. It came in a manner which startled the Radicals. Major General O. E. C. Ord, commander of the "military district" of Mississippi and Arkansas, became unduly offended by the exercise of free press by one William H. McCardle, editor of the Vicksburg *Times*. Ord proceeded to exercise his new power. A squad of soldiers filed into McCardle's newspaper office on November 13, 1867, arrested him, and took him to military prison. A military commission tried and convicted him.[8] The charges, likes those against Milligan, were vague, but they filled much space in print, alluding to "libellous and incendiary articles," and concluded by citing him for the high crime of "impeding Reconstruction."[9]

The unterrified McCardle, however, appealed to the United States Circuit Court for a writ of habeas corpus. The object obviously was

[6] *Welles's Diary*, April 29, 1867.
[7] 6 Wallace, p. 77.
[8] J. W. Garner, *Reconstruction in Mississippi*, p. 168.
[9] 6 Wallace, p. 320.

to test the constitutionality of the Reconstruction Acts, but the Circuit Court ruled that the Acts were constitutional and that trial under them by military commissions was therefore legal. McCardle was remanded to the custody of the military authorities.[10]

So far the proceedings had been wholly orthodox and gave the Radicals no concern. Now, of a sudden, they took a startling turn.

The Radicals, in their zeal to protect their major generals at the South from local courts and officials, had passed a special Act authorizing all habeas corpus cases to be appealed to the United States Supreme Court.[11] To be sure, when the Democrats in 1855 had so tried to protect the Federal officials in the *Ableman* vs. *Booth* case, the abolitionists had denounced it as a monstrous act[12] and had helped to defeat the bill. But new days, of course, require new laws, and being without a new one they dusted off this old discarded one.

To their amazement, however, and to their consternation, Black, acting for McCardle, sprung their own trap upon them by appealing to the Supreme Court for a writ of habeas corpus under this new Radical law. The Supreme Court released McCardle from prison under bond.[13]

On January 10, 1868, Black moved before the Supreme Court that the case be advanced for speedy hearing. Henry Stanbery, the Attorney-General, having advised the President that the Reconstruction Acts were unconstitutional, stated to the court that he could not act for the Government. A week later the Supreme Court granted Black's motion.[14]

Before the real hearing came a preliminary skirmish, beginning upon January 31, upon whether jurisdiction of the case had been granted the Supreme Court by the new Act of 1867. Counsel for the government moved to dismiss McCardle's appeal upon the ground that the Act gave no jurisdiction. Senators Lyman Trumbull of Illinois and Matt H. Carpenter of Wisconsin, with James Hughes, argued for dismissal. "I spoke two and a half hours today," wrote Carpenter to his wife. "I had half of the Senate for an audience." Evidently it was a great effort. "I am praised nearly to death," he continued in this letter. When he had finished, Edwin M. Stanton, with tears in his eyes, exclaimed fervently, "Carpenter, you have saved us."[15]

The next day Black, with William L. Sharkey, answered Carpenter. The text of these arguments has not been preserved, nor is there any testimony upon whether half the Senate was again present. But two days later, on February 3rd, Chief Justice Chase delivered the opinion

[10] *Ibid.* [11] *Statutes at Large, XIV*, p. 285.

[12] *Cong. Globe*, 33 Cong., 2nd Sess., Appendix, pp. 211-213.

[13] 6 Wallace, p. 320.

[14] Warren, *op. cit.*, III, p. 187.

[15] *Ibid.*, p. 195.

of the court, rather curtly refusing to dismiss the McCardle appeal. "We are satisfied . . ." said Chase, "that we have such jurisdiction under the Act of 1867."[16]

The Radicals of Congress, already disturbed in mind, were now rudely jolted. They could not help but know that the Reconstruction Acts were unconstitutional. The Fifth and Sixth Amendments were unmistakably plain, even to a layman. The Supreme Court already had ruled upon military commissions in the Milligan case—and in the McCardle case, the same lawyer was to argue the same principle over again before the same court. Only one result was possible.

A Radical Caucus, therefore, called upon the Judiciary Committee of the House for action, and that committee gave birth to a plan saving the handiwork of Congress from the Supreme Court. James F. Wilson, of Iowa, chairman of the committee, introduced a bill into the House that would require a two-thirds majority of the Supreme Court, instead of a bare majority, to declare unconstitutional any law of Congress. In a long speech he set forth the blessings to posterity which such a bill must bring.[17]

Its enemies pounced upon it with vigor. Black's old friend and former colleague upon the Supreme Bench of Pennsylvania, George W. Woodward, was now in Congress. He denounced the bill as unconstitutional. Samuel S. Marshall of Illinois labeled it a "confession of guilt."[18] The House machinery, however, was oiled and the bill was passed by 116 to 39, a straight party vote.[19]

The Senate, however, hesitated before such an obvious tampering with the Supreme Court. Democratic Senators taunted the majority with fearing that even a two-thirds law would not prevent the Supreme Court from declaring the Reconstruction Acts unconstitutional. Finally the bill was dropped.

The arguments upon the McCardle case were begun on March 2. They lasted four days. Black's argument consumed two days. No complete and accurate text of his speech was preserved. What purported to be a complete text appeared in the *National Intelligencer* for March 3 and 4, 1868. This report was so defective that Black repudiated it altogether and undertook to dictate a correct report of it, but he dropped the matter before the task was completed.[20] Presumably, however, the newspaper edition offers the text of his argument, even though it is defective in reporting the style.

The argument was second in power only to that in the Milligan case, indeed some critics judged it to be the better of the two.[21] To

[16] 6 Wallace, p. 327.

[17] *Cong. Globe,* 40 Cong., 2nd Sess., pp. 478-489. Delivered on January 13th.

[18] *Ibid.,* p. 489. [19] *Ibid.*

[20] C. F. Black, preface.

[21] *National Intelligencer,* March 11, 1868.

those who heard or read them both, they constituted a single exposition of the rights of civil liberty, thought of together, spoken of together.

The ultimate issue was whether the "rebellion" had changed the status of people in the South. Once more, as in the Milligan case, Black swept through an historical argument upon the effect of rebellion upon the rights of citizens. "There was a rebellion against the English government in the reign of George II," he said, "which was put down . . . at the battle of Culloden. The rebels were scattered and the rebellion was at an end. . . . A great many violent things were done after the close of the rebellion. But there was not a living man in the island of Great Britain who undertook to assert that the rebellion had the consequence of increasing the power of the English government. The Act of Union between Scotland and England continued to be precisely the same as before."

"Take another case, the case of the Monmouth rebellion against James II. There not only all Scotland rose up . . . but all of the western counties of England. . . . It ended at the battle of Sedgemoor; the leader of it became a fugitive, and was finally captured and beheaded. The rebellion was completely suppressed and the successful government was conducted by a class of men who would have done anything in the world . . . in order to wreak their vengeance . . . James II, . . . Sunderland, . . . Jeffries. . . . But neither Jeffries nor Sunderland, nor the King himself ever pretended to say that the suppression of the Monmouth rebellion enabled them to govern contrary to the laws of the realm any more than before."

The day upon which he was speaking was March 3, 1868. Already Andrew Johnson had been impeached for "high crimes and misdemeanors," and the Senate was preparing to sit in trial upon his case. The Chief Justice had been served with a notice to preside at this trial and was about to withdraw from further hearing in the McCardle case. Alluding to this theme, Black arose to the climax of his argument.

Not only do citizens owe allegiance to the Constitution, but the Constitution owes her citizens the obligation of protection, he said. "But if your Honors think differently from me, then I think it is pretty nearly over with us. . . . This is the third day of March; it may last a year and a day. But certainly it cannot survive that period. . . . I am not old enough to have sat by the cradle of constitutional liberty; but if it is now to receive its death blow at the hands of Congress and with the consent of this Court, I shall claim to be one of that melancholy throng who will follow with the hearse, and lift up the voice of lamentation over its grave."[22]

It was the "most powerful and magnificent political speech of the day," exclaimed the *National Intelligencer*, after the trial had closed,

[22] *National Intelligencer,* March 4, 1868.

and although this paper had reported the speech in full upon the day following its delivery, it now went over its contents again in a one-column editorial.[23]

The Supreme Court took the case under advisement on March 9. The Radicals were now wildly alarmed and resolved to prevent a decision at all hazards. Pending in the House was an unimportant Senate bill relating to jurisdiction of the Supreme Court in cases involving customs and revenue officers. Without explanation and without debate, James F. Wilson of Iowa, upon March 12, attached to this bill an amendment, repealing the Habeas Corpus Act of 1867 under which the McCardle case was being tried. But Wilson's amendment did not stop with a mere repeal of this Act. It forbade the exercise of jurisdiction *in appeals which already had been made*![24] In other words, it forbade any decision in the McCardle case.

The Democrats were taken unawares, and the bill was passed without any comment whatever. It went to the Senate. There also it was passed upon the same day without debate, with sixteen Senators absent. Charles R. Buckalew of Pennsylvania, a warm friend of Black, raised a question of the purpose of this bill, but Williams of Oregon deliberately misinformed him. Buckalew was suspicious, however, and asked for a postponement of action. This the Senate refused.[25]

When the bill appeared in print, the truth at last dawned upon the nation. Welles, in his diary, wrote these impassioned words: "The Radicals in Congress are in a conspiracy to overthrow not only the President but the Government. The impeachment is but a single act in the drama. . . . By trick, imposition and breach of courtesy, an Act was slipped through both houses, repealing the laws of 1867 and 1789, the effect of which is to take from the Supreme Court certain powers and which is designed to prevent a decision in the McCardle case."[26]

The *Nation*, with unconscious irony, explained the whole situation. The Act of 1867, under which the McCardle appeal was taken, said this organ, was intended "for the blacks and Unionists of the South." Therefore, when the Supreme Court consented to hear the McCardle case, although "it has no right to review it"—reason why unstated—its decision was "very properly avoided" by this law.[27] The *Independent* expressed its view more pointedly. "This Congress will not brook opposition from the court in political matters. . . . If the court interferes, the court will go to the wall."[28]

[23] *Ibid.*, March 11, 1868.
[24] *Cong. Globe*, 40 Cong., 2nd Sess., p. 1860.
[25] *Ibid.*, p. 1847.
[26] *Welles's Diary*, March 14, 1868.
[27] *Nation*, April 2, 1868.
[28] *Independent*, April 21, 1868.

The bill was sent to the President for his signature or his veto. Already six days had passed since the conclusion of the McCardle argument. Ten days more would elapse before the President would return the bill to Congress. Would the Supreme Court assert its rights by handing down a decision before the bill, depriving it of jurisdiction, could become a law? Congress, plainly, was worried. The anxiety was too much for Wendell Phillips, and he erupted with a public statement that "the most menacing danger" to the nation "is the probable decision . . . of the Supreme Court in the case of McCardle that the reconstruction laws are unconstitutional." He called for "a voice from the North, loud and deep enough to . . . drive the Supreme Court with its equivocal chief into silence."[29]

Gradually it became evident that the Supreme Court had no intention of defending its own dignity. Andrew Johnson, however, was of a different mold. He may have been a reckless man, he may have been at times untactful, but his bitterest foe never could accuse him of lacking in courage. His impeachment trial already had begun. A veto of this bill inevitably must aggravate the feeling which the Senate held against him. His chances at best of being acquitted were doubtful, and any aggravation of his judges must injure his cause. Yet without flinching before this danger, Johnson returned the bill to Congress with his veto.

Upon the successive days, March 26 and March 27, the Senate and House overrode his veto, "with," said *Harper's Weekly* in smug review of the case, "the usual two-thirds majority."[30]

Welles expressed the feelings of conservative Republicans over the meekness of the Supreme Court. "The Judges of the Supreme Court have caved in, fallen through, failed, in the McCardle case. . . . Things look ominous, and sadden me. I fear for my country."[31]

On March 30, Black again appeared before the Supreme Court. Fearlessly, he called attention to their delay in handing down the McCardle decision, and stated that the purpose could not have been other than to wait for the Act of Congress which clipped their wings of power to render any decision.[32] Elijah, in pronouncing the sentence of the Almighty against Ahab, could not have been more daring than this "angry baron of King John," standing in the shadow of contempt of court, yet fearless in his arraignment of that high tribunal.[33]

The court as a body made no reply, nor did it cite him for con-

[29] *National Intelligencer*, March 20, 1868. See also New York *Tribune*, March 19, 1868.

[30] *Harper's Weekly*, April 11, 1868.

[31] *Welles's Diary*, March 23, 1868.

[32] *National Intelligencer*, March 31, 1868.

[33] Whitelaw Reid, in the New York *Tribune*, August 20, 1883, doubtless had this instance in mind in saying that Black was allowed greater freedom before the Supreme Court than any other man.

tempt, but Judge Grier was "visibly agitated and with emotion observed that he felt called upon to vindicate himself" from whatever obloquy or censure might be attached to the inaction of the court.[34] The meaning of his remark seems not to have been grasped at the time, but it was made unmistakably clear when he read in court upon April 6[35] a public protest against the postponement of the McCardle decision. His opinion is a remarkable indictment of the court by one of its members:

This was fully argued in the beginning of this month. It is a case which involves the liberties and rights, not only of the appellant, but of millions of our fellow-citizens. The country had a right to expect that it would receive immediate and solemn attention of this Court. By a postponement of this case this Court will subject themselves (whether justly or unjustly) to the imputation that we have evaded the performance of a duty imposed on us by the Constitution, and waited for Legislative interposition to supersede our action, and relieve us of the responsibility. I am not willing to be a member of the eulogy or opprobrium that may follow. I can only say,

Pudit hoc opprobria nobis
Et potuisse dici, et non potuisse repelli

(or, literally translated, I am ashamed that such opprobrium should be cast upon the Court, and that it cannot be refuted).[36]

So closed the McCardle case.[37] According to the short view, the Radicals in Congress had won. They had saved their Reconstruction Acts. But in the longer view, they had paid a heavy price for their victory—for into the official Acts of Congress they had been forced to write a confession of guilt, signed by the Speaker of the House and the Chairman of the Senate, and to make it a part of the enduring records of the nation. It gleams out, as fitfully today as then, at all who examine these records. It disturbs those who might be tempted to defend the course of the Fortieth Congress.

As to Black's arguments in behalf of Milligan and McCardle, a biographer is tempted to write many solemn things—that they are essays upon the rights of man, which rise above any dry and tedious detail of legal treatment, and are entitled in their own right to "the heritage of immortality,"[38] . . . to point out that the first of them led to a decision "long recognized as one of the bulwarks of American

[34] *National Intelligencer*, March 31, 1868.

[35] Black Papers, April 6, 1868.

[36] *National Intelligencer*, April 6, 1868. The translation of the Latin passage, given in parentheses, was omitted in this paper but included in other papers. Whether it was a part of the original document is not clear.

[37] Officially the case closed a year later when, after a hearing, the court decreed that the new act of Congress had taken away their jurisdiction. 7 Wallace, p. 506. Black had no part in this hearing.

[38] W. H. Snyder, *Great Speeches by Great Lawyers*, p. 483.

liberty,"[39] . . . that they constitute his greatest service to the nation. These facts indeed are true. They are today well recognized. But they were not so well recognized at that time. The editor of a Pennsylvania newspaper set forth a better exposition of the opposing lights in which they were then viewed. In his newspaper he published the following letter which he had received from a rather prominent physician: "Dear Sir: Please find herewith $2.50, which I wish to invest in copies of Judge Black's speech. It is the most perfect demonstration I ever read of any proposition, and should be read and preserved by every man in the land."

The editor thereupon added this comment: "What on earth a *Doctor* wants with so many of Black's speeches we cannot imagine, unless he uses them for blister plasters on the stomachs of his Abolition patients. We doubt not, that so applied, they would prove far more efficacious than Spanish flies, while administered internally they would be worse than nitro-glycerine." In the next issue of the paper the editor pursued the subject further: "Receipt of various orders from *other* physicians in different parts of the State, calling for extra copies of Black's speech" had convinced him that "our first conjecture of its medicinal virtues when used in the treatment of malignant cases of negro-phobia, was in the main correct. This opinion is further strengthened by the fact that the Marysville demand came from a leading druggist in that city, who has no doubt had a perfect run upon his establishment for this wonderful and world astounding remedy."[40]

[39] Warren, *op. cit.*, III, p. 149.
[40] Press clipping, Clayton MSS.

24

THE IMPEACHMENT COUNSEL OF ANDREW JOHNSON

THE impeachment of Andrew Johnson is one of the comic strips of American history. The actors in the drama took themselves so seriously, recited with sober faces so many ridiculous lines, and plagiarized so boldly from Burke's *Impeachment of Warren Hastings*, that one is saved from a flippant treatment of it as a farce only by the grim fact that it so nearly resulted in tragedy.

The movement for impeachment began early and had an undulating career. As early as December 1865, eight months after the death of Lincoln, the New Orleans *Tribune* launched an impeachment campaign.[1] Wendell Phillips, in May of 1866, began his attack against Johnson[2] and soon after was violently calling for impeachment. Benjamin F. Butler, at Cincinnati in October of 1866, was crying out "Impeach him and remove him now," and threatening to call out the Civil War "Boys in Blue" to overawe Johnson and the standing army.[3]

James M. Ashley of Ohio moved impeachment in the House on January 7, 1867, while Congress was drafting the Reconstruction Acts.[4] The Judiciary Committee began its labors and by November had filled a 1200-page Congressional volume with "evidence." No impeachment proceedings, however, were voted on during the first session of the Fortieth Congress. Thaddeus Stevens, with his finger on the national pulse, was holding back the Radicals to await the further rise of a public delirium.

Meanwhile Congress had passed a Tenure-of-Office Act forbidding the President to remove any official "during the term for which he was appointed." This Act was aimed to protect Stanton, now serving the Radicals as watchdog and spy in Johnson's Cabinet. But Johnson, on August 6, 1867, deliberately removed Stanton from office—acting upon the ground, first, that the Tenure-of-Office Act was unconstitutional; and second, that Stanton was Lincoln's appointee, not Johnson's, and that the term for which he was appointed had ended March 4, 1865.[5]

Congress now had its long-awaited cause for action. Thaddeus Stevens—old, tottering, slowly dying, with ghastly parchment skin

[1] *Welles's Diary*, Dec. 11 and 18, 1865.

[2] C. Martyn, *Wendell Phillips*, p. 353.

[3] *Cincinnati Commercial*, October 8, 1866.

[4] *Welles's Diary*, January 7, 1867.

[5] *Ibid.*, August 5, 1867.

and sunken burning eyes—struggled to his feet and moved "that Andrew Johnson be impeached of high crimes and misdemeanors in office."[6] As if to emphasize the mockery of the whole proceeding, Stevens made the motion on Saturday, February 22—Washington's birthday! After a Sunday of seething public interest, the motion passed the House on Monday by a strict party vote.[7]

The Senate prepared to sit in judgment upon the charges and Johnson began to draw about him a counsel to serve in his defense. The first three members of the counsel assembled consisted of Henry Stanbery, at that time Attorney-General; Benjamin R. Curtis, formerly associate justice of the Supreme Court, and Jeremiah Black. At their early consultations, however, Black stated frankly that, although he was anxious to participate in the defense of Johnson, yet he feared that his appearance upon the counsel might prejudice the case; since the Radicals were hostile toward him because of participating in the Milligan and McCardle cases. Both Stanbery and Curtis had apprehensions of this also. The three men referred the matter to the President and his Cabinet for their opinions.[8]

In the Cabinet, McCulloch opposed the retention of Black; "the Republicans were hostile to Black," he said. Seward agreed with this view and felt that "someone as capable and not so obnoxious might be found." Welles, however, differed with them. "Would it be wise or politic to exclude from the managing counsel any prominent Democrat whatever? It appeared to me important that there should be one such lawyer among them, and while I had no great intimacy with, or partiality for, Black, I knew of no one who was . . . in all respects, his equal. We wanted something more than a mere lawyer for such a case as this—a politician and statesman, one who made the Constitution and public affairs a study." To this the Cabinet agreed in principle. "Thurman of Ohio was named." He was thought to be less objectionable to the Republicans than Black. "But," objected Welles, "he had no such national reputation as Black."[9]

Heavy pressure was put upon Johnson to reject Black as a member of his counsel. Thomas Ewing, an old Whig leader from Ohio, wrote Johnson on March 1. Of Black he said, "His very presence there . . . will injure your cause. He is known as a violent man—has talents but no discretion, and he would in the heat of his nature sacrifice your cause rather than omit saying a bitter thing."[10] Soon after the Cabinet discussion of March 7, Seward called upon the President to urge

[6] *Cong. Globe*, 40 Cong., 2nd Sess., p. 1336.

[7] *Ibid.*, p. 1401.

[8] *Welles's Diary*, March 7, 1868.

[9] *Ibid.*

[10] Quoted in W. A. Dunning, "More Light on Andrew Johnson," *Amer. Hist. Rev.* XI, 1906, p. 593.

against retaining Black. Johnson, however, replied that "the retention of Mr. Black was not an open question."[11]

The entire counsel as finally announced was composed of Black, Stanbery, Curtis, William M. Evarts of New York, and Thomas A. R. Nelson of Tennessee, a personal friend of Johnson. In surveying this distinguished counsel even the radically hostile *Harper's Weekly* was moved to comment, "Judge Black is called by Republican politicians at Washington the 'brains of the Opposition.' "[12]

But in the end Black did not serve upon the impeachment counsel of Andrew Johnson. Abruptly and without public explanation he resigned, severed all connections with the impeachment proceedings and left Johnson to continue, for better or worse, without his aid. The repercussions of this rupture shook Washington at the time, were echoed in the halls of Congress during the impeachment trial, found their way into newspaper columns for the succeeding two months, and have plagued historical writers upon that era down even into this decade. Neither Black nor Johnson ever offered a public explanation of the breach.

Why did Black resign?

Before entering the historical facts of the case we must pay our respects to that version of the rupture which has only recently appeared but which has been given wide circulation in the writings of Claude G. Bowers, Paul Lloyd Stryker, and George Fort Milton.[13]

This version attempts to make of Black a corrupt bargainer and a scoundrel.

Now readers of this biography doubtless already have discovered that its primary viewpoint is neither praise nor blame of its subject, but is instead the setting forth of historical facts concerning his unique and unusual influence on his age. This primary purpose has indeed compelled the author to evaluate good and evil in the forces which drove the American people by turns into the hysteria of Civil War and into the paranoia of Reconstruction, but Black's part in both tragedies has been reported rather than eulogized. It is of no great moment to the purpose of this biography whether Black was a scoundrel or hero in this impeachment episode. It is of greatest moment, however, to know which he was, if either. In order to do so we must turn aside to examine the version of Bowers, Stryker, and Milton concerning Black's part in Johnson's impeachment trial and to test its historical accuracy. The author does this with sharp regret at being forced into a criticism thereby of these historians, two of whom in his judgment have written the most accurate interpretations of the catastrophe of Reconstruction that have yet appeared.

[11] *Welles's Diary*, March 9, 1868. [12] April 4, 1868.

[13] Bowers, *The Tragic Era*, p. 180; Stryker, *Andrew Johnson*, pp. 612-17, and appendix, 829 *et. seq.*; Milton, *The Age of Hate*, pp. 534-39.

Bowers cites no authority whatever for his version of the Black-Johnson controversy.[14] Since, however, his phraseology is identical at all points with Stryker's account, there can be no question that Bowers has taken his version from Stryker. Therefore, it is Stryker whose interpretation must first be analyzed. Milton's version will be discussed separately.

According to Stryker's version, Benjamin F. Butler "had been gathering guano from a small island called Alta Vela, which Santo Domingo claimed to own, and which had objected to any more forceful taking of fertilizer." Black "seems to have been counsel for Butler," and when appointed as a member of Johnson's impeachment counsel, he took instantaneous advantage of his position. "He now demanded the dispatch of an armed vessel" to Alta Vela "to safeguard American interests." This demand was first made to Secretary of State Seward, who refused to comply, "relying on the precedent established by Black himself, when in 1857 as Buchanan's Attorney General, he had rejected an American claim to Cayo Verde, an island in the Caribbean."

Black then, the story goes, made the demand upon Johnson himself and in order to force Johnson to yeld, Black secured a written opinion favoring his claim from Benjamin F. Butler, Thaddeus Stevens, and two other members of the committee appointed by the House of Representatives to prosecute Johnson in the impeachment trial. On March 18, 1868, Black called upon Johnson in person and made it clear that he had struck a trade with these members of the prosecution counsel, and that if Johnson would protect Butler's guano interests, the prosecution would put on the soft pedal and allow him to be acquitted. Johnson toyed with the idea, told Black to return the next day, and that night took the matter up with Seward in a personal conference. Then, when Black returned the following day, Johnson flatly refused to send a vessel to Alta Vela, since "he had no constitutional right" to do so.

According to the story, Black now grew indignant and retorted: "I have pointed the way to your acquittal and advised you to pursue it. You decline to do so. You will be convicted and removed from office. I prefer not to have you convicted upon my hands, therefore I resign as one of your counsel from the impeachment case."

But Johnson, under this story, looked his tempter in the face and rendered a modern version of get-thee-behind-me-Satan in these words: "You try to force me to do a dishonorable act contrary to law, as I see it, and against my conscience, and rather than do your bidding I'll suffer my right arm torn from its socket. . . . I regard you as a damned villain, and get out of my office or, damn you, I'll kick you out." The next day, however, Black relented, and wrote the President: "Let bygones be forgotten; I am willing to continue as one of your

[14] *The Tragic Era*, p. 180.

counsel." But Johnson retorted to the bearer of the note: "Tell General Black he is out of the case and will stay out."[15]

Such is the story. What of its truth? Its authority hangs upon the unsupported memory of an 88-year-old man, a Colonel E. C. Reeves of Tennessee. This Colonel Reeves does not tell how he learned the story. He merely recited it, without any shred of evidence, authority, or proof of any sort. To be sure he had known Johnson during the latter's advanced age; but he does not even claim that he learned the story from Johnson, and Johnson is not known to have repeated such a story to any other being.[16] On the other hand this story bears a most remarkable resemblance to certain street gossip which made its rounds in 1868, and which was wholly discredited before it got under way.[17] It would seem probable that Colonel Reeves's mind, in its advanced age, must have resurrected this old and discredited gossip and attempted to give it the dignity of history. However he may have learned the story, he offered no proof of its authenticity. It was a story that had been carried around in his mind through a long life. He never gave it the light of publicity until the exact day of his 88th birthday. Upon that day—after reading what he felt to be "a mendacious attack upon the character of Andrew Johnson," written by George Creel and appearing in *Collier's Weekly* of November 27, 1926—this aged man sat down and, in his pent-up eagerness to defend Johnson, reproduced from memory many stories of Johnson's courage and honesty.[18]

Among these reminiscences were the details of the Johnson-Black episode. The supposed events had occurred fifty-nine years earlier and Reeves had not been present at the happening. Yet, without the aid of a note or a document to sustain his memory, with nothing to correct any errors of imagination, or any deviations from fact which might spring from his eagerness to defend the character of Johnson, he nevertheless reproduced in full the details of the affair, even to the exact words uttered. Mr. Stryker regarded such an unreliable feat of memory a "valuable first-hand historical document,"[19] and elevated it to the dignity of history.

Application, however, of a few tests of historical accuracy puts this "historical document" in a different light. In the first place, Black never was an attorney for Benjamin F. Butler, nor did Butler have one cent of interest in the guano industry. Examination of more than

[15] Paul L. Stryker, *op. cit.*, pp. 612-17; see also Appendix, pp. 829-30.

[16] Johnson's voluminous papers in the Library of Congress contain no document even suggesting such an episode. Welles criticized Black for resigning, but he had no knowledge of a corrupt bargain.

[17] See *Nation*, May 7, 1868.

[18] Stryker, in his Appendix, pp. 825-37, prints the Reeves version in full and cites Reeves in the text as his only authority.

[19] Stryker, *op. cit.*, p. 825 n.

a hundred documents of the Alta Vela affair, not only among the Black papers in the Library of Congress but also in the private collection now in possession of Mr. Carey Etnier of York, Pennsylvania, has failed to reveal any connections whatever between Black and Butler. The official report of the Secretary of State also failed to list Butler as one of the contesting parties.[20] Butler himself testified that he never in his life had a cent of interest in the guano business, and this fact was also sworn to in an affidavit by Chauncey F. Black (son of Jeremiah Black) and by another attorney, J. W. Shaffer.[21]

Secondly, according to the Reeves story, Black went to the committee appointed by the House of Representatives to prosecute Johnson at the impeachment trial and from four of these members—Butler, Stevens, Logan, and Bingham—secured an opinion favoring forcible intervention in Alta Vela. This opinion, however, was supposed to be the overt evidence of the bargain he had struck with these managers of impeachment to acquit Johnson if the latter would protect the guano interests. It is definitely established, however, that this opinion was secured, without the advice or knowledge of Black, by J. W. Shaffer, a friend of Butler. Butler, Chauncey F. Black, and J. W. Shaffer all three testified to this under oath at the impeachment trial.[22] Even Johnson's personal friend and spokesman on the defense counsel at the impeachment trial, T. A. R. Nelson, admitted this fact at a time when it would have been to his interest to have kept silence.[23] Black himself made no public statement upon any point in this controversy. But in a private letter he reminded Johnson that "I knew nothing about it, had no communication with the signers, direct or indirect, verbally or in writing. I saw the paper first when you showed it to me."[24] Black was hot tempered and often partisan, but so impeccable in character that no historian could question this testimony on his part, even were it not supported, as it is, on all sides by corrobating evidence.

In the third place, Black is supposed to have made his corrupt proposal to Johnson upon March 18, 1868. Now Johnson did not *that* day rise up in virtuous wrath and kick Black out of his office. Instead, he invited him to call again the next day, and in the interim held a conference with Seward over the question of accepting this evil offer. We pass by the moral point involved, that Seward was keeper of the keys to Johnson's character, and go at once to the greater issue. Johnson did consult with Seward on March 18, according

[20] *Senate Executive Documents,* 40 Cong., 2 Sess., I, no. 38.

[21] Trial of Andrew Johnson, *Congressional Globe,* 40 Cong., 2 Sess., *Supplement,* p. 336.

[22] *Ibid.*

[23] *Ibid.,* pp. 294-95.

[24] Letter of April 28, 1868; York (Pa.) *Democratic Press,* May 15, 1868; Clayton MSS.

to this story, and as a result of this conference, rejected Black's corrupt bargain on the following day. *But Seward was not in Washington upon that day, or that week!* The diary of Secretary of the Navy Gideon Welles, the most authentic source of information upon the daily activity of the Cabinet, reveals that throughout this whole period, Welles was bitterly complaining that Seward had run away and was staying away so the President might not reach him. According to Welles, Seward left Washington for New York on or before March 12.[25] On March 20—two days after Seward is supposed to have told Johnson that it was wrong to disobey a law—Welles was again complaining that "Seward is still absent."[26] Seward did not return to Washington until about March 24.[27]

In the fourth place, a thorough student of Johnson's life and habits concludes that he was more careful than any predecessor that ever sat in the presidency to preserve "every bit of correspondence, private and official, that came into the White House."[28] Johnson's files contain all of the letters known to have been written him by Black. But the famous Black letter supposed to have been written on March 19, "Let bygones be forgotten; I am willing to continue as one of your counsel," is not found among these papers. For sheer self-defense, this letter was imperative to Johnson—for it was the only written evidence in existence to prove that any such affair as alleged had occurred between him and Black. Yet it is not found among the papers of this man who was the most careful, of all presidents down to his time, in preserving all correspondence. The most obvious explanation is that it is missing because it never was sent.

In the fifth place, it must be remembered that Thaddeus Stevens was czar of the House as few men have been before or since. With a fanatical cunning almost diabolic he had held back the eager Radicals on impeachment until the time was ripe, and had carefully laid the Tenure-of-Office trap. No bargain, corrupt or otherwise, could have been made to acquit Johnson without Stevens's consent. Now what historian knowing Stevens would contend that he would trade Johnson's acquittal for a guano dump, or for any monetary price whatsoever?

Obviously the Reeves version will not hold. Its collapse in turn wipes out the interpretations of Stryker and Bowers. Even George F. Milton, who clings to this view of the Black-Johnson quarrel, finds it "difficult to give full credit" to Reeves—this after interviewing him in person.[29]

[25] *Welles's Diary*, March 12, 1868.

[26] *Ibid.*, March 20, 1868.

[27] *Ibid.*, March 24, 1868.

[28] Howard K. Beale, "The Decision of Reconstruction." (Ph.D. Thesis, Harvard Library), p. 94.

[29] Milton, *op. cit.*, pp. 743-44, n. 41.

Let us now examine the version of Milton. In his behalf it must be said that he made a sustained effort to secure the direct historical evidence upon this controversy[30] but that the keystone evidence which would have admitted him to the complete story was not available at the time of his search. Whatever may be said below against his interpretation of the Black-Johnson controversy must be understood only as a criticism against conclusions which he was forced to draw from incomplete evidence. It does not impair the general conclusions of his splendid treatment of Andrew Johnson, the best perhaps that has yet been written.

To one who checks Milton's account against the sources which he cites, there appears a striking defect. Careful as he is usually in documenting his sources, fourteen of the twenty paragraphs which contain this account are wholly undocumented; and of the six documented paragraphs, not one contains any direct proof. Not being able to obtain any such proof, Milton did what every historian must do—utilize what sources he had and draw whatever inferences they seem to indicate. The method was right, the inferences were wrong. When the direct evidence, unavailable to Milton, is examined there arise the following criticisms of his interpretation:

(1) The origin and issue of the Alta Vela controversy was misunderstood. Milton's account infers that the whole Alta Vela affair was framed to force Johnson, while under threat of impeachment, to despoil Santo Domingo of a rich island for the benefit of Black's clients. Actually this was only one episode of a twelve-year effort by Black to recover a guano island, once owned by his clients, who had been robbed and driven out by certain Dominican officials; and who were protected in this thievery by William H. Seward for private reasons of his own.

(2) Milton infers that the letters between Black and his guano clients show intent to influence Johnson improperly through Black's personal association with him. Only the discredited Reeves document sustains this inference. The letters between Black and his client indeed show them desperately anxious to prevent further theft of guano, then rapidly being carried on, from their Alta Vela property, but they show no deliberate effort to have Black resort to improper influence.

(3) Milton infers that Black did in fact urge his claim upon Johnson on personal grounds. Johnson was indeed once purported to say in the heat of anger that Black had done so, though one cannot be entirely sure that he did say so. At any rate Black completely denied making any personal appeal[31] and in the complete folio of letters now among the Black and the Johnson Papers in the Library of Congress

[30] Letters to the author, September 13 and 19, 1932.

[31] Letter to Johnson, Johnson Papers, March 24, 1868.

there is none of the many Black wrote to Johnson on this question that suggests appeal on personal grounds.

(4) Milton infers that Black's guano clients voted stock which was used to bribe Benjamin F. Butler, and possibly other Congressmen including Garfield, Bingham, Blaine, and Thaddeus Stevens, into urging Johnson to protect the Alta Vela claim. In proof of this Milton cites a document, dated March 6, 1868, now among the Black Papers in the Library of Congress. Milton here was frankly in error. The exact purpose for which this stock was voted was for "Compensation to Such person or persons as they the Said Black and Winder in their discretion may employ to aid in the prosecution of the Claim," and the document which Milton cites as inferring Butler bribery had no reference to Butler, direct or indirect, remote or immediate. It was merely a deed conferring guano to an attorney, John L. Dawson, for his legal services.[32] The attorneys—Black, Lamon, Shaffer, Winder, and Dawson—were all paid in this manner. No inference, not even a suggestion of inference, toward bribery can be drawn from this document.

There are several significant omissions also in Milton's version, but the space required to detail them would not justify the answer, especially as they will become apparent later in this chapter. In short, Milton, for lack of data which he attempted unsuccessfully to obtain, was forced to make inferences which more complete evidence renders invalid.[33]

In the light of this evidence, the entire Black-Johnson quarrel takes on a different aspect. The guano fertilizing industry sprang up in the early Fifties. In 1856 Congress passed an act authorizing any United States citizens discovering a guano island to take possession and register their ownership. It also empowered the President to use both land and naval forces to protect the guano rights of any discoverer.[34] This clause empowering protection is of especial significance when it is remembered that, under the Reeves version, Black was supposed to have urged Johnson to grant protection thus afforded by law, while Johnson swore that such protection (specifically au-

[32] Black Papers, March 6, 1868.

[33] Specifically this evidence comes from five sources: (1) Black Papers now in possession of Carey E. Etnier, York, Pa. (2) Clayton MSS., collected by Black's daughter, Mary Black Clayton; now in possession of his granddaughter, Dr. Mary Clayton Hurlbut, Lockport, New York. The data in these two sources open a trail leading back to three official sources, namely (3) *Statutes at Large*, XI, 119-20, act of August 18, 1856, containing guano laws under which the case was being urged. (4) The official report of the Secretary of State on Alta Vela, *Senate Exec. Doc.*, 40 Cong., 2nd Sess., I, no. 38. (5) Archives, Department of State, through which the tangled skein of the Alta Vela affair ran for more than a decade.

[34] *Statutes at Large*, XI, pp. 119-20.

thorized by this act) was unconstitutional, and vowed that he would "suffer my right arm to be torn from the socket" rather than grant it. Reeves, Bowers, Stryker, and Milton all seem to be unaware of this base act of Congress. Instead of consulting it, they rest this part of their case upon Seward's citation of a decision made by Black in 1857 while Attorney-General against the Cayo Verde guano claimants. An examination of that decision, however, shows a vital difference between it and Alta Vela. On Alta Vela American citizens had been attacked, American property destroyed, and all reparations refused; whereas Cayo Verde was merely a disputed island whose status was being peacefully settled by negotiations.[35]

But to return to the guano story. A Baltimore firm, Patterson & Murguiondo, on February 23, 1860, had discovered a guano island, one-half by three-quarters of a mile in area and some fifteen miles south of Haiti, known as Alta Vela. Under provisions of the 1856 Guano Act they registered ownership with the Secretary of State, occupied the island and began to dig guano.[36] But after seven months of occupation this company was attacked without warning by an expedition from Santo Domingo. Its laborers were seized, its tools, buildings, and entire property were destroyed. This act, it will be noted, was not committed by the government of nearby Haiti but by the more remote Santo Domingo.[37]

Patterson & Murguiondo at once appealed to the Secretary of State for protection of their rights under the Guano Act of 1856.[38] Black himself was at this time Secretary of State. Upon January 14, 1861, he wrote Patterson & Murguiondo that "the Government is entirely disposed to protect you in the enjoyment of any rights which you may have legally acquired to the guano" on Alta Vela. "Inasmuch, however, as the Dominican Republic is understood to claim jurisdiction over Alta Vela . . . the Department deems it proper before taking other steps in the matter to address a communication to its special agent" at Santo Domingo to ascertain the "grounds upon which its claim to the island is based."[39]

Upon the day following, Black instructed W. L. Cazneau, the American special agent in Santo Domingo, to "at once, if you have not already done so, request the attention of the authorities to this event,

[35] *Official Opinions of the Attorneys General of the United States*, 1859, IX, p. 406.

[36] Official Report of the Secretary of State on Alta Vela, *Senate Exec. Doc.*, 40 Cong., 2 Sess., I, no. 38. Hereafter cited as *Alta Vela Report*.

[37] Report of William L. Cazneau (Special U. S. Agent in Santo Domingo); Archives, Department of State, Washington, D. C., Special Service dispatch of February 19, 1861. Hereafter cited as "Cazneau."

[38] Black Papers, P. H. Sullivan to Black, Dec. 24, 1860 and Jan. 16, 1861; Patterson & Murguiondo to Black, January 1861.

[39] Archives, Department of State, Domestic Letters, LIII, 389.

and learn particularly the grounds upon which they claim jurisdiction of the island in order that this government may know what measures are necessary to protect the interests of our citizens in that quarter."[40]

Cazneau made a thorough investigation and rendered his report. As to the Dominican right to the island, it lay fifteen miles off the south coast of the island of Haiti. "I cannot ascertain that this Republic has ever exercised the sovereign duties of protection or government on . . . Alta Vela, since it has been a nation." Indeed the Santo Dominican foreign minister was forced to admit that not even de facto jurisdiction ever had been exercised; and of the two governments upon the island of Haiti—the Haitian and the Dominican—the Haitian "exercises the only visible jurisdiction" of the coast line nearest Alta Vela. Patterson & Murguiondo had registered their ownership only after ascertaining that no jurisdiction was exercised by either of these governments. When they first began removing guano the Haitian authorities "made a visit of inquiry to the Americans at Alta Vela," but after ascertaining the nature of the enterprise they "withdrew without offering any molestation." The Dominican government made no protest for seven months, although the American flag floated daily over the island of Alta Vela. Then, with still no word of protest to the American government, they seized the island, destroyed the buildings and tools of the company, and claimed the guano as their own.[41]

This report reached the Department of State on March 31, 1861, after Black had left the office and Seward was in charge.[42] Yet Seward made no move to restore the rights of the American citizens. More significant in light of his later actions, he made no request of the Dominican Government to set forth its right to claim this island. Black, meanwhile, had returned to the practice of law and was engaged by Patterson & Murguiondo to represent their interests. He at once petitioned Seward to secure redress for the injury inflicted upon his clients.[43] Through the next seven years, he made repeated application for redress, but Seward made no move whatever. He gave sundry excuses for the inaction. To W. H. Lamon, a partner with Black in the affair, he promised on June 22, 1866, that he would make demand upon the Dominican government for restoration. To Black, on October 23, 1866, he wrote saying that the obstacle to prosecuting the claim was that the present Dominican government was only

[40] Archives, Department of State, Special Missions, American Hemisphere, II, p. 18.

[41] "Cazneau," *loc. cit.*

[42] *Alta Vela Report*, p. 7.

[43] Black Papers, March 27, 1861. This is probably the first case undertaken by Black after returning to private life.

provisional. To Black he gave assurance on November 13, 1867, that he had written the United States Consul at Haiti to call on the Dominican government and that the case would be wound up in a few weeks.[44]

Thus seven years dragged by. One guano case after another arose and was settled. But in all these seven years Black could not get Seward to take action on Alta Vela, either to affirm or deny the claim. Once the matter came up for discussion in Johnson's Cabinet; whereupon Seward "politely informed us," recorded Welles, "that he required the attention of no one but the President and the Attorney-General."[45] Yet the examination of the opinions of the Attorney-General shows that Seward, although calling upon him for opinions upon other guano claims, never referred to him the Alta Vela claim.[46]

At last it became obvious even to Seward's Cabinet colleagues that his course of action was peculiar. "For a little matter," noted Welles in his diary, "Seward has manifested deepest anxiety in the Alta Vela business. I do not think he has any pecuniary interest in it, but he is solicitous for his friend Weed, who has."[47]

Here was the key; Seward's friendship for Thurlow Weed. For the Dominican government, after destroying the property of the Baltimore firm which had discovered Alta Vela, had sold the guano right on this island to a New York company—Root, Webster, Clark & Co.—in which Thurlow Weed had a financial interest.[48] This company was rapidly removing the guano claimed by Patterson & Murguiondo of Baltimore. The longer the delay in settling the dispute, the more guano could be removed. If the delay was long enough, all of the guano would be removed before any settlement was reached.

Finally Black took the matter over Seward's head to Congress and, as a preliminary to action, the Senate on February 13, 1868, called on the President for the correspondence relating to the whole affair. Seward at last prepared the information and Johnson transmitted it to the Senate on March 8, 1868—*the day before the impeachment summons was served upon him.* Three days later it was printed and made public.[49]

One is tempted to linger over the contents of this report. It purported to give the full documentary history of the Alta Vela affair. Yet a comparison with the original papers in the Archives of the Department of State shows that Seward had included only that which

[44] See Black Papers, end of 1868, for the summary of these various reasons offered by Seward.

[45] *Welles's Diary,* March 20, 1868.

[46] See *Official Opinions of the Attorneys General,* X and XI.

[47] *Welles's Diary,* March 7, 1868.

[48] Clayton MSS.

[49] *Sen. Exec. Docs.,* 40 Cong., 2 Sess., I, no. 38.

he desired to include and suppressed that which he desired to suppress. It was not a government report, but a political pamphlet.[49a]

But we hasten on to the results of its publication. Here is the reason why the Alta Vela issue reached its crisis after Black became a member of Johnson's impeachment counsel—not because Black was a member of the counsel, but because the issue was precipitated by Seward's report made public two days after the summons was served on Johnson. As attorney for Patterson & Murguiondo, Black must act at once or give up their cause. Since Seward refused to act, Black took the case directly to Johnson and asked him to proceed under the Guano Act of 1856 which specifically authorized the President to use land and naval forces to protect the guano claims of American citizens. But Johnson had the impeachment trial hanging over his head and he seemed loath to commit any act which would both antagonize Seward and injure his chances of being acquitted.

At this stage, however, another attorney in the case, J. W. Shaffer, took a hand.[50] Shaffer formerly had been an aide-de-camp to General B. F. Butler. Now he went to Butler and secured from him a written legal opinion which recognized the validity of the claim and pointed out Johnson's right to use force in protecting American interests. This Shaffer carried to John A. Logan, another member of the prosecution counsel in impeachment, who willingly added his signature.[51] Later, Garfield and several other Congressmen endorsed the statement. Among them was Thaddeus Stevens, who signed it gladly because, he said, "Seward has acted the scoundrel." [52]

[49a] Among the documents suppressed were: (1) First Cazneau dispatch no. 15, giving details of injuries inflicted on Americans at Alta Vela; (2) dispatch of American Consul at Porto Rico relating to Alta Vela attack; (3) Patterson's private report to Seward on the Alta Vela situation; (4) the correspondence with Root, Webster, & Clark, which revealed the interest of Thurlow Weed in the company then removing guano claimed by Patterson & Murguiondo.

These omissions were discovered by J. W. Shaffer, an attorney, and filed with Johnson, who made this comment a part of the official report now extant (See *Alta Vela Report*, p. 65), but 2,000 copies were published and distributed, marked "for use of the State Department" which omitted this part of the report. (Clayton MSS.)

Another mutilation was discovered by the present author which was unknown either to Black or Shaffer, namely that only five of the eighteen pages of the important second Cazneau report of February 19, 1860, were included. The other thirteen pages were suppressed, although they treated of important phases of injuries done to American citizens by the Dominican government. The original report is still in the Archives of the Department of State.

[50] Milton assumes that Shaffer was a member of the Black law firm. (See *The Age of Hate*, p. 535.) This is an error. Except for about five years Black had neither law partner nor office. (See *infra*, p. 220.) Shaffer was an independent counsel in the case.

[51] *Cong. Globe*, 40 Cong., 2 Sess., *Supplement*, p. 336.

[52] *Nation*, May 7, 1868.

Of Shaffer's maneuver, Black testified to Johnson: "I knew nothing of that paper until after it went into your hands, heard nothing about it, had no communication with the signers, direct or indirect, verbally or in writing. I saw the paper first when you showed it to me.[53]

Why did Shaffer secure the names of impeachment managers to this letter that was intended to influence Johnson in protecting the guano claim of Patterson & Murguiondo? In the first place, Shaffer was an old friend of Butler. In the second, Johnson was facing serious trouble in the impeachment trial and any act of his that tended to aggravate the Radicals in Congress would certainly diminish his chances for acquittal. Shaffer felt that if he could show Johnson that the protection of American guano interests would not aggravate the impeachment situation, at least Johnson would be free to act in the matter. Indeed there is good evidence to believe that Johnson had, in fact, "angled a little for some of the signatures" of these members of Congress.[54] If so, it was a perfectly proper act. The matter of Congressmen endorsing claims is certainly neither new nor unique in administrative procedure.

Nevertheless the Alta Vela matter was now at a head. After seven years of delay, a report was finally rendered which promised resulting action. Either the claim of Patterson & Murguiondo must be protected or given up. Black, who had been their attorney for seven years, had been Johnson's attorney for ten days. He called upon Johnson, as he often had called before,[55] to urge protection of the claim of American citizens. Johnson gave him his final answer. The claim would not be protected. Johnson's reasons for thus refusing are seemingly quite apparent and practical. Nor was his policy out of line with political expediency. By his election on the ticket with Lincoln he had alienated the Democrats. By his policy on Reconstruction he had alienated the Radical Republicans. The only element to which he might cling for personal support in his struggle was the ex-Whigs, and Seward was indisputably the leader of these ex-Whigs. Yet Seward was so violently opposed to any protection of American claims on Alta Vela that for Johnson summarily to overrule him would be to make an open enemy of this ex-Whig leader at the moment when the President needed every vote he could muster in Congress.[56]

Milton states that Andrew Johnson's courageous "conduct in the Alta

[53] Letter of April 28, 1868; York (Pa.) *Democratic Press*, May 15, 1868; Clayton MSS.

[54] *Nation*, May 7, 1868.

[55] For previous correspondence on this subject see Black's letters to Johnson of July 22, and August 7, 1867 (*Alta Vela Report*) and of October 23, 1867 (Johnson Papers).

[56] For other evidence of repeated occasions where Johnson was unwilling to antagonize Seward, see *Welles's Diary*, March 12, 14, April 17, May 31, 1867; and especially September 4, 1867.

Vela case approached closely to Immanuel Kant's categorical imperative . . . right was right and wrong was wrong, and it was . . . wrong to violate the rights of Santo Domingo";[57] Johnson therefore resisted this wrong even though it threatened to cost him conviction at the impeachment trial. But this statement was made, and could be made, only because Milton lacked access to all the documents on the Alta Vela controversy. In plain truth, every code of justice demanded that Johnson protect Patterson & Murguiondo's legal claim to Alta Vela; and the Guano Act of 1856 authorized this protection. But political expediency demanded that he sacrifice these claims as the price of retaining the good will of Seward and its influence on the ex-Whigs in Congress. Johnson chose the politically expedient course. His action was perhaps wise in view of the titanic constitutional issue at stake in the impeachment trial. But it cannot be called a courageous act.

Black's position, however, was untenable. He was counsel for Johnson, and he was counsel for Patterson & Murguiondo whose interests demanded action over Johnson's head to Congress. Black thereupon resigned from Johnson's impeachment counsel. His reasons were well stated in a letter to Johnson:

> Although I thought it your clear duty to protect these persons, as the law requires by restoring them to their lawful possession, I did not ask you to do so as the condition on which I would appear as your counsel in the impeachment case. I never even referred to the embarrassments which it might create until after you had given what I took for your last word on the subject. I told you too, verbally, and in writing, that I did not ask it on the score of personal kindness (for it was no kindness to me) but a matter of justice to the unfortunate men who were robbed and ruined by Mr. Seward's protégés. The trouble is that your decision, or rather your refusal to decide, places me in a situation where I may be compelled to do what your counsel cannot and ought not to do.[58]

The last sentence refers to Black's intention to seek action from Congress for safeguarding his clients' rights in Alta Vela. "I cannot advise them to submit in silence to the outrage perpetrated upon them," he wrote Johnson. "They must seek elsewhere for the justice which you deny them."[59] Toward this congressional action Johnson was quite cordial; so cordial indeed that his personal spokesman on the impeachment counsel, T. A. R. Nelson, went out of his way to assure Congress that Johnson was of the opinion that Congress alone had power to order a warship to Alta Vela.[60] In other words, John-

[57] *The Age of Hate*, p. 539.

[58] Johnson Papers, March 24, 1868.

[59] Johnson Papers, March 19, 1868.

[60] Trial of the President, *Cong. Globe*, 30 Cong., 2 Sess., *Sup.*, p. 337.

son, knowing it "wrong to violate the rights of Santo Domingo," was not unwilling to have it suggested that Congress do it.

But what of Black's duty toward the great constitutional issue at stake? Upon the outcome of Johnson's trial, it was then generally believed and doubtless correctly, depended whether the United States should continue to have a tripartite and equally authoritative government, or one in which the legislative branch was supreme and the other two definitely subordinated. Should not Black have joined in sacrificing his clients' property to Seward's interest and have remained with Johnson? But assuming even the willingness of the clients sacrificed, there is something to be said on the other side.

Johnson's impeachment trial was no judicial hearing. It was a political inquest. Black's great constitutional knowledge and his rare skill as a pleader would undeniably have been of aid to Johnson before a judicial hearing. But facing a political inquest was another matter. Black was the towering legal opponent of the Radical's Reconstruction policy. He had appeared in every important Reconstruction case on the Supreme Court docket. The Radicals feared and hated him. So hostile indeed were they that many in Johnson's Cabinet believed that his presence on the counsel would injure Johnson. Ex-Whigs had implored Johnson not to permit him to serve. At least two members of the counsel had the same fears. Black himself when first approached had expressed this fear.[61] The Reconstruction historian, William Archibald Dunning, was convinced that Black's withdrawal improved Johnson's chances of success.[62]

Certainly Black, in withdrawing, was not sensible of injuring Johnson's chances of acquittal. Upon the day following his resignation—the exact day in which the Reeves version would have him writing his "Let-bygones-be-forgotten;-I-am-willing-to-continue-as-one-of-your-counsel" letter—Black in fact wrote to Johnson as follows:

> My retirement from your cause will not probably diminish the chances of its success. When you first expressed the desire that I should be one of your counsel, I gave some reasons why it might be better for you that I should not consent. Upon Messrs. Curtis & Stanbery these considerations had some weight, but you over-ruled them without hesitation. If you will reflect upon them again, you will probably see that you have no reason to regret my present decision to retire. . . . I hope you see plainly that I have adopted the only possible mode of relieving myself from embarrassment and complications which would be wholly unendurable if I did not get rid of them in some way.[63]

[61] *Welles's Diary*, March 7, 1868.

[62] W. A. Dunning, "More Light on Andrew Johnson," *Amer. Hist. Rev.*, XI, 1906, p. 594.

[63] Johnson Papers, March 19, 1868.

Such are the facts of Black's retirement from the impeachment counsel of Johnson. Stryker places full and sole reliance upon the version of an 88-year-old man who, writing under great emotional stress and without a document to sustain him, made Black to appear a renegade and a rascal. Milton, admitting that Colonel Reeves's marvelous memory was due to advanced age, nevertheless allowed the Reeves version to influence him unduly. Against them both stands William Archibald Dunning, careful scholar, who after half a lifetime of study on the Reconstruction and an examination of all the documents then available decided that "there was in the episode nothing whatever discreditable morally to any party concerned."[64] The examination of all the currently available documents confirms Dunning's view with an emphasis as it pertains to Black.

Unquestionably Black's appearance at the impeachment trial would have added an element of picturesqueness to the scene. Always a bold and brilliant pleader, he gave color and energy even to the most obscure legal proceedings. His withdrawal, although it cannot be said to have injured Johnson's chances for acquittal, was nevertheless keenly regretted by certain Washington newspaper correspondents who had looked forward to another Black-Butler tilt such as they had witnessed in the *ex parte Milligan* argument. Among these was Mack, correspondent for the Cincinnati *Enquirer*, who poured out his regret in the following news letter:

> There is no man in the House who can successfully take the offensive against Butler, and I doubt if there is any man in the country who can do it, except Jere Black. Jere gets after him occasionally in Court, and they say he shakes him into a condition of utter mutilation. The great dread of Butler's existence during the impeachment trial was that A. J. would employ the ex-Attorney General as one of his counsel. It is a great pity that he didn't—or rather it's a great pity that after he had employed him he should have quarreled with him, and allowed him to withdraw from the case. The old fellow would have had Butler's scalp in his belt before the close of the second day's proceedings. And if the people of his district want to serve their country to an appreciable extent they will send him to Congress as soon as possible to take charge of Benjamin on the floor of the House. He is the only man I know of who could be relied upon to meet Spooney at all points and under all circumstances, and in less than a month after his advent the gentleman from Massachusetts would sing smaller than the smallest of his colleagues.[65]

[64] Dunning, *op. cit.*

[65] Cincinnati *Enquirer*; press clipping, Clayton MSS.

25

RESTRICTING RECONSTRUCTION IN THE COURTS

ONE of the important post-war cases arising in the Supreme Court was that of the Floyd Acceptances. Floyd, it will be remembered, was Secretary of War under Buchanan. In that position, he had accepted commercial paper from a transportation company in advance of services rendered. The discovery of this action led to Buchanan's instantly demanding his resignation.[1]

This company, meanwhile, had sold the paper. Some of it fell into the hands of T. W. Peirce of Boston, who brought the case before the Court of Claims. This court refused to allow the payment. Thereupon Peirce and three others, who also held this paper, took their case to the Supreme Court. Eighteen more claims were pending in the lower court which would depend upon the outcome of this suit. The case was argued during the December term of court in 1868.[2]

Black appeared as senior counsel for Peirce. He argued that the United States, through Floyd, already had accepted the bills; and that the claimants had purchased them in good faith and through payment of good money; that by a previous decision, the Supreme Court itself had ruled that such conditions constituted a binding contract. "If you reverse that judgment . . ." he argued, "you tell the world that it has stood for twenty-five years like an open man-trap in the public highway, baited with Government paper; at last it has become full of innocent victims against whom the War Department happens to have a grudge, and it may be sprung upon them to their ruin and dstruction. The decision that you substitute in the place of it will be another trap, baited in the same way, until some other obnoxious individual happens to put his foot into it, and he will suffer as these men, women and children are expected to suffer now." "It is a stab at national honor. Like Mercutio's wound, it is not as wide as a church door nor as deep as a well, but it will do your business for you in the course of time."[3]

With Black were two other outstanding lawyers, Benjamin R. Curtis and C. B. Goodrich. But the Supreme Court rejected their arguments and refused to allow payment to the holders of this paper. Peirce, who was a vigorous letter writer, poured out his troubles to Black:

[1] See *supra*, p. 93.
[2] 7 Wallace, p. 666.
[3] C. F. Black, pp. 481, 486.

We are at sea without helm, sail or pilot. The old captains and guides with chart and compass are put on shore and the old ship of state is in the breakers with no sheet anchor and if she reaches shore it will be a miracle, but is it not your duty to help to save? You have more than once kept her off the rocks and now when she is fast filling with water you must help to bail. . . . I thought you had got them [the Supreme Court judges] educated to duty. You had but they have forgotten the lessons you taught them. . . . I have been despoiled of over two millions of hard earned money . . .[4]

Even in defeat, however, Peirce admired the lawyer who lost his case. "I got your argument in my case," he wrote to Black, "and gave it to Goodrich who desired me to express to you his deep sense of its great power exhaustive of every point and principle of the case, and ought alone to have won it and would have done so in any Court in Christendom but that Court. . . . Curtis is equally indignant; feels and says it is a judicial outrage . . ."[5]

The next great case in which Black appeared before the Supreme Court was the Blyew case, which involved an interpretation of the Thirteenth Amendment, and of the Civil Rights Bill, passed by Congress to secure negro rights. Before passing to this case, however, it should be observed that a change had come over the Supreme Court by the year 1870. The Radical Congress, with its assault upon the Supreme Court in the McCardle case, had reached the limit of its power. In the impeachment of Johnson, they had overstretched it. The acquittal of Johnson marked the beginning of their decline. Like Mercutio's wound, to which Black referred, this defeat was not at once fatal, but it did the business in the end. By 1870 the Supreme Court once more was freed in spirit from any threat of control by Congress. The Blyew case was tried in 1872 before an unimperiled judiciary.

The Civil Rights Bill, which was involved in the Blyew case, had been passed by Congress on April 9, 1866. It gave citizens of "every race and color, without regard to any previous condition of slavery," the same right to "give evidence . . . and to full and equal benefits of all laws and proceedings for the security of person and property as is enjoyed by white citizens." And to the *Federal* courts it gave all cases affecting persons who might be denied those rights.[6]

Kentucky, however, had a law dating from before the Civil War which forbade slaves, negroes, or Indians from testifying against any white person. Therefore, when Blyew was indicted in the courts of Kentucky for the murder of a negro woman, the case was taken out of the hands of that State and thrown into the Federal court on the

[4] Black Papers, March 15, 1869.
[5] Black Papers, March 16, 1869.
[6] *Statutes at Large,* XIV, p. 27, Act of April 9, 1866.

grounds that negro witnesses were denied the right to testify against the defendent, solely on account of race or color.[7]

Kentucky claimed the right to punish her own criminals, and appealed the case to the United States Supreme Court. Before that court Black appeared, with I. Caldwell, in behalf of Kentucky. The case was not widely different in principle from those of Milligan and McCardle. Where the former had involved an encroachment against the rights of persons, this one involved an encroachment upon the right of a State. The argument was heard on February 21, 1872.

"A murder was committed," said Black to the court. "It was within the limits of the State of Kentucky, and on her soil. . . . Her law and the law of God alone were offended by it, and none but the Almighty and the State of Kentucky had a right to enter into judgment with the perpetrators of it. . . . It was no more an offense against the United States than it was against the Republic of France or the Empire of Germany." Yet the case had been dragged from state to Federal jurisdiction.

To what end did this point? "If a fight takes place at a militia muster, or a cross-roads meeting, or a general election, or a barbecue, or at any other public gathering, in the presence of a thousand white persons who can testify to it, though it concern nobody but white men, though it is between white men entirely, they can not be indicted for the offense in a State court if one single negro or mulatto in that whole crowd saw the thing done." If this law of Congress be valid, then "any man that pleases may . . . commit any crime he pleases against the State of Kentucky, with perfect immunity from the State authorities, if he will simply take a negro along with him when he does the deed. . . . If a negro steals a hog, or robs a hen-roost, the suffering party must let him run unpunished or else go to Louisville for justice, and that would cost twenty times as much as the pigs and chickens are worth. . . . Nine-tenths of the lower class of crimes committed by negroes and by white men under protection of negro witnesses, must go unwhipped of justice."

"The autonomy of a free State is not a thing to be trifled with," and with this thought lingering in the mind of his hearers, Black swept into an avalanche of argument to show the unconstitutionality of the Civil Rights Bill.

But we cannot encompass the whole argument. Senator Alexander H. Garland of Arkansas was among these who heard it. Garland was himself an exceedingly able lawyer and later became Attorney-General of the United States. He had heard Black but once before, and that was preceding the Civil War. But this speech, he thought, "was the finest combination of law, rhetoric, and eloquence I ever listened to. . . . He became not only his client, but his client's cause;

[7] 13 Wallace, p. 581.

he was wrapped up and lost in it; he moved and acted in it. So great were his earnestness and power of assertion, I . . . fancied I could see the convictions of judges giving away reluctantly before him and surrendering to him as he spoke."[8]

The opinion of the Supreme Court was a remarkable document. It decided the case entirely in favor of Black—yet without pronouncing the Civil Rights Bill unconstitutional. It merely decided that the Act did not mean what its makers had tried to make it mean, that it could not be interpreted to take such jurisdiction away from any State.[9]

Public temper was returning to normal. The press as a whole accepted the decision without a murmur. The New York *Tribune* made no comment whatever.

The last important Reconstruction argument which Black gave before the Supreme Court was in the famous Slaughter House Cases arising out of an interpretation of the Fourteenth Amendment. The setting of this case began when the Carpetbagger Government of Louisiana, apparently under the influence of corruption and bribery, passed a law granting a monopoly of the slaughterhouse business of New Orleans to one favored company. This act deprived more than 1,000 persons of their means of livelihood, and its obvious favoring of a certain interest aroused a community feeling of outrage.[10]

Unmistakably, here was a call for relief—if the Federal courts could find the power to deliver it.

The deposed slaughterhouse dealers took their case to the Supreme Court of Louisiana and lost it. Following that they took an appeal to the Supreme Court of the United States, alleging a violation of both the Thirteenth and Fourteenth Amendments—the former prohibiting "involuntary servitude"; and the latter prohibiting the States from abridging "privileges or immunities of citizens of the United States," or from depriving them of "liberty or property" without due process of law.[11]

But a greater—a more far-reaching issue—was involved. Undeniably the injured slaughterhouse dealers were in need of redress, and redress had been denied them in their own State. Undeniably also, the first section of the Fourteenth Amendment had been written with the deliberate intent to nationalize all civil rights, to make Federal power supreme over the States, "to bring the private life of every citizen directly under the eye of Congress." To gain this power over the States, the Radicals in Congress had attached this section as a rider to three other sections punishing the South. The Northern States, in

[8] C. F. Black, p. 26.
[9] 13 Wallace, p. 590.
[10] 16 Wallace, p. 38.
[11] *Ibid.*, p. 43.

a fervor of post-war righteousness, had embraced the punitive sections and failed to understand the rider. The Southern States had been forced to ratify the Amendment as a condition of escape from military rule.[12]

But suppose the Supreme Court should rule that the slaughterhouse dealers of Louisiana could secure no redress under this Amendment? The effect of such a decision would be a lasting thing, cutting out bodily this part of the Amendment. It would smash the intent of the Radicals. It would restore civil rights to the States. In the end, it would leave Louisiana free to deal with Carpetbaggers in her own way as soon as military force should be removed.

To a trenchant defender of States Rights and a militant follower of Jefferson, as was Black, there could be but one side to such a controversy. Before the Supreme Court he appeared as counsel for Louisiana—to argue that the Fourteenth Amendment gave the Federal government no power to interfere with State control over civil rights. Distinguished counsel appeared upon both sides of the case. With Black were Matt H. Carpenter, Charles Allen, and Thomas J. Durant. Opposing them were P. Phillips, J. Q. A. Fellows, and John A. Campbell. Durant was expected to be President Grant's choice for a vacancy upon the Supreme Court. Campbell formerly had been a member of the Supreme Court, and had resigned at the beginning of the Civil War to follow the fortunes of the South.[13]

The final argument was held on February 3, 4, and 5, 1873. The Court's opinion was delivered by Justice Samuel F. Miller of Iowa,[14] who pointed out that for the first time the Court was called upon to interpret the Thirteenth and Fourteenth Amendments.

Gravely Miller admitted the "great responsibility" of such a duty. "No questions so far-reaching and pervading in their consequences . . ." he said, "have been before this court during the official life of any of its present members."[15] With this dedication to duty, Miller then reviewed the history of the Fourteenth Amendment and its "pervading spirit." In the end he concluded that it had never intended to take from the States "the entire domain of civil rights," and transfer it to the Federal government. Therefore, no relief could be afforded in the Federal courts to the injured slaughterhouse dealers of Louisiana.[16]

In vain did the minority of the Supreme Court, including Chief

[12] See Warren, *op. cit.*, III, p. 262; Burgess, *Polit. Sci. and Const. Law*, I, p. 325; Blaine, *op. cit.*, II, p. 419.

[13] Warren, *op. cit.*, III, 258.

[14] 16 Wallace, p. 44. No copy of Black's argument in this case was preserved, and no résumé is reported in Wallace.

[15] Nathan Clifford, appointed in 1858, was the senior member of the court. In other words, the court felt this to be the gravest decision since that of Dred Scott.

[16] 16 Wallace, p. 61.

Justice Chase, point out such an interpretation practically made a nullity of that clause in the Fourteenth Amendment forbidding States to abridge privileges and immunities of a citizen. The majority of the Supreme Court had spoken. This rider of the Amendment—forced upon the South at the point of the bayonet and foisted upon the North by its attachment to punitive measures against the South—was severed from the Constitution.

Here indeed was one of the epoch-making decisions of the Supreme Court. It is not an overstatement to say that, by it, State sovereignty was saved from annihilation. For had the decision been otherwise, States would have been hopelessly subordinated to the National Government. All control of civil rights would have passed from State into Federal hands—and with the passing of civil rights, much or most of State autonomy would have vanished. Except for historical interest, State entities would have faded into pale colors. Even John A. Campbell of the defeated counsel in this case admitted in later years that this decision was best for the country.[17]

Yet in writing this Amendment the Radicals had "intended to occupy the whole ground," said Burgess, "and thought they had done so."[18] James G. Blaine, who had been one of the manipulators of this Amendment, said that by the Slaughterhouse decision "the Amendment has been deprived, in fact, of the power which Congress intended to impart to it."[19]

The public, however, as a whole failed at the time to grasp the significance of the decision. The Washington *National Republican* saw it merely as "important and interesting," as one which would "clear up many doubtful points" upon which there was "much confusion and laxity of thought."[20] The New York *Tribune* devoted a full column editorial to explaining the meaning of the decision. But its author either was ignorant of the true significance, or was exceedingly careful to refrain from touching upon it.[21] The *Nation* applauded the decision as "showing that the Court is recovering from the war fever, and getting ready to abandon sentimental canons of construction."[22] Even the *Independent* hailed it as the just and true interpretation of the Fourteenth Amendment, intended by its framers.[23] Verily had this journal experienced a rebirth since the days of Milligan and McCardle.

Reconstruction was now drawing to a close. For eight years in this tragedy Black had played a dramatic and dynamic role in defense of the Constitution. The valiant minority in Congress had been over-

[17] Warren, *op. cit.*, III, p. 268.
[18] Quoted in Warren, *op. cit.*, III, p. 262.
[19] Blaine, *op. cit.*, II, p. 419.
[20] Washington *National Republican*, April 16, 1873.
[21] New York *Tribune*, April 15, 1873. Greeley had died the year previously.
[22] *Nation*, April 24, 1873.
[23] *Independent*, May 22, 1873.

whelmed by sheer numbers; the President himself had been stripped of more power than any other in the history of the nation, and had escaped removal from office by the slender margin of a single vote. Yet without office of any kind, Black had achieved as great a measure of success, if not a greater, than any man who had planted himself across the course of the Radical Congress. He had written the veto message upon the original Reconstruction Act. He had defended Milligan—and won a decision freeing the North from military rule. He had defended McCardle—until Congress was forced to repeal one of its own Acts of Reconstruction in order to salvage its main policy. He had played a major role in clipping the wings from the Civil Rights Bill. He had aided in cutting off bodily from the Fourteenth Amendment that portion of it which took civil rights from the States and gave it to the national government.

Now the tragedy of Reconstruction was nearly over, and Black's role in this tragedy had ended. He stood without dispute as the boldest and ablest defender of the Constitution and of personal rights which this era had produced.

26

POLITICS

BLACK'S preëminence in the legal phases of Reconstruction maintained him as a potent figure in Democratic politics, and in 1868 the Democracy of Pennsylvania brought him forward as their choice for President. The Williamsport *Standard* initiated the move and it found a ready support among other Democratic papers of the State. "Judge Black is *the* man" said the Carlisle *Volunteer*. The Harrisburg *Patriot and Union* endorsed the movement. It pointed out that "leading Radical organs in the North from the New York *Tribune* down, via *Harper's Weekly*" had taken "special pains to traduce and misrepresent the Hon. Jeremiah S. Black, who, though only private citizen, (i.e. neither an office-holder nor a seeker after office) is unquestionably the ablest expounder of the Constitution in the land." Such misrepresentations sprang from their fear of his nomination. "Judge Black . . . is a Radical Democrat," continued the *Patriot and Union*, "*not* a 'copperhead' or 'sympathizer with rebellion' as lying Radical sheets like *Harper's Weekly* and Forney's 'two papers—both dailies' would have the world believe, but simply a sound unflinching Democrat of the Jeffersonian and Jackson stamp, whose politics, like his moral character, is without stain or blemish."[1]

The Hanover *Citizen* professed a certain conservatism in the matter. It "refrained from bringing our favorite forward until we could hear from other States." Then it added, "we have not waited in vain. From every section of our extended country, we hear the cheering voice of Pennsylvania's favorite son. Wisconsin, Ohio, New Jersey, Maryland, nearly all the New England States, have spoken out for our choice. . . . Being thus satisfied, we shall henceforth urge the claims of Judge Black." The Chambersburg *Valley Spirit* proclaimed him "beyond dispute the boldest and best Defender of the Constitution and of Popular Rights now living," and urged that "the country has need of a statesman like Judge Black in the Presidential chair." A few Maryland papers took up the cause,[2] but beyond these two states the movement did not spread. As for the "cheering voice" from Wisconsin to New England, heard by one of these papers, it was silent when the Democratic Convention met in New York.

Black himself had little itch for office. "Though I have seen many

[1] Press clippings, Clayton MSS.
[2] *Ibid.*

cases of presidential fever," he said, "have watched with interest its malignant effects, have seen it more fatal than small-pox or yellow fever, yet I may truthfully say that I have never felt the slightest touch of it."[3]

His indifference was not unknown to these newspapers which urged his nomination for President. The Harrisburg *Patriot and Union* had commented upon it. The Chambersburg *Valley Spirit* had admitted that "we do not know with what degree of favor Judge Black himself would look upon a movement in his behalf."[4]

The probable cause of this indifference was not that Black possessed less desire for fame than the common run of men, but that public office did not offer him the outlets which his peculiar nature preferred. He was a man of intense passions, and often of intense prejudices. He was unmatched in phrase making and in invective by any lawyer in his generation. Out of office he had gained a singular distinction for his "surgical ability" to dissect a legal argument and to puncture the armor of the most pachydermatous man who stood before him in lone combat. This skill had brought him both fame and fortune. It offered him an outlet of political satisfaction during the era when his political party was eclipsed by the shadow of discredit and defeat. Radicals in Congress might suppress debate and smother the opposition by an avalanche of votes, but in the court room they must meet him in naked intellectual combat and parry his blows, if they could, single handed.

Had he held public office, he must have quit the arena of the court room. He must have put a curb upon his terrible invective. He must have uttered in public, not the untrammeled thoughts which his nature prompted, but politic thoughts which would not lose his votes at the polls. There would be compromises with politicians and pacifying of office seekers. Both were alien to a temperament which loved a fight without quarter to the finish. In short, out of office he enjoyed not only fame but complete freedom of speech and action. In office, his freedom must be restricted and his arena of combat given up. He was well content to remain unrestricted by office.

Horatio Seymour and Francis P. Blair were nominated by the national Democratic Convention, and Black at once plunged into an active campaign in their behalf. His most prominent speech of this campaign was given at a State Democratic rally held in his home city of York, on August 24, 1868. One reads in that speech, not only his political views, but his attitude toward the conduct of the Civil War and the personal attacks which had been launched against him during Reconstruction.

Through praising Seymour, he struck at those who had attacked

[3] Clayton, p. 89.
[4] Clayton MSS.

himself. "The Scripture says, 'woe unto you when all men speak well of you' which means that you cannot possibly be an honest man and at the same time be popular with the rascals. There is enough said against Mr. Seymour to take that curse away from him."

In discussing Blair, he deftly delivered a thrust at the barbaric conduct of certain army officers during the Civil War. "General Blair . . . was a *fighting*, not a *stealing* general. . . . Whenever he went on duty he wore *two uniforms*—the uniform coat of a soldier, and the uniform *conduct* of a gentleman."

But for the Radical Congress was reserved his especial respects. After detailing the gross unconstitutional nature of their handiwork, he summed it up: "You must presume that members of Congress had read the Constitution. . . . They could not help but see that it provides a jury trial and habeas corpus for every citizen . . . forbade searches and seizures of person and property without a warrant, . . . declares that no act of attainder . . . shall be passed."[5]

But Grant and Colfax were elected, and Black uttered dark prophecies of the corruption which must follow the continuation of the Radicals in power. In response to one of these utterances, his friend George W. Woodward wrote:

> Like yourself I have no hopes of the future of our country. The money power has got possession and will control the labor of the country. . . . The aristocrats of the old world were not so smart as our money Lords, for they provided no better currency for themselves than for their serfs, whereas our aristocrats have helped themselves to gold instead and put us off with paper currency worth from 60 to 70 cts. in the dollar. Never have a people been so chained to the chariot wheel of wealth as we the people of this country. . . . The people are bought like slaves. . . . Oh how I wish I could sit at your feet and listen to you. Do come and see me. I will be at home all this month.[6]

These fears were realized with a vengeance. Never in the history of the American people, and few times in the history of any modern state, has stark naked corruption walked so openly in the light of day as in the administration of Grant. It is impossible for an historian to put his finger upon any major spot of that administration without the oozing of political pus. There was no hiding it. Toward the close of that administration, Senator George Frisbie Hoar—a Republican and a supporter of the administration—burst the seal upon his lips and wrote the story in a few dramatic strokes.

> My own public life (he said) has been a very brief and insignificant one, extending little beyond the duration of a single term of Senatorial office; but in that brief period I have seen five judges of a high court of the United States driven from office by threats of im-

[5] Clayton MSS.

[6] Black Papers, November 11, 1868.

peachment for corruption or maladministration. . . . I have seen the chairman of the Committee of Military Affairs in the House . . . rise in his place demanding the expulsion of four of his associates for making sale of their official privilege of selecting the youths to be educated at our great military school. When the greatest railroad of the world, binding together the continent and uniting the two great seas which wash our shores, was finished, I have seen our national triumph and exaltation turned to bitterness and shame by the unanimous reports of three committees of Congress . . . that every step of that mighty enterprise had been taken in fraud. . . . I have heard that suspicion haunts the footsteps of the trusted companions of the President.[7]

By the end of Grant's first administration there was hope for the falling of this rotten fruit. The Democratic Executive Committee of Pennsylvania called upon Black to prepare a manifesto to the voters of Pennsylvania. The document was short, precise, and powerful—a philippic upon the constitutional usurpations and the corruption of the party in power.

The manifesto attracted wide attention. "We propose," said the Savannah (Ga.) *Republican*, "that the Democracy of all the States adopt Jeremiah Black's address as their platform, and that the Democratic National Convention, when it meets, forego the usual string of resolutions and whereases, and put forth the same address as the Platform of the National Democratic party," Then it added: "And we don't care if they put Jeremiah Black himself upon it as a candidate." Commented the *Boston Post*: "Terser, more logical, or clearer writing than Judge Black's has never been published since the days of the Federalist. . . . In every line is a most powerful arraignment of Radicalism." The Pennsylvania Democracy again took up the Black boom for President. "Judge Black would make a strong Democratic candidate and most excellent President," said the Pittsburgh *Post*.[8]

There also was arising within the ranks of the Republican party an organized opposition toward the widespread corruption. Leaders like Carl Schurz, William Cullen Bryant, David Davis, Horace Greeley, Lyman Trumbull, and Charles Francis Adams joined in a "Liberal movement" to separate themselves from the Republican party.[9] From the first they had an eye toward a coalition with the Democrats. The Democrats were not unwilling to profit by this split within Republican ranks. Therefore, as the day approached for the assembling of the national convention at Cincinnati of this new Liberal movement, the leaders of each group manifested a sensitiveness toward the views of the other.

[7] *Cong. Record*, 44 Cong., 1st Sess., Trial of Belknap, p. 63.
[8] Press clippings, Clayton MSS.
[9] New York *Tribune*, April 30 and May 1, 1872.

On April 29th, two days before the Cincinnati Convention met, the Washington correspondent of the New York *Sun* came to York for an interview with Black upon the important question of coöperation between the Liberal Republicans and the Democrats.

"I determined yesterday to seek out one of the great lights of the Democracy, and interview him," said this correspondent. "I had no difficulty in deciding who the right man was. The Hon. Jerry Black, in point of ability, integrity, and influence, is second to no man in all the land. . . . He is the idol and champion of his party. He also wields the most trenchant pen of any writer on political matters in the Union, and as an orator he has few equals and no superiors living. Whatever emanates from his pen or falls from his lips is received as law and gospel by the voters of his party."

The whole theme of the interview was whether Black would support any man nominated by the Liberal Republicans at Cincinnati. On this Black refused to commit himself. "If," he said, "the Convention will pledge itself and its constituents to stand upon the Constitution, to restore the liberties of the people, and to introduce honesty and economy into the administration of the finances; if they will put their opposition to Gen. Grant's administration upon the specific ground that it is corrupt, lawless, and oppressive; and if they will crown their work by nominating a candidate of known integrity and ability," then, felt Black, he believed that the Democratic party ought to support them.

"Who is your candidate for the Presidency?" inquired the correspondent. "Charles O'Connor," answered Black, although of the Liberal candidates he was particularly disposed toward Charles Francis Adams and Judge David Davis.[10]

But the mountain was in labor and brought forth a mouse. The Cincinnati Convention met and brought forth Horace Greeley as their leader for the Presidency. Of all available men, one cannot conceive of another so unfit to lead this movement. Some of the leaders of the Liberal movement were seeking escape from the dread of centralization; to them he offered no hope of relief. Others were demanding a tariff reform; so bitter was his opposition to them that even while the Convention sat in Cincinnati, Greeley was hammering the cause of a high tariff in his editorials.[11] To the Democrats, he stood as an abolitionist fanatic, and against every time-honored principle of the Democratic party. Yet they were now expected to yield him their support.

As for Black, the support of Greeley was at first unthinkable. His very name was a synonym for abolitionism—a red flag to a Spanish bull. Of all the Radical organs which had taken a special delight in

[10] Press clipping, Clayton MSS.

[11] New York *Tribune*, May 3 and 4, 1872.

personal assaults upon Black for his attacks upon Reconstruction, those of Forney and Greeley had been the most virulent—and Greeley's voice had carried the farther.

To the editor of the York *Gazette*, Black addressed an open letter: He could not agree with those "Liberal Republicans" who were "so extremely liberal"? that they thought "it mean in the Democratic party not to surrender their organization into the hands of its enemies." "There are many thousands of men in the party," he continued, "who will refuse to be dragooned or bullied into the support of that ticket. The Greeley men had better suspend their plan of operation immediately. The longer they continue the less likely they are to succeed either in July or November. 'We the people,' the rank and file, the yeomanry of the country, cannot be driven to the polls as negroes are driven in the South by carpet-baggers and scalawags."[12]

There was no hope of success against the corruption of Grant's administration, however, except through Greeley. Besides, certain Democratic leaders already had committed themselves. Therefore the Democratic Convention at Baltimore on July 10th adopted both the platform and candidate of the Liberals. Then Pennsylvania delegation was defiant, however, and cast twenty-one votes for Black.[13]

Unquestionably was Greeley the bitterest political pill ever swallowed by Black. Yet he swallowed it without even the outward manifestations of a wry face. He even did it skillfully. Upon the day following Greeley's nomination, Blanton Duncan, in behalf of the 700,000 members of the Labor Reformers, wrote Black begging him to allow his name to be brought before their Louisville Convention. He promised these 700,000 votes to Black in the national election, if Black would allow his name to go before that convention.[14] The answer to this request is not preserved, but without doubt Black refused. He was too ardent a Democrat to break with his party. At any rate his name was not brought forward at the Labor Reformer's Convention.[15]

But would he support Greeley, the anathema? Scores of letters poured upon him from wavering Democrats, inquiring his position. At last he gave a full and formal answer to these inquiries through an open letter to the Baltimore *Gazette*. "If I take more time and space than might be expected," he wrote to the editor, "you will please remember that I and a great many other Democrats are in a position which requires something more than a mere definition. We cannot avoid misconstruction without furnishing a rather full explanation. . . . The next President must be Greeley or Grant. The circumstances of the political situation limit our choice to these two men."

[12] York *Gazette*, May 21, 1872.
[13] New York *Tribune*, July 11, 1872.
[14] Black Papers, July 11, 1872.
[15] Stanwood, *A History of the Presidency*, I, p. 339.

Grant's administration was unthinkable:

> "Make the hoar leprosy adored; place thieves,
> And give them title, knee and approbation,
> With Senators on the bench."

As to Greeley, "it cannot be pretended that his political life is very symmetrical. He was in the ranks of the radical abolitionists for a good many years. That is bad; for such associations have a natural tendency to debase him." Yet he had never yielded to their fanatical assaults upon the Constitution, nor had he yielded to the other fanatics who made religious intolerance an issue of politics. In summary, "the reluctance which many of us feel to vote for either of them is hard to overcome." Yet the next President must be Grant or Greeley. "Even if we find no *good* in either of them, we must take the one who shall appear to be *least bad*." And that one was Greeley.[16]

This letter was broadcast over the nation by the Democratic and Liberal press. Three days later, Black's personal friend and political enemy, James Speed,[17] read it in a Kentucky newspaper. At once Speed wrote to Black: "Voting for Greeley will have the same effect upon you that a nauseous dose of medicine does upon a patient over charged with bile . . . it will purge away many of your prejudices and leave you with that feeling of love and charity, so beautifully conspicuous in convalescents." Then, in a genuine expression of his warm friendship for this inveterate enemy of his party, Speed closed, "If Greeley should be elected—which God forbid—I think I will go all the way to York to spend a day or so with you and enjoy with you what I know will be the happiest days of your life."[18]

Speed was saved the trip. Many Liberal Republicans abandoned their own candidate. Democrats sulked at home, refusing to support the man whose life had been devoted to their vituperation. Grant was reëlected, 286 to 76. Greeley died, a madman, three weeks later.

But the rotten fruit was overripe and some was falling even as voters went to the polls. The Credit Mobilier was the greatest of these scandals in the sheer amount of money involved and in the number of politicians who were fattening off of its proceeds. Only by wild efforts was it kept from public light until after the elections were over—then its rottenness was laid open to the public view. But the story must be started at the beginning.

The Credit Mobilier Company of America had been chartered under the laws of Pennsylvania, as a speculative venture in high finance. It

16 Black Papers, August 3, 1872; Clayton MSS.

17 Speed had been Attorney-General, 1863-1865. He had opposed Black in the Milligan case and had received terrific manhandling in that case from Black; see *supra*, p. 153. But the two were warm personal friends.

18 Black Papers, August 6, 1872.

seems to have been organized to turn its hand to any sort of enterprise. In 1867 its head, Oakes Ames, made a contract with the Union Pacific Railroad to build 667 miles of railroad for that company. For this work, Credit Mobilier was to receive $47,925,000 in cash or in Union Pacific securities.[19]

It was a bargain highly profitable to Credit Mobilier. If one wonders why the Union Pacific Railroad should pay so terrific a price for its roadbuilding, the answer is simple. All of the large stockholders in the Union Pacific were also stockholders in the Credit Mobilier.[20] Holding their Union Pacific stock in their left hand, they made a bargain with their right hand which held the Credit Mobilier stock. If the left hand had made a bad bargain, the right hand had made a good one—and the little stockholders in the Union Pacific would be the only ones to suffer.

Not even all of the Credit Mobilier stockholders, however, were to be allowed the fat from roadbuilding. By no means. Therefore, on October 15, 1867, a triple contract was drawn up between Oakes Ames (manager of Credit Mobilier), seven trustees, and the Credit Mobilier Company. This contract gave to the seven trustees the power to execute the roadbuilding contract and to divide among themselves and a few picked stockholders the main profits of the project.[21]

All might have gone well, except that one of the stockholders, H. S. McComb, claimed to have bought 250 shares of this stock, by payment of $25,000 cash, which was never delivered to him. He claimed that the inner ring had taken his cash and refused to deliver the stock. He therefore engaged Black to enter suit in his behalf to compel the company to deliver, not only his original 250 shares, but the 125 other shares, plus the huge amounts of cash, which had accrued as dividend upon this stock.[22]

Through the investigations preparatory to bringing this suit, Black discovered appalling evidence of corruption. Upon the financial side, the Union Pacific Railroad had issued bonds and stock to the amount of $131,000,000 for the building of the railroad. Yet the construction of the road seemed to have cost only $27,000,000. This left a surplus of $104,000,000. He prepared for McComb a statement to the public upon the affair. "The Credit Mobilier," said this statement, "was *supposed* to have built the road or most of it under a contract which Oakes Ames made and which they [the Credit Mobilier] guaranteed. But in point of fact the Pacific Railroad Company bought all of the materials, employed all the labor, superintended the whole work, reported the amount expended, and left to Mr. Ames and the Credit

[19] *Poland Report of Credit Mobilier*, Report No. 77, 42nd Cong., 3rd Sess., p. II.

[20] *Ibid.*

[21] *Ibid.* See also Garfield, *Review of Transactions of Credit Mobilier Company*, p. 7.

[22] 10 Philadelphia Reports, p. 2.

Mobilier the lighter duty of appropriating the profits." Whence and whither went the $104,000,000? If the whole sum did not go to Credit Mobilier, its whereabouts was not known.[23]

In the two years 1866-68, the Credit Mobilier Company had paid dividends to the staggering total of 1,059%—or dividends enough to have covered one hundred years with a return of 10% per year. Yet McComb had been left out. The 375 shares which he claimed were carried upon the books in the name of "Oakes Ames, *Trustee*," and as such Ames had been collecting all of the dividends.[24]

For whom was Ames "trustee" for these 375 shares of stock? None less than Senators and Congressmen of the United States, to whom he was distributing it. According to his books Black found that the stock had been distributed to them at par, although it was worth many times that amount. Some of them had never paid even a cent of cash for it, but merely agreed to take it, allowing Ames to carry it for them without payment. Two swift Credit Mobilier dividends, one for 80% and the other for 60% of the par value, paid off the full purchase price of the stock, and left them besides with a fat 40% cash dividend. There was promise of more such dividends to follow.[25] It was high finance indeed.

Ames's object, in thus initiating Congressmen into the inner circle, was to prevent Congress from regulating by law the rates of transportation over the Union Pacific Railroad. Congressmen, having no direct ownership in this railroad, were supposed to be safe from public criticism. But owning stock in Credit Mobilier, which was fattening off of Union Pacific property, they were expected to look with a friendly eye upon any legislation which might favor the railroad, and to oppose any which might regulate its operation.

Who were the Congressmen involved? McComb had copied the list from Ames's books. This he showed to Black. The list included James G. Blaine, Henry F. Wilson, Schuyler Colfax, Henry L. Dawes, George Boutwell, J. W. Patterson, and James A. Garfield.[26] Later additions added the names of James F. Wilson and William B. Allison of Iowa, J. A. Bingham of Ohio, and "Pig Iron" Kelley of Pennsylvania.[27]

James A. Garfield was one of Black's closest personal friends. He was credited with ten shares. According to Ames's books he had never paid down a cent for these shares, but had allowed the high dividends to pay it off and had taken a cash dividend of $329 after his stock had been thus paid for.[28]

Black at once went to Garfield. He insisted that no Congressman

[23] Black Papers, January, 1878 (1873?).

[24] *Ibid.*; Poland, op. *cit.*, p. III.

[25] Poland, *op. cit.*, p. VII.

[26] McComb submitted this copy to the Poland Committee; see p. 6.

[27] Poland, *op. cit.*, pp. 212, 304, 197.

[28] Poland, *op. cit.*, p. VII.

could allow his name to be connected with Credit Mobilier, that the company was not only defrauding the Union Pacific, but even its own stockholders, and that they literally were giving the stock to Congressmen under the pretense of "selling" in order to influence action upon any legislation that might arise.[29]

Whatever might have been the motives which led Garfield into buying this stock, he convinced Black that he had acted honestly in the matter and without any knowledge whatever of the true nature of the Credit Mobilier enterprise.[30] Ames was still holding the stock as "trustee" for Garfield. Therefore, at Black's insistence, Garfield refused to take up the stock or to receive further dividends.

These events had occurred in the winter of 1869-70. More than two years passed and still McComb was unable to get any settlement from Credit Mobilier for the 375 shares of stock which he claimed to have bought and paid for. Black meanwhile was pressing the claim with vigor and in order to avoid the net, the stockholders of Credit Mobilier voted, on June 12, 1872, to dissolve their corporation. Under the laws of Pennsylvania, in which Credit Mobilier was incorporated, a dissolution would extinguish all debts due to and from a corporation[31]

This, of course, would allow the inner ring of Credit Mobilier stockholders to keep the fat already fried out of the Union Pacific Railroad; it would leave the Congressmen in possession of the profits derived from the 375 shares of stock which McComb claimed belonged to him. Black and McComb, however, did not propose to allow Oakes Ames and his colleagues to escape so easily. Black demanded a settlement out of court of the money due McComb. The Credit Mobilier officials refused and carried on their petition for dissolution. Thereupon, Black entered suit for McComb in the Court of Common Pleas at Philadelphia to prevent a dissolution.[32]

A part of the evidence filed by Black in this suit consisted of two incriminating letters written by Ames to McComb. These letters revealed the red line of corruption which ran from the treasury of Credit Mobilier through the halls of Congress. They were now laid open to the public view.[33]

The first of these incriminating letters, written by Ames, told of him placing McComb's stocks "where they will do most good to us," and named the various States whose Congressmen and Senators had

[29] J. A. Garfield, *Review of Transaction of Credit Mobilier,* p. 12.

[30] Black to Blaine, Feb. 15, 1873, Garfield, *op. cit.,* p. 14.

[31] *Pa.* vs. *Credit Mobilier,* 10 Philadelphia Reports, p. 2.

[32] *Ibid.*

[33] R. Hazard, in *The Credit Mobilier of America,* p. 34, insinuated that Black was using these letters as blackmail. Either Hazard was ignorant of or ignored the lawsuit over the dissolution of Credit Mobilier which was the cause of the release of these letters. Hazard's paper is an attempted defense of Credit Mobilier. As such it is ingenious, but omits too many historical facts.

bought the stock. The next letter remarked that "we want more friends in this Congress" so that "we should not be interfered with."[34]

They appeared first in the New York *Sun* on September 4, 1872—two months before the Presidential election. Later there appeared rumors naming the Congressmen who were supposed to have bought the Credit Mobilier stock. A wild panic swept the Republican ranks. Denials were heard upon all sides. Among those whom rumor connected with buying stock was James A. Garfield. In an effort to clear his name, he called upon Black for aid. Black's reply is, without doubt, the most significant document yet uncovered concerning Garfield's connection with Credit Mobilier:[35]

Don't attempt any defence of O. A. or his ring. You have, I believe, no idea of what it is like. It will turn out to be the most enormous fraud that has ever been perpetrated. Oakes & his confederates are indefensible—drunken, destroyed—gone, hook and line. The party will hold them above water until the election and then let them go. What I think you ought to do, sooner or later, is give the public the explanation which you gave me and wh. nobody can doubt is the true one. The following are the points of it according to my recollection:

1. You regarded O. A. as a perfectly upright man . . .

2. He offered you some stock in Cred. Mob., offered to sell it at par . . .

3. You declined at first to take it (tho you believed what he said about it) because you had not the money . . . and then he offered and urged you to take it on credit which you did.

4. When you made the contract you . . . had no reason to believe that the Cred. Mob. had any connection with the Un. Pac. RR. Co or anything else which Cong. could by any possibility be called on to legislate.

5. At a subsequent time when you proposed to adjust your indebtedness, for the stock, Mr. A. put you off . . .

6. At a still later time he showed you an acc't in wh. you were charged with the price of the stock at par, & credited with the dividends rec'd by him for you. This left a balance in yr. favor wh. he then paid.

7. During all this time you were not informed and did not suspect that the Cred. Mob. was connected with the U. P. R.R. Co. or that

[34] New York *Sun*, September 4, 1872; copies of these letters appear in Poland, pp. 4, 7.

[35] Garfield, before the Poland Investigating Committee, denied ever having purchased any stock or receiving any money as dividends. That committee refused to accept his version, whereupon Garfield then published a "Review of the Transactions of Credit Mobilier Co." still denying having bought the stock. In this Review he quoted a letter from Black. But in this letter Black merely said that Garfield "was perfectly unconscious of anything evil." It offered no denial of Garfield having purchased the stock. The letter cited in the above text is good evidence that Garfield had admitted to Black of having bought Credit Mobilier stock.

either of those companies was committing anything wrong against the U. S. or anybody else.

I think I am accurate substantially. It relieves you entirely from every imputation wh. A's statement, unexplained, might case upon you. It shows that you were not the instrument of his corruption, but the victim of his deception.[36]

Garfield and Black, evidently, had further conferences upon the matter, for upon November 7th Blaine wrote to Garfield, "I have a note from Judge Black based on a conversation you had with him in regard to the investigation of which we talked at Cleveland. I sincerely hope you have not talked with anyone else in regard to it, as it would kill the whole thing to have it get in the papers and a very little talk will send it there."[37]

After the election, in which Grant was overwhelmingly reëlected, the administration assumed a pious air and undertook to wash its dirty linen through investigating committees of Congress.

The appalling facts revealed by these committees were well summed up as follows by the *Nation*: "Total loss, one Senator; badly damaged and not serviceable for future political use, two Vice-Presidents and eight Congressmen."[38]

Who were the "eight Congressmen"? They included the chairman of the appropriating committee, the ways and means committee, the naval committee, the banking and currency committee, and the judiciary committee. Of these eight Henry Wilson (Vice-President elect), J. A. Bingham, James F. Wilson, Henry L. Dawes, William B. Allison, "Pig Iron" Kelley—all admitted buying Credit Mobilier stock.[39] Schuyler Colfax (outgoing Vice-President), James A. Garfield, and James G. Blaine chose to deny it.[40] Black was present as attorney for McComb when Garfield took the stand. He intervened and put a few questions himself. Garfield could have admitted his purchase and called upon Black to testify that he had refused to keep the stock when Black had warned him of its danger three years before. But instead he chose to deny having taken the stock and having ever received any dividends.[41]

Schuyler Colfax was caught red-handed. Ames produced a check for $1200 that he had paid Colfax in dividends. Colfax denied having received it, but his bank statement showed that on the day following he had made a $1200 deposit. He was thereupon called on to explain the coincidence. For ten days his mind was blank. He left Washington,

[36] Black to Garfield, Black Papers, September 29, 1872.
[37] Black Papers, Nov. 7, 1872.
[38] Quoted in Bowers, *op. cit.*, p. 397.
[39] Poland, *op. cit.*, pp. 187, 191, 212, 113, 304, 197.
[40] *Ibid.*, pp. 83, 129, 1.
[41] *Ibid.*, p. 130.

left Congress in session, and went off over the country, attending religious and temperance meetings, preaching about "unjust aspersions," and receiving wild applause.[42] After ten days his memory cleared. He now remembered all the details. A Mr. Nesbit, friend of his, had sent him a $1,000 "gift," and his father-in-law had at the same time paid off a $200 debt. And $1,000 plus $200, of course, equaled $1,200. He remembered Nesbit's gift most clearly for at the time it struck him as a remarkable and astonishing gift.[43]

The committee was satisfied with his arithmetic. Besides, Nesbit, most conveniently, was now dead and could not himself testify. But the *Nation* was unkind enough to inquire why—if this singular gift had so remarkably impressed Colfax at the time—it took him ten days to recall it to mind?[44]

Oakes Ames also was a member of Congress. Naturally there was no saving him. Besides, why should he be saved? Had he not turned state's evidence? No punishment was too severe for such a rogue. Also in this select company, there was one Democrat—James Brooks of New York. So the committee made its investigation and rendered its report. Ames and Brooks, the committee found, were guilty of the terrible crime of corruption. Blaine was completely exonerated. Henry Wilson, James Wilson, Allison, Dawes, Schofield, Bingham, and Kelley, all had admitted buying the stock. Therefore, they were innocent of evil thoughts or intent. Garfield and Colfax both denied buying the stock. They had perjured themselves. Therefore, they too were innocent.[45]

If the party could not "point with pride" to these leading members, at least it could point to a tub of whitewash expediently used.

"The Poland Committee Report . . ." said the *Nation*, "is hardly worth discussing." Brooks and Ames were recommended to be expelled from Congress. As for the others who had admitted taking the stock and receiving dividends, "none of these men . . . had any corrupt motives in buying the stock." They "were not in common decency bound to inquire what the Credit Mobilier was."[46]

Oakes Ames wrote the final epitaph of the affair. "It's like the man in Massachusetts," he said, "who committed adultery and the jury brought in a verdict that he was guilty as the devil, but that the woman was as innocent as an angel. These fellows are like that woman."[47]

The Credit Mobilier of America was having likewise a checkered career in the courts. During the very days in which the Poland Com-

[42] *Nation*, February 6, 1873.
[43] Poland, *op. cit.*, p. 502.
[44] *Nation*, February 20, 1873.
[45] Poland, *op. cit.*, pp. V-XIX.
[46] *Nation*, February 12, 1873.
[47] New York *World*, February 19, 1873; quoted in Bowers, *op. cit.*, p. 401.

mittee was plying its whitewash in Washington, Black was resisting in court the Credit Mobilier effort to escape its payment to McComb. The Court of Common Pleas in Philadelphia handed down its decision, in the same month that the Poland Committee reported to Congress. By this decision, the prayer for dissolution was refused, and the company thus defeated in its initial effort to avoid payment.[48] McComb's suit dragged through the courts for another five years, ending finally in the United States Circuit Court, by a decision rejecting his claim to the stock.[49]

The prolonged corruption of the Grant administration was bearing fruit at last. In 1874 the Democrats swept into control of the House of Representatives. In Pennsylvania, to their own surprise, they captured the Legislature whose first function on meeting in January would be to elect a United States Senator. At once a movement was launched to send Black to the Senate. Hardly had the election returns been completed when the Lancaster *Intelligencer* exclaimed of Black, "Thou art the man!"[50] Three days later the Louisville *Courier-Journal* declared that "To the world outside, the election of a Democratic United States Senator in Pennsylvania irresistibly suggests the name of Judge Black. . . . The Democracy of the whole country *en masse* asks Pennsylvania to send him to Washington."[51] The press of Maryland, Alabama, Ohio, New York, and Indiana took up the cause. Even the far-off tiny Dubuque, Iowa, *Daily Telegraph* had its word: "We go for Black. There is no superior to him . . . and but few his equal."[52]

The conservative and influential New York *Sun* believed that if the question "Who shall be Senator? were submitted to the Democratic voters" of Pennsylvania, Black "would beyond doubt receive nine-tenths of the votes cast." Yet that paper had no false illusions as to the chances for his election. "He will probably fare about as well in a Democratic caucus at Harrisburg as Charles Francis Adams would in a Republican caucus at Boston."[53]

Black was not unwilling to accept the office, although he refused to undertake a campaign. To A. A. Chase he wrote:

I know less about it than probably any other well informed man in the State. Partly this ignorance is wilful and partly it happens very naturally because I am not in the confidence of those who are most active in carrying on the business. I do not expect to learn much more of the subject until after the 19th of January when the Legislature itself will effectually post me. I have not thought from the first that I was likely to be elected. I did not offer myself, but I could

[48] 10 Philadelphia Reports, p. 2.
[49] 13 Philadelphia Reports, p. 468.
[50] Lancaster *Intelligencer*, November 7, 1874.
[51] November 10, 1874.
[52] Clayton MSS.
[53] December 2, 1874.

not say then and cannot now say that if chosen I would not serve. I would on the contrary give my whole heart and mind to the promotion of certain great measures upon which I think the future prosperity of the country, and the entire restoration of liberties depends.[54]

But there was a legion of hungry office seekers, at least fifty for every place "on the hill" and for every mite of patronage. Three of the most powerful politicians of the State, each with the power of patronage behind him, were seeking the Senatorship. Black had no patronage, no political power, only reputation. The Senatorship went to William A. Wallace.

In truth, Black seems to have thrown all of his political strength to the support of his son Chauncey. The latter was very active in helping to make Samuel Randall Speaker of the House of Representatives.[55] Chauncey Black about this time, 1875, began the steady writing of editorials and political articles for the New York *Sun*. He finally was elected Lieutenant Governor of Pennsylvania in 1880.

Nevertheless, as the Presidential campaign of 1876 came around, there again arose an effort to place Black upon the national Democratic ticket. A New Orleans paper began urging "Thomas A. Hendricks for President and Jeremiah S. Black for Vice-President." *Harper's Weekly* commented that "The battle-cry would obviously be 'Tom and Jerry.' "[56]

Black's friends, however, were urging his nomination for the Presidency itself. The Pittsburgh *Post* led the campaign and the Democratic press of that State solidly backed the movement although, as the Lewistown *True Democrat* remarked, "His very pre-eminence of intellectual ability and purity of moral character would, in all probability, help to defeat rather than secure his nomination."[57] A few outstate papers took up the cause, notably the Minneapolis *Tribune*. "As Republicans," said that paper, "we look forward with ardent hope . . . to the success of the nominee of our party," yet if the Democrats "can nominate Judge Black, they will startle the country with an evidence of vitality not yet visible."[58] That paper's evening contemporary, the Minneapolis *Daily Evening Mail*, likewise Republican, reported that "there is undoubtedly a strong feeling among the Democrats of Minnesota in favor of Judge Black."[59]

At the Pennsylvania Democratic Convention, held on March 22nd, Black's old friend George W. Woodward moved that the delegates

[54] Black Papers, December 24, 1874.

[55] The Black Papers from January to June, 1880, show fifty letters from Randall to Chauncey Black upon affairs of the House. Their correspondence from 1874 to 1880 was extensive.

[56] *Harper's Weekly*, April 15, 1876.

[57] Clayton MSS.

[58] Minneapolis *Tribune*, March 7, 1876.

[59] Clayton MSS.

be instructed to support Black, "but although a strong sentiment in favor of Judge Black for President pervaded the convention, a majority thought it best" to leave the delegation uninstructed. Considering the strong sentiment both in and out of the State in favor of Black, it is difficult to understand why the majority of delegates should have thus withheld their formal support. But in truth the Democratic Party in Pennsylvania since 1860 had been dissevered by internecine strife, and even in victory was seldom able to work together in harmony.

Nevertheless Black's strong newspaper support continued and even grew. But on May 1st he formally withdrew his name. "I have never encouraged in the slightest degree any effort to make me a candidate," he wrote to the editor of the Pittsburgh *Post*. "But I could not interfere . . . without being offensive to persons for whom I felt greatest respect and affection." Nevertheless he now desired that "my name be dropped from the list of possible candidates" for reasons "some of them private and personal, others personal and political."[60] The *Post* and the Democratic press of Pennsylvania, however, refused to surrender their advocacy of his nomination. Said the Lancaster *Intelligencer*, "We do not suppose that Judge Black himself thinks he has the power to withdraw his name from the consideration of the people."[61]

There was likewise some correspondence between Black's friends and other national party leaders. Henry Watterson of the Louisville *Courier-Journal* wrote to one of these friends: "There is not a man in America whom I think more of than our friend Judge Black and if the wheel at St. Louis turns his way, he may be sure of all the consideration he could expect of you or Chauncey. I take it that he will not be presented directly. But there is no knowing what may not happen."[62]

But at St. Louis, Samuel J. Tilden was nominated on the second ballot. By 1880 Black had passed the age of availability as a national candidate.

[60] Letter to James P. Barr, Clayton MSS.
[61] Lancaster *Intelligencer*, May 8, 1876.
[62] Watterson to "Peter," Black Papers, 1876.

27

THE GENERAL PRACTICE OF LAW

FROM the time of Black's first connection with the land cases of California until his death he carried on an enormous general practice in the law. At first he formed a partnership with his son-in-law, James F. Shunk. But this partnership was dissolved within two or three years, probably because of Shunk's failing health. Shunk seems to have withdrawn entirely from the practice of law and to have undertaken the writing of Buchanan's biography after Black withdrew from that project,[1] but his health continued to fail and shortly afterward he died.[2]

After the dissolution of partnership with Shunk, Black then took Ward H. Lamon as a junior partner.[3] This partnership maintained an office in Washington. It carried on business for about five years. But Lamon had contracted with Chauncey F. Black to write a biography of Abraham Lincoln. Lamon was to furnish the materials, Chauncey Black to do the entire writing of the biography, for a stipulated sum of money, and the completed work was to be published under Lamon's name. The biography was thus written and published, and is still known today as Lamon's *Life of Lincoln.* But Lamon and the publishers changed so many portions of it that Chauncey Black entered suit to prevent the publication in its altered form. In this he was unsuccessful, but the book as published was a complete financial loss, leaving him with the satisfaction of knowing that he alone derived a profit from the enterprise. This estrangement caused Lamon to withdraw from his partnership with Black.

Thereafter Black practiced law alone. His relations with the partnership office in Washington always had been casual. Now he practiced without the pretense of having an office. His home was in York. His chief practice was in Washington. His clients might find him, however, in New York, Philadelphia, Baltimore, Texas or Michigan—in county courts, or in the highest State or Federal courts—wherever large interests might claim his talents.[4]

Clients often complained that they received no answers to their

[1] *Buchanan's Works,* XI, pp. 449, 450.

[2] Forward-Black Family Bible.

[3] New York *Tribune,* December 20, 1865. Lamon formerly was a law partner of Abraham Lincoln.

[4] Hensel, p. 193; Niles to the author, January 10, 1930.

letters. Black replied that their letters never reached him. In truth his habits of business were beyond the power of any postal system to render service. Not only did he have no office, but he did not maintain even a secretary to receive and dispose of his mail. The matter was left to members of his family. The house in York usually was closed during the winter and he took up quarters with his family in Washington. Letters, forwarded there from York, might find him in Philadelphia or Galveston. In following him around, many letters were lost. Others were saved by his friends holding them and writing to learn his whereabouts before sending them on. Nevertheless he continued to go from court to court, trying cases, and winning so large a portion of them that clients who one day were complaining of his neglect of their correspondence, were the next day pouring out their gratitude on paper for his winning of their suits.

Even before Black had initiated Garfield into the practice of law in the important Milligan case, he attempted to induce Garfield to join him in a partnership. "The judge talks very hopefully," wrote Garfield, "and thinks we can reap large mutual advantages from such a partnership. My present impression is that I shall at first make a conditional and temporary partnership which . . . [will] leave me free to go on in Congress to the end of my term and then I can make a final decision."[5] But Garfield was then engrossed in an oil land business and the partnership was not formed. Apparently it was not until Garfield decided not to enter partnership that Black formed his partnership with Lamon.

Nevertheless, after the Milligan case, Black and Garfield continued to practice together without any regular agreement of partnership. Their first important case together was in the famous Alexander Campbell Will controversy. Campbell was one of the founders of the Disciples Church, of which both Black and Garfield were members. At his death, two groups of Campbells, descended from two successive wives, became involved in a controversy over his will. Black was called upon to defend the will left by Campbell, and engaged Garfield to aid him in the enterprise. The case was tried at Wellsburg, the county seat of Brooke County, in which Bethany was located. After a series of postponements, the case came up February 17, 1868. Black had prepared the brief. Together with Garfield he appeared at the opening day of the trial. The second day he left, turning the full case to Garfield. The hearing of evidence took six days; the argument took two and a half more. The verdict was in favor of the defendants, represented by Black and Garfield.[6]

After the firm of Black and Lamon had dissolved, Black again attempted to induce Garfield to join him in a full and formal partner-

[5] April 10, 1865. Smith, *Garfield*, p. 825.
[6] *Ibid.*, p. 829.

ship. Garfield was still in Congress. "I am, at this moment, greatly tempted to resign," he wrote. "At any rate, I shall think further of the proposition." But shortly after this he was unanimously renominated by his district in Ohio and so again deferred it. Garfield's most serious objection to joining Black was that such a partnership would force him to change his residence to Washington. He would thereby lose his citizenship in Ohio. He feared that he might not succeed as well in the law as he hoped and might desire to return to political life. He therefore hesitated before this project of giving up his Ohio citizenship.[7]

The two men, however, continued their occasional practice together. Their last important case together was that of Phillips' Appeal in 1870 before the Supreme Court of Pennsylvania. The four Phillips brothers were personal friends of Black, and their entire estate was at stake in this trial. They were defendants in a suit for payment upon certain contracts. The issue was whether the payment should be made in cash or whether it should be made in oil stocks at par value. But the oil stocks were worth several times their par value, and to count them at par would, in effect, increase the payments by about four hundred per cent. A master had examined the claims and reported the amount due from the Phillips brothers to be $246,688.04. A lower court had affirmed the judgment. The Phillips brothers had then appealed to the Supreme Court, engaged Black to appear for them, and Black had called in Garfield.

The outcome of the trial was a brilliant triumph for Black and Garfield, for the Supreme Court rejected the master's report and reduced the amount to be paid down to $62,489.53—or approximately one-quarter of the original sum.[8]

Through a clever manipulation, however, the plaintiffs managed to get a nominally distinct case back into the courts in the following year which again involved the Phillips brothers with this claim. Again Black and Garfield appeared for the defendants. This time their triumph was even more brilliant. The first award of $62,489.53 was shrunk to $30,000.00.[9]

One of the most famous cases in which Black appeared was that of the Goodyear Rubber Company. The history of this case began when Goodyear sued the Providence Rubber Company for infringements upon the Goodyear patents. Black was first drawn into this case in 1862,[10] on the side of the Providence Rubber Company, although it was more than seven years before the case came to a final settlement.

[7] *Ibid.*, p. 831.
[8] 68 Pa. State Reports, p. 131.
[9] Smith, *Garfield*, p. 834.
[10] A. Payne to Black, Black Papers, Dec. 8, 1862.

Meanwhile it had gone through the United States Circuit Court of Rhode Island and at different times had been heard by three of the judges of the United States Supreme Court, sitting in these circuit hearings. Each of them had sustained the Goodyear suit. Therefore, when the suit came before the Supreme Court for a final hearing in 1869, the attorneys for the Providence Rubber Company were in a position where they must win the opinion of all five of the remaining judges upon the bench or lose the case.

Besides Black, for the Providence Company, were Caleb Cushing, James A. Garfield, J. H. Parsons, Abraham Payne, and W. W. Boyce. For the Goodyear Company were W. E. Curtis, W. M. Evarts, E. W. Stoughton and J. H. Ackerman. The testimony in the Circuit Court had covered 1200 pages. The arguments before the Supreme Court covered another 700 pages.[11]

The Supreme Court sustained the Circuit Courts and upheld the Goodyear patents.[12] The Providence Rubber Company was enjoined from infringing upon these patents, and all motions to file further petitions and crossbills were denied.[13]

This was the largest suit that Black ever lost.

The railroads at this time were in an age of bitter competition and with little government regulation. Railway lawsuits filled the courts and there was not a year after Black retired from public office when he was not engaged in from one to half a dozen of these cases. In 1862 the Minnesota and Pacific Railroad offered him five sections of land to represent them in a suit with the North Western Railroad Company, then pending before the United States Supreme Court.[14] But Black does not seem to have taken their case.

One of the earliest railway cases in which he appeared illustrates the type of litigation that was common in this period. Four railways—operating in the three different States of New York, Ohio, and Pennsylvania—had combined under one system, known as the Atlantic and Great Western Railway, whereupon the Attorney-General of Pennsylvania brought suit to dissolve this combination, and to force the four roads to continue operation as separate units. The case became one which was to set a precedent of whether railways in the United States were to be allowed to operate as interstate trunk lines, such as we take for granted today, or whether they were to end at each state line in the manner that characterized and so long throttled the commercial development of Australia.

Black appeared for the railway, defending the right of consolida-

[11] 9 Wallace, p. 788.

[12] *Ibid.*

[13] *Ibid.*, pp. 805, 807. Black did not appear in these attempts to reopen the case.

[14] Black Papers, Jan. 30, 1862.

tion. The Supreme Court of Pennsylvania in 1866 delivered an epoch-making decision, sustaining this right.[15]

Immediately thereafter there arose with this consolidated road the issue of whether a stockholder in one of the original four companies, who refused to exchange the original for the amalgamated stock, could have any stockholder's rights in the new company. In effect, it again opened the issue upon the legality of consolidation. The Atlantic and Great Western Railway lost the case in the lower courts, but carried it to the Pennsylvania Supreme Court. Again Black appeared in their behalf. The Supreme Court reversed the lower court, declaring that unless a stockholder converted his stock, he could have no rights in the new corporation.[16] The distinct effect of these decisions was to promote the consolidation of short railways into trunk lines.

T. W. Peirce, whom Black had represented in the Floyd Acceptances case, persuaded him with great difficulty to handle a suit over the ownership of the Galveston, Houston and Henderson Railroad, held in Galveston, Texas, during the year 1868. Black lost the first hearing of this case.[17] He thereupon took an appeal to the Circuit Court of the United States and won it.[18] The other contestants for the ownership of the road then carried an appeal to the United States Supreme Court. For some reason Black did not appear in this argument, stating to Peirce that he feared his appearance would prejudice it. Benjamin R. Curtis headed the counsel in this argument and lost the case. Black and Peirce then exchanged some correspondence upon a reopening of the case, but its procedure in the courts is lost from view. Later, however, Peirce turned up as President of the railroad. Presumably he was successful in the end.[19]

The Pittsburgh, Fort Wayne and Chicago Rail*way* Company also engaged Black in an unusual case. Formerly the road had gone under the name of the Pittsburgh, Fort Wayne and Chicago Rail*road* Company. But certain alleged creditors of the rail*road* company brought suit in the Federal Courts to foreclose it. This company thereupon sought relief by appealing to the Legislature of Pennsylvania and secured from that body an act providing for a reorganization of the company. The Pittsburgh, Fort Wayne and Chicago Rail*road* Company thereupon dissolved. The effect of this dissolution was to extinguish all debts and alleged debts. Being thus freed from creditors seeking foreclosure, the bondholders then reorganized themselves into

[15] *Attor. Gen.* vs. *At. & Gr. W. Ry.*, 53 Pa. Reports, p. 9. One great incentive toward consolidation was to standardize the width of track. One of these roads had a 6 ft. gauge; another had a 4 ft. 8 in. gauge.

[16] *Scott* vs. *At. & Gr. W. Ry. et al*, 53 Pa. Reports, p. 20.

[17] Black Papers, July 7, 1868.

[18] Black Papers, July 13, 17, 1868; March 15, April 3, May 28, 1869.

[19] Black Papers, September 1, 1873; June 21, 1875.

the Pittsburgh, Fort Wayne and Chicago Rail*way* Company. At once the old alleged creditors brought suit for collection of the old debt, claiming that the so-called two corporations were in reality the same. The case passed through the lower courts and into the Supreme Court of Pennsylvania. Here Black entered the case as counsel for the rail*way* company. The Supreme Court sided with Black's client, decreeing that the rail*way* company was not the same as the rail*road* company, and hence not liable for its debts.[20] Perhaps the most famous of these railroad cases in which he appeared, however, was the Osage Land Case—a case remarkable for the extent of property involved and for the vast number of people interested in the decision. It was heard before the Supreme Court in 1875, but its beginnings dated from fifty years previous. Let us, then, run the story back to 1825.

In that year the Osage Indians ceded a part of their lands to the United States Government, reserving the remainder for themselves.[21] But in 1865 these Indians, being impoverished with an excess of land, disposed of their surplus to the Government. The Government was to *sell* this land and turn the money into an Indian trust fund.[22] Meanwhile, two years before this, in 1863, Congress had authorized the State of Kansas to make land grants for stimulating the construction of railway and telegraph lines. The State was allowed to grant railway companies every alternate section for ten sections in width upon each side of any road that might be built, but not thereby to disturb any rights of persons who might already have acquired such lands by homestead or purchase. In such cases, other lands were to be given to the railway.[23]

Kansas accepted this grant and designated a railroad route through the Osage lands.

Settlers had begun pouring into the Osage lands as soon as it was opened to sale by the treaty with the Indians. They had selected their sites, recorded them in the land offices, and begun their payments of $1.25 an acre. Meanwhile houses had sprung up, barns appeared, sod had been broken. A wild prairie had been turned into farms. The railroad would soon be finished and the hand of civilization be extended farther into the great West.

Then came the disastrous news that the Secretary of Interior had refused to accept payments upon any of the odd-numbered sections within ten miles of the new railroad. Such lands, he claimed, had been granted to the new railroad.[24]

[20] 22 Smith, p. 29, which reports this case, does not show Black as being upon the counsel. But Black Papers, November 25, 1872, June 7, 1873, and May 28, 1874, show him to have represented the railroad in this case.

[21] *Statutes at Large,* VII, p. 240.

[22] *Ibid.,* XIV, p. 687.

[23] *Ibid.,* XII, p. 772.

[24] 2 Otto p. 738.

Few others than those who themselves have lived in a new country can realize the full extent of this disaster. Men, women—whole families—had packed their earthly possessions into a wagon, had severed ties with their life behind, and followed westward the course of empire. Upon the fringe of civilization, where the Indian menace still haunted the horizon, they had driven their stakes, planted their hopes, and invested their last cent. Now, one-half of these settlers throughout five counties were to be torn from their lands and sent forth destitute—leaving behind a bruised welt of twenty miles for a railroad to plunder.

The settlers about to be thus driven out banded together for protection. At one meeting alone 5,000 were present. It was quiet, orderly, but "very earnest." The Governor and Congressman of Kansas came down and pledged their support.[25]

The settlers appealed their case to the Circuit Court of the United States—alleging that the Government could not grant any of the Osage lands to railway companies, since it had bound itself by an Indian treaty only to sell these lands. From the lower court, the case went by appeal to the Supreme Court of the United States. The settlers then engaged Black to assist their local attorneys in defending their title to the lands.[26]

The case was argued on October 20, 21, 22, 1875.[27] The settlers in Kansas nervously awaited the decision. By the middle of the following month, the tension was acute. From day to day they were expecting the news. "I cannot describe the intense anxiety felt by our people for the result," wrote their attorney in Kansas to Black. "I dare not think of a defeat. I could not bear it, and should this Court inflict it upon me, I am sure I should never be fit for 'self-government' any more."[28]

November passed, . . . December . . . January . . . February . . . and no decision came from the Supreme Court. Spring came and the winter wheat was shooting up. Would its harvest belong to the settlers or the railroad? At last, upon April 10, 1876, came the decision. The lands belonged to the settlers.[29]

This case had meant more to Black than an ordinary one. It was an issue of human rights against corporate rights. It was another Milligan, another McCardle. In a grim joy over the triumph, he wired the news to Kansas in the following telegram:

"Opinion by Davis, Miller affirmed. Lawrence sustained. Shannon

[25] Philadelphia *Press*, October 3, 1873.

[26] Black Papers, May 1, 1873.

[27] 2 Otto, p. 733. No copy of Black's argument in this case has been preserved.

[28] G. R. Peck to Black, Black Papers, November 15, 1875.

[29] *National Intelligencer*, April 11, 1876.

honored. Peck glorified. Justice vindicated. Truth triumphant. Settlers protected. The Lord God Omnipotent reigneth!"[30]

The Leavenworth (Kans.) *Daily Times* carried this telegram to its readers beneath headlines eight inches deep. The typesetter evidently was excited, for the headlines read: "The Settlers Protected, and the Lord Still *Raineth* [sic] Supreme."[31]

Lithographs of the telegram were scattered among the settlers whose land titles had been involved.[32]

The Vanderbilt Will Case was another of the famous suits in which Black appeared. "Commodore" Vanderbilt, at his death, had left to William H. Vanderbilt, his eldest son, $80,000,000, which was the bulk of his estate. To another son, Cornelius, he had left but $200,000.[33] The latter—already $300,000 in debt—entered suit to break the will, claiming that the Commodore had been of unsound mind and unduly influenced by his eldest son. The old Commodore, however, had been one of the original specimens of ruthless American captains of industry—a man who at seventy had taken his fortune of $11,000,000, made in the shipping industry, thrown it into railroads, and came out at eighty with $104,000,000. It was no mean task to establish insanity in such a species. Nevertheless Scott Lord, who was manager of the case for Cornelius Vanderbilt, pushed it with vigor and engaged Black to appear in the argument.[34]

For two years this case was fought out in the courts of New York.[35] As the end approached, through the final hearing before the New York Supreme Court, it became the sensation of the hour. Crowds jammed the courtroom and at times overflowed into the streets. On March 5, 1879, however, it came to an unexpected end. Abruptly the suit was withdrawn. The family row had been settled out of court, by William H. Vanderbilt paying to Cornelius $1,000,000 instead of the $200,000 granted in the will.[36]

The last great case in which Black was engaged was the Mormon case arising out of the Edmunds Act of Congress. A Congressional Act of 1862 had prohibited polygamy. The Edmunds Act of 1882 enlarged upon this and set up a commission to supervise the election of territorial officers in Utah. But the commission reached Utah too late to hold an election in 1882, and the Territorial Governor filled all offices by appointment. The Governor and the Mormon Church al-

[30] Davis and Miller were Supreme Court judges. Lawrence was a Congressman from Ohio who argued the case with Black. Shannon and Peck were Kansas lawyers who aided in the case but did not argue.

[31] Leavenworth *Daily Times*, April 11, 1876.

[32] Clayton, p. 118.

[33] B. J. Hendrick, *McClure's Magazine*, November 1908, p. 62.

[34] Black Papers, April 2, 3, 1879.

[35] March 13, 1877, to March 20, 1879. See New York *Tribune*, March 20, 1879.

[36] New York *Tribune*, March 5, April 8, and April 9, 1879.

ready were in conflict and the Mormons claimed that he had deliberately wrested control of electoral offices from their hands and turned them to bitter enemies of the church. For a while they threatened to resist the right of appointed officers to take over the government, but finally yielded and took the case to the courts. The new Territorial officers at once undertook to disenfranchise all polygamists who were ex post facto offenders, as well as those who had contracted polygamous marriages after its prohibition by Congress.[37]

Black took the case for the Mormons as it came up for final hearing before the United States Supreme Court. He prepared to argue again the great issue of personal rights before this court, where so often he had argued it before. But the case was postponed and he did not live to see its final settlement.[38]

These cases which have been discussed are, of course, only the more outstanding ones with which Black was connected during the last twenty years of his life. They are merely a fraction of the total number—a total which would run into the hundreds. He successfully defended the right of Washington College and Jefferson College to unite, as Washington and Jefferson College, in a sensational suit which was carried by the minority of the trustees of these colleges from the Supreme Court of Pennsylvania to the Supreme Court of the United States.[39] He was one of the advisers to the counsel for Robert E. Lee's son in securing an indemnity for the confiscation of the Lee estate at Arlington.[40] He was chief counsel for the Choctaw Nation in their claim presented to Congress for payment of ceded lands east of the Mississippi.[41] For fifteen years he represented the interests of General John C. Frémont in litigation over railways and western lands.[42]

His correspondence in 1872 shows him to have been engaged during that year with thirty-seven cases. Yet not only are his preserved papers incomplete, but during a part of this year he was serving as a member of the Constitutional Convention of Pennsylvania and was unable to devote full time to his practice. The year 1874 was more typical, since practically his full time was given to the law. During this year he was engaged in at least fifty-two cases. All of them apparently were before higher courts, either State or Federal. Seven of them were

[37] Black Papers, end of 1882.

[38] The case was decided March 23, 1885—*Murphy* vs. *Ramsey*, 114 U. S. Reports, p. 15. Black's brief was used in the case. The court upheld the Edmunds Act, but declared as void all the self-made rules of the electoral commission and decided against any ex post facto application of the law on polygamy.

[39] 13 Wallace, p. 190.

[40] Black Papers, January 24, 1871.

[41] Black Papers, June 25, July 18, 1868; and through 1875.

[42] Black Papers, Nov. 14, 1860; Jan. 21, 1861; Dec. 20, 1870; through 1872-1875.

railway cases—in which he appeared either for or against the Reading, the California and Texas, the Parkersburg, the Atlantic and Great Western, the Flint and Pierre Marquette, and the Southern Pacific railways.[43]

Black's income from this practice was enormous. Exactly how large it was, is impossible now to calculate. He kept no records. He did not himself know his income except in a general way. He cannot be said to have practised for the lure of money alone. Seldom, in taking a case, did he set a fee in advance. As a general rule, he never did so unless at the request of his client. Even if the figure was agreed upon, ordinarily it was never drawn up in contract, but was merely a verbal agreement. More often his method was to accept a retainer to handle a case, with the agreement for a contingent fee if he won it. The amount of the contingent seems to have been left for settlement after the argument of the case. Often it was left to the judgment of the client. In practice, of course, this custom resulted in the value of his services appearing to be much smaller to a client after the case was won than it would have appeared beforehand.

His memory showed a remarkable twist in the matter of fees. The facts of law and history, the exact language of literature, were upon the tip of his tongue. He spoke before courts without notes, yet he cited legal references accurately and without hesitation. He quoted from literature apparently almost at will. He was never known to misquote. Yet he could settle with a client upon the amount of a fee—and the figure would pass completely out of mind.[44]

Such loose methods of business could not help but lose him money. Some of it was lost by indulgence to clients—as in the Osage Land Case where he was offered a large fee, but was paid chiefly in gratitude.[45] Some was lost by the plain dishonesty of clients who availed themselves of his known simplicity and easiness in business methods.[46] But such losses did not unduly concern him. His income was out of all proportion to his needs, and he had no taste for the sheer accumulation of money.

Perhaps he enjoyed the distinction which such habits brought him, for often he was called upon to settle disputes over fees between other lawyers and their clients, and always it seems to have been the client, not the lawyer, who made the appeal.[47] One woman, previously unknown to him, went even further. She sent him a draft for

[43] Black Papers, 1872, 1874.

[44] In the Phillips Case, he not only forgot the amount of the fee, but forgot what proportion of it was due to Garfield. Black Papers, July 29, 1871.

[45] Clayton, p. 119.

[46] C. F. Black, p. 25.

[47] See H. S. McComb to Black for a typical case wherein Black was called upon as arbitrator of a fee. Black Papers, Feb. 1, 1876.

$1,000, merely to have him find out if her regular lawyer was honestly pushing her case.[48]

In spite of these losses, however, his income was large. For handling the Pittsburgh, Fort Wayne, and Chicago Railway case, the incomplete records show him to have received $5,000.[49] Undoubtedly, however, these figures are incomplete. For his argument in the first Atlantic and Great Western case, he received at least $5,500,[50] although here too the figures are probably incomplete. Upon one occasion he also received $500 merely to examine a mortgage for this railway.[51] For the Credit Mobilier prosecution, he received during the first year $6,000.[52] This case continued in the courts for twelve years. For the Phillips brothers' appeal the fee was $5,100.[53]

For the Osage Land case, he was offered $500 as a retaining fee and a part of "three forty thousand dollars,"[54] but was paid very little for handling it.

In a few instances, it is possible to ascertain positively his full fees. For handling the Choctaw claim, the fee was $28,000.[55] For two arguments in the Vanderbilt Will case, he was paid a like amount—$28,000.[56] But for handling the first argument in the Galveston, Houston, and Henderson Railway case—which he lost—he received a larger fee than any of these here mentioned. The case was held in Galveston, Texas, during the month of June 1868. Three times he had been asked to take the case. Each time he refused. Finally a telegram reached him at York: "Name your fee." He showed the message to a friend, V. K. Keeser, complaining, "I don't want to go down there. It's too hot." "But," answered Keeser, "they said to name your fee." Whereupon Black chuckled and said, "All right. I'll fix them," and he telegraphed that his fee would be $1,000 a day from the time of leaving York until his return. "I guess they will let me alone now," he remarked. But before he had left the downtown of York to return home, came a telegram accepting his terms.[57]

He was absent from York for thirty days.[58]

[48] Black Papers, 1874.

[49] Black Papers, Nov. 25, 1872; June 7, 1873; May 28, 1874.

[50] Black Papers, Feb. 27, 1865; Sept. 28, 1866.

[51] Black Papers, April 28, 1869.

[52] Black Papers, October, 1868; March 26, 1869.

[53] Black Papers, July 29, 1870. One-third of this went to Garfield.

[54] Black Papers, May 1, 1873.

[55] Black Papers, June 25, 1868; July 18, 1868.

[56] Black Papers, April 2, 3, 1879.

[57] W. F. Bay Stewart to the author, Jan. 11, 1930. Stewart was witness of the event.

[58] Press Clipping, Clayton MSS. Through Black's records are strewn many small fees and part payments. For the year 1874 they total $8,500, in addition to other letters noting fees enclosed but not giving the amount. These records, of course, are not complete.

Yet with the enormous fees which Black received for handling the California land cases—together with the continuously large income which he enjoyed throughout the last twenty years of his life—he left only a modest estate at his death. He owned two farms just south of York, totaling about 200 acres; another in Franklin County, purchased from Buchanan, of about 250 acres; a fourth in Maryland of 312 acres; and, jointly with Garfield's widow, a very small farm in Virginia just across the river from Washington. His equity in the latter brought less than $3,000. The total value of the others did not exceed $65,000. Also he owned a house in Washington. His personal estate, including bonds and household effects, was appraised at $113,870.57. The total estate did not reach $200,000.[59]

Yet this estate was remarkable in one aspect. Throughout his life, Black had never invested a dollar on speculation.[60] At his death, he had among his securities only one depreciated investment—and that was a stock taken in payment of a fee from a personal friend. With this exception, every one of the other stock and bond investments which he had made, were marketable above their par value.

[59] Black Will, Will Book, York County (Pa.), C. C. No. 3, pp. 346-51; Executors' Inventory, *ibid.* This will had been made six months before Black's death and had been carelessly placed between the pages of one of the books upon the library shelves. It was not found until fifteen days after Black's death.

[60] C. F. Black, p. 25.

28

A PERSONAL SKETCH

ONE year after Black's first argument of the railway case at Galveston, he started again to Texas for an argument of the appeal in a higher court. This was in May of 1869. With him were his wife and Judge Noah H. Swayne of the United States Supreme Court. When the train was about twenty miles south of Louisville, Black met with a terrible accident which maimed him for life and came near killing him.

The corner of a freight car, stationary on a siding, had been left with an end thrust over the main line of rails far enough to scrape against the cars of his train. Black was seated at an open window, with his right arm carelessly resting on the sill. As the train passed this freight car, its projecting end ripped through the whole side of the car in which Black was seated. All but two of the passengers, however, escaped injury. One, a young doctor, was injured only slightly. But the freight car projection caught Black upon the palm of the hand and dragged it backward against the window casing. His arm was broken in seven places between the wrist and elbow alone. The elbow joint was crushed, and most of the bones in the fingers and the hand were broken.[1]

The train was stopped and a special train was sent from Louisville to take him back to that city. The slightly injured physician administered brandy and gave first-aid treatment. Black left the train, and walked a quarter of a mile to a house to await the special train, carrying with his left hand the jelly of crushed flesh and bone which, a few minutes before, had been a good right arm. The special train arrived, and he was taken to a hospital in Louisville.[2]

Here he remained for seven weeks, his wife by his side during the whole time. Physicians decreed that the arm must be taken off, but Black refused to allow it. They warned him that an amputation was necessary to save his life. He flared back, "I won't have my arm taken off. And I warn you surgeons, if you take it off while I am under anæsthetic, I will hold you responsible for the act."[3]

They left it on. But even the highest medical skill could not restore the use of the mangled arm. That was forever destroyed. When

[1] Black to Chauncey Black, Black Papers, June 5, 1869; Clayton, p. 142.
[2] Clayton, p. 144.
[3] W. F. Bay Stewart to the author, January 11, 1930.

informed of this, Black replied characteristically, "Then I'll never enter the prize ring."[4] So the arm remained, utterly useless, but "more ornamental than an empty coat sleeve."

At the first moment his condition allowed, he dictated letters to his children. To his son Chauncey he wrote, "I am utterly and perfectly helpless as I lie on my back but I sleep now with the assistance of opiates." Then, from his restless bed, he poured out to this eldest son his innermost and uncensored feelings. In the letter, one has a fleeting glimpse at another side of his nature—a side so often hidden under his vehement public life. Here was not the Nemesis of the abolitionists, anathematizing them as enemies of law and reason. Nor was it the defender of the Constitution, startling the echoes of the court room. It was an anxious father, writing to his son. It was a man who had gazed at death, writing to one he loved.

"Looking back upon you all from this bed," he said, "I cannot help but feel that I have loved you as my children, more than I ought to have done; that is to say, I realize more than I did, that you are and are to be men and women. My trouble now consists in thinking what I shall do for your future. I know very well that you will never blame me, but continue as long as you live 'to yearn o'er my little good and pardon my much ill.' To gratify my natural affection I would not bring any of you here, but I feel sometimes as if I could not do without your presence."[5]

To his daughter Mary he wrote that his draft of a will started previously was incomplete, but "Mr. Thompson has now prepared another, intended merely to serve in case I should not reach home. . . . If serious apprehension should arise that I will not be able to reach home, you shall be promptly informed of it, and in time to reach here. So long as the accounts continue favorable to my recovery, you may feel secure in the hope of seeing me, for there will be no attempt to impose upon you."[6]

No complications developed, and on July 25th he was able to leave the hospital. But the right arm was useless, and henceforth he required a servant in constant attendance upon his person. Yet there was no outward murmur or grumbling at this visitation of affliction. Although he was but a few months under sixty years of age, he set himself to mastering a finer use of his left hand. He learned to shave himself. He learned to write.[7]

His papers show the interesting development of his progress in writing with the left hand. Four days after he left the hospital—July 29, 1869—is found his first attempt. The draft of the letter is in an

[4] Washington *Evening Star*, August 20, 1883.
[5] Black Papers, June 5, 1869.
[6] Clayton, p. 150.
[7] *Ibid.*, p. 153.

unknown hand, with corrections in Black's hand. These corrections consist of an occasional scratching out of words, and here and there the insertion of a single word. Every stroke of his pen is pitifully uncertain, and the words inserted by his hand are pathetically irregular and almost impossible to read. A second paper, on August 9th, however, shows a marked improvement. Within five months, that is to say by the December following, he was writing an even and legible backhand. Indeed by this time it was better than much of the script in his right hand just previous to the accident.[8]

He wrote, of course, much more slowly. He gave up the use of a pen, and did all of his writing thereafter with a pencil. Often he dictated letters, but the first draft of legal briefs and of all the numerous magazine articles, which he began to write shortly after this accident, were done in full with his left hand, then copied by some member of his family.[9] His legal work, and his newspaper and magazine controversies, required an enormous amount of writing. Yet his legal work was continued without decrease and his controversial writings grew in number and in length after this injury. His speaking in public apparently suffered no impairment. Many of his most effective arguments were made under this handicap. That in the Goodyear Rubber case was given within less than five months after he left the hospital. The last two of the Reconstruction arguments—those in the Blyew and Slaughterhouse cases—were given shortly afterward. The Osage Land case and the Vanderbilt Will suit, of course, came many years later. Life in general flowed as smoothly after the accident as before.

An event two years later, however, threatened completely to disrupt the tenor of his life. This was the death of his youngest daughter, Anna. She died on August 8, 1871,[10] at the age of nineteen. Perhaps Black was no fonder of her than of his other daughters. But she was his youngest. She had barely touched womanhood. The Washington correspondent of the New Orleans *Times* had noted the intimacy between them. "He had with him," said this correspondent after meeting Black, "a daughter, in whose beauty, innocence and fascinating sprightliness, his whole heart was wrapped. It was touchingly beautiful to see the affectionate intimacy between the grand old man and his lovely, graceful daughter."[11]

After her death, all of the fortitude which had sustained him during the arm accident deserted him. His grief, for a while, was violent and unmanageable. Then it settled into the bitter outward calm of hope-

[8] Black Papers, July 29, August 9, end of 1869.

[9] Clayton, p. 154.

[10] Forward-Black Family Bible. Anna seems to have been known to her friends as "Nannie."

[11] Press clipping, Clayton MSS.

as evidence that it will be unfairly tried or unjustly decided for mere party reasons. At all events neither I nor any of my colleagues have ever thought of advising resignation in any possible contingency. Moreover if such advice were given no matter by whom the President would reject it with becoming scorn. The trial will proceed unless the House of Representatives shall see fit to withdraw from it which is not at all probable and we have not yet seen any reason to doubt that Senators will meet their responsibilities by patiently hearing the defence as well as the accusation and honestly deciding the cause according to the truth.

J. S. Black

Phil'a. March 5. 1870

My Dear Sir

I enclose certificate of 2000 shares of stock in Niagara Oil Co. and agreement of Mr. [illegible] Phillips concerning it which please to keep until I return home. As I do not go back directly I thought it better to send it this way than to carry it about me.

Yours truly

J. S. Black

Hon. A. J. Glossbrenner

BLACK'S RIGHT AND LEFT HANDWRITING

less resignation.[12] "When we met after the event," said a friend of his, "we did not once refer to the sad event. Once we approached by accident, then both hastily retreated in opposite directions, well knowing that on that subject we could not trust ourselves. On the contrary, we talked and laughed more heartily and louder, feeling instinctively that we were so near the graveyard that if we stopped for an instant, voices would be heard."[13]

But Black's nature was too strong to be conquered by grief. In the end he folded his coat over the wound, and marched on. Never again did he mention this daughter's name to any mortal.[14] He determined to leave even the house in which she died, the home in which they had lived for nine years in York.[15]

By piecemeal he had been purchasing land upon the southern slope of the Codorus valley, about two miles south of York. A part of his land topped the highest knoll in the county, and offered a twenty-mile view down the valley with the city of York in the foreground—a cluster in color, against a background in landscape. Halfway down the knoll was a grove of ancient oaks and under their shade was a spring of water, limpid and cool. It had long been known as *Brache* spring, from an old Dutchman whose ghost was supposed to haunt the place. Black had fancied the name, but his family did not take kindly to thus perpetuating the memory of Brache's ghost. Both achieved their wish. The spelling was changed to *Brockie* and the name was kept.[16]

For some years Black had talked of building a country home at Brockie. Now his decision to leave the house in which his daughter had died offered the immediate incentive. Also it gave a task to his restless mind. So by the edge of the group of trees surrounding the spring, he built a country home. It was a solid, massive, brick building, was a mansard roof and a tower on the front side. It was flanked with ample porches. The landscaping was carried out in a manner fitting to the house. Roads and terraces were laid out, trees and shrubbery were planted. The spring was opened up and a tiny lake created. The land at this particular spot was a poor clay, too poor to grow even good grass. But better soil was brought in, and presently not only grass, but roses, honeysuckles, and geraniums sprang up about the place. Nearby were vineyards and a peach orchard. In the stables were horses and Jersey cows. So on March 31, 1873, the family moved

[12] Clayton, p. 156.

[13] Press clipping, Clayton MSS.

[14] Clayton, p. 156. In the same way did the death of Black's younger brother affect him in his youth. He seldom mentioned the event, or even the name of the brother.

[15] Mrs. J. V. L. Finley to the author, Jan. 11, 1930. Mrs. Finley was a classmate of Anna Black. Also Clayton, p. 156.

[16] Clayton, p. 141.

into the new home. Black began farming more industriously than before. His "best agricultural implement," as he termed it, was neither a plow nor a cultivator—but a large field glass through which, from his home, he could look over his fields, observe his men at work and enjoy his growing crops.[17]

Here he lived, a country gentleman, through the remainder of his life. No longer did he date his letters from York, but from "Brockie." Clients came to him at Brockie. Newspaper reporters interviewed him at Brockie. Friends visited him at Brockie. With no office save this country home, he remained one of the leaders, if indeed not *the* leader, of the American bar. Here he composed philippics upon the administration of government by the Radicals, and wrote polemics that were compared with those of Junius.

He had long been known as an eccentric character. His very physical appearance gave color to this eccentricity—the enormous eyebrows "very white and very shaggy," the glittering grey eyes that "lie in ambuscade" underneath, the sternness of expression in repose and the instant softening into a smile, his "sense of alertness, of vigilance, of quick large consciousness" in spite of his bulky frame. Long after his immense eyebrows had turned snow-white he persisted in wearing his red-brown wig. "When a man as wise as Jere Black wears a red-brown wig above snow-white eyebrows," wrote an observer, "we conclude he abides in that supernal sphere of mental action where the thought of anything so trivial as a wig never enters in."[17a]

His natural taste for disputation lent an added hue. After removing to Brockie, he reveled more than ever, if that were possible, in this taste. He still attacked Reconstruction in the courts, still defended Buchanan, and anathematized the abolitionists. He remained the militant champion of Democracy. To his friends and to most of his party, whatever emanated from his pen, or fell from his lips, was received as law and gospel.[18] Nor could his enemies ignore his attacks.

Through his curiously egocentric life there ran a martial note. Unwittingly this note was struck by contemporary biographers and eulogists. Note their descriptive figures—a "mail-clad knight"; a "militant champion of minority rights," whose words are a "trumpet call"; "one of King John's barons . . . reappeared upon the earth."

Many a tale was repeated of his eccentric habits and striking mannerisms. Friends nearest him delighted to repeat them.[19] Newspapers broadcast them in print. It is not improbable that Black himself secretly enjoyed these stories which gave him so unique a distinction.

His powerful frame, and the unusual markings of his personal ap-

[17] *Ibid.*, p. 157.

[17a] Mary Clemmer, letter to the New York *Independent*, Clayton MSS.

[18] See "Sappho," New York *Sun*, about April 30, 1872. Clayton MSS.

[19] Hensel, p. 196.

pearance in general, commanded attention wherever he went.[20] Yet he paid little if any attention to his wardrobe. Never would he order a suit of clothes for himself, and he disliked to change a familiar old suit for a strange new one. Unknown to him, his family would order clothes from his tailor in Philadelphia. Whenever this tailor needed a new measurement, he must resort to strategy in capturing Black for the ordeal. Usually, however, Black's first intimation of a new suit was its arrival—whereupon further persuasion was necessary to induce him to abandon the old suit and wear the new one.[21]

He still continued to maintain his home in Washington during the winters, and to travel extensively at all seasons of the year. Many a time he was known to leave home for a short trip without taking a cent of money. He knew the conductors; they knew him, and passed him along to his destination on credit.[22]

He never questioned a bill, was lavish in tips, and, when he took money with him, was an easy prey for pickpockets. He would pace the platform of a railway station, oblivious to all surroundings, pondering upon a theme, speech, or essay—twirling with his good hand that famous silver tobacco-box which always was in evidence and which for years figured in every description of him. The first of these silver tobacco-boxes had been given him in 1866 by Ward H. Lamon, his junior partner at law. Engraved upon it were the words: "An honest man is the noblest work of God," and a figure of the scales of justice. Within a few years the inscription was entirely worn out by constant handling. Later the box followed the inscription. But another took its place, then another. Always it was filled with "fine cut" chewing tobacco, from which he drew frequent and copious quids. Almost always it was in his hand, even in arguments before the Supreme Court, and was constantly in motion, described by his daughter as "a peculiar, rapid, indescribable twist of his hand by which he turned it over alternately sidewise and 'end for end,' never twice in succession the same way."[23]

After his injury, Black had with him at all times a valet. His most famous one was an excessively pompous negro named George Washington. This valet took a cue from the eccentric nature of his master. In traveling with Black, he carried a hatbox marked "The Honorable George Washington, care of J. S. Black."[24]

Black had abated no whit in his harsh opinion of New Englanders. "He held New England answerable to posterity and to God," said James G. Blaine, "for all heresies which afflicted either church or

[20] Press clipping, *Woman's Campaign*, Clayton MSS.
[21] Philadelphia *Record*, August 20, 1883.
[22] Hensel, p. 196; Mrs. J. V. L. Finley to the author, Jan. 11, 1930.
[23] Clayton, p. 126.
[24] W. F. Bay Stewart to the author, Jan. 11, 1930; Clayton, p. 136.

state." "The New Englander, individually, I greatly affect," Black often said, "but, in the mass, I judge them to be stark mad." Thereupon he would add enigmatically, "If you are going to make much of a New Englander, he should, like Dr. Johnson's Scotchman, be caught young."[25]

Yet many of Black's friends were New Englanders. And in spite of his anathematizing of the Republican party, he counted among his personal friends many members of that party—particularly Garfield, Matt Carpenter, James Speed, and Benjamin Curtis. As individuals he esteemed them; but their political views were no less heretical because of this esteem. Nor did he offer apologies for his opinions upon the subject. Upon one occasion a Republican friend, Congressman G. W. Schofield of Pennsylvania, undertook to convert Black to the faith. "It's a pity, Judge," said Schofield, "that a man of your splendid mind should not be in the public service; you are too great man to remain in the minority."

Black responded with a shrug and a grunt, and Schofield continued: "Judge, you had better come over to us; we would do handsomely by you."

"I have thought sometimes about that, Mr. Schofield," replied Black, "but there is one obstacle in the way."

Schofield warmed to his task: "Ah, Judge, what can that be? Is it a serious one? Can't something be done to remove it? You are too great ——"

Black cut in with finality. "Yes, sir, a serious one, a very serious one. *I believe in a hell!*"[26]

To be sure, the men were speaking in tones of banter, yet Black's remark was not altogether in jest. In different words, the same inflection was heard upon other occasions. One month after Black moved to Brockie, Salmon P. Chase, Chief Justice of the United States Supreme Court, suddenly died.[27] Grant at this time was beginning his second term and there were many rumors and opinions of whom he would appoint to succeed Chase. Two appointments were in turn rejected by the Senate and speculation increased upon whom the next appointment would fall. Inevitably Black was mentioned as a possibility. Indeed a few newspapers took up his cause with vigor.[28]

A friend met him pacing the corridor at the Ebbitt House in Washington. "Judge, is it true," this friend asked, "that President Grant has signified his intention of nominating you for Chief Justice in case Mr. Cushing is rejected?"

Black, of course, held the corruption of Grant's administration in

[25] Blaine, *op. cit.*, I, p. 231.
[26] Clayton MSS.; *American Law Review*, XVII, 1883, p. 786.
[27] May 7, 1873—less than a month after the famous Slaughterhouse decision.
[28] Press clippings, Clayton MSS.

utter contempt. Added to that, the odor of the Credit Mobilier scandal was still lingering in the halls of the Capitol. Very deliberately he replied to this question: "The President has tendered to me, and I have accepted, the highest and most honorable position which can be held under his administration."

His friend waited expectantly, while Black added with grim emphasis, "the proud position of a private citizen!"[29]

So the stories of his eccentric nature grew and often departed from the perpendicular truth. The Washington correspondent of the Cleveland *Leader*, for example, set down his impressions of Black in this form:

> He is a tall, grizzle-haired, big-nostriled, long-nosed man, who smokes perpetually, except when he chews. Being of a nervo-lymphatic habit, he sits down with his hat on around the hotel parlors, and rolls great clouds of meditative smoke, seldom conversing with anyone and then in a Diogenes-like way. In the Supreme Court he has a spittoon set in the middle of the floor, and walks up and down as he talks with the precision of an Elizabethan dramatist, spitting as straight as a syllogism all the time. The power of his argument is measured by the number of spittoons he fills. A small and easily surmountable case takes two spittoons; a good tough argument requires four; for a great feat of legal gymnastics he requires as many as nine successive spittoons of the size of those great stone or India rubber ones. In the McCardle case this great expectorationist is said to have spit even full eighteen vases. When he had reached the seventeenth, the opposing counsel whispered: "We are gone up; he has another spittoon in reserve."[30]

In commenting upon this "Bohemian description" the York *Republican* added:

> We question the . . . smoking attributed to the subject, and also the "seldom conversing" and the cynic tone, for we have always understood that Judge Black was a copious and most agreeable conversationalist. . . . The chewing of the weed and the abundant expectoration, we believe, cannot be denied, though the writer has let his pen run wild upon the topic.[31]

As a conversationalist Black was, in fact, greatly renowned. "I had the good fortune to sit beside him for some three hours," wrote a press correspondent. "It was a great intellectual treat, as he is not only full of humor, but brings it to bear in recalling historical reminiscences of the most entertaining sort."[32]

[29] Clayton, p. 138; Clayton MSS.
[30] Press clipping, Clayton MSS.
[31] *Ibid.* The York *Republican* was correct. Black did not smoke, but chewed and conversed most copiously.
[32] Washington correspondent, New Orleans *Times*, Clayton MSS.

"In a book of American *ana*," commented another acquaintance, "his wise and witty sayings and eloquent observations, flung out on the spur in his animated talks, would, to the delight of readers, fill a good many pages. He needed but a Boswell to make him in that respect appear equal to Johnson. Talk was his kind of dissipation—his intoxicant—the means for exhilaration, like wine to the more sluggish."[33]

Much of this exhilaration of conversation marked his most serious forensic arguments. In his final Credit Mobilier argument before the United States Circuit Court in Philadelphia, for example, he inserted this allusion upon the subject of legal technicalities:

If you come upon my premises and carry away my cow or convert her to your own use, and I bring action against you, the question to be submitted to the Court and the Jury, and which they will decide between them, will be, not whether the cow is yours or whether the cow is mine; but whether I kept her in a square field or a round field, or in a three-cornered field; and whether it was a red cow with white spots or a white cow with red spots; whether she had crooked horns or straight horns, or a long tail or a short tail.[34]

So, famed as a conversationalist and renowned for his eccentricities, he reveled in the luxury of both. Twirling the famous silver tobacco-box and followed by his negro valet, he was a familiar figure in the court rooms of a dozen states. At Brockie he lived in summer, enjoying his country home, his fields and crops. To Washington he moved in winter, near the Supreme Court, where his voice so often was heard. His right arm indeed was useless—but the polemics written with a stub pencil in his left hand had lost none of their power and invective.

"He was debater to the very last . . ." wrote Whitelaw Reid. "There was hardly a time in his life when he was not involved in some controversy, yet few public men had more staunch friends in both parties. With his kindly nature and his fierce rhetoric and abundant humor, he was one of the most interesting characters in public life."[35]

[33] Thomas J. Keenan of Pittsburgh, quoted in C. F. Black, p. 30.
[34] Black Papers, May 2, 1877.
[35] New York *Tribune*, August 20, 1883.

29

THE CONTROVERSIAL WRITER

THAT little dash of bitterness, which Black thought would have given a more consistent tone to Judge Gibson's life,[1] happily was not wanting in his own. He loved a fight. He lived in a turbulent era, where the echoes of conflict over mighty issues were still resounding, even in the hour of his death. The man fitted the age; the age demanded his type. Opportunities abounded to satisfy his natural taste for disputation; he never failed to seize a proffered opportunity. In his cases at law, he was not only the lawyer but also the dexterous and aggressive Democrat who managed usually to score a point in one stroke both for his client and his party. In his Reconstruction arguments, he rose to the highest level of all his forensic efforts—and as conflicts over the issues of Reconstruction gradually drew to an end in the courts, he turned to a new weapon of attack.

This new weapon was the potent one of Junius and Burke—that of pamphlets, newspapers, and magazines.

A summary of Black's use of this weapon, both interesting and valuable, has been given us by David Miller Dewitt in *The Trial and Impeachment of Andrew Johnson.*

Black was one of the profoundest and at the same time one of the acutest lawyers of his generation (said Dewitt) and, besides, he was one of the most brilliant advocates—brilliant before a jury and brilliant before the full bench. He had been a great judge as well as a great lawyer, and at a perilous crisis he showed his mettle as a statesman when Attorney General and Secretary of State under President Buchanan.

But great as he was as a lawyer, judge and statesman, as a controversial writer he was greatest. In this field, his habit of driving home a proposition ill-conceived, and half-comprehended by the average man, by a seeming audacity in its statement became of marvellous service. The ease with which the clear-cut sentences grow out of each other and, finally, with an epigrammatic clinch culminate in what one rejoices over as an absolutely demonstrated truth, has the effect of humor. The completeness of his refutation of an opposing argument by a single wave of his pen has the effect of wit. Compassion over the decapitation of his adversary is swallowed up in admiration at the deftness of the stroke. His epithets are photographic. His sarcasms are syllogistic. His invectives carry with them the force of intuitive

[1] *Supra,* p. 31.

reason. His logic is so severely perfect that it becomes rhetoric raised to the highest power.[2]

Yet, excepting the one controversy with Douglas over Popular Sovereignty, Black was past sixty years of age before he turned to the general writing of controversial articles. His début was made through the magazine *Galaxy*.

The immediate cause was an article written by Senator Henry Wilson of Massachusetts in the *Atlantic Monthly* on Edwin M. Stanton.[3] Wilson was an able politician, although his colleague and friend, George Frisbie Hoar, thought that he carried partisanship and party organization further than a scrupulous sense of honor would warrant, or than the American people as a whole expected of their statesmen.[4] He was at this time tainted with Credit Mobilier profits—a fact already known to Black, but not yet revealed to the public. Wilson seized upon Stanton's death in 1869 as an occasion to write an article concerning the latter's part in the Buchanan Cabinet—denouncing Buchanan, Black, and the whole Cabinet save Stanton, whom he praised for his underhanded conduct of serving as a spy for the Republicans.

In Wilson's article one finds such statements as these: "The President and his Attorney General surrendered the government's right of self-preservation." The Secretary of Treasury "was deranging the finances and sinking national credit." The Secretary of Interior "was permitting the robbery of trust funds." Stanton, on the other hand, was boldly urging Buchanan to "coerce the seceding States." Secretly, he had "put himself in communication with the Republicans in Congress," in an effort to prevent Congress from supporting Buchanan. This, Wilson labeled as "intense patriotism." It was typical of the post-war paranoia which still lingered five years after Appomattox.

One need not be told how such an article affected Black. He had been out of the hospital, with his injured right arm, less than six months. But already he was able to write smoothly, if not rapidly, with his left hand. Wilson's veiled attack upon the Democratic party was a red flag. His palpable half-truths allowed full sway for Black's logical powers in destroying them. Invective and logic combined to produce a powerful polemic. Under the title "To the Honorable Henry Wilson, Senator from Massachusetts," his reply appeared in the June 1870 issue of *Galaxy*.

"My principal object," he began, "is to satisfy you that you have . . . grossly injured" Mr. Stanton "by what you supposed to be a panegyric. But before I begin that, suffer me to correct some of your errors about other persons." As to Buchanan, "I will make no effort

[2] P. 203.

[3] *Atlantic Monthly*, February, 1870, pp. 234-46. Wilson was elected Vice-President in 1872.

[4] Hoar, *op. cit.*, I, p. 216.

to convince you that Mr. Buchanan was right in standing by the Constitution which he had sworn to preserve, protect, and defend. That I know would be altogether hopeless. The declared admirer of John Brown, the political ally of Jim Lane, the partisan of Baker, the advocate of general kidnapping and special murder by military commissions, the open supporter of measures which abolish the right of trial by jury . . . —such a man would entirely misunderstand the reason (simple as it is) upon which I put the justification of a dead President for refusing to perjure himself. But, if I cannot *justify*, perhaps I can *excuse* him."

The chief premise of justification was that "Mr. Buchanan was born of Christian parents and educated in a Christian community. . . . The corruptions introduced into the Church by the political preachers of New England never reached him . . ."

From the defense of Buchanan, Black took up in turn each of the Cabinet officers attacked by Wilson—Floyd, Toucey, Cobb, and Thompson. At last he came to Stanton.

According to your account, he was all the while waiting and hoping for the time to come when he could betray the Constitution and its friends into the cruel clutches of their enemies. For this cold-blooded and deliberate treachery you bespeak the admiration of the American people. You might as well propose to canonize Judas Iscariot.

As to Stanton's alleged suggestion to certain Republicans that his colleague Toucey "ought to be arrested," Black disposed of it with the retort: "It is only necessary to recollect the fact that kidnapping of American citizens was at that time wholly unknown and absolutely impossible. We were living under a Democratic Administration, the country was free, and law was supreme."

As to Stanton's alleged secret visits and reports to Sumner's house at midnight, Black queried whether it was "possible that the fearless Stanton of your 'Cabinet scene' "—browbeating Buchanan—"could be the same Stanton who, at one o'clock in the night, was 'squat like a toad' at the ear of Sumner—

Essaying by his devilish arts to reach
The organs of his fancy."

But Black had not done with his adversary. "You seem wholly unconscious of defaming the man you meant to eulogize. But if your facts are accepted, the honor and honesty of them will not be measured by your standards. It may be true that public opinion has of late been sadly debauched; but the American people have not permanently changed their code of morality. . . . Fraud may abolish the Constitution, but the Ten Commandments and the Golden Rule are beyond your reach." Stanton, he pointed out, had been violently accused of other crimes during the Civil War—of encouraging Secession, of betraying McClellan, of refusing even to receive starving Federal prisoners from Andersonville when offered without ransom or exchange. "But," concluded Black, "if he wore the cloak of constitutional Democracy with us, and put on the livery of abolitionism with you, why should he not assume the garb of a secessionist with men of the South? If he tried to get his friend Toucey kidnapped, what moral principle could hinder him from contriving the ruin of his friend McClellan? . . . You cannot safely blacken a man with one hand and neutralize the effect by daubing on the whitewash of patriotism with the other . . . He needs a more discriminating eulogist than you."[5]

This reply to Wilson created a newspaper sensation beyond anything that might be imagined today. The *Grand Army Journal* undertook an elaborate defense of Wilson. John W. Forney's Washington *Chronicle* disagreed with Black's view but handled the matter with heavy gloves—until one of Forney's competitors accused him of fearing to draw Black's "scathing invective upon himself, for he dreads annihilation. He has seen the victims of that terrible pen writhing and squirming beneath the agonies of its inflictions." Upon the other hand, the Louisville *Courier* omitted whole sections of miscellaneous matter in order to print Black's article in full, noting that the "reader will soon see how much attaches to the averments of Mr. Wilson." The New York *World* likewise carried it in full—and added more than a column of editorial comment. Already the *World* had asserted Wilson's article to be "a silly piece of egotism." Now it commented that Black's reply "in point of vigor of style and force of logic, is certainly calculated to make its mark on the pachydermatous exterior of the Natick Senator. We do not see how he can avoid noticing it if he means to hold social intercourse with gentlemen." The New Orleans *Times* agreed, gleefully quoting large passages from the article. The Baltimore *Gazette* gave it two colums, terming it "the challenging clang of a trumpet amid the shrill, discordant noises" then heard in politics.[6]

Even Salmon P. Chase, although he could not agree of course with the theme, wrote to Black that "it is marked as every one who knows you would expect by great power."[7]

Perhaps, however, the most balanced criticism of it came from Alexander K. McClure, a moderate Republican who could see both sides of the controversy. To Black he wrote, greatly admiring the strength of the reply, but "suggesting that your invective marred your article," referring "especially to your rating Wilson both morally and mentally below the standard that the country now gives him . . . You make him at times wholly imbecile—again wholly wretch and

[5] *Galaxy*, June 1870, pp. 817-31.
[6] Press clippings, Clayton MSS.
[7] Black Papers, July 4, 1870.

scoundrel . . ." However, "I do appreciate the feelings you must have under the tide of passion that made Buchanan its objective point." McClure closed by joining with Black in an earnest desire to "resist the efforts of miserable pretenders and camp followers to rake up the passions of the war to perpetuate their power. . . . Until the people do overthrow such men, there can be no peace."[8]

Montgomery Blair, however, took another position. "The first impression made by Wilson's performance," he wrote, "is, how low the moral standards must have been in New England, when one of their Senators writes into its leading literary journal to lavish praise upon a man for the barest acts of treachery to those who lifted him into position."[9]

With this uproar whirling about his head, poor Wilson could not ignore Black's attack. Soon he gave out a notice to the press that he would "take occasion to reply."[10] The promised reply appeared in the *Atlantic Monthly* of October 1870.[11] In this reply he accused Black's article of being "as vulgar as vituperative, as ill-mannered as ill-tempered, with effrontery as strange and fatuous as it was brazen, his article falsifies history, and defames the dead." Thereupon he entered into an elaborate attack upon Black and a defense of his own former position.

But Wilson made a tactical blunder. Had he chosen to offer a moderate and dignified answer, he might have won sympathy and respect for his position, even if he were unable to match Black's logic and force. Instead, Wilson chose invective as his main weapon. This left him vulnerable at all points, for invective and logic were Black's own thunderbolts—and Wilson became a plaything in his hands.

"You take violent exceptions to my former letter as being vituperative and ill-tempered," Black wrote. "Let us see how the account stands between us on the score of mere manners. . . . You wrote, or caused to be written, . . . an article in which you attacked the reputation of certain persons. . . . What was I to do? My first impulse was—no matter what; I did not obey it. . . . But you affirm my denial to be an act of 'reckless audacity'; in your eyes my *de*fense is an *of*fense. I really cannot understand this, unless you suppose that . . . slander, like other injuries, is consecrated by loyalty when a Democrat is the sufferer."

Wilson had declared that "contemporary history has already pronounced against" Black. In reply, Black retorted that Wilson's pamphlets of "judgment" were not history, but "mere sewers into which the

[8] Black Papers, June 18, 1870.
[9] Black Papers, June 16, 1870.
[10] Press clipping, Clayton MSS.
[11] *Atlantic Monthly*, October, 1870, pp. 463-75.

filth of the party is drained off," adding that "I hope I am tolerably secure from the praise of this venal tribe."

Wilson had again repeated his charges against Thompson, Cobb, Toucey, and Floyd. Black this time went to the government records for his reply, bringing forth exact figures and documents. The effect was overwhelming.[12] "I said this narrative of yours was mere *driveling*," he summarized, "and I think I paid it a flattering compliment."[13]

The keen interest exhibited by the press in the first article had scarcely abated when the second appeared, even though the controversy was old. Again the New York *World* reprinted the article in full.[14] Editorial comments once more went the rounds. "There has certainly been nothing written since the days of Junius so perfectly withering and merciless," exulted the Democratic press.[15] The Republican press as a whole did not welcome the controversy, however. It was lukewarm in its defense of Wilson. Even the predicatory New York *Tribune* limited itself to an eight-line comment tucked among its miscellaneous items.[16]

Black's next venture in controversial writing was a year later, in *Galaxy* of March 1872. "A Great Lawsuit and a Field Fight," he entitled the article. His chief attack was upon the new code which had replaced Common Law in New York. "The new code," he said, "encourages ignorance, rapacity, and fraud by inviting everybody to practise it who cannot live by any other trade. . . . We venture, though with some diffidence, to pronounce this a rather poor substitute for the trial by battle which would have been accorded in the Middle Ages. So thought the parties in the Susquehanna and Albany Railway suits; for they actually loosened the deadlock by physical force. It is true that the champions did not go out on the open plain, and after taking an oath against witchcraft, beat each other with sandbags to show whose cause was holiest in the sight of God; but they did try whose judges had made the most righteous injunctions by rushing against one another with colliding locomotives."[17]

[12] So thorough was Black's uncovering of the facts of Floyd's alleged arms shipment, that no general history has gone back of them. Rhodes, III, p. 239, takes his version from Black's article.

[13] *Galaxy*, February, 1871, pp. 257-76.

[14] New York *World*, January 17, 1871.

[15] Press clippings, Clayton MSS.

[16] New York *Tribune*, January 19, 1871. Black had not confined himself to *Galaxy* articles in this controversy. When Attorney-General E. R. Hoar repeated some of the alleged facts on Stanton, Black addressed him an open letter calling for proof. This letter likewise was circulated through the press, but Hoar did not reply. Black refused, however, to let it rest. He then addressed an open letter to the New York *Herald*, later widely circulated among other papers, refuting the charge that Stanton was a spy in the Buchanan Cabinet. Clayton MSS.

[17] *Galaxy*, March, 1872, pp. 376-92.

Shortly afterward, he again appeared in *Galaxy*—this time in a polemic upon the public life of Seward. Black's unvarnished opinion of this statesman had been expressed before. It sprang chiefly from Seward's course in the Alta Vela affair. To Johnson, Black wrote after detailing an account of Seward's conduct: "And you keep this driveling charlatan in office. . . . He will never be faithful to the right, and he has not ability enough to make the wrong seem plausible."[18] Therefore, when Charles Francis Adams delivered a Memorial Address, rather tending to rate Lincoln as a figurehead, and Seward as the chief power in that administration, Black was driven to protest.[19]

His open letter "To the Honorable Charles Francis Adams," however, was markedly different from his previous letters to Wilson. There was no hint of the utter contempt which dripped from every line of his indictment of Wilson—for Adams he held in high personal esteem, both in ability and personal integrity. Adams' "naked assertion would go further," he said, than any other American "at home or abroad." But Adams had compared Seward to Pericles. With this, Black could not agree and advised Adams to "a little reflection and another reading of Plutarch."

For Seward, greatness was impossible, either as a lawyer or a statesman—not from want of ability, but by "inherent defects in his moral nature." His "higher law" was an example, though not the only one.

"Mr. Seward taught disobedience to the Constitution as a duty and contempt for it as a patriotic sentiment." His higher law was "not law at all, but license to use political power in any way that will promote the interests and gratify the passions of him who wields it. . . . Called by other names, the Higher Law was practised often before it was introduced here . . . Herod . . . Nero . . . Mme. de Pompadour filling the Bastile . . . Lola Montez setting her dogs on the students at Munich."[20]

Black's next important venture in this field was against his good friend Garfield. The latter had made a speech in Congress in which he called the Democrats "not a party" but "an organized appetite . . . of the belly." He furthermore had set forth the theory that two great sets of ideals early had been planted in America. One in Virginia, from which slavery and the ills of government flowed; the other at Plymouth, from which freedom and all the blessings of freedom and equality came.[21] It was, of course, a political speech, made in August of 1876, and intended to serve as a halyard for hoisting the bloody

[18] Black to Andrew Johnson, July 29, 1868; Press clipping, Clayton MSS.

[19] Black was not the only man to protest. See *Galaxy*, October, 1873, for Gideon Welles's protest.

[20] *Galaxy*, January, 1874, pp. 107-21.

[21] *Garfield's Works*, II, p. 351.

shirt. Doubtless Garfield did not himself believe it. But he had the temerity to send a copy of it to Black.

At once Black retorted with an open letter "To the Honorable James A. Garfield, Member of Congress from Ohio." From Moore's *History of Slavery in Massachusetts* he traced the Puritan slave code—the earliest in America and the most cruel. He reviewed the persecutions "carried on systematically against Baptists, and Quakers, and Catholics," and the treatment of Roger Williams. "I think you will find," he added as a parting shot, "that the crew of the Mayflower brought over and planted no 'germ of an idea' which has flourished with more vigor than their canting hypocrisy."

"Secession, like slavery, was first *planted* in New England. . . . It was while England had her tightest grip on the throat of the nation, that the Hartford Convention was called to dismember it; and this, Mr. Jefferson says, they would have accomplished but for the battle of New Orleans and the Peace of Ghent."

"You tell us that the Republican party 'will punish its own rascals.' The newspaper report of your speech says that this was greeted with laughter from the Republican side of the House. . . . How did the Republican party 'punish its own rascals' " in the Credit Mobilier Case? "They were promoted, honored, and advanced. . . . What makes this worse is your closing declaration that you will take no step backward. There is to be no repentance, no change of policy, and consequently no peaceful or honest government. 'Onward' you say is the word. Onward—to what? To more war, more plunder, more oppression, more universal bankruptcy, heavier taxes, and still worse frauds on the public treasury?"[22]

In discussing the Credit Mobilier scandal, Black had not laid on his blows with the usual power. He was, no doubt, unwilling to expose such a personal friend as Garfield to any individual embarrassment in this scandal. At once C. A. Dana of the New York *Sun* wrote to Black, "What I object to most is the compliment you pay to this rapscallion. . . . In my judgment, nobody, except perhaps Schuyler Colfax, came worse than he out of the Credit Mobilier business."[23] B. F. Meyers, editor of the Harrisburg *Patriot*, also took Black to task for this leniency. "So far as Gen. Garfield's connections with the Credit Mobilier and the other corruptions of the Republican party are concerned, I am inclined to think your letter is a little mild; but I can appreciate your desire not to be too severe upon one in whom you have had confidence."[24]

The most famous, probably, of any of Black's controversial writings was his debate with Robert G. Ingersoll upon the Christian

[22] Pittsburgh *Post*, Sept. 15, 1876; C. F. Black, pp. 292-311.
[23] Black Papers, September 13, 1876.
[24] Black Papers, September 18, 1876.

religion. Black himself was a sincere believer in Christianity. His sincerity of religious practice was, indeed, often a subject of comment. "To many it seemed strange," commented the editor of the *Albany Law Journal*, "that when many in these days of unbelief are drifting far away from God and from hope, that a man of such wide attainments and high intellectual gifts should have adopted and lived" by the gospel of Christ, "and that too in one of his humblest forms of communion."[25]

At the same time, he had no patience with religious intolerance or with the "political preaching" of his day. Many years earlier, in 1856, a professor of Dickinson College had delivered a lecture in defense of the Know Nothing party, urging the dangers of Catholicism in America. He had been inspired to this by his desire for a seat in the United States Senate, but Black felt that when such virulence had crept into centers of learning, it was time to utter a protest. Therefore when called upon, shortly after, to address the Phenakosmian Society at the annual commencement of Pennsylvania College, he chose the theme of "Religious Liberty." In treatment of this theme he drew, with artistic skill, the portraits of Roger Williams, Protestant, and Lord Baltimore, Catholic. Conversely, from the Spanish Inquisition to the "curse of Cromwell" in Ireland, he traced the baneful influence of religious strife. "It takes its adversary by the beard and affectionately inquires, 'Art thou in health, my brother?' while it stabs him under the fifth rib."[26]

Ten years later, in 1866, he had engaged Dr. Alfred Nevin of Philadelphia in a discussion upon the evils of "political preaching." The mission of Christianity, held Black, was to reform and elevate individuals—not to ally itself to governments or to form a "vulgar partnership with politicians." "You believe in the first day of the week as a Sabbath, and, so believing, your duty is to exhort all persons under your charge to observe it strictly; but you have no right to preach a crusade against the Jews and Seventh-day Baptists . . . for keeping Saturday as a day of rest . . ."[27]

Black's views upon Christianity, therefore, were well known. In the meantime, Robert G. Ingersoll had been attacking the Christian religion in press and platform, and the editor of the *North American Review* planned a debate upon this subject in his magazine. At first he considered an Ingersoll-Beecher debate, but finally dropped Beecher and came down to Brockie, persuading Black to answer Ingersoll.[28]

The two articles appeared together in the August 1881 issue of the *North American Review*, under the title of "The Christian Religion." There was in Black's answer none of the moderation found in his

[25] *Albany Law Journal*, XXVIII, p. 259.
[26] C. F. Black, p. 65.
[27] *Ibid.*, p. 71.
[28] Black Papers, October 1881.

reply to Adams or Garfield. He looked upon Ingersoll as a political scandalmonger of the Henry Wilson type, and singled him out for a surgical dissection. "Why should I," he began, "an unlearned and unauthorized layman, be placed in such a predicament? The explanation is easy enough. This is no business of priests. Their prescribed duty is to preach the word . . . I am no preacher. . . . My duty is more analogous to that of a policeman, who would silence a rude disturber of the congregation by telling him that his clamor is false and his conduct an offense against public decency. . . . Let Christianity have a trial on Mr. Ingersoll's indictment, and give us a decision *secundum allegata et probata.*"

The first weakness of Ingersoll's position into which he probed was that it offered, or assumed, no explanation of the origin of organic laws of the universe—save that the whole structure stumbled into existence by sheer accident. This notion of "the fortuitous concurrence of atoms" Black termed a "kind of lunacy."

In particular had Ingersoll attacked "wars of conquest" as being "simply murder," and condemned the Bible for containing accounts of such affairs. To answer this, Black pointed out that, at every point of attack against Christianity, Ingersoll had delegated to himself the authority of judgment. Having established this premise, he turned upon Ingersoll's private conduct as being a better standard of judgment than his mere words. "Mr. Ingersoll is himself a warrior who staid not behind the mighty men of his tribe when they gathered themselves together for a war of conquest. He took the lead of a regiment as eager as himself to spoil the Philistines, 'and out he went a-coloneling.' How many Amalekites, and Hittites, and Amorites he put to the edge of the sword, how many wives he murdered, or how many mothers he 'unbabed' cannot now be told. . . . But it is certain that his refined and tender soul took great pleasure in the terror, conflagration, blood, and tears with which the war was attended, and in all the hard oppressions which the conquered people were made to suffer afterward. . . . If his own conduct . . . was right, it was right on grounds which make it an inexcusable outrage to call the children of Israel savage criminals for carrying on wars of aggression to save the life of their government."[29]

Inevitably this controversy provoked a wide discussion. "It has fallen to the lot of a layman of God's Church," exclaimed the Philadelphia *Press*, "to crush 'the first of living infidels.' No theologian in this or any other country could have done a neater or more complete job. . . . An avalanche of reason—Ingersoll's school delights in reason—has struck him and his creed of destruction, and both have been swept out of sight."[30]

[29] *North American Review,* August 1881, pp. 128-52.

[30] *Philadelphia Press,* July 11, 1881, probably written by A. K. McClure.

The Reverend Dr. H. L. Wayland, editor-in-chief of the *National Baptist*, did not agree with this opinion, however. "The quality of the paper," he complained, "is so lowered by personality, by errors, by a virulent partisan spirit, that its value as a contribution to Christian literature is naught."[31]

The Dr. Wayland, of course, was a "political preacher," of the type whom Black had denounced for forming a "vulgar partnership with politicians." Nevertheless a section of the press agreed with Wayland that both men had yielded too freely to invective and personalities, even though for the most part Black's reply was hailed as a "powerful article" and a "masterly reply." Perhaps the most rational and conservative comment came from the editor of *Harper's Magazine*: "Judge Black's article is marked by the legal astuteness and strong logic that are characteristic of the man. . . . We think Judge Black won."[32]

In these controversial writings Black gained a fame out of all proportion to the actual amount of writing that he did. In part this was due to the issues which he discussed and to the wide heralding given his articles by the newspapers. Yet the influence of his style of writing cannot be ignored. At times its invective was perhaps too severe. His attacks were too merciless and personal. Yet there is some truth in defense of this manner of writing made by a friend of his—"there is no polish of phrase that can conceal the poison in telling a man that he is an aider and abetter of fraud."[33] And he lived in an age that, unquestionably, was the most corrupt in American annals.

His great delight was to "have at" his subject or his victim. The hammer and anvil were his favorite weapons. However stinging his indictment, he never was forced to strain his rhetoric to an unnatural level. He was a master both of invective and dialectic.

His rare skill with these weapons was a frequent subject of comment and comparison. He had "not been excelled," thought one critic, "since Swift . . . and reminds us of that melancholy writer."[34] More often, however, the comparison was made with Junius—that unknown eighteenth century English genius of satire and sarcasm. "His diction was richer than Macaulay's and more brilliant than that of Junius."[35] "He was as much superior to Junius as an equal skill in the use of language, combined with a vastly superior legal knowledge, could make him, to say nothing of the superior manhood which made him sign his name even to the bitterest of his philippics."[36]

[31] *Ibid.*, August 8, 1881.
[32] September 1881, p. 638.
[33] Clayton, p. 168.
[34] Editor, *Albany Law Journal*, XXVIII, p. 259.
[35] J. Hubley Ashton, quoted in C. F. Black, p. 30.
[36] Z. B. Vance, quoted in C. F. Black, p. 26.

30

THE FORENSIC ORATOR

NO COMPREHENSION of Black's life can omit or slight his power as an effective speaker. It was the *raison d'être* for his preëminence as a constitutional defender during Reconstruction. It was the mainspring of his success in the law. Indeed, although this success seldom has been paralleled in American law, there was a minority among his contemporaries who denied him the right to the highest legal rank. They sought to deprecate his legal learning and to explain away his rare success at law wholly in terms of his eloquence.

He was "a brilliant rather than a profound lawyer," said one of these critics. "Whatever he said was invariably so happily put, or aptly illustrated, as to attract attention, be taken up, commented upon, and generally remembered."[1] "That he was really a great lawyer," commented another, "was not so universally admitted as that he was a bold pleader and an eloquent, forcible, and most interesting speaker. If he did not always persuade the court, he never fatigued it. If his audience was sometimes unconvinced, it never failed to be delighted."[2] This criticism, to be sure, misses the essential point that he not only invariably delighted the court, but he also persuaded it to a degree seldom equaled in American forensic annals. Yet it is a valuable commentary from unwilling witnesses upon the admitted moving power of his forensic eloquence.[3]

Most of his qualities of eloquence already have been witnessed in the treatment of prominent individual speeches, but here we shall draw the more outstanding of them together into a semblance of form.

Preëminently Black was a forensic speaker. Always his greatest efforts were before a court. It is true that he was also unusually popular and effective before the general public. His eulogy on Andrew Jackson, when still a young man, brought him first into state-wide prom-

[1] Ed. Washington *National Republican*, August 20, 1883.

[2] Ed. Philadelphia *Press*, August 20, 1883.

[3] This view of Black's legal shortcomings was distinctly a minority view. "That he belonged to a giant race of lawyers, now almost if not quite extinct . . . that he was the greatest advocate at the bar this country has seen since Pinckney . . . these are well known and now, I believe, conceded facts," said J. Hubley Ashton. (C. F. Black, p. 30.) This represents the other extreme. There may have been more profound students of the law in his generation than Black, yet in certain particulars there was not his equal. His success with the California land cases, for example, was in no small degree due to the fact that he excelled all contemporaries both in the mastery of Mexican law and of the Spanish language.

inence. His eulogy on John Bannister Gibson was long quoted in Pennsylvania as a classic. At the unveiling of a bust of Alexander Campbell at Bethany College, Black pronounced a eulogy upon Campbell which was nearly the equal of his tribute to Gibson.[4] In the rough and tumble of political campaigns, he was a keynote speaker of rare power. Upon the centenary of Grattan's declaration of Irish independence, in 1882, Black addressed a great audience in Baltimore. Although he then was past seventy-two years of age, this address in its written form impresses one with its rhetorical perfection and its sustained power. Its immediate effect upon the audience was electric.[5] He was begged in turn to address the State centenary meetings in New Jersey and Massachusetts.[6] Centenary meetings in this year were numerous. Many speeches were heard. But among them all, this one of Black so stood out that the *Catholic World* four years later pointed back to it as the epitome of these addresses, one that would unite Black's memory with that of Irish "champions in all the centuries of her misrule."[7]

Yet there is nothing among these public addresses to compare with Phillips at Faneuil Hall, Beecher at Liverpool, or Henry before the Burgesses of Virginia. Nor do they equal Black's own greatest efforts at the bar. Black was himself well aware of his limitation in this direction. "I have often envied the gentlemen," he once said during a speech dedicating a county courthouse, "in possession of that gift which nature had denied to me. . . . The faculty of speaking readily and fluently upon any side of any case upon the shortest possible notice. [Laughter.] . . . I do not perform well in what rhetoricians call demonstrative oratory—that is, the sort of speaking which has no particular object or purpose [Laughter] except that of talking." [Laughter.] He cited a distinguished friend who, when called upon for such speeches "would take his position on the outer edge of created space and crack away at all eternity." [Laughter.] "Now I cannot do that."[8]

The Grattan centenary may justly be termed a great speech, a very great one, but it is not the equal of the Milligan, McCardle, or Blyew arguments before the Supreme Court. Those were efforts not again equaled before that court in Black's generation, and it may be that the Milligan argument never has been equaled there, before or since.

This much certainly may be stated as true: That upon no other occasion in Supreme Court history was so signal a victory gained under so great a handicap. For Black faced the court under a cloud—a man

[4] Clayton, p. 72.
[5] Baltimore *Sun*, April 19, 1882.
[6] Black Papers, April 28, May 24, 1882.
[7] *Catholic World*, September 1886, p. 758.
[8] The Hollidaysburg, Pa., *Standard*, July 4, 1877.

scorned as a "Copperhead." He faced a body of men politically opposed to him and to his views. He faced it at a moment when the dogs of passion had been unleashed in legislatures and courts throughout the land, and even in Congress. He defended a man whose alleged crimes aimed at the life of the nation and whose blood Congressmen had petitioned to have spilled. A military commission had condemned him with a scant gesture. A civil court had recoiled from its plain duty to save him. Public temper was in no mood for niceties in the law. Seldom in such throbbings of history have victims escaped vengeance. The Earl of Lancaster, Stormont, Monmouth, and Dreyfus will serve as examples. In order to save Milligan, the Supreme Court must pronounce void Lincoln's whole conduct of the Civil War in the matter of habeas corpus and military commissions. Yet this the Supreme Court unanimously did. But at doing this it did not stop. It took the amazing step of going beyond the case before it—and of stating that Congress could never legalize military commissions outside the zones of actual war. Here was victory enough. But an additional touch of drama consummated the whole episode—by having this decision come from David Davis, Lincoln's warm personal friend and the former judge upon his famous circuit. There is no parallel to this in American forensic history.[9]

The superiority of Black's forensic speaking over his public oratory sprang from inherent qualities. To begin with, he was essentially a lawyer in all modes of thought. Law was the religion of his life, as sacred as theology. Justice was godliness, "the practical enforcement in daily affairs of the Golden Rule."[10] In the Bible, his first study was of the Hebrew Judges. In politics, to the end, he was the lawyer. His views upon the great issues which swayed the passions of the nation—slavery, Secession, Reconstruction—were undiluted legal views. This sharp legal focus which disqualified him for the highest rank in popular oratory enhanced his powers before the bar. He had far less eagerness for the plaudits of the multitude than is seen in Beecher, Phillips, or Bryan. But twelve men in a jury box, or nine upon the court bench—these were a challenge to highest effort.

There were, of course, other contributing qualities. He loved a fight without quarter. The court room satisfied that side of his nature better than popular audiences. It is worth mentioning, and it may have some significance, that the two California land cases which he lost, out of the sixteen in which he appeared during the years 1861-65, were the only two insignificant ones which he argued. In one of these, there was not even a counsel upon the opposing side.[11] Even out of the court

[9] For the details of this argument, see *supra*, p. 151 *et seq.*

[10] Niles, p. 429.

[11] *U. S.* vs. *Wilson*, 1 Black, p. 267. The other case was *U. S.* vs. *Vallejo*, 1 Black, p. 283.

room his speeches were purely argumentative. They rang with the clink of steel. But a swordsman without an adversary becomes a shadow fencer. His highest skill is seen only when parrying the lunges and thrusting behind the defenses of a skilled opponent.

Likewise his mind was severely logical. The final judgment placed upon it by a contemporary critic, A. F. Faust, is not overdrawn:

> There is a degree of skill in the constructive and destructive methods which Judge Black employs rarely to be met with in argumentation. Persuasive and eloquent as he may appear at times, all the links in the chain of his reasoning are carefully forged and welded together. . . . Every fact and every argument follow in strictest sequence and when complete exhibit both a consummate power in art and an unrivalled perfection in presentation.[12]

Logic is a more powerful weapon before the judges upon the bench than before the general public. If one doubts that, take a page at random from Phillips or Bryan—then measure its logic beside a page from Webster or Erskine.

Perhaps also in the matter of physical endowment, Black was better adapted to the court room than to the public platform, although here it is not possible to speak with certainty. In person, he was a man of striking appearance, physically large, imposing in manner, marked in features. The "magnetic eye," so fabled among great speakers, he possessed in unusual degree.[13] These are advantages more imposing at close range than long, in a court room than upon the platform. On the other hand, although both appearance and voice are high assets to a speaker under all conditions, yet before the multitude a powerful and resonant voice outweighs appearance alone.[14]

As to Black's voice, there is not a word of testimony extant regarding its quality. If any conclusion can be drawn from this negative evidence, it must be that his voice had in no way impressed itself upon his friends, newspaper reporters, or contemporary biographers. It must have been a mere ordinary speaking voice—neither shrill or strident, nor yet deep and resonant. It could not have possessed the penetrating and vibrant qualities traditionally common to most great public orators.

On a few occasions he disappointed large public audiences by not reaching them with the range of his voice. Particularly were there places in the Belknap impeachment trial,[15] and even in his Grattan centenary address,[16] where the fringe of the audience missed a few

[12] *Catholic World*, September 1886, p. 759.

[13] Hensel, p. 196; Clayton, p. 46; Niles to the author, Jan. 10, 1930.

[14] No small part of Bryan's triumph in 1896 before the Chicago Convention, for example, came from the singular fact that his was the only voice distinctly heard by auditors in every part of the poorly constructed Coliseum.

[15] New York *Tribune*, July 25, 1876.

[16] Baltimore *Sun*, April 19, 1882.

parts of his speech. Whether this was due to his well-drilled habit of talking to a handful of men in a court or jury, or due to sheer lack of power in his voice cannot, of course, now be determined. At all events, his could not have been a voice of extraordinary power.

On the other hand, his manner of speaking, in at least one respect, gave him an advantage over many of his contemporaries at the bar. He spoke wholly without notes. Many times there would be long decisions to adduce, page references to cite, yet through his long career at the bar one seeks in vain to find a time when he ever stood before a court or jury with notes to sustain his memory. Repeatedly the court, jury, and spectators marveled at his unerring memory in speaking uninterruptedly for two or three hours without a scrap of paper before him—citing decisions even to the exact page, reviewing evidence and testimony, reciting poetry, and startling with apt quotations of literature.[17]

Take as an example, his argument in the Goodyear Rubber Case. He had been out of the hospital with his maimed hand less than five months, yet he "spoke for three hours without notes," said a press correspondent, "making one of the most masterful arguments heard for years. His ridicule of Goodyear and his clients as a scientific inventor, kept the Court in constant laughter, while his splendid bursts of eloquence in reciting the benefactions to mankind of Galileo, Newton and others . . . were acknowledged by the almost breathless silence of Court and spectators. He handled the testimony with equal skill, never at loss for the name of a witness, and quoting his language so accurately, that the opposing counsel in no instance corrected him. He read no law book, but from his vast stores of knowledge cited decision after decision, giving book, title and page. . . . He enriched his argument with illustrations drawn from nature, science, history, the Bible, literature, art and poetry."[18]

As to the method by which Black so thoroughly prepared these speeches very little is known. His daughter recorded that "in preparing his speeches, he studied through and through upon his subject until his mind was literally saturated with it. When he came to delivery his sentences rolled off his tongue . . . without a scrap of paper to guide him."[19] At another place, she recorded that he often dictated letters after his arm injury, but never long articles, for these "required long pauses, talking to himself and charging about the room."[20] The Washington correspondent of the Cincinnati *Commercial*, after once writing that "Black is a very curious character, full of idio-

[17] Hensel, p. 195; Levi Maish cf. Clayton, pp. 126, 131, 203; newspaper reports, cf. Clayton MSS.

[18] Press clipping, Clayton MSS.

[19] Clayton, p. 126.

[20] *Ibid.*, p. 154.

syncrasies," added that "he prepares most of his arguments at home, walking up and down the floor at night, where he would walk the whole night long if his wife did not appear along toward one o'clock and lead him to bed."[21] Perhaps this correspondent knew; perhaps he was guessing; but his remark is reminiscent of the testimony of many who knew Black intimately.

These facts are scanty, yet taken together with the manner and quality of his speaking, they afford a general idea of his method. It was purely extemporaneous. That is to say, with all of the careful preparation in organization and arrangement, the collecting of legal decisions and assembling of apt quotations from prose and poetry, which his speeches show, they were not written out and memorized. His arguments were too adaptable to the moment, the court, and the opposing counsel; and his repartee was too quick and devastating to have been hampered by frozen manuscripts. Nor is there to be found among his papers even one draft or outline of any speech he ever prepared—although there are many stenographic reports of his speeches as they were actually delivered.[22]

Yet these speeches, as they come unrevised from his lips, are better "literature" than his carefully written articles. Like the poet and the prophet, he thought more profoundly and phrased more eloquently when impassioned. But with him passion came, not in the sequestered calm of the study, but in the heat of forensic combat, facing a jury or a court.

Dunning admired Black's power of language, but regarded him as violent tempered and unable at times to control himself. In this Dunning was in error, yet his criticism is a key to one significant fact in Black's nature and his style of speaking. For Dunning passed judgment from Black's writing, not from his speeches,[23] and the fault of which Dunning complained—lack of restraint in language—is found there to an immoderate degree. In his writings apparently Black was not conscious of a goal or an audience. He wrote to sting, to produce a welt. Not so when he spoke. Before him was the court. He had in view a goal, a decision to be won, and he allowed no uncontrolled language to injure his efforts. True, he used invective. He used it at times with a terrible effect. But it was not a malicious or sneering invective. It was intrepid, sustained with logic and seasoned with anecdote, until even the victim seldom bore malice.[24] Likewise Black knew its limits. He never turned it upon the court.

[21] Press clipping, Clayton MSS.

[22] Cf. Credit Mobilier Speech, Black Papers, May 2, 1877.

[23] *Amer. Hist. Rev.*, XI, 1906, p. 593.

[24] A noteworthy example of this is his devastating invective of Attorney-General Speed in the Milligan case. Yet Speed took no personal affront, remained an intimate friend. See *supra*, p. 153.

There was indeed a fearlessness in his manner toward the court which gained him the reputation of being allowed more freedom in speech than any other living man at the bar.[25] But the very fact that Black, throughout his private practice in the law, faced courts politically opposed to him, constantly argued political cases, yet was allowed freedom of speech in a measure beyond that accorded to other attorneys, is proof that his fearless manner was not offensive to courts. Only once was he known to reflect upon the dignity of any judicial body, and that was when the Supreme Court surrendered to Congress in the McCardle Case.[26] On that occasion he appeared boldly before it, and standing in the shadow of contempt he arraigned its conduct. Yet so respectful were his manner and words that the court heard him, if not in meekness, at least in silence and without reproof. But this was a deliberate protest, pitched upon a high level. It was not a mere overboiling of the kettle produced out of heat in controversy.

So far from being uncontrolled in speech, before a court, few men knew better than Black how to promote his cause by the tactful assumption of expecting nothing less than even justice from the bench. One finds this vein running through all of his great speeches. In the Almaden Quicksilver Mine Case, he stated the assumption openly.

> There is nothing really *in* this case which gives me the slightest embarrassment; but certain occurrences *outside* of it have caused me some uneasiness. . . . We are here asking for legal justice; and that we expect to get, neither more nor less, for we are in a court where the scales are held with an even hand. We are not begging favors, but demanding a right. If we do not show our right, let our claim be rejected.[27]

Let us come to the qualities that mark Black's style of oratory. We shall not content ourselves with what Wichelns calls the "lesser strokes of literary art,"[28] but shall include as well what the Romans termed invention and disposition.

Consider first Black's drive of ideas. He never appealed to mere passions, yet there was always a powerful emotional drive behind his arguments. Indeed one of his great sources of power sprang from a rare ability to unite argument with the springs of action in human beings. He could premise logic upon impelling motives—self preservation, progress, honor—things that men live for and at times die for. When he had finished, not only had he impelled the mind to accept his logic as true, but he had aroused emotions to *want* what the mind proclaimed as true. But this was not *argumentum ad populum*. It was logic surcharged. "I make no appeal to the passions," he once said

[25] Cf. New York *Tribune*, August 20, 1883.

[26] See *supra*, p. 177.

[27] C. F. Black, pp. 430, 431.

[28] H. A. Wichelns, "The Literary Criticism of Oratory, p. 185.

scornfully to the Supreme Court after they had listened to an address of this sort. "Let the stump and the newspapers do that."[29]

The argument which followed in this case will illustrate the drive behind his logic. The issue was whether Kentucky or the Federal Government had the right to try a murder case in which a negro was witness to the crime. Black's propositions were simple: *First,* that the effect of the Civil Rights Bill of Congress in 1866 was to abolish the autonomy of the States. *Second,* that such an act was a "flat, sheer, naked breach of the Constitution." The treatment of these propositions click with logical precision, but behind the logic were powerful turbines of emotional drive. He was arguing before the Supreme Court. They were judges, learned in the law; they were high in cultural level, versed in the rudiments of history; they were human beings, proud of their country and its form of government. To all of these qualities, he supplied the elements of drive. Consider in brief the drive in his argument upon the first proposition—abolishing the autonomy of States.

The State of Kentucky—and therefore every State of the Union—would be stripped by this law of power to administer justice, "even to the smallest and lowest cases." State lines would fade into dark shadows and Federal prosecutors, like the proconsuls of Rome, would rule with a heavy hand. But the prosecutors went further than proconsuls, for the Empire of the Seven Hills in her most vicious days had never interfered with the local tribunals to the degree that the Civil Rights Bill empowered Federal Courts. Justice, removed to these distant courts, would leave nine-tenths of the lower class of crimes "unwhipped of justice," until people "graduate in crime from the lowest to the highest and society is altogether broken up." "The autonomy of a free State is not a thing to be trifled with," and out of Megara and Corinth, Thebes and Athens, he lifted examples of disaster which flowed from such triflings; and fitted them in outline to the disaster which hung over Kentucky, and through her, over all States of the Union. . . .

But one must read the full score to test the logic and sense the full drive behind it. The judges before him had lived through the Civil War and Reconstruction. They had listened to his arraignment of dangers in the Civil Rights Bill. They were, therefore, fitted to feel the force of his closing appeal to rise above the astigmatic temper of the time and to return a verdict averting these dangers:

When the Prophet Elijah stood on the mountain-side to look for some token of divine will, he did not see it in the tempest, or the earthquake, or the fire, but he heard it in the "still small voice" which reached his ears after those had passed by. We have had the storm

[29] Blyew argument, C. F. Black, p. 541.

of political debate; we have felt the earthquake of civil war; we have seen the fire of legislative persecution. They are passed and gone, and now if we do not hearken to the still small voice which speaks to our consciences in the articulate words of the Constitution from the graves of our fathers, then we are without a guide, without God, and without hope in the world.[30]

The basis for the contention of some critics that Black knew less about the law than many of his contemporaries was his method of argument from broad and sweeping principles of law, rather than confining himself to specific and technical details. If we were here arguing that issue, we would premise the case upon the contention that little minds must cling to little things, and only a great mind can assemble the details of law into broad principles of jurisprudence. But we pass by the argument and go to the fact. Black, in fact, did argue almost entirely from broad principles of law, principles which ranged behind all statutes and charters of government. One great source of his power as a pleader sprang from this method of argument.

In this particular, he was the opposite of William M. Evarts, another great lawyer, somewhat younger than Black, whose career partly overlapped Black's. Evarts' arguments, like his sentences, were involved and complicated. He was profound. He was a great and successful lawyer. But his method was the opposite of Black's. A layman, lost in following Evarts, follows Black with greatest ease. The one argued from involved legal propositions. The other from bold and sweeping maxims of law. Both adapted themselves to the court before them—Evarts wholly to the lawyer in the judge, Black to both the lawyer and the man.

In the Milligan Case one sees Black's method at its best. Stanbery was endeavoring to argue the subtle legal point that, since Milligan had been sentenced to hang the year previous, the legal presumption was that he had been hanged, and, therefore, there was no point in discussing the liberty of a dead man. Butler was insisting that, although the Constitution did in fact prohibit military trial of civilians, this part of the Constitution was "silent amid arms." Speed was entangled with the various Acts of Congress upon the subject.[31]

Black brushed aside these involved propositions and subpropositions. The opposing counsel had been toying with leaves and twigs. He went boldly to the body of the Great Charter Oak itself. "I prove my right to a trial by jury," he said, "just as I would prove my right to an estate if I held in my hand a solemn deed conveying it to me. . . . There is the charter by which we claim to hold it. It is called the Constitution of the United States. It is signed with the sacred name of George Washington, and by thirty-nine other names, only

[30] C. F. Black, pp. 539-57.

[31] 4 Wallace, p. 2.

less illustrious than his. . . . The Attorney-General [upon the opposing counsel] himself became a party to the instrument when he laid his hand upon the Gospel of God and solemnly swore that he would give to me and every citizen the full benefit of all that it contains.

"What does it contain? . . .

"*'The trial of all crimes except in cases of impeachment shall be by jury,'*" and "*'except in cases arising in the land and naval forces.'*"

"Is there any ambiguity there? . . . No; the words of the Constitution are all-embracing—

As broad and general as the casing air."

But Black did not stop with the Constitution. He went behind it—to the Petition of Right, the Bill of Rights, the Magna Charta, Alfred, Tacitus, the Saxons of Germany—until he had erected a mountain range of jurisprudence, extending unbroken for twenty centuries. There was his Alps protecting Italy. The Constitution was the weapon in hand. Let invaders try to overturn right of trial by jury with the puny weapons of mere Acts of Congress or Proclamations of a President.[32]

From this fleeting picture, one may grasp some idea of the broader aspects of Black's style. Cicero lays stress upon two things a forensic speaker should be able to do—delight his audience by wit and move them to tears.[33] The first of these Black could do in a rare degree, but the second was wholly alien to his temperament. He did not, and could not, do it. Yet he could move his audience in a way more effective in modern annals than any excitement to tears. He could arouse in them the desire to "fight Philip." He did so through a peculiar surcharging of logic with passion, and through attaching his arguments to broad and sweeping maxims of law.

We now come to the lesser strokes of style—the management of words, the coining of phrases. He was, said Alexander H. Garland, "a rhetorician without a superior—the best phrase-maker I ever heard. He used the English language after the style of Shakespeare."[34]

Black indeed compounded much of Shakespeare into his language, yet the finished product was not "after the style" of that writer. It more nearly approached the forensic style of Macaulay. Yet it is not Macaulay's. It is Black's own. It is his personality, delineated into language. If any one word can be found to express its quality, that word is *strength.* True it has beauty of a kind, but it is the rugged beauty of a sky-scraper; not the slender lines, nor the fine etchings, of a Gothic structure. It has a music too, but it is not the music of the flute that one hears in Burke, nor yet of the trumpet that resounds

[32] C. F. Black, pp. 510-39.
[33] *De Oratore,* Bk. II, Ch. 44-71.
[34] Quoted in C. F. Black, p. 27.

from Webster. It is the raw clang of steel on shield, echoing with grim purpose, but it is tempered steel of which Damascus might be proud, and both clang and echo are music of a kind.

As to "phrase-making" Garland was right. Black was indeed a phrase-maker, seldom content with the common currency which serves the purpose of more placid men. His phrases were of special mintage, coined with precision, and marked with distinctive hues. This quality, above all others, was the trade-mark of his style. In part it sprang from his choice of colorful words and striking figures; arguments were made vivid by the flash of a metaphor, and deepest philosophy was illumined by tropes. The most distinctive source of his phrase-making, however, was derived from allusions and apt quotations of Shakespeare and the Bible.

When once he desired to warn the Supreme Court that repudiations of a small debt might lead to large disasters, he took the phrase from Romeo and Juliet. "*Like Mercutio's wound*, it is not as wide as a church door nor as deep as a well, but it will do your business for you in the course of time."[35]

But a more sustained example better illustrates the method. During the course of the Goodyear Rubber argument, Black had occasion to disagree with an *obiter dictum*, clung to by the opposing counsel, once made by Judge Grier, who just three days prior had resigned from the Supreme Bench. Grier, in effect, had said that "we could know nothing of matter, except by its qualities," and that "the matter was new if its quality was changed." Therefore if rubber be changed in its sensitivity to weather, though it still be rubber, yet it was new "matter." Black undertook to overthrow this *obiter dictum*. Not until one has read the sinfully heavy philosophy of Locke, Berkeley and Hume in the original, can he appreciate Black's brilliant phrase-making summary of this philosophy and his attack upon its soundness.

"This," he argued, "is specious enough to have received the assent of some great thinkers long before Judge Grier uttered it. The metaphysical philosophy of the last century was full of it." Locke asserted that "color existed in the eye, the odor of a violet in the nose, and the temperature of a hot iron in the nerves that shrunk from its contact"; or, as Butler put it,

'There's no more heat in the fire that heats you,
Than there is pain in the stick that beats you.

"Berkeley, by the same reasoning, showed the unreality of the primary qualities, and removed the seat of their ideal existence to the mind. . . . It was a dismal theory. It abolished the created universe without restoring the reign of Chaos and old Night. It dissolved all human relations, for the bodies of men were merely '*such stuff as*

[35] Floyd Acceptances argument, C. F. Black, p. 486.

dreams are made of.' It did not *'strike flat the thick rotundity of the globe,'* but it did worse, for it made it a nonentity. *'This brave o'er-hanging firmament, this gorgeous canopy, fretted with golden stars,'* was not even what Hamlet called it, *'a pestilent congregation of vapors'*; it was a huge phantasm, hung on high to cheat and delude us." This assumption of knowing matter only by its qualities was " *'nonsense piled on nonense to the skies.'* . . . If you adopt it, you will craze the law, and make it as mad as the metaphysics of Berkeley and Hume."[36]

In one sense, however, Black's speeches are not the "literature" claimed for Burke or Webster. There are redundancies on occasion and, more rarely, digressions in the midst of argument. But the digressions flow from interruptions of the opposing counsel or questions from the court. They break the unity of the discourse, yet they add immensely to the immediate effect of the argument. They reveal a speaker ready, on the instant, to meet all obstacles and to turn his argument into whatever channels the moment demands.[37] The redundancies flowed from the inherent nature of extempore speaking. They are the price paid by every speaker who phrases thoughts before an audience, the overhead for the compensation of direct composition. Comparison in this regard with Burke or Webster is impossible, for Burke's masterpieces were perfected upon manuscript before delivery; and Webster's were revised *afterward* until slovenly sentences—"caught," as he said, "in the hurry of the moment"—were replaced by smooth and stately periods.[38] Black, upon the other hand, spoke wholly from extempore preparation, and left to posterity his speeches exactly as uttered. The copies of them are stenographic reports, and among his papers there is not one alteration made to polish the style. The reporting of the McCardle speech was so defective that he repudiated it altogether and undertook to dictate a revised report of what he actually said, but even in this he lost interest before the task was completed and gave it up.[39] Style with him was not a matter of glitter, grace, and beauty. It was a weapon to win decisions, and when the speech was over, the purpose was served. There was no polishing for the plaudits of posterity.

Nevertheless, taken as a whole, it was a style always lucid and forceful, and at times brilliant. "We confess in reading him," commented a discriminating editorial critic, "to a sort of editorial pang, such as Kent avows, with professional pride, in regard to Blackstone's chapter on Contingent Remainders: We read 'with mingled emotions of admiration and despair.' He makes the most difficult question plain to

[36] C. F. Black, p. 501.

[37] Cf. Almaden Quicksilver argument, C. F. Black, p. 456; Goodyear Rubber argument, *ibid.*, p. 403; Milligan argument, *ibid.*, p. 528.

[38] E. P. Whipple, *Daniel Webster*, p. XXIV.

[39] C. F. Black, preface.

a child's comprehension. He gives to each familiar topic a novel grace of expression. . . . It is all done, too, with an ease that gives the highest impression of strength and power. He never seems toiling and 'spreading himself.' . . . It is, to our mind, the perfection of the '*proprie communia dicre.*' Horace might well say *difficile est.*' "[40]

The sheer effect of his speaking cannot be passed without comment. Court decisions speak their own language, but there also are other earmarks of effect. Whenever great cases were pending and a galaxy of famous lawyers had gathered for argument—it was not Evarts, Curtis, Cushing, or even Charles O'Conor, who drew the greatest crowds to the courtroom. It was Black.[41] Others certainly were as profound in argument. But presumably Black's broad maxims of law were easiest to follow and most instructive. Certainly his anecdote was the liveliest, his invective was the most scorching, his phrase-making and power of apt quotation was the most thrilling.

We "had a crowded court room nearly all day yesterday in anticipation of the argument of Judge Black," noted a Philadelphia reporter; and again, "as though by magic the usually empty court room filled up with listeners" when it was learned that Black was about to speak. "Judge Black began his argument about a quarter before one o'clock," noted a reporter before the Pennsylvania Supreme Court, "and when it became known that he was speaking the little room that was left was rapidly filled up."[42]

On one occasion he was arguing a California land case before the Supreme Court. Scarcely was the speech over when a man, whom Black never saw before, rushed up to him, tugging at his own watch-chain as he went. He held out the chain to Black and exclaimed, "Here, Judge Black, for God's sake take this. It is all I can do to show my admiration for you." Before Black could recover his surprise, the man had slipped back into the crowd and disappeared. To his death, Black never knew who he was. The watchchain was made of gold nuggets, as they came from the mine, alternated with burnished gold, curious in workmanship and of great value. It remained among his historical collections.[43]

"He could," said Edgar Cowan, "pack up the conclusion of a hundred pages of argument in a little bundle no larger than a greenback; and yet the whole was there, every light and shade of meaning which played over it was full of significance which seems to have been compressed by the argument as it rolled along into the smallest possible space. Then there was a merry twinkle in the corner of the eye

[40] Ed. Upper Marlborough (Md.) *Prince Georgian*, Sept. 4, 1868.

[41] Cf. McCardle Case, *National Intelligencer*, March 3, 1868; and Belknap Trial, New York *Tribune*, July 25, 1876.

[42] Clayton MSS.

[43] Clayton, p. 134.

and a patient half-jocular smile as he watched that greenback fall over and crush his antagonist."[44]

Often in his life, however, there came greater tributes to this power of persuasion than mere praise from friends or critics. The following is an example of one such, coming to Black from Henry W. Palmer of Wilkes-Barre—then a very young attorney, but later a famous lawyer and Attorney-General of Pennsylvania: "I am in a bad scrape and want help," wrote Palmer. "I defended a fellow for shooting his Mother-in-law and the jury convicted him. The court gave him a new trial. On looking over the case thoroughly I concluded if it was mine, I would rather take my chance before the Court and advised my client to plead guilty and let the Court fix the degree. That tribunal disappointed me also by fixing the first degree. I took a writ of error. . . . This chap has no money but I can rake up $100 *if you will come down here and tell the Supreme Court that my client ought not to be hung.*"[45]

In a railway case before the Supreme Court of New Jersey, Black once appeared in an attempt to break up the interstate operations of the Pennsylvania railroad ring. An outstate newspaper correspondent came down to hear his speech and wrote this account:

> His argument was listened to throughout with the greatest interest both by the court and the large audience which had collected in the court room. It is admitted by all who heard him that he gave the death-blow to the case. . . . The great force of his argument lies in the plain and homely way in which he goes to the very pith of the subject, and clears away all the flimsy, sophistical cobwebs which his opponents may have thrown around it. He has a great fund of wit and genuine humor also, and his sallies invariably brought down the house and forced a broad grin and sometimes a hearty laugh from the sedate Chancellor. There is no other subject spoken of in Trenton this afternoon but "Black's great argument." You hear it on the street, in the hotels, and on the fair-grounds, and it is held by all to have settled every phase of this great case.[46]

After another such argument before the United States Supreme Court, Judge David Davis called the Marshal of the Court to his side, remarking. "It is useless to deny it, Judge Black is the most magnificent orator at the American bar."[47]

[44] Black Papers, April 11, 1884.
[45] Black Papers, February 26, 1874. (Italics mine.)
[46] Press clipping, "A.M.G.," Clayton MSS.
[47] Hensel, p. 194; Press clipping, Clayton MSS.

31

IN THE PUBLIC SERVICE OF PENNSYLVANIA AND MARYLAND

THE menacing lack of control over railroads, and the general corruption diffused throughout the State government, led the citizens of Pennsylvania in 1871 to call for a convention to amend their constitution. This convention met on November 12, 1872, and sat through most of the following year, struggling with the despairing problem of improving the evils of State government through constitutional provisions.

The State had sent its most eminent men to the convention. Among them were William M. Meredith, formerly Attorney-General of Pennsylvania and Secretary of the Treasury under Zachary Taylor; Andrew G. Curtin, war Governor of Pennsylvania; and George W. Woodward, formerly Chief Justice of the State Supreme Court and a life-long friend of Black.

Black came to the convention as a delegate-at-large. "He was," said Niles, "possibly the most conspicuous figure. His position was unique. He was a statesman of experience, a profound jurist, a brilliant debater. He was without political ambition or desire or preferment."[1] He remained in the convention for eleven months, at a loss of many thousands of dollars in his practice, yet refusing to accept a dollar in payment, giving his services to purge the State of its distempers. His colleagues treated him with peculiar respect. The printed debates show that, whenever they had occasion to differ with him upon the floor of the convention, they did so only after prefacing a tribute to his learning, character, or eminence.

He came to the convention, hoping much. His friends expected much of him. In a few of the things he hoped for, he succeeded. But in most of them he failed. Partially he failed because he stood politically in the hopeless minority, where failure was inherent and inevitable. But also he failed in some things because he was not fitted by temperament for the task at hand. No longer was he in the court room where a case was won or lost, but never compromised. Invective and surgical dissection of the opposing counsel or the evidence served his ends before the judiciary; but they were not the most tactful of weapons in the legislative chambers where fellow members must be conciliated. He therefore stood out in the convention more as a pic-

[1] Niles, p. 432.

turesque and striking figure, than as a practical and successful one. Still the convention would have lost much of its savor without him and the news value of his brilliant speeches added much to the general interest and knowledge in the proceedings.

Upon the third day occurred his first major difference with the majority. He was a member of a Special Committee to report on standing committees and rules. Notwithstanding the fact that the 4th Section of the Act authorizing the convention specifically forbade it "to change the language or alter in any manner the several provisions of . . . the Declaration of Rights", in the old Constitution, this Special Committee recommended the appointment of "one Committee to consist of nine members upon Declaration of Rights." Black signed a minority report, protesting against this violation of powers. He took his protest to the floor of the convention in a long and able speech, but was overruled by a vote of 106 to 18.[2]

Again, when the Committee on Legislature reported a provision, aimed at Philadelphia, to forbid any city or county to elect more than four Senators, Black joined the ranks of protestants. "I think it partakes a little too much of the spirit of the Pharisees," he said, "for those from the country to say to the inhabitant of the city: 'Stand aside, I am holier than thou.'" His good friend Woodward had argued that people of the great cities were not engaged in productive industry, but were in effect "a set of idlers and drones." Retorted Black: "The fact is not so. . . . Somebody has been victimizing him. Somebody has taken the advantage of his youth and inexperience and imposed upon him most grossly"—while the convention roared its delight at this sortie between friends.[3]

His greatest and bitterest fight was against the corrupt ring which had plundered the State for more than a decade, the corporation lobbyists, or "third House" as he called them, who elected members of the Legislature, muzzled the Governor, and dictated legislation. On March 10, 1873, he delivered a great speech upon the subject, caricaturing this "third House" as a "buzzard, digesting his filthy meal . . . upon the prostrate carcass of the Commonwealth." After detailing the particulars of its activities, he glanced at the other side of the house, remarking sarcastically: "There are about seventeen gentlemen on this floor who were formerly members of the Legislature. Of course they passed through the furnace of that temptation without the smell of fire upon their garments." He set forth an elaborate program intended to protect the State in the future from this ring—including the defining of bribery to include corruption of all kinds, empowering the courts to declare void all fraudulent acts of the Legislature, and the

[2] *Debates of the Constitutional Convention,* I, pp. 55, 57. Hereafter cited as *Debates.*

[3] *Debates,* II, p. 191.

swearing of all officials both into office and out of office with an "iron-clad oath."[4]

On June 28th, this question came to a vote. Black had drafted an oath as tight as any rogue ever could hope to avoid. Not only must members swear themselves into office, but upon leaving it, they must also swear that they had not "listened to private solicitations" of any sort, had not "voted or spoken on any matter" in which they "had or expected to have a private interest," nor had they "done or permitted to be done" any act which would make them guilty of bribery. Upon the eve of the vote, he made his final defense. With a discouraged voice, he prophesied its defeat: "We are out on a forlorn hope. . . . The utmost I expect is a square vote against me. . . . The proposition will be voted down, corruption will be throned and sceptred and crowned. . . . Let all the rings rejoice." But the section was carried. The iron-clad oath was saved.[5]

This was his greatest contribution to the work of the convention. When the first Legislature assembled under this new constitution, in January of 1874, a correspondent of the Philadelphia *Press* wrote his impressions of the change thus wrought. The administration of this oath, he thought, would "be of novel interest, if not dramatic effect. The oath is one of the most binding and searching . . . ever administered to a legislature, cutting off with one sweep of the sword all the rich pickings which sent more than one man out of Harrisburg rich who came here poor. It is an oath without a single hole for a knave to escape through . . . and leaves no room for somersaulting. The man who takes it must keep it in spirit and practice or suffer the penalty of perjury. . . . It will be interesting to see some of the old and tried legislators . . . take this oath."[6]

When, however, Black attempted to define bribery in the constitution so as to include all private solicitation of legislators by interested parties, the convention voted him down. He retired with this good-humored but defiant salvo: "Every proposition made by a friend of reform is answered by a thundering *no*. Our opponents rush at us like a herd of buffalo on a western prairie. They crush us down by mere weight of body and hardness of hoof. (Laughter.) . . . Here they come, with horns down and tails up. (Much laughter.) I mean to get out of the way."[7]

The last sentence was not a jest. On the next day, October 2, 1873, he resigned from the convention. His friend George W. Woodward, who presented the resignation in Black's behalf, submitted as the rea-

[4] *Ibid.*, II, p. 485.

[5] Press clipping, Clayton MSS.

[6] Philadelphia *Press*, January 12, 1874.

[7] *Debates*, VII, p. 409.

son that Black's professional business in the Supreme Court demanded his presence.[8]

This undoubtedly was true. His legal business had suffered heavily. But there also were other reasons. By temperament and training he was unfit for the legislative work of compromising. He stood in the minority. He felt the majority to be palliating the evils which had marked the State as conspicuous, even in that age of corruption. At the Belknap Impeachment Trial, three years later, he gave the more fundamental reason for his retirement. "I found myself shooting at the stars," he said. "I was told that I was trying to make the officers of the Commonwealth righteous overmuch."[9]

Though members of the convention would not vote with him, they heard of his resignation with regret. They begged Woodward to persuade him to reconsider—or even to return later and sign the new constitution. For eleven days his resignation lay before them without action. At last, upon October 13th, when the last hope of his returning had been given up, they voted to accept it.[10]

In spite of his temperamental unfitness for legislative work, and his failure in many of the direct measures he undertook, Black did, however, stand among the influential members of the convention. His iron-clad oath led to the practical extinction of the famous "third House" in the Legislature. Also, as Woodward remarked, the convention was largely an educational institution—arousing honesty and patriotism of the voters—and Black's fiery invective and stirring anecdote became the greatest news factor of the sessions.[11]

The convention voted its members $1500 each as compensation. It was a modest reward, but Black protested that only the Legislature had power to fix the compensation. He held such an irregular procedure to be a usurpation of power and therefore refused to accept any pay whatever.[12]

The following year, 1874, Black was chosen by the Legislature of Maryland as one of the arbiters to settle the long-standing boundary dispute between Maryland and Virginia. "Our papers have hailed this selection with great pleasure," wrote Governor W. P. Whyte.[13] The other two arbiters were Governors Charles L. Jenkins of Georgia, and W. A. Graham of North Carolina.

This dispute was an old and famous one, dating back into early Colonial history. Under the Articles of Confederation friction had arisen between these two States over the control of commerce upon the

[8] Philadelphia *Press*, October 3, 1873.

[9] *Trial of William W. Belknap*, 44 Cong., 1st Sess., part 7, p. 314.

[10] Philadelphia *Press*, October 14, 1873.

[11] Niles, p. 466.

[12] Black Papers, June 24, 1873; Niles, p. 465.

[13] Black Papers, May 18, 1874.

Potomac River. Once there had been a convention at Alexandria which led, by devious routes and through the good intervention of George Washington, to the Annapolis Convention and thence to the great Constitutional Convention. Still, after more than a century, many phases of this dispute were still unsettled.

For three years this board of arbiters gathered evidence and heard arguments, sitting by turns at Sulphur Springs, Washington, Philadelphia, Cape May, and Saratoga. Among the interesting old documents which were searched out for authority was an original map of Captain John Smith's which had been but recently discovered. At last, in 1877, the board rendered its decision and the aged and famous dispute was brought to an end.

In general, the entire Potomac River was awarded to Maryland, up to the low-water mark on the Virginia shore, but all indentations of bays, creeks, and rivers in Virginia were declared to be exclusive territory of that state. Also was Virginia given full use of the Potomac beyond the low-water mark to the extent necessary for the enjoyment of her riparian ownership.[14] Maryland, therefore, was secured in her fishing rights to the Potomac and her sportsmen left to the monopoly of duck hunting.

[14] *Opinion and Award of Arbiters on the Maryland and Virginia Boundary Line*, pp. 29-31.

32

THE BELKNAP IMPEACHMENT TRIAL AND THE TILDEN-HAYES ELECTION DISPUTE

IN THE elections of 1874 the Republicans once more hoisted the bloody shirt to its halyards, but the public was weary of this guidon and nauseated from the stench of corruption. The Democrats carried Pennsylvania, Ohio, New York, Connecticut, and the governorship of Massachusetts. The House of Representatives, safely Republican by 198 to 88, was rudely upset and the Democrats swept into control, 168 to 108. It was an ill omen for the Presidential election of 1876.

Upon the eve of this election, William W. Belknap, then Secretary of War, was discovered to have been receiving $6,000 a year as an annuity for appointing a certain Caleb P. Marsh to the post-tradership at Fort Sill, Oklahoma. He was at once impeached by the House of Representatives,[1] but the forehanded public servant had outpaced the House by five hours in resigning from office.

The Republicans, with an eye on the November elections, demanded Belknap's blood. But Black recalled their management of the Credit Mobilier affair in the election of 1872. He was convinced that this was merely the act of Pharisees praying in public. He appeared before the Senate at the impeachment trial, defending Belknap in what assuredly was the most remarkable type of argument ever submitted upon such an occasion. Baldly put, his argument was that Belknap was no worse a crook than his political associates, and must not be made "the scapegoat to carry the sins of the whole off into the wilderness."[2]

His development of this proposition must have been an unanaesthetized probing into the conscience of many who heard him. The transfer of money from Marsh to Belknap, he argued, was a "mere exchange of gifts." It offered only a "bare plausibility" of any corruption. Proof of how bare it was could be found upon every hand. The Credit Mobilier managers, for example, had given stock and bonds to the wife of Senator Henry Wilson. Wilson knew it, voted in Congress for a Credit Mobilier charter and later to extend its privileges, but this was considered no proof that his vote was bought with the stocks and bonds, and he "died in the odor of sanctity."

[1] *Trial of William W. Belknap*, part 7, 44 Cong., 1st Sess., p. 111. Hereafter cited as *Trial*.

[2] C. F. Black, p. 27.

Grant also had taken huge gifts openly—money, lands, houses, goods,—and conformed his policy of government to the wishes of donors. "Nay, he did more . . . he appointed those who bought him by these gifts to the highest offices which he could bestow in return. . . ." Yet he was regarded still as "one of the greatest heroes and sages the world has produced. Instead of being impeached and ignominiously removed from office, he was flattered and re-elected." Specifically, Black recited the gift of a library by E. R. Hoar to Grant and of Grant rewarding Hoar with the office of Attorney-General; also Judge Pierrepont's gift of $20,000, and of Grant's bestowal upon Pierrepont of the Ambassadorship to England. Was the House "afraid to take the Chief Magistrate by the throat, or did they suppose the Senate would use one measure of justice for Grant and another for Belknap?"

From Grant he passed to other members of the administration, referring with irony to "these good and great men" who "constantly practice" the act now complained of against Belknap. With grimness of humor, he closed: "You will no doubt be glad to hear me say that I am done."[3]

The greatest crowd of the long impeachment trial had gathered to hear Black,[4] and the backfire was deliciously interesting. Belknap was acquitted by almost a straight party vote, the Democrats refusing to have him singled out among the many culprits of the administration.[5] But upon the instant the final vote was over, adjournment was delayed while a letter of protest was read from Congressman George F. Hoar, claiming that his brother never had given Grant a library. Senator George F. Boutwell then demanded the floor to explain away Henry Wilson's interest in Credit Mobilier.[6] The New York *Tribune* referred to Black's "singular precedents" for justifying Belknap's action, but was meticulous in avoiding any discussion whatever of these precedents.[7]

Closely upon the heels of the Belknap episode came the discrepant election of 1876. It had been preceded by excitement intense and prolonged, and the result, instead of affording relief, added to the tension. Out of 185 votes necessary to elect, Tilden had the undisputed control of 184, with the 19 votes of Louisiana, Florida and South Carolina in riotous dispute. Every one of these 19 votes was necessary to put Hayes in office, and there was grave doubt whether he was entitled to any one of them. Particularly in Louisiana was there evi-

[3] *Trial*, pp. 314-18.

[4] New York *Tribune*, July 25, 1876.

[5] *Trial*, pp. 346-57. The official reason given was that the Senate lacked jurisdiction because of Belknap's resignation.

[6] *Ibid.*, p. 357.

[7] New York *Tribune*, July 25, 1876.

dence of barefaced fraud. The gross returns from that State gave Tilden a majority of 8,957 votes, but the Returning Board of Louisiana had yet to finger the ballots. A most remarkable body, was this Returning Board. In defiance of law, it possessed not one single Democrat among its members. Its president was one James Madison Wells whom General Sheridan had caught with hands thrust deep into a $4,000,000 levee appropriation, had booted from office and branded as "a dishonored man," whose conduct was "as sinuous as . . . a snake." Two other of its members were ignorant negroes, one of whom had been indicted for the low crime of larceny and had admitted his guilt.[8]

Wells and his cohorts pondered with a purpose before submitting a final report. To the Democrats, Wells offered to sell the vote of Louisiana for $200,000.[9] When this marked-down bargain was refused, the fate of the election was sealed. Three days before the work of the Board was completed, the United States Marshal at New Orleans wired to Washington: "Have seen Wells who says Board will return Hayes sure. Have no fear." Wells was a gentleman of his word. His Board threw out 13,250 Democratic votes and 2,042 Republican, until Louisiana was made safe for Hayes.[10]

Said the *Nation*, "We do not ourselves see how Mr. Hayes can, if he be the man he has been represented, take the place under the circumstances."[11] But Hayes made no move to prove himself such a man. Twenty-five years later Rhodes felt called upon to apologize for his conduct: "If Hayes had envisaged the facts as I now do he would have refused to accept the presidency from the Louisiana Returning Board."[12] Yet the facts neither had been altered, nor made more accessible after twenty-five years.

In Louisiana, as in Florida and South Carolina, two sets of returns were sent to Congress, one set delivering the electoral votes of these States to Tilden, the other delivering them to Hayes.

Who should count the ballots? And which ballot should they count? The House was Democratic. If the election was thrown to the House, Tilden would become President. But the Senate was Republican. If allowed to "count" the ballots, it would count in Hayes.

The Constitution provided no remedy. There was no law upon the subject. Violent men upon both sides were talking by turns of unarmed citizens, and of disciplined Civil War veterans, marching on Washington to install their candidate. But the more sane-minded preferred

[8] *Nation*, December 14, 1876.

[9] *Nation*, March 8, 1877; Black in the *North American Review*, July 1877, p. 1, compiled the legal proof for this bargain. Rhodes, *op. cit.*, VII, p. 233, used most of it and agreed to its authenticity.

[10] Rhodes, *op. cit.*, VII, p. 232.

[11] *Nation*, December 14, 1876.

[12] Rhodes, *op. cit.*, VII, p. 236.

barriers to barricades, and at last a special Act was passed in Congress creating an Electoral Commission, composed of five members each from the House, Senate, and the Supreme Court, to determine the counting of these disputed votes.[13]

The Electoral Commission met upon January 31, 1877, to hear the evidence and argument. Before this Commission appeared Black as one of the Democratic counsel to defend the cause of Tilden. "The Democrats are better provided with counsel," commented the *Nation*. "It can hardly be called an equal fight with Messrs. Stoughton, Matthews, and Schellabarger on one side, even when assisted by Mr. Evarts,—and Messrs. O'Conor, Trumbull, Black, Merrick and Field against them."[14]

A superior counsel the Democrats might have, but in the end it was not the counsel, it was the Electoral Commission, which was to decide the election—and upon that Commission sat eight Republicans and seven Democrats. Among them was Black's friend Garfield, who had strenuously opposed the creation of the Commission and argued bitterly that Hayes was entitled to the Presidency. When the Republicans first set up Garfield as a member of the Commission Black had gone to him, protesting that he already had committed himself and therefore could not serve without embarrassment. "There was some force in the suggestion," wrote Garfield in his journal, "but after consulting with Messrs. Hoar and McCrary and others of my friends I found that I could not withdraw without displeasing my own party in the House."[15] Garfield therefore sat, already committed, upon the Commission.

Nevertheless, the Democrats entered the argument with high hopes, conscious of the enormous superiority of their case. The Florida vote was the first to be considered. R. L. Merrick opened for the Democrats, followed by Black and then by O'Conor. "Must Congress," argued Black, "blindly accept the result of votes as announced to them by the Vice President or can they go behind to learn if the votes presented to the Vice President are genuine or fraudulent?" This, of course, was the ultimate issue of the entire case, for there could be no question but that the Carpetbag Governor of Florida had delivered the vote of that State to Hayes. Nor could it be disputed that there was fraud in the Florida election returns.

The opposing counsel had argued that Congress had no right to go behind these returns. Agreed, said Black, but Congress does have the power to go behind the fraudulent act of the Carpetbag Governor to learn what were the true returns. Not only does Congress have that power, but it has exercised it before. In the election of 1838, the

[13] *Statutes at Large*, XIX, p. 227.

[14] *Nation*, February 8, 1877.

[15] Journal, Jan. 27th, quoted in Smith, *Garfield*, p. 631.

Governor of New Jersey certified five members to Congress who had not been elected. The House was confronted with the same issue as now. Then as now it was argued "that the certificate of the Governor was conclusive evidence." But after a struggle of four or five weeks, Congress went behind the Governor's seal to the people's act and denied these five claimants a seat.[16]

This speech reads like terse, driving, and unified argument, brief and to the point. Garfield's comment in his journal, therefore, becomes peculiarly significant. "I fear Judge Black is falling into the loose and garrulous ways of an old man." Of Charles O'Conor, who followed Black in an argument which the *Nation* said was a brilliant one, Garfield wrote, "he is suffering from feebleness."[17]

Six days later, on February 9th, the Commission returned the first of its famous 8 to 7 decisions, giving Florida to Hayes.[18] On February 15th "the great fraud" of Louisiana, as Rhodes termed it, likewise was sanctified by the Commission, and on the 23rd the abortive Oregon dispute was decided in favor of Hayes. In both cases, the vote was 8 to 7.[19]

In neither of these cases, however, did Black have a part. In truth it must be said that, after the Florida decision, the Democrats showed decidedly inferior management of their case. The Republicans maintained their counsel of four—Evarts, Stoughton, Matthews, and Schellabarger—throughout the entire hearing. But the Democrats passed thirteen lawyers in review before the Commission, with no one in active charge and a decided lack of consistency in their arguments. O'Conor argued the Florida case and vanished. Lyman Trumbull, John A. Campbell, and Matt Carpenter appeared in the Louisiana arguments, and they too disappeared. After the Florida case Black also departed until he was called in at the eleventh hour and the last minute in the South Carolina hearing.

Nevertheless the case cannot be said to have been lost by poor management, for in reality it was decided when eight Republicans and seven Democrats were chosen to sit upon the Commission. Against that handicap Democratic arguments were a mere "ocean of dreams without a sound." In the Florida argument there was neither lack of power nor unity, yet it brought forth an 8 to 7 decision, and twenty-three times hand-running upon major and minor issues that monotonous vote, 8 to 7, was repeated.

The South Carolina case was taken up on February 26th. The result

[16] *Proceedings of the Electoral Commission,* part 4, 44 Cong., 2nd Sess., p. 24.

[17] Journal, Feb. 3, quoted in Smith, *Garfield,* p. 634; *Nation,* Feb. 8, 1877. This impartial magazine felt that the Democrats (i.e., Black) had driven the Republicans completely off the field in their claim of a Governor's certificate being final.

[18] *Proceedings,* p. 276.

[19] *Ibid.,* pp. 279, 282.

was known in advance. The Commission, for the twenty-fourth time, would reiterate its formula. Nevertheless the Democrats, like Mr. Britling, resolved to see it through. Two young Congressmen, Hurd of Ohio and Cochrane of Pennsylvania, were sent in for a baptism of fire. For the Republicans, Congressman Lawrence of Ohio promised not to speak, and then read a pile of manuscript for about an hour. Suddenly Black and Montgomery Blair appeared, both having been summoned at the last minute.[20] Blair spoke for half an hour, rambling, embarrassed, and unprepared.

"The duty of closing the case thus shiftlessly and feebly opened," commented the *Tribune*, "devolved upon the venerable and eccentric Judge Black."[21] And Black closed it with a vengeance, not with an argument, but with a branding iron. The case was lost. Argument was futile. So with a master's touch he applied the smoking heat of invective to the vitals of the "sanctified Eight." "Its bitterness," thought the *Tribune*, "was relieved now and then by gleams of good-natured humor which are so much a part of Judge Black's nature that he could not wholly suppress it,"[22] but there was as little humor in him at this moment as any of his life.

"I had not, and have not now, any intention to argue this case," he began. "I am, I suppose, the very last man in this whole nation who should be called upon to speak here and now . . . I . . . am degraded and humiliated. . . . A President deriving his title from a shameless swindle, not merely fraud, but of fraud detected and exposed. . . . But you are wise, you are calm. You can look although this awful business with a learned spirit. . . . No passionate hatred of this great fraud can cloud your mental vision or shake the even balance of your judgment. You do not think it wrong that a nation should be cheated by false election returns. On the contrary, it is rather a blessing which Heaven has sent us in this strange disguise. . . . Give then your cool consideration to these objections and try them by the standard of the law."

Briefly, then, he touched upon the proof of legal fraud committed with deliberate intent in the South Carolina returns. But logic was not his weapon of the hour. He closed by evoking the searing words of Isaiah. "Well may you say, '*We have made a covenant with death, and with hell we are at agreement; when the overflowing scourge shall pass through, it shall not come unto us; for we have made lies our refuge, and under falsehood have we hid ourselves.*' . . . Wait; retribution will come. . . . The mills of God grind slowly, but they grind exceeding fine," and fiercely he looked at Garfield and Hoar

[20] New York *Tribune*, Feb. 28, 1877.
[21] *Ibid.*
[22] *Ibid.*

as if they especially were to be put into the hopper.[23] Then he added significantly, "wait until the flood-gate is lifted."[24]

Having finished with the gentlemen, Black turned his back upon them and strode out of the room. There followed a moment of painful silence.[25] Then the Commission filed out of the room and, by a vote of 8 to 7, denied Tilden the Presidency.

The reception of Black's cauterizing speech affords interesting reading. He had spoken barely twenty minutes, yet to Garfield the torture seemed like three-quarters of an hour.[26] A judge of the Supreme Court, sitting upon the Commission, vowed that had Black uttered such words before a court he would have been punished for contempt.[27] "Sunset" Cox, however, and his colleagues in the House, rejoiced that "this grand old statesman of Pennsylvania" had gone "'to the book of the avenging Jehovah,' to voice in our own tough Teutonic tongue, his *anathema maranatha* against these spoilers of our election liberties."[28]

Black did not desist, even after Hayes had been enthroned on March 4th. In the July issue of the *North American Review* there appeared under his name an article upon "The Great Fraud," supported by documents, laying bare the plot of the Louisiana Returning Board to sell out to the Democrats for $200,000, and the violation of State Law in every step of their procedure.[29]

The Republicans felt called upon to take some notice of this argument, and therefore E. W. Stoughton, a member of the Republican counsel before the Electoral Commission, undertook a reply. But Stoughton was hardly equal to the task, relying so largely upon personal abuse of Black that the latter branded it "as the scolding of a fish-woman." Stoughton's misstatements, Black continued, may not have been deliberate.

> But wrong is wrought for want of thought
> As well as want of heart,

and Stoughton had showed a want of thought. He had, for example, not explained the remainder of the election in Louisiana. The Returning Board had awarded the Carpet-bag candidate for Governor a thousand more votes than to Hayes, yet the would-be Governor fled the State the instant Federal troops were withdrawn, and Hayes had repudiated the very regime that had set him in office, confessing to its cor-

[23] *Ibid.*
[24] *Proceedings,* pp. 190-91.
[25] New York *Tribune,* Feb. 28, 1877.
[26] Smith, *Garfield,* p. 645.
[27] New York *Tribune,* August 20, 1883.
[28] Cox, *op. cit.,* p. 663.
[29] *North American Review,* July 1877, pp. 1-34.

ruption, by lifting no finger to defend it. "When your masters at Washington," concluded Black, "intrusted you with the defense of the Great Fraud, they put the business into most incompetent hands."[30]

Both articles, like the closing speech before the Electoral Commission, were saturated with fiery invective, yet it cannot be said that they overstepped the bounds of truth. Black's unvarnished opinion of Stoughton's part in the Tilden election, however, was best expressed in a private letter to Congressman James Proctor Knott of Kentucky. Knott had addressed several letters to Black while the latter was preparing his reply to Stoughton, but had received no reply. At last he became urgent and Black wrote: "My dear Knott: I really have not time to answer your letters just now. Am busy skinning a dog."[31]

[30] "Reply to Mr. Stoughton," New York *Sun*, November 11, 1877.
[31] Clayton MSS.

33

IN THE RIPENESS OF LIFE

BLACK approached the biblical allotment of three score years and ten in more serenity than ever he had enjoyed before. The political cloud, under which he had lived for twenty years, gradually was melting away as time lengthened the span stretching backward to the Civil War. Fame was his, fortune, and a host of friends. His party had lost the election contest of 1876, but Reconstruction in the South was over, the Constitution in his view at last was reënthroned. The future was rich with promise. A few lingering disputes remained, enough to satisfy his hunger for disputation.

During the summer of 1878 he visited California with his wife, looking after a few mining interests, visiting for the first time the well-known sites, cities, mines, and lands which he had long before defended for their owners in the land controversies before the Supreme Court. Everywhere he was welcomed, honored, and feted.[1]

In the spring of 1880 he took at last the long-deferred trip to Europe, accompanied by his wife and granddaughter.[2] He enjoyed the trip, but found sight-seeing more wearing than his strenuous life at home. On May 9th, he wrote his daughter Mary from Killarney, Ireland: "I am cut off from the usual sources of that mental excitement which has heretofore been so healthful. . . . I feel as if my faculties were rusting for want of somebody or something to fight."[3]

Landing in England he went at once to Runnymede, passing by all other historic sites, that he might stand first upon this ground where the Barons of King John had forced that pandering monarch to yield their civil rights in the Magna Carta.[4] One is tempted to dwell upon the tumultuous thoughts which must have surged within the mind of this defender of Milligan, McCardle, and of trial by jury, as he stood upon the bank of the Thames gazing at the historic ground where men, eight centuries before, had risked their necks in the same great cause. But we forego the speculation. The mere act of hastening there first is significant enough.

Shortly afterward he wrote to Germany, making inquiries about

[1] Black Papers, July 29, 1878; Clayton, p. 173; Clayton MSS.

[2] Black Papers, April 14, 1880. Twenty-three years before, in 1857, he had engaged a passage to Europe when the trip was prevented by his unexpected appointment as Attorney-General.

[3] Clayton, p. 177.

[4] Hensel, p. 196.

the passion play at Oberammergau,[5] but he does not seem to have attended this play. By the first of June he was anxious to return to America. "My spirit wearies by absence from home," he wrote. Still he found deep pleasures in Westminster Abbey, which he termed "a wilderness of wonders." He had just attended a dinner with half a dozen distinguished authors. "I never heard so much curious talk," he said, "or saw such magnificent strawberries."[6]

Nevertheless he lingered in Europe until August, landing in New York on the 24th.

While in London he had heard of the unexpected nomination for President of his friend Garfield, by the Republican party. Why these two men had remained such warm friends is, in some ways, an enigma. Black was twenty-one years the older. They differed so violently in politics that it seems a sheer miracle that their friendship should have outlasted a single election. Yet it lived on. Once Garfield had been marooned at York, in a sleeper, while a porter had transferred both bag and clothes to another car. Left to the scant resources of his nightclothes, Garfield upon awakening called upon Black. "The noble old Judge," he wrote, "put on me one of the Judge's shirts with a fixed standing collar," and thus attired, with presumably other additions, he continued his journey. They delighted in table talk of all kinds. "Had Judge Black and Professor Newcomb at dinner," noted Garfield in his journal in 1872, "and discussed until a late hour the 'Transit of Venus,' and its value to science." The following year he commented in his journal, "I never meet Judge Black without a feeling what power and culture and genius of mind have done to overcome all the roughness of partisan feeling and made a man a great and delightful friend." Garfield had sat upon the Electoral Commission which denied Tilden the Presidency, yet even while the deliberations were going on, they visited together over Sunday.[7] They had tried cases together, they owned a farm together, but never did they see eye to eye in politics, and even the nomination of Garfield for President could not reconcile their differences.

From London, upon hearing of this event, Black at once wrote Garfield a letter that surely is as remarkable a document of its kind as ever was penned.

I suppose I ought to be glad for two reasons at least. In the first place it opens the way by which a very dear friend will probably reach that great office which makes ambition virtue; and secondly it saves the country from the calamity of Grant or Sherman. . . . Perhaps it diminishes our chances of getting a president whose views of consti-

[5] Black Papers, May 23, 1880.
[6] Letter of June 2, quoted in Clayton, p. 180.
[7] Smith, *Garfield*, pp. 634, 792, 831, 906.

JEREMIAH SULLIVAN BLACK
At About Seventy Years

tutional duty are sound, but I have described you as thought [of] truly, at home and here, since the nomination and before, as the first man of your party, with a very long interval between you and the second. . . .

I am sure that if elected you will try your best to do justice, to love mercy, and to walk humbly before God. But to a certain extent you are bound to fail, for in our country the leader of a party is like the head of a snake—it can go only as the tail impels it, and your tail will be a very perverse one. Whatever you may do, or think, or feel as a public man, the obligations of social fidelity, fraternal affection and love of truth will compel me to see to it as far as I can that you are not wronged by any aspersion from which I can vindicate. . . .

Win this prize, therefore, if you can without endangering our great and wise institutions.

> But howsoever thou persist this act
> Taint not thy soul, nor let thy heart contrive
> Against thy country aught.

. . . It may seem to you that I am taking too much upon myself when I talk in this strain, but I am very serious in my feelings today. In the course of all my life only one political event has made me feel so strange to myself. Whatever I may be called to do, to be, or to suffer, I intend to remain, Yours faithfully, J. S. Black.[8]

The last sentence was prophetic of Black's share in the campaign.

Amidst the busy rush of this campaign, Garfield at once answered Black in his own hand.

I know how grounded you are in the ways of political thinking which seem to you just and for the highest good of your country—and so all the more for that reason I prize your words of personal kindness. . . . Succeeding or failing I shall none the less honor your noble character, great intellect and equally great heart.[9]

Black returned from Europe in August. Winfield S. Hancock, the hero of Gettysburg, had been nominated by the Democrats. Hancock and Black long had been friends, though never so intimately as had Garfield and Black.[10] But Hancock was championing the cause of Democracy and, when called upon to campaign in his behalf, Black agreed to do so. "Whatever I may be called on to do," he had written Garfield, "I intend to remain, yours faithfully." But as he plunged into the campaign his promise became harder and harder to keep, except perhaps in the heart. Once more Garfield was accused of having held Credit Mobilier stock and having received dividends. Black

[8] Black Papers, June 9, 1880.

[9] Black Papers, July 20, 1880.

[10] Letters of Black to Hancock, Nov. 30, 1867 (Clayton MSS.); and July 9, 1870 (Black Papers).

was called upon to testify. He could do none other than admit that Garfield had, in fact, done both.[11]

Later Black was led to believe, rightly or wrongly, that Garfield had sealed a bargain with the stalwarts of New York by which the latter, in return for supporting Garfield, were to have E. D. Morgan made Secretary of Treasury and Stanley Matthews placed upon the Supreme Bench. "Taint not thy soul," he had written Garfield, but this he felt was taint, "worse than the Hayes bargain of 1876 or the Adams-Clay cheat of Jackson." He denounced the believed bargain and took the stump aggressively against Garfield.[12]

They never saw or corresponded with each other again. But not even this break in the heat of campaign could sever the inner feelings of either man for the other. When Garfield was struck down by an assassin, Black broke his silence and was among the first to reach him with a telegram. He followed this with a solicitous call at the White House, although by physician's orders none was allowed to see Garfield. Arousing from his lethargy, about a week after he was shot, Garfield at once asked, "Have you heard from Black?" "Yes," replied the attendant, "his was among the earliest telegrams, and one of the most sympathetic. He has been here and is anxious about you." With great emotion Garfield answered, "*That almost pays for this.*"[13]

During the summer of 1881, Black's memoirs were released to the public. They appeared as a series of interviews with Black, made by a well-known political writer, Frank A. Burr. From Black, Burr secured letters, documents, and verbal testimony concerning the latter's part in the closing days of the Buchanan administration. Added to this he obtained also the letters and testimony of other men who had been associated with Black, as Philip Thomas, John Dix, Joseph Holt, and Jacob Thompson. These interviews and documents were published both in the Sunday and weekly editions of the Philadelphia *Press*, through August and September of 1881.

The result amounted almost to a revolution of public thought concerning Black's part in the Secession crisis. Heretofore, loyalty to Buchanan had sealed his lips. Now came the incontrovertible proof not only of his loyalty to the Union in that crisis, but of his aggressive leadership of the entire Cabinet in this loyalty.

When Buchanan was fuming in 1862 to hasten with his vindication

[11] Smith (Cf. *Garfield*, p. 936) states that Black reversed his utterances of 1873 in saying this. This is an error. Black's private letters to Garfield in this year show that he knew it. His public letters were exceedingly careful to refrain from touching upon this delicate point. He believed Garfield to be originally innocent of wrong-doing in the affair, but beyond that he scrupulously refrained from testifying. See *supra*, p. 214.

[12] Cf. Philadelphia *Herald*, August 20, 1883.

[13] C. E. Henry to Black, Dec. 21, 1881. Henry obtained the account from Mrs. Dr. Edson, attendant to Garfield while ill. Quoted in Clayton, p. 197.

to the public, Black had urged delay. "You speak of laying facts before the public," he wrote. "*There is no public.* . . . Let your vindication await . . . the restoration of the popular mind to its wholesome normal condition."[14] Events now justified his wisdom. Twenty years had passed. The public temper was at least nearer normal than at any previous time since the resounding of guns at Sumter. With but the rarest of exceptions, both public and press received Black's vindication with proud acclaim. He was hailed as the "grand old statesman" who had fought disunion to the bitter end. He was even evoked as an oracle by some who, at the beginning of the war, had denounced him as a traitor. "No American wields a. more trenchant pen or speaks with more eloquent lips," acclaimed his erstwhile bitter enemy, the Philadelphia *Press*,[15] continuing in a long editorial to retract its former view and to eulogize Black as one of the saviors of the nation in the crisis of 1860. This view found generally a universal echo, in which the press agreed that Black's name was wholly, and for the first time, cleansed of the unfair stain long laid upon it.[16]

Down in Washington sat another Pennsylvanian in the office of Attorney-General which Black once had held, Benjamin H. Brewster. Brewster had made his initial appearance before the Supreme Court of Pennsylvania while Black sat upon that bench. In spite of political differences, he admired the trenchant and grizzled old warrior. To him Black had made a personal request for the disposition of some legal business, and Brewster not only at once complied with the request, but answered Black with a warm note of personal friendship. This note betokens the general softening of the harshness with which political enemies once held him.

"Now please remember," wrote Brewster, "that you must treat me in this way always. I wish to keep alive between us the most cordial and pleasant relations. . . . My respect and admiration for you binds me to you closely and I am never so happy as when every now and then since I have been in public office you have displayed your sense of friendship by your personal appeals to me in such matters as interested you, for I know that a man of your noble nature—I should say heroic nature—would never make personal requests unless he felt an affinity of strong personal regard."[17]

On April 18, 1882, Black delivered the greatest popular address of

[14] Black File, Buchanan Papers, March 1, 1862.

[15] Philadelphia *Press*, August 22, 1881. This paper was no longer owned by John W. Forney, but was still Republican in policy.

[16] Cf. Philadelphia *Press* of August 9, 10, 11, 1881, carries reprints from the tributes of Philadelphia *Chronicle-Herald* and *Evening Bulletin*, Pittsburgh *Dispatch* and *Post*, Lancaster *New Era* and *Examiner*, New York *Evening Mail*, Springfield (Mass.) *Republican*, Boston *Journal* and *Post*, Cleveland *Herald*. The New York *Tribune* later added its acclaim; see Aug. 20, 1883.

[17] Black Papers, 1881.

his life, at the Maryland centenary celebration of Grattan's declaration of Irish Independence. The old Concordia Opera House could not hold the crowd. William Pinkney Whyte, Mayor of Baltimore and formerly Governor of the State, was the first speaker of the occasion. Following him was Congressman W. E. Robinson of Brooklyn, and then Black, chief speaker of the day. "When Judge Black was introduced," reported the Baltimore *Sun*, "the cheering was so deafening that the music of the band could not be heard." As he spoke "laughter and applause . . . fairly shook the hall. There was no spread eagle in his style."[18]

The speech rose to the level of magnificent proportions in eloquence and in scope. "On that night," commented the *Catholic World*, "years before Mr. Gladstone . . . outlined his policy of Home Rule, this greatest of American jurists . . . developed a plan for self government of Ireland in harmony with the integrity of the British Empire."[19] The tribute was not in the least exaggerated.

Step by step, Black traced the causes for the ills of Ireland—the tenant land system, and the misrule of government. He then turned to a discussion of the cure, setting for a plan of Home Rule which would protect both the British Empire and the long-suffering people of Ireland. In closing he spoke words of counsel to the Irish sympathizers in America. Unlike Wendell Phillips, in the latter's celebrated Irish address at the O'Connell centennial seven years before, Black indulged in no wanton abuse of England, not even to gratify the taste of her bitterest enemies among his hearers.

"We must speak respectfully of England . . ." he said. "Her armies circle the earth; her fleets cover every sea; the long reach of her diplomacy perplexes where it does not control the councils of other States. This is power and power is always honored. . . . But England has other and higher claims upon our respect. Her literature is our own, and from her we derive much of our science and art. . . . The Magna Carta, trial by jury, habeas corpus, and the bill of rights are her inventions." Yet calmly and frankly he dissected and exposed the long misrule of Ireland.

In the peroration Black voiced his grave fears for the future of America, speaking words of disturbing prophecy.

> Here, as elsewhere, unjust legislation and cunning arrangements of business grind the workman to swell the colossal fortunes of the upstart adventurer. Here, as elsewhere, the hastening evil is upon us of a community "where wealth accumulates and men decay." The struggle to be free, which land and labor are making in Ireland, is not an exclusively Irish affair. We make it a common cause, not merely because the love of justice and the sense of right impel us, but because

[18] Baltimore *Sun*, April 19, 1882.

[19] A. F. Faust, *Catholic World*, September 1886, p. 758.

this is an united effort to deliver ourselves, as well as them, from the hand of the spoiler. If we assist Ireland to win the victory she hopes for, we expand our own principles, perfect our own practice and strengthen our own courage for a contest, perhaps more arduous, which we may have to wage on our own account.[20]

It was a great address, great in its conception, its execution, in its immediate and indirect effect. The Irish of New Jersey and of Massachusetts appealed to him to address their State centennials.[21] At Trenton, New Jersey, Ludlow McCarter, a brilliant and rising young attorney, wrote:

Judge Black speaks and writes the English language with more power than any living man. No matter how much a subject may have been discussed nor by whom discussed, whenever he writes or speaks on that subject, he seems to throw new light on it. It is not too much to say that he is to prose what Shakespeare was to poetry. . . . And he is perhaps today recognized—I mean take him all in all—as the foremost lawyer of the American bar.[22]

For Black, these were the halcyon days of Indian Summer.

[20] Baltimore *Sun*, April 19, 1882.
[21] Black Papers, April 28, May 24, 1882.
[22] McCarter to Atkinson, Black Papers, April 28, 1882.

34

CLOSING DAYS

DURING the winter of 1882-83 Black spent most of his time as usual in Washington. He was still in vigorous health, "and his friends," wrote his daughter, "never found him more genial and vigorous, bodily and mentally." Yet something prompted him to leave Washington in the midst of the Supreme Court session and return to Brockie. Here he revised his will and spent a few days in quiet and solitude.[1]

His last public appearance was before the Senate Judiciary Committee of the Legislature of Pennsylvania on March 9, 1883. Railway legislation was then pending before the Legislature. The various corporations affected had been heard through officials and attorneys, but "the plundered people," noted a reporter, "had as yet no champion" to put the railroads' "lance in rest."[2] It was indeed the day of the railroad, wherein the public were "to hastening ills a prey." Black long had been gravely perturbed over corporate invasion of public rights. In his early decisions from the Supreme Court of Pennsylvania, through his arguments before the Supreme Court of the United States, and down to his solemn closing words in the Grattan centenary address, runs the unbroken vein of this grave concern. The proposed legislation in Pennsylvania was the embodiment of his fears. The railroads, knowing his great influence, attempted to control it by employing him as counsel, offering to pay whatever retainer he might name. "I cannot take your case," he replied. "I am pledged to the whole people of the Commonwealth of Pennsylvania."[3]

He announced the intention of giving his views upon this disturbing topic to the Senate Judiciary Committee, charged with task of formulating railway legislation. He came to the State Capitol "quietly and unostentatiously," noted a reporter, with the intention of addressing the Committee in its rooms, but at the earnest request of friends he at last consented to speak in the Senate Chamber. Let us take the account from an eyewitness: "At a little after eight o'clock Judge Black . . . came down the main aisle of the Senate Chamber. . . . He was immediately surrounded by all the men of mark and note

[1] Clayton, p. 203. His will was dated February 21, 1883; Cf. York Co. Will Book, C. C. No. 3, p. 346.

[2] Clayton, p. 203.

[3] Niles, p. 468.

who could reach him. There was no question of politics here. The men about him were of all parties. . . . Soon he was addressing the Committee, and who among all that throng will ever forget the flood of pathos, humor, logic, and irresistible eloquence that fell from his lips for over three hours. Notes had he none, but . . . he covered every phase of the question and left nothing to be added." After closing the address, he announced he was ready to be catechized upon any points, and for another hour he stood "calmly and rapidly answering great questions of constitutional law as they were propounded to him."[4]

Black had passed his seventy-third birthday, yet his address shows an unflagging mental energy. Forcibly and cogently he argued a proposition then bitterly denied by the railroads, but now universally admitted, that the "companies are not owners of the railroads," but are "public agents," and therefore subject to regulation "to prevent those agents from betraying their trust." Against the bitter opposition to this view by the railroads he marshaled a chain of law, court decisions, and the incorporation of this view as "fundamental law" into the State Constitution of 1874.[5]

There was a touch of melodrama in this epilogue of Black's public career, that he should have crowned and rounded it by this unsolicited defense of human rights. He was a Roman to the end.

Throughout the spring he remained at Brockie, superintending the planting of crops. To his daughter Mary, now the wife of an army officer stationed in New Mexico, he wrote on June 9th: "There never was such a glorious looking place as Brockie just now. The woods are a deeper green than you ever saw them. The grass is richer. Every tree is loaded with fruit. . . . The wheat promises to be the best crop we have ever had. The bull that Mr. Tilden gave me is a perfect beauty. The cow got her horn torn off. The old Dick horse is as much a fraud as ever. . . . I made nothing out of my bullocks except an enormous pile of manure which is telling in its effects all over the farm." Again, on August 7th, he wrote her, "I never felt better in my life, inside and out, than I do today."[6]

The old love of disputation remained, yet there was a mellowness about it never seen before. Jefferson Davis, having just read Black's memoirs, heatedly denied some of the facts contained, and in answer wrote a long controversial letter to the Philadelphia *Times*. Five years earlier Black would have rejoiced in a tilt with Davis, or any other man, but now he was prompted to ignore the challenge. Nevertheless

[4] Quoted in Clayton, p. 203.

[5] C. F. Black, pp. 172-88. This speech was chosen as the representative specimen of Black's arguments by the board of editors for Brewer's *The World's Best Orations*. See II, p. 75.

[6] To Mary Black Clayton, quoted in Clayton, p. 207.

he did not lack for defenders. The *Press* once more extolled him as a statesman "who honestly and patriotically labored to prevent that collision" in 1860. Humorously it added, "but we are not troubled about Judge Black and his fate in the matter. Past observation leads us to reserve all our sympathy for Mr. Davis. He will need it when Judge Black's answer appears."[7]

A week later this paper published an interview with the Confederate General, Joseph E. Johnston, who had said "there was no call for the letter of Jefferson Davis in what Judge Black had written," and had "serenely smiled at the idea of Jef. being a match for Jeremiah with the pen."[8]

When F. A. Burr, the chronicler of Black's memoirs, came down to Brockie on August 9th, he found Black in a most placid mood. He had not even read Davis's article. But he welcomed Burr most cordially and they seated themselves upon the great porch. Burr handed Black the article. Carefully Black read it, then looked off across his fields a moment, wrapped in deep thought. At last he turned to Burr with a twinkling, humorous expression in his eyes, saying "I fear Jeff has lost his temper."[9] Burr urged him to make a reply, and with some reluctance, Black finally agreed to do so.

Then they talked of other matters. Black remarked laughingly that his trouble right then was too many clients. He spoke of going to Kansas soon to argue a great railroad case. Shaking Burr by the hand as the latter left, he said good naturedly: "I've been taking it very easy. The truth is I am healthier and lazier now than at any time during the past twenty years. I get up in the morning and think I will work, but I walk out and look at the fruit and crops and come in and sit on the porch awhile, then go and look at them again. I really need a little spurring up."[10]

Two days later, however, he started the reply to Davis. With a pencil in his left hand, he drafted a few pages in that curiously interesting back-slant writing. "I do not see," he wrote, "as clearly as some of my friends the necessity of answering General Davis. . . . But his weapon is smeared with venom, which, if not attended to, may fester in the scratch. . . ."[11]

These were the last lines Black ever wrote. He had just received a copy of *The Life of Buchanan*, by George Ticknor Curtis. He turned away from his reply to Davis and eagerly took up the work. He opened it, not at the beginning, nor even at that part which concerned himself. Those pages were neither torn nor cut. He never saw them.

[7] Philadelphia *Press*, August 9, 1883.
[8] *Ibid.*, August 17, 1883.
[9] F. A. Burr, Philadelphia *Press*, August 20, 1883.
[10] *Ibid.*
[11] C. F. Black, p. 33.

But he turned at once to the closing pages, bearing the account of the religious experience and death of his old friend. Evidently this portion was read with a deep interest, for the pages were rudely torn apart by running his thumb through them. Having read of the closing days of his friend, he walked out upon the great veranda, "gazed thoughtfully at the shadows of the clouds chasing each other across the moonlit hills," and retired to bed.[12]

This was late on a Saturday night. Before the dawn of Sunday he was ill. The illness proved to be an acute urinary trouble, caused by enlargement of the prostate gland and spasmotic stricture. Physicians were summoned from Lancaster, Philadelphia, and Washington. But ordinary appliances failed to reduce the enlarged gland. Upon Monday the physicians were forced to puncture the bladder to gain relief. This temporary relief sufficed until Wednesday, when it was repeated. The bulletins given out to the press that day pronounced him "in a very precarious condition" with "little hope entertained for his recovery." However, on Thursday the three physicians "proceeded to make a radical operation for permanent relief, with the most happy results," and his condition was pronounced as "greatly improved," and a "speedy recovery certain unless some unforeseen complication should arise."[13]

During this crisis the newspapers followed his condition with great solicitousness. Daily bulletins were published and editorials written wishing a speedy recovery. "The Judge is in his 74th year," commented the New York *Tribune*, "but his intellectual vigor is as great as ever. Everybody will hope to see him engaged in many a fierce but good natured controversy yet."[14]

Indeed his controversial nature remained almost to the end. His first remark at returning to consciousness after the operation was, "I will now proceed to answer the criticisms of Mr. Jefferson Davis."[15] But this flash of the old nature was but momentary. Complications developed, toxæmia set in, and the end was but a question of time.

As this end stood plainly in view, his mind turned from the controversial nature which had marked one side of his life, to the inner religious nature which had marked the other side. He was perfectly resigned to go. To his wife he said, "How can I fear to cross the dark river when my Father waits for me on the other shore?" To Chauncey, his son, he added, "I would that I were as comfortable about what I leave behind in this world. I thought that there was yet some work for me to do here, but I am resigned to the will of God." Then in an

[12] *Ibid.*, p. 32.
[13] Daily bulletins, Aug. 14-17, esp. Philadelphia *Press*, August 17, 1883.
[14] New York *Tribune*, August 18, 1883.
[15] *Ibid.*, August 20, 1883

ordinary voice he proceeded to give instructions regarding certain of his business affairs.

As he neared the parting moment, he uttered this simple and earnest prayer: "O Thou beloved and most merciful Father, from whom I had my being and in whom I ever trusted, grant, if it be Thy will, that I no longer suffer this agony, and that I be speedily called home to Thee. And, O God, bless and comfort this my Mary."[16]

At ten minutes past two o'clock on the morning of Sunday the 19th of August he passed from life, a calm and courageous soul prepared to render "an account of deeds done in the body."

Brockie was still rich with the splendor of foliage and flanked with its canopy of flowers when, near sunset on the evening of August 21st, its master passed through the gates for the last time. Down the long hill he went, upon this last journey, across the winding Codorus, through the city of York, to the cemetery on the hills beyond. The marble monument which marked the resting place could be seen, gleaming in the trees, from the porch of Brockie.[17]

At Washington, in the hall of the Supreme Court, where his mighty voice for a quarter century had been heard, where his ringing words in defense of civil rights and trial by jury still echoed in the minds of men who had heard them, the Court paused in its affairs of justice. Before it gathered the members of that eminent bar "to pay respect to the memory" of this man who once had walked among them, and to hear words of tribute upon his character and eminence.[18] For a brief moment was his world thus suspended, and it then moved on.

[16] N. Y. *Tribune* and Phila. *Press*, Aug. 20, 1883; C. F. Black, p. 32.
[17] Clayton, p. 211.
[18] 109 U. S. Reports, p. V.

BIBLIOGRAPHY

MANUSCRIPTS

Archives, Department of State, Washington, D. C.; Domestic Letters LIII; Special Missions, American Hemisphere, II; Special Service, Reports of William Carey Jones and William L. Cazneau.

Beale, Howard K., The Decision of Reconstruction; Harvard University Library, Cambridge.

Black File, Papers of James Buchanan; Historical Society of Pennsylvania, Philadelphia.

Black-Forward Family Bible (containing the Black genealogy); in possession of Carey E. Etnier, York, Pennsylvania.

Clayton Manuscript; a collection of newspaper clippings and pamphlets relating to the life of Jeremiah S. Black, made by Mary Black Clayton, now in possession of Mary Clayton Hurlbut, Lockport, New York.

Last Will and Testament of Jeremiah S. Black (including inventory of personal estate and final account of Executors of Estate); Register of Wills, Will Book, CC No. 3, 346-351, York, Pennsylvania.

Papers of Jeremiah S. Black, 1813-1904; 73 Volumes, Manuscript Division, Library of Congress, Washington.

Papers of Jeremiah S. Black, 1863; in possession of Carey E. Etnier, York, Pennsylvania.

Papers of Andrew Johnson, 1865-1868; Manuscript Division, Library of Congress, Washington.

Papers of Edwin M. Stanton, 1857-1865; Manuscript Division, Library of Congress, Washington.

PUBLIC DOCUMENTS

Court Reports:

Pennsylvania:

Grant's Cases, Vol. 1, H. C. and R. H. Small, Publisher, Philadelphia, 1859. Pennsylvania State Reports, Vol. 17-27, cited as:

Harris, Vols. 5-12.

Casey, Vols. 1-3.

Philadelphia Reports, Vols. 2, 10, 12.

United States:

Hoffman, Ogden, *Reports on Land Cases Determined in United States District Court of Northern California*, Vol. 1, 1862.

United States Reports (Supreme Court) Vols. 62-109, cited as:

Howard, Vols. 21-24.
Black, Vols. 1-2.
Wallace, Vols. 1-23.
Otto, Vols. 1-17.
Davis, Vols. 1-2.

Wisconsin State Reports, Vols. 3 and 14.

Debates of the Convention to Amend the Constitution of Pennsylvania. Convened at Harrisburg, November 12, 1872. State Printer, Harrisburg, 1873.

Garfield, J. A., *Review of the Transactions of the Credit Mobilier Company*, Government Printing Office, Washington, 1874.

Official Opinions of the Attorneys General, Vols. 9-12.

Official Records of the Union and Confederate Armies, (War of the Rebellion) Series I, Vol. 1. Government Printing Office, Washington, 1880.

Opinion and Award of Arbiters on the Maryland and Virginia Boundary Line. McGill & Witherow, printers, Washington, (no date).

Poland Report, Credit Mobilier Investigation; House Report No. 77, 42 Congress 3rd Session.

Private Land Claims of California. A Report of the Attorney General to the President; Executive Document 84, House of Representatives, 36 Congress, 1st Session, 1860.

Proceedings of the Electoral Commission; Part 4, 44 Congress, 2nd Session, 1877.

Proceedings of the Senate Sitting upon the Trial of William W. Belknap; Part 7, 44 Congress, 1st Session, 1876.

Report of the Committee upon the Impeachment of the President; No. 7, 40 Congress, 1st Session, 1867.

Richardson, James D., *Messages and Papers of the Presidents,* Vol. 6.

Statutes at Large of the United States of America, Vols. 7-19.

Trial of the President. Supplement to Congressional Globe, 40 Congress, 2nd Session, 1868.

United States Treaties, 1776-1909; Senate Document 357, 61 Congress, 1st Session.

NEWSPAPERS

Baltimore *Sun*
Gazette
Chambersburg (Pa.) *Valley Spirit*
Cincinnati *Commercial*
Enquirer
Chicago *Tribune*
Cleveland *Leader*

Lancaster (Pa.) *Intelligencer*
Leavenworth (Kans.) *Daily Times*
Louisville *Courier-Journal*
New York *Herald*
Times
Tribune
Sun
Philadelphia *Herald*
North American
Press (Daily and Weekly)
Record
Public Ledger
Daily News
Times
Pittsburgh *Post*
Upper Marlborough (Md.) *Prince Georgian*
Washington *Constitution*
Evening Star
National Intelligencer
National Republican
York (Pa.) *Democratic Press*
Gazette
Republican

MAGAZINES

(Editorials and News)

Albany Law Review
Harper's Weekly
Harper's Magazine
Independent
Nation
Pennsylvania Law Journal

(Articles)

Black, J. S., "Mr. Black to Mr. Adams;" *Galaxy*, XVII, January 1874; 107-121.

Black, J. S., "Mr. Black and Mr. Wilson;" *Galaxy*, XI, February 1871; 257-276.

Black, J. S., "The Christian Religion," a Debate with Robert G. Ingersoll; *North American Review*, CXXXIII, August 1881; 109-152.

Black, J. S., "The Electoral Conspiracy;" *North American Review*, CXXV, July 1877; 1-34.

Black, J. S., "Senator Wilson and Edwin M. Stanton;" *Galaxy*, IX, June 1870; 817-831.

Corwin, E. S., "The Dred Scott Decision in the Light of Contemporary Legal Doctrines;" *American Historical Review*, XVII, October, 1911; 52-69.

Dunning, W. A., "More Light on Andrew Johnson;" *American Historical Review*, XI, April 1906; 574-594.

Faust, A. F., "Jeremiah Sullivan Black;" *Catholic World*, September 1886; 753-765.

Hendrick, B. J., "The Vanderbilt Fortune;" *McClure's Magazine*, XXXII, November 1908; 46-62.

Hensel, W. U., "Jeremiah Sullivan Black;" *The Green Bag*, II, May 1890; 189-197.

Wilson, Henry, "Jeremiah S. Black and Edwin M. Stanton;" *Atlantic Monthly*, XXVI, October 1870; 463-475.

Wilson, Henry, "Edwin M. Stanton;" *Atlantic Monthly*, XXV, February 1870; 234-246.

GENERAL WORKS

Auchampauch, P. G., *James Buchanan and His Cabinet;* privately printed, 1926.

Baker, G. E., *Works of William H. Seward;* V Vols., Houghton Mifflin, Boston, 1889.

Bancroft, H. H., *History of California;* VII Vols., The History Company, San Francisco, 1888.

Beale, H. K. (See Manuscripts).

Beveridge, Albert J., *The Life of John Marshall;* IV Vols., Houghton Mifflin, Boston, 1916.

Black, Chauncey F., *Essays and Speeches of Jeremiah S. Black;* D. Appleton, New York, 1885.

Black Papers (See Manuscripts).

Black Reports (See Public Documents, U. S. Court Reports).

Black Will (See Manuscripts).

Blaine, James G., *Twenty Years in Congress;* Henry Bill, Norwich, Conn., 1884.

Bowers, Claude G., *The Tragic Era;* Houghton Mifflin, Boston, 1929.

Brewer, David J., *The World's Best Orations;* X Vols., Ferd P. Kaiser, Chicago, 1923.

Brown, David Paul, (Chapter on J. S. Black) *The Forum,* Vol. II, 102-117; Robert H. Small, Philadelphia, 1856.

Buchanan, James, Works of, ed. by J. B. Moore; XII Vols., Lippincott, Philadelphia, 1911.

Burgess, John W., *Reconstruction and the Constitution;* Scribner's, New York, 1902.

Burr, Frank A., Interviews with J. S. Black, Philip Thomas, and Joseph Holt; Philadelphia *Press*, August 7, 14, 21, 28, 1881; also *Weekly Press*, August 11, 18, 25, Sept. 8, 1881. Supplementary articles on these interviews were also published in the *Press* on March 16, 1882, August 20, Sept. 10 and 17, 1883.

Butler, B. F., *Ben Butler's Book* (An autobiography) ; A. M. Thayer, Boston, 1892.

Callender, E. B., *Thaddeus Stevens;* A. Williamson, Boston, 1882.

Casey Reports (See Public Documents, Pa. Court Reports).

Chadwick, F. W., *Causes of the Civil War;* Harper, New York, 1906.

Cicero, Marcus Tullius, *De Oratore;* (Trans. by J. S. Watson,) David McKay, Philadelphia, 1897.

Clay, Mrs. Clement C., *A Belle of the Fifties;* Doubleday, New York, 1904.

Clayton, Mary Black, *Reminiscences of Jeremiah Sullivan Black;* Christian, St. Louis, 1887.

Clayton MSS. (Manuscripts).

Corwin, E. S. (See Magazines).

Cox, S. S., *Three Decades of Federal Legislation* (A Memoir) ; Reid, Providence, 1886.

Crawford, Samuel Wylie, *The Genesis of the Civil War;* Charles L. Webster, New York, 1887.

Curtis, B. R., *The Life and Writings of Benjamin R. Curtis;* II Vols., Little, Brown, Boston, 1879.

Curtis, George Ticknor, *Life of James Buchanan;* II Vols., Harper, New York, 1883.

Davis, Varina Howell, *Jefferson Davis;* II Vols., Belford, New York, 1890.

Day, Sherman, *Historical Collections of the State of Pennsylvania;* G. W. Gorton, Philadelphia, 1843.

Dewitt, D. M., *The Impeachment of Andrew Johnson;* Macmillan, New York, 1903.

Dix, Morgan, *Memoirs of John A. Dix;* II Vols., Harper, New York, 1883.

Dunning, William A., *Reconstruction;* Harper, New York, 1907 (See also Magazines).

Faust, A. F. (See Magazines).

Federalist, The; (ed. of John C. Hamilton,) Lippincott, Philadelphia, 1869.

Garfield, James A., Works of; II Vols., ed. by B. A. Hinsdale, Osgood, Boston, 1883.

Garfield, James A., (See also Public Documents).

Garner, James W., *Reconstruction in Mississippi;* Macmillan, New York, 1901.

Gorhan, George C., *Life and Public Services of Edwin M. Stanton;* II Vols., Houghton Mifflin, Boston, 1899.

Grant, U. S., *Personal Memoirs;* II Vols., Century, 1895.

Grant's Cases (See Public Documents, Pa. Court Reports).

Harris Reports (See Public Documents, Pa. Court Reports).

Hart, A. B., *American History as Told by Contemporaries;* IV Vols., Macmillan, New York, 1906.

Hart, A. B., *Salmon Portland Chase;* Houghton Mifflin, Boston, 1899.

Hazard, Rowland, *The Credit Mobilier of America;* S. S. Rider, Providence, 1881.

Hazard, Samuel, *The Register of Pennsylvania,* Vols. VII-XII (1831-1833).

Hensel, W. U. (See Magazines.)

Hoar, George F., *Autobiography of Seventy Years;* II Vols., Bickers, London, 1904.

Hodder, F. H., *Some Aspects of the English Bill for the Admission of Kansas;* American Historical Association Report, 1906, I, 201.

Hoffman, Ogden (See Public Documents, U. S. Court Reports).

Howard Reports (See Public Documents, U. S. Court Reports).

Jefferson, Thomas, Writings of; X Vols., ed. by P. L. Ford, G. P. Putnam, New York, 1895.

Johnson Papers (See Manuscripts).

Klingelsmith, Margaret, "Jeremiah S. Black;" in *Great American Lawyers,* ed. by Wm. Draper Lewis, Vol. VI; Winston, Philadelphia, 1909.

Martyn, Carlos, *Wendell Phillips;* Funk and Wagnalls, New York, 1890.

Milton, G. F., *The Age of Hate;* New York, 1930.

Nichols, Roy F., "Jeremiah S. Black;" in *American Secretaries of State and Their Diplomacy,* ed. by S. F. Bemis and J. F. Jameson, Vol. VI, Knopf, New York, 1928.

Niles, Henry C., "Jeremiah Sullivan Black and His Influence on the Law of Pennsylvania;" *9th Annual Report of the Pennsylvania Bar Association,* 1903, 400-471.

Otto Reports (See Public Documents, U. S. Court Reports).

Pickett, George E., *Soldier of the South* (War Letters to His Wife); Houghton Mifflin, Boston, 1928.

Pierce, Edward L., *Memoirs and Letters of Charles Sumner;* IV Vols., Sampson, Low, Marston & Co., London, 1893.

Philadelphia Reports (See Public Documents, Pa. Court Reports).

Poland Report (See Public Documents).

Polk, James K., Diary of; IV Vols., McClurg, Chicago, 1910.

Pollard, E. A., *Lee and His Lieutenants;* E. B. Treat, New York, 1868.

Rhodes, J. F., *A History of the Civil War;* Macmillan, New York, 1917.

Rhodes, J. F., *A History of the United States, 1850-1877;* VII Vols., Macmillan, New York, 1896.

Richardson, James D. (See Public Documents).

Scott, Henry W., *Distinguished American Lawyers;* Charles L. Webster, New York, 1891.

Seward, F. W., *Seward at Washington;* II Vols., Derby and Miller, New York, 1891.

Sherman Letters; *Correspondence between General and Senator Sherman from 1837 to 1891;* Sampson, Low, Marston & Co., London, 1894.

Smith, Theodore Clarke, *Life and Letters of James Abram Garfield;* Yale University Press, New Haven, 1925.

Smith, Theodore Clarke, *Parties and Slavery;* Harpers, New York, 1906.

Snyder, W. H., *Great Speeches by Great Lawyers;* Baker, Voorhis & Co., New York, 1881.

Stanwood, Edward, *A History of the Presidency from 1788 to 1897;* Houghton Mifflin, Boston, 1898.

Statutes at Large (See Public Documents.)

Stryker, Lloyd Paul, *Andrew Johnson, A Study in Courage;* Macmillan, New York, 1929.

Thayer, Eli, *The Kansas Crusade;* Harpers, New York, 1889.

Tribune Almanac, 1838-1868; New York, 1868.

Wallace Reports (See Public Documents, U. S. Court Reports).

Warren, Charles, *The Supreme Court in United States History;* III Vols., Little, Brown, Boston, 1922.

Welles, Gideon, Diary of; III Vols., Houghton Mifflin, Boston, 1911.

Whipple, E. P., *The Great Speeches and Orations of Daniel Webster with an Essay on Daniel Webster as a Master of English Style;* Little, Brown, Boston, 1897.

Wichelns, Herbert A., "The Literary Criticism of Oratory;" in *Studies in Rhetoric and Public Speaking in Honor of James Albert Winans,* Century, New York, 1925.

Winston, Robert W., *Andrew Johnson;* Henry Holt, New York, 1928.

Wisconsin Reports (See Public Documents, Wis. Reports).

Woodburn, James A., *Life of Thaddeus Stevens;* Bobbs Merrill, Indianapolis, 1913.

PERSONS

Finley, Mrs. J. V. L., York, Pennsylvania; daughter of V. K. Keeser, an executor of the Black Will; classmate of Nannie Black and a frequent visitor at the Black home.

Kooser, Francis J., Somerset, Pennsylvania; brother-in-law of Jeremiah S. Black.

Niles, Henry C., York, Pennsylvania; a law student, 1870 et seq., in the office of Black's intimate friend, Robert J. Fisher.

Stair, Mrs. William, York, Pennsylvania; a sister of Mrs. Finley.

Stewart, W. F. Bay, York, Pennsylvania; one time next door neighbor of Black.

INDEX